The 7 Secrets of Financial Success

How to Apply Time-Tested
Principles to Create, Manage,
and Build Personal Wealth

The 7 Secrets of Financial Success

How to Apply Time-Tested Principles to Create, Manage, and Build Personal Wealth

Jack B. Root
Douglas L. Mortensen

IRWIN
Professional Publishing®
Chicago • London • Singapore

Times Mirror
Higher Education Group

Library of Congress Cataloging-in-Publication Data

Root, Jack B.
    The 7 secrets of financial succes : applying the time-tested
principles of creating, managing, and building personal wealth /
Jack B. Root. Douglas Mortensen.
      p.   cm.
    Includes index.
    ISBN 0-7863-0459-6
    1. Finance, Personal—Planning.   I. Mortensen, Douglas
II. Title.
    HG179.R6424   1996
332.024—dc20   96–3564

Printed in the United States of America
1 2 3 4 5 6 7 8 9 0 DO 3 2 1 0 9 8 7 6

Dedication

This book is dedicated to

Wilma Root, wife of Jack
and mother to all the rest of us.

Thank you for your never ending encouragement and for saying
"I think you can do better."

Foreword

I've grown tired of seeing volumes on book racks that tout financial practices the authors themselves have never followed — or if they did, they got in trouble with the IRS, the SEC or the NASD (some have). I'm tired of TV "money editors" and magazine writers who insist that everyone should be their own planner and immediate success will come from buying no-load products that just "incidentally" advertise quite heavily in that publication. I'm sick of infomercials which insist that some cassette, book, or seminar will lead to instant and effortless wealth. I've nearly worn out my TV remote clicking off financial pundits who make snide comments about accountants, bankers, attorneys, financial planners, and salespersons.

Just when I'd despaired of finding an objective, informative, and interesting book, what should arrive but *The 7 Secrets of Financial Success*. What a treat! I thoroughly enjoyed reading this book because it was well laid out, had lots of illustrative stories, and had an incredible array of charts and graphs. Never did I reach a paragraph which caused me to recoil at errors or misrepresentations. All of the professionals in the financial services industry were treated fairly, as were the institutions and associations.

You'll probably buy several of these books. Who for? This one is for yourself, for future reference next time some bad advice comes your way. The next copies will be for your family members. They will help start your children or grandchildren in the right direction. After that, you may buy copies for friends or business associates. A small gift can have major impact.

Perhaps one of the reasons *7 Secrets* is so objective is that it was written by financial educators, rather than practitioners. The authors, Jack Root and Doug Mortensen, are authors of the Successful Money Management Seminars. However, there is no bias in this book toward seminars. There is a discussion of product compensation and loads, but it is fairly presented. Neither a fee-based nor a commission-based planner will be offended or compromised. This book is not pro-insurance or anti-insurance, nor does it advocate real estate or mutual funds as the one true path. However, it will definitely advance your understanding as a consumer.

The language, charts, and stories are just what you'd expect from experienced financial educators. All technical terms are clearly explained and there is very little industry jargon to turn the reader off.

You will make a considerable investment in this book — a small amount of your money and a large amount of your time. If you decide to take action, and in fact have started doing so before reading the last page, then it will make a major contribution to your economic life.

However, some readers will not take action despite the need to improve their money management. If you fit into the latter category, I urge you to seek professional guidance as suggested in Chapter 7. Your money is too important to procrastinate about! *The 7 Secrets* will have suggested where you need assistance, helped you gather the facts, and provided guidance on selecting an advisor. Register for a financial seminar, if available, or call a qualified financial advisor. This book will equip you to use professional advice more wisely. Whether acting alone, or with advice, if you follow the fundamentals of this book, you will achieve financial success.

Edwin P. Morrow, CLU, ChFC, CFP, RFC
Financial Planning Consultants, Inc.
Middletown, Ohio

Acknowledgments

As we put the finishing touches on this book, we are reminded how much others have contributed. First, we want to acknowledge our many clients. Before we built our company, Successful Money Management Seminars, Inc., we taught our personal finance courses to thousands of adults in local schools and community colleges and through their employers. As many of our students became clients, we were able to experience their lives up-close and personal. In helping prepare their financial plans, we saw the fruits of their hard work, examined their spending habits, and vicariously participated in their lives. We listened to their uncertainties, monitored their careers, and experienced joy in their achievements. We joined in their hopes for their children, shared their dreams and aspirations, and appreciated their wishes for their heirs. In short, we observed their lives from an intriguing point of view — their money. Our clients' lives, their financial plans, and what we learned through our years of counseling are embodied in this book.

Second, much of what you will discover in the pages ahead is based upon two sources. They are the input from hundreds of professional financial advisors who are instructors of our seminars and upon the insights of our trusted and knowledgeable employees. They educated and subsequently helped literally hundreds of thousands of families to achieve financial success. We have gained much from the shared experiences and knowledge of these fine professionals.

Several individuals deserve special mention for making *The 7 Secrets of Financial Success* a reality. Jack Root, Jr., was the chief editor, contributing writer, researcher, and project manager. He made our dream a reality. Janet Enge, CFP, a writer and journalist, helped us structure the book, organize chapters, and polish the text. Her contributions were invaluable. Yvonne Carlascio helped with the early research and created the first draft of several chapters. Amelia "Mimi" Bushart, a great and creative designer at our company, proved in this book that the seemingly complex can be explained clearly through well-constructed graphics and charts. We give Mimi a special thanks for really bringing *The 7 Secrets* to life. Wilma Root, and Linda Thomas once again, demonstrated their always-appreciated attention to detail by expertly proofreading the entire text.

We also extend thanks to the outstanding staff at Irwin Professional Publishing, especially Jeffrey Krames. Our clients, families, associates, and seminar instructors spent years recommending that we write this book. Then Jeffrey flew to Portland, took us to dinner, and enthusiastically showed us how our book could help millions of additional Americans on the path to financial security. He left with our commitment, and we began to write it in earnest.

Finally, we thank you, our reader. Whether you purchased this book at a store, received it as part of an employer sponsored program, borrowed a copy from a friend or relative, or were provided it by your financial advisor, you are helping make *The 7 Secrets of Financial Success* an important book.

Introduction

Why You Should Know the Seven Secrets: Principles for Achieving Financial Success

Are You Getting Ahead Financially as Well as You Would Like?

"Oh sure," you say. "We're doing great! I have a good job, my spouse works, we're bringing home more money now than we ever have before. We have everything we need, a new boat, water skis. Last year we went to Hawaii for two weeks. Well, we haven't exactly paid for that trip yet; it's still on the credit card. It's going to take a while to pay that off.

"Retirement plans? How could I worry about retirement plans? Every time we get some money saved, the dryer quits working, or the transmission falls out of the car.

"In four years, we'll have two kids in college. I guess they'll have to work their own way through. We can't save anything. The utility bills are killers, tennis shoes cost $70, and our son needs a tutor. Our property taxes went up so the mortgage payment is higher now.

"We don't talk much about it. We just go to work, pay the bills, and go to work again. We're doing the best we know how. I used to dream of retiring early, but that seems impossible now. Now that you mention it, I guess we're not getting ahead after all. I wish I knew the secrets to getting ahead."

If any of this sounds even in the least familiar, this book is for you. We wrote this book because we truly believe it is possible to get off the

"Money gives a person 30 more years of dignity."
– Chinese Proverb

treadmill and get your finances on the fast track to building your personal wealth. We want to share the secrets with you. The knowledge in this book will not only make your success probable, it will make it nearly impossible to avoid — if you dedicate yourself to the secrets we disclose.

Do you dream of becoming wealthy . . . imagine being financially independent . . . of not having to work for a living . . . of not worrying about paying the bills? Whatever it is that success means to you — and it's always very personal — your financial success is our goal.

What is Financial Success?

Financial Success means being in control of your money. It means enjoying a comfortable lifestyle and still paying your bills on time. It means having money set aside for small emergencies and having adequate insurance coverage for major disasters. It means having the resources to buy a nice house, educate your children, or start a business. It means preparing to achieve and maintain your chosen lifestyle throughout your retirement years. It means freedom from financial stress and worries that interfere with your relationships, personal happiness, and physical well-being. To sum it up, financial success means peace of mind.

Your income level does not determine whether or not you are financially successful. Think of the movie stars, professional athletes, or lottery winners who earn and spend a million dollars a year and end up with nothing. We've known many people who make six-figure incomes who have more financial troubles than people with seemingly meager incomes. Similarly, we've known people who have earned hundreds of thousands of dollars in their lifetime, yet come to retirement dead broke. We've known couples who work hard their entire lives, salt away what seems to be a comfortable nest egg, then realize their assets will only last four or five years after retirement. Millions of people earn comfortable incomes but spend as much, if not more, every year until they arrive at retirement with virtually nothing to fall back on. Hardly the golden years they expected.

Yet over the years, we have also met and worked with many ordinary people with ordinary jobs who have achieved extraordinary financial success simply by using the principles outlined in this book. These are self-made people who have reached their goals by careful planning and personal incentive. Their's is the triumph.

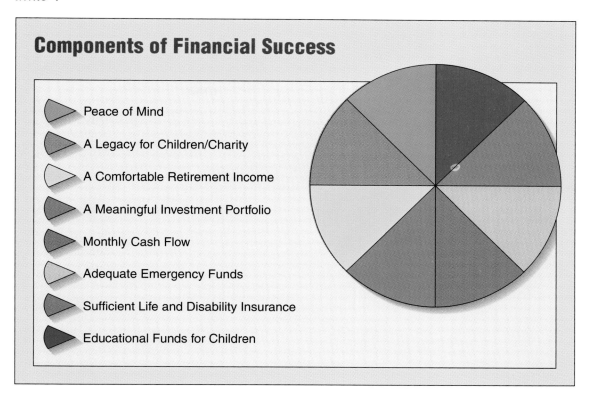

Components of Financial Success

- Peace of Mind
- A Legacy for Children/Charity
- A Comfortable Retirement Income
- A Meaningful Investment Portfolio
- Monthly Cash Flow
- Adequate Emergency Funds
- Sufficient Life and Disability Insurance
- Educational Funds for Children

America has the highest standard of living and one of the highest per capita incomes of any country in the world. The tragedy is that nearly 45 percent of Americans over age 65 have less than $15,000 annual income and only 30 percent have incomes over $25,000 per year. These figures include Social Security benefits! Just as significant, 59 percent of people over age 65 have a total net worth of less than $100,000. How does this happen?

Many of these people believed their pensions, Social Security, and Medicare would support them through retirement. They didn't believe that they needed to plan for any other retirement income. These are the same people who will spend their twilight years in disappointment, impoverished and struggling to make ends meet. The truth is, Social Security accounts for only one-third of most retirement incomes. Medicare has many shortcomings and Medicaid doesn't contribute anything until people are nearly penniless.

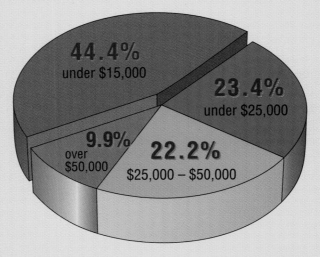

Household Incomes of Americans Over Age 65

44.4%
under $15,000

23.4%
under $25,000

9.9%
over
$50,000

22.2%
$25,000 – $50,000

The choices you make today will determine how well you live during retirement. Will you live the life you dream of, with vacations, material comforts, and enough money to pursue your hobbies and interests? Or will you join the almost 45 percent of Americans over age 65 who survive on an annual household income of less than $15,000?

Source: U.S. Bureau of the Census

Why do these people live their retirement years dependent upon their families, the government, and charity? Because they failed to take advantage of their earning years. They certainly didn't plan to fail; they simply failed to plan for success. *Financial success is attained through what you do with your income, not through how much you earn.*

Financial success is attained through what you do with your income, not through how much you earn.

A comfortable retirement isn't the only goal of planning your financial affairs. Financial success is a process, and there are benefits at each stage. The ability to have substantial assets available to begin a business on your own is one possibility. Daily freedom from worry over your finances is another, and financial independence is the ultimate end goal of financial planning.

The Information Overload Syndrome

It is becoming increasingly difficult to come up with excuses for our poor performance in managing our money. We live in the Information Age, flooded with technology, with access to many excellent, substantive financial information sources. The problem is sorting through it all to get what we need.

Herein lies the paradox: We blame this glut of information for our reluctance to dive right into a self-directed financial education. Library shelves are bulging with books on mutual funds, stocks, or some other special area of finance. It's all terribly intimidating. There's almost too much to read, and it's tempting to just walk away from it all.

This book is your opportunity to view your financial situation in the world of finance as a whole. It is your chance to rise above the trees (mortgage payments, utility bills, and pensions plans), take a look at your direction, and develop a dynamic synergy between your personal money and the financial markets of the world.

Knowledge is Power

During our combined 54 years in the financial industry, we've met many terrifically smart people who were doing tragically stupid things with their money. They didn't want to be financially ignorant; they simply didn't know where to turn to learn the nuts and bolts of money management — and they hadn't learned the Seven Secrets.

> **"An investment in knowledge always pays the best interest."**
>
> **– Benjamin Franklin**

America's Financial Education Crisis

Part of the success of America as a nation can be attributed to education of the masses. But, unfortunately, the country with the highest rate of wealth per capita suffers from a money management education gap. High schools have only begun to offer courses about principal and interest and balancing checkbooks in the last few years, and many of us earned a college degree without ever learning about compound interest. We expected to receive a financial education to teach us to manage our money properly. Did we? For most of us, probably not.

To further complicate the problem, many of us were raised to believe conversations about money were rude. Many people don't feel comfortable exchanging thoughts about their personal finances among peers and acquaintances, even though it is an excellent forum for testing ideas. The school of hard knocks is a harsh and costly way to learn about money and is selective in the courses. A little preparation can save you from a lifetime of costly mistakes.

Get Rich Slowly

We don't propose a get-rich-quick plan. This is a practical and realistic get-rich-slowly book. It would be wonderful to offer you — in good conscience — surefire strategies for short-term riches, but the truth is, we can't. What we can offer you are old-fashioned, common sense methods for accumulating wealth that have worked since people started trading furs.

The Roots

The beginnings of this book reach back to 1977. We already had more than 20 years in the investment business, and we knew how hungry people were for the truth about investments. People are bombarded with misinformation and inadequate information. Between the stockbroker on the phone, the insurance salesman wanting to sell life insurance, and the tips from the barber, it's hard to separate truth from sales pitch.

We sat down and wrote *The Successful Money Management*® *Seminar* to take our message to the public. We did it to leverage ourselves. Instead of meeting with one client and teaching that person the basics of investing, our clients could come to our comprehensive seminars for 10½ hours of generic education. It wasn't a doctorate in financial analysis, but it worked. Today, more than 25,000 people a month attend our seminars to learn critical information that helps them make educated decisions about their money.

> **"I've found there is one thing money can't buy — poverty."**
>
> Jack Root

Nearly 20 years later, our goals haven't changed. We intended to help people in the confusing world of personal finance then, and we want to do so now with our book. It isn't a lengthy treatise. It doesn't need to be. There are plenty of books that do an excellent job of putting you right to sleep. We want to keep you awake. We want to take you from hanging out on a limb to flying high. We want to give you the secrets you will pass down to your children and your children's children.

We hope, above all, that young people will grasp the concept of combining time with compound interest and perceive the staggering results obtainable from the two. Older people are more than ready to grasp it, but they're out of time. Young people have the *time* to turn $100 a month into a million dollars.

This is a concept that could turn the whole economy of our country around. We wouldn't need to be looking to the government for support, because capital made available for investment rather than consumption, contributes to the formation of more wealth. America was built — and made great — on the willingness of its people to invest their money in productive businesses. We know the secrets to personal wealth. We have a vision of helping people become financially independent at an early age. This is our dream. Our book tells you how to apply the time-tested principles to create, manage, and build personal wealth: *The 7 Secrets of Financial Success.*

Contents

PART II   The Success Triangle

Secrets or Proven Principles?

"Money makes money. And the money that money makes, makes money."
– Benjamin Franklin

The Seven Secrets of Financial Success are revered principles for creating, managing, and building personal wealth. These principles have stood the tests of time throughout the ages and are not really secrets at all. Nearly everyone will find that the implementation of these secrets can be effective in building financial independence regardless of the amount of money available to work with.

If you are just beginning your career or have been struggling for years to make ends meet, reading this book and applying the not so secret secrets throughout your life will be one of the best things you can ever do for yourself. In our experience, we have seen that it is quite difficult for people to have the other aspects of their lives in harmony when their finances are in a miserable state. Even if you are one of the minority who has your financial house in order, you will still probably learn many new ideas that will help magnify your returns and preserve the wealth that you have accumulated.

In any case we aren't going to say it's easy. It's actually easier to do nothing, and let the tides of time and chance carry you along. The secrets themselves are simple to understand, but a certain amount of knowledge is needed to apply them. And there is one ingredient that only you can add: the determination to succeed. This is your dream . . . only *you* can add *commitment*.

Set Goals
Plan for Financial Success

They had more than 700 successful glider flights behind them. They had an engine that they had built themselves when no automobile manufacturer would take on the task. No one else had a record of manned flight when the Wright brothers gave it a try. We don't actually know what Orville said to his brother Wilbur when he made his bumpy landing on that isolated beach in North Carolina on December 7, 1903. We're willing to bet, though, that Orville jumped out of the Kitty Hawk with soaring spirits and shining eyes, and shouted to his brother Wilbur, "I always wanted to fly!"

Like Orville and Wilbur Wright, you accomplish what you set your mind to. That's it. Secret Number One. *You must set goals.*

Goals are the starting point of all achievement. They are the creation of the mind that must occur before the beginning of the reality. They are the blueprints, born of ideas and dreams, that are fully drawn out before the first shovel full of dirt is ever moved.

Setting goals is no secret. We do it all the time. In our jobs, we set sales and production goals. And it works, doesn't it? Achieving those goals brings in revenue for the company or business. The secret is to apply the goal-setting process to our personal spending and saving.

Who needs a plan to spend their money? No one; it just happens. There are numerous demands on your money each day. But wait, what if you had a long-term plan for spending your money? Wouldn't that prioritize the demands? Wouldn't the unnecessary demands become

"Nothing happens unless first a dream"
– Carl Sandburg

immediately apparent? If you know goal setting works, why haven't you set goals to make your money work for *you?*

Put simply, people achieve financial success by setting goals and then formulating a plan of action to reach them. Napoleon Hill, author of the motivational classic *Think and Grow Rich,* defines goal setting as developing a definiteness of purpose. Success is never an accident.

Study financially successful people and you will find their achievements are driven by their goals. These high achievers write down their goals and stick to them through changes and setbacks. Goals are the target. Successful people aim — and keep aiming — until they hit the mark.

Most people spend more time planning a dinner party than they spend on their financial plans. There is the guest list to whittle, the menu to ponder over, and the table decorations to order. Grocery shopping alone takes hours, before the food preparation, setting the table, and writing out placecards begins. All for a meal that will be consumed in less than an hour; yet, they haven't spent ten minutes planning the financial direction of the rest of their lives.

We Simply Fail to Plan

You can spend hours daydreaming about where you'd like to be in the future — on a mini-farm, retired at age 55 to travel, or owning a roadside nursery. You can daydream until the sun goes down, but the reality is that most dreams need money to materialize. Money is the tool with which we carve our future, but too many of us believe we need vaults full of cash and other assets to make even a modest dream, such as owning a small bed and breakfast business, come true.

Overwhelmed, we find ourselves casting our dreams aside and waiting for a windfall. In our experience, a plan, a commitment to the plan, and a little money create an amazing potential for achieving a goal. A formula that always works, without fail.

Goal creators turn invisible dreams into visible goals. Daydreamers wish for riches and end up bitter that luck was never with them. Dreams remain forever unrealized until goals are set.

When we say things such as "I'm going to get my Christmas shopping done early this year," or "I'm going to work out three times a week," we are setting goals for ourselves. Yet, when it comes to financial goals, too many people sit back and wish for financial success but take no action. Again, we don't plan to fail; we simply fail to plan.

It's neither realistic nor practical to verbalize an objective and expect it to materialize while jetting about on cruise control. Hard

Many years ago, I idly wrote down about 10 goals on a small piece of paper. I remember that at the time they seemed fantastic because they meant an entire change of lifestyle and career. I didn't take care of those goals or consult them every day. In fact, I lost track of that paper completely.

Six years later, I was cleaning my desk and found my list. I was amazed to find that little piece of paper after all that time. I had achieved almost every single one of those goals, including creating and selling a business. There's only one goal left: I still haven't done any skydiving.

work alone isn't the answer, either. Many hard-working people never enjoy financial success, because they haven't planned for success.

Where you are today isn't important. It's where you want to go that matters. Once you clearly define your goals, you'll realize that you are immediately filled with enthusiasm, initiative, and motivation. And as your plan gains momentum, your enthusiasm and energy will grow in proportion to your progress.

If you believe in your carefully crafted goals, become committed to them, and implement action, the odds are that you will achieve them. You really can plan financial success.

> **Warning! The odds are if you believe in your carefully planned goals, become committed to them, and implement action — you will achieve them.**

A Guide to Successful Goal Setting

Write Them Down

Goals in your head are no more than daydreams floating about, confused and ungrounded. Written goals are tangible, capable of being realized, and inherently worthy of your attention. You become especially committed to their attainment when you can actually see them.

Clear your head, and sit down in a quiet room with some blank sheets of paper and ask yourself this question: What do I *really* want out of life? Write down every potential financial goal that comes to mind. We'll consider their probability later. For now, write with abandon. When you've drained your brain of every desire involving you and money, set the list aside for a day.

Don't be surprised that you have learned something about yourself. You may have written some things you never thought about

FIGURE 1–1

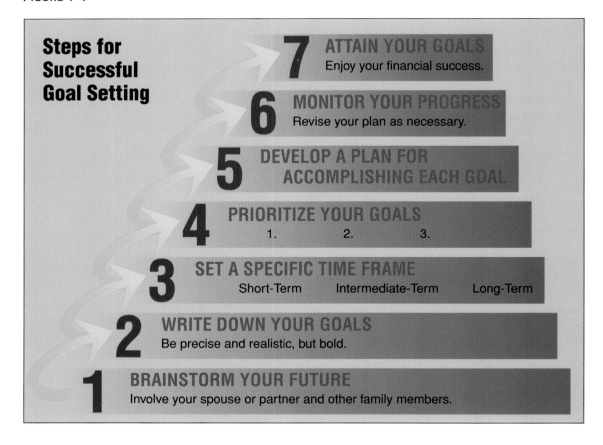

Steps for Successful Goal Setting

7 ATTAIN YOUR GOALS
Enjoy your financial success.

6 MONITOR YOUR PROGRESS
Revise your plan as necessary.

5 DEVELOP A PLAN FOR ACCOMPLISHING EACH GOAL

4 PRIORITIZE YOUR GOALS
1.   2.   3.

3 SET A SPECIFIC TIME FRAME
Short-Term   Intermediate-Term   Long-Term

2 WRITE DOWN YOUR GOALS
Be precise and realistic, but bold.

1 BRAINSTORM YOUR FUTURE
Involve your spouse or partner and other family members.

before. Some of what you thought were your pet goals may not have appeared at all. Goals that deal with money and the way we use it are inextricably intertwined with the deep fundamental principles that make us who we are. How different our lives can be from what they are now, once we discover what is truly most important to us! We change and grow with life.

Be Realistic, but Think Big

We agree with your grandmother: Aim for the moon. If you miss, you'll still have the stars. Don't make the mistake of limiting yourself. We're asking you to have the courage to believe in yourself, to believe in your ability, to believe in your own determination.

Now go over your goals a second time, adding an element of realism. The things that matter most will be self-evident. Write them down on a fresh sheet of paper under the heading Goals. Next, examine the list for the things that, in retrospect, you don't really want or need, and cross them off.

Move anything you have mixed emotions about to a column called Future Reference. You might not feel the need to pursue them immediately, but keep them. After you know how easy it is to achieve your goals, you'll probably have to set some new ones.

Finally, ask yourself, Is this what I really want or what I am expected to want? Be honest with yourself. Make your goals truly your own. Clearly identify what you want and your focus will shift toward acquisition almost effortlessly.

Be Specific

Generalities are fine for brainstorming, but real goals need to be written in specific terms. If your goal is to be rich, get to the point. What does rich mean to you? $100,000, $300,000, or a million dollars? Write the goal: "I want to have $1,000,000 accumulated by the time I reach age 60."

Be specific. A goal that reads: "Start investing some money," is not nearly as useful as setting a goal of investing $167 each month in an IRA (Individual Retirement Account) in XYZ mutual fund.

Right now, you may not feel you know enough to set specific goals. We promise you will by the time you have finished this book. Keep reading for now, and get the full particulars later. Moreover, you will probably discover completely new ideas about making and specifying goals.

Set a Time Frame

Goals are dreams with deadlines. Provide a time frame for the implementation and completion of the steps that you will take to achieve each goal. Mark a starting point and an ending point. For example, say specifically that you will "invest the money from the pay raise to take effect next month," or "accumulate $3,000 in a savings account to use for our vacation next summer." It's easier to mark progress when you have a time frame for your goals.

Now that your goals are clearly defined, it is time to arrange them in categories. On a clean sheet of paper — a thick one to last your lifetime — separate your goals into long-, intermediate-, and short-term objectives.

FIGURE 1–2

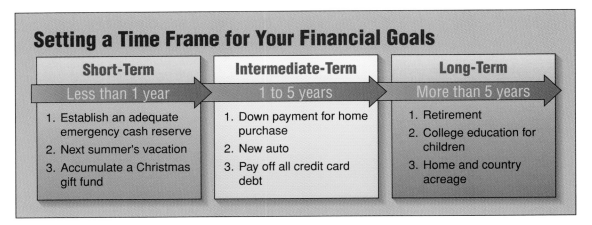

Short-term goals have a time frame of less than one year, such as saving $1,000 for Christmas gifts this year. *Intermediate-term goals* are those requiring one to five years to complete, such as saving $250 per month for the next four years to use as a down payment on a new home. *Long-term goals* are those requiring more than five years, such as saving for a child's college education or retirement.

Break Large Goals Down

To complete your plan, outline each step that you must take to attain the goal. Initially, large goals may seem impossible, so break them down into smaller, easily managed subgoals. As you achieve each subgoal, you will enjoy a feeling of accomplishment that will keep you focused on the primary objective.

Here's an example of what we mean. Maybe you are getting a raise next month of $100 a month. You have been paying your bills regularly, but haven't started any investment programs at all. While reading *The Seven Secrets of Financial Success* you have decided to begin saving the money from your raise. Further, when your furniture is paid off in 14 months, you will have another $60 a month to add to your investments. Your goals could be written like this:

GOAL: Begin an investment program to accumulate $100,000.

Subgoals:

1. Research savings accounts and money market fund yields.
2. Start a savings account with the $100 raise and add to it monthly.

RULES FOR SUCCESSFUL GOAL SETTING

1. Write down your goals.
2. Be realistic.
3. Be specific. Quantify your goals.

4. Set a time frame for your goals.
5. Break large goals down into easily managed subgoals.

3. In 10 months, open a money market fund with $1000 at a higher interest rate. Continue adding $100 monthly to the money market.

4. In 14 months, raise monthly additions to $160 and continue until cash reserve needs have been accumulated.

5. Research investments that should provide a better return and begin investing in them.

Subgoals will help you weather the tough spots that everyone hits sooner or later. When luck goes against you, you can look at your list and say, "See, I haven't achieved my main goal, but I have achieved A, B, and C. I'm that much closer in spite of this setback." Subgoals also give you little rest stops to review your goals to make sure you are on track or that your values and objectives haven't changed.

Once these simple exercises are completed, you'll be amazed at your sense of accomplishment. You have used your power to seize control of your financial future. You have refused to give the power of your future to other people or circumstances. And all this with only the first secret of financial success!

TWO

Pay Yourself First
Keep a Part of All You Earn

" ay to yourselves, *'A part of all I earn is mine to keep.'* Say it in the morning when you first arise. Say it at noon. Say it at night. Say it each hour of every day. Say it to yourself until the words stand out like the letters of fire across the sky."

– from The Richest Man in Babylon

"A penny saved is a penny earned."
– Benjamin Franklin

Look carefully at your next paycheck and think, "How much of this really belongs to me?"

"I worked for it," you say. "It's *all* mine!" What about the rent? That's not yours. And you must buy groceries, clothing, and pay the utility bills. And just when you think there might be a little money left over, the insurance premiums and the car payment are due, and that dreaded Visa bill arrives in the mail.

We work hard to make a living and it's frustrating when everyone except us receives a portion of our money. Isn't it about time we start paying ourselves something?

During our years in the financial planning business, we've met people with modest incomes who save a large portion of what they earn. We've also met people with substantial incomes who save virtually nothing. We've discovered that savings rates rarely parallel earnings. It's human nature to increase our spending to meet our income, regardless of how much we earn. *Financial success originates from the amount we save, not the amount we earn.*

Americans are terrible savers. We have one of the lowest personal savings rates of any country in the industrialized world. Depending on the age group, we save only from 1 to 8 percent of our disposable incomes; our overall average is less than 5 percent compared to 10 to 20 percent in many countries.

As we've said, financial dreams and goals need money to materialize. Unless you win the lottery or receive a hefty inheritance, you are dependent on saving a portion of your earnings to reach your goals and achieve financial success.

You are probably thinking, "Sure I want to save but I can barely pay my bills as it is. The money always seems to be gone before the end of the month. Maybe I can start saving next month; I'll just have to see how things go."

The secret is to *save first,* then spend what is left over. Isn't your future as important as your landlord's, your grocer's, or your local restaurateur's? Those who spend first and plan to save what is left usually have nothing left to save. Savings should be the first item in your budget every month.

But most people still believe they will start saving as soon as they earn just a little more money. How much is just a little more? They receive a raise and reward themselves by buying a new stereo this month, a new piece of furniture next month, more dinners out, a better car — and then say, "I could start saving if I earned…just a little more. Maybe next month." This self-destructive thinking disappears when you understand Secret Number Two: *pay yourself first.*

Why We Overspend

The marketing wizards of Madison Avenue have one mission: to get us to spend our money. The average person sees up to 100 advertisements a day, most of which show beautiful people enjoying wonderful lives because of some unique product or service they bought. The message? You too can have this lifestyle when you buy our product or service.

Advertising targets consumers who believe their self-esteem will be enhanced by a particular product or service. These consumers believe, for instance, that their peers will think more of them when they drive a certain make of car. Historically, consumers are easy to sell; their money slips easily right out of their hands.

To tempt us further, instant gratification is easy to achieve. Retailers offer a painless payment plan of your choice — "No payment due until July of next year. Buy now and enjoy our easy payment plan. All

FIGURE 2-1

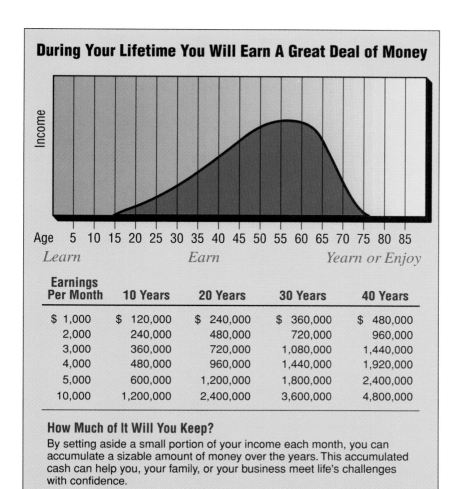

During Your Lifetime You Will Earn A Great Deal of Money

Income

Age   5   10   15   20   25   30   35   40   45   50   55   60   65   70   75   80   85

Learn   *Earn*   *Yearn or Enjoy*

Earnings Per Month	10 Years	20 Years	30 Years	40 Years
$ 1,000	$ 120,000	$ 240,000	$ 360,000	$ 480,000
2,000	240,000	480,000	720,000	960,000
3,000	360,000	720,000	1,080,000	1,440,000
4,000	480,000	960,000	1,440,000	1,920,000
5,000	600,000	1,200,000	1,800,000	2,400,000
10,000	1,200,000	2,400,000	3,600,000	4,800,000

How Much of It Will You Keep?

By setting aside a small portion of your income each month, you can accumulate a sizable amount of money over the years. This accumulated cash can help you, your family, or your business meet life's challenges with confidence.

major credit cards accepted." By making access to our money so much easier, technology has also become an accomplice in our overspending. We'll talk more about debt in Chapter 5.

Above all, spending money is fun. It makes us feel good and it's easy to justify. We work hard and deserve to spend our money, right?

If you are a consistent over-spender, we challenge you to move beyond the hype, to realize that your value as a person has nothing to do with your possessions, and to simply change the way you think about using your money. Turn the idea of instant gratification into the concept of ultimate gratification. Think beyond the moment. Pay yourself first.

The Price of Spending It All

When we spend all we earn today, we guarantee a future in jeopardy. As some previously high-income earners who suddenly lost their jobs have discovered, without an income or savings, homelessness is just a few months away. There is enough uncertainty in life without deliberately asking for more.

If we don't set aside money for emergencies, such as a broken appliance or a major auto repair, we are forced to borrow to pay for the emergency. Future income is used to repay the loan (plus interest), resulting in an overall lowering of our standard of living. The accumulation of debt is an automatic consequence for those who spend everything they earn.

> **The accumulation of debt is an automatic consequence for those who spend everything they earn.**

Provided we continue working and don't spend more than we earn, we can enjoy a nice standard of living until we are no longer able to work. Lifelong jobs are becoming obsolete. Illness, accidents, or disability are extremely unpredictable. Do you think you'll want to — or be able to — work all your life? Many people must work into what should be their retirement years just to make ends meet. Others are forced to accept a lowered standard of living.

Without saving a portion of what you earn, your dreams and financial goals have little chance of materializing. Handling your money is nothing but a vicious treadmill when you haven't learned to pay yourself first.

Living within Your Means

Many people cannot save simply because they are living beyond their means. Financial success requires tough choices: learning how to earn more or spend less. Think for a minute; we'll bet you can think of several people who earn less money than you do and still manage to live comfortably within their incomes.

Spending limits your choices. Money used in one way isn't available to use in another way. Evaluate lost opportunities before you spend. Center your thoughts on your goals.

What Do You Spend?

Most personal finance authors recommend you work out a budget and learn to stick to it. In our experience, however, few people have the desire or the self-discipline to stick to a budget for any length of time.

Secrets or Proven Principles?

FIGURE 2–2

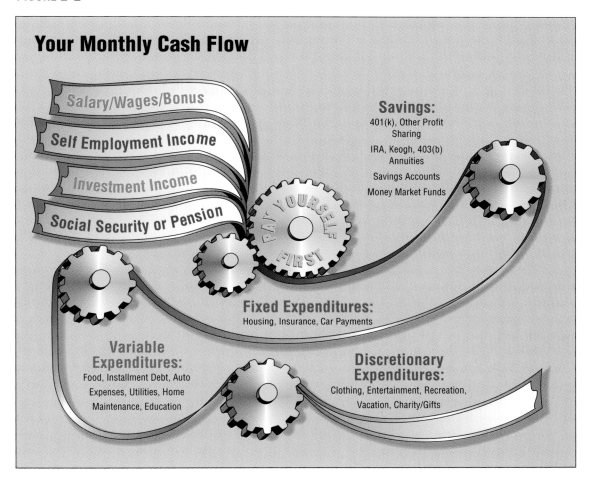

Your Monthly Cash Flow

Salary/Wages/Bonus

Self Employment Income

Investment Income

Social Security or Pension

PAY YOURSELF FIRST

Savings:
401(k), Other Profit Sharing

IRA, Keogh, 403(b) Annuities

Savings Accounts

Money Market Funds

Fixed Expenditures:
Housing, Insurance, Car Payments

Variable Expenditures:
Food, Installment Debt, Auto Expenses, Utilities, Home Maintenance, Education

Discretionary Expenditures:
Clothing, Entertainment, Recreation, Vacation, Charity/Gifts

Nonetheless, it is a useful exercise to write out a list of all your monthly payments and expenditures. This list simply helps you to see where your money is going. Let's take a look at what should be on this list.

First come the *fixed expenditures.* These are the things that cost the same every month, such as your mortgage payment, car payment, and insurance premiums. It would take major adjustments in your life to eliminate any of them.

Next are the *variable expenditures,* which include the bills you pay every month, but at different amounts, such as credit cards, fuel, and utilities.

TIPS FOR CUTTING YOUR SPENDING

- Leave your credit cards at home — save them for emergencies and rental cars.
- Drive a less expensive car — save on fuel, repair, and insurance.
- Shop for the best value, especially on big ticket items such as cars and appliances — the savings are often quite impressive.
- Buy in bulk at large shopping club stores.
- Eat out less often.

- Drink less when you do eat out — drinks are very expensive.
- Rent a place with fewer amenities — you probably don't use most of them anyway.
- Maintain higher deductibles on your insurance policies.
- Ask yourself whether you really need an item before you buy it.

Finally, there are *discretionary expenditures* on items such as clothing, vacations, and entertainment that contribute to your lifestyle, although you could do without some of them.

Even if you can't stick to a budget, use it to gain a better understanding of where your income is spent. Add up your monthly expenditures. Figure out what you actually earn, before and after taxes.

Chances are your income exceeds the expenses you've listed, probably by as much as 20 to 40 percent. So where is the difference going? Much of this is usually spent fifty cents or a few dollars at a time.

We've found that people usually fall into one of the following categories:

1. People who spend *more* than they earn and thus accumulate debt.
2. People who spend *all* they earn but save nothing.
3. People who spend *less* than they earn and save the difference.

Which category are you in? Hint: Category 3 is where you should be.

It is sad to see how many people go through their entire working lives without ever gaining control of their spending. The good life is reserved for those who employ self-discipline in their spending and save to accomplish their financial goals. Ultimate satisfaction only comes when you have learned to pay yourself first.

How to Pay Yourself First

The secret is to **make savings the first item in your monthly ~~budget~~ expenditures,** then do whatever you like with the rest. Have fun — live it up — and enjoy the fruits of your labor. Once you are saving

Secrets or Proven Principles?

For 40 years, I never saved a dime. My earnings grew, my spending grew more. At the end of every month, I could never pay all the bills. Then I read *The Richest Man in Babylon*.

Now I'm saving $1,000 a month. Every paycheck, without fail, I pay myself first. My savings are growing faster than I ever believed they would. I haven't had to change my lifestyle all that much and I'm still comfortable — at the end of the month, *I still can't pay all the bills.*

---

part of your income first, before spending anything, financial success is virtually guaranteed. *Whatever you have left is yours to spend.*

The amount you need to save is dependent on the financial goals you have set for yourself. We generally recommend saving a minimum of 10 percent of your income. Initially, that may seem very difficult. If so, start with less. Maybe just 5 percent, then increase it whenever possible. Young people will be able to accumulate a nice retirement nest egg if they save just 10 percent, but people in their 40s and 50s who are only now beginning to save for retirement should aim for more. The important thing is to begin by saving something. Once you form a savings habit by paying yourself first, you won't even miss the money you are saving.

Saving is the only way you keep any of your money.

Don't be deceived by thinking of saving as a negative expenditure or self-punishment that deprives you of your money; this attitude couldn't be further from the truth. Saving is the only way you *keep* any of your money. A commitment to paying yourself first is the second secret of building personal wealth.

Saving Priorities

True saving is money saved *and invested to increase in value*, not just set aside for a short time to purchase consumer goods. Once you have decided on and prioritized your financial goals, determine what action is necessary to accomplish them. Parts II and III are quite specific about where to invest your savings, but for now we'll just touch on a few ideas.

Some savings vehicles, or financial instruments, are better suited to short-term goals than longer time periods. The first place to start

FUN SAVINGS SCHEMES

You can grow a money tree—one that is all yours—from your daily spare change. Every day, when you empty out your pockets or purse, put all of your change and one dollar bills into a jar. When the jar is full, go directly to the bank and deposit the money into your savings account. As the account grows, invest it to fund a financial goal. You will never miss that spare change, and over the years you will amaze and dazzle yourself as you watch the account grow and grow and grow.

Fund a child's college education on just a dollar a day. When your child or grandchild is born, immediately begin saving one dollar a day to fund their college education. As your daily dollars grow, buy long-term investments such as mutual funds. If you can average an annual return of just 10 percent, the child will have a college fund of almost $17,000 at age 18. If parents and both sets of grandparents all contribute a dollar a day ($3/day compounded at 10 percent for 18 years grows to $54,535), the child probably won't have to work during school.

saving is in a cash reserve fund for emergencies. Money market funds or passbook savings accounts are ideal vehicles for emergency and short-term goal dollars because these are easy to access and don't suffer from fluctuations in asset value.

Money for your intermediate-term goals (1 to 5 years) can be put into various conservative investment vehicles such as certificates of deposit, bonds, or conservative mutual funds. These vehicles provide better returns than money market funds and passbook savings accounts but are not as accessible and may be subject to fluctuations in asset value.

Savings destined to fund your retirement and other long-term goals should be stashed away in places where you have a hard time getting to them. Retirement plans, such as IRAs, annuities, and 401(k) plans, allow your money to accumulate tax-deferred — you don't pay taxes on the income until it is taken out of the plan. Savings destined to finance your long-term goals should be invested in investments with long-term growth objectives, such as growth mutual funds, common stocks, or real estate. As we'll discuss in detail later, these vehicles generally produce the best long-term returns but are subject to market cycles and significant fluctuation in value.

Secrets or Proven Principles?

Summary

Remember to pay yourself first. You are the most important person in your world. Your family is the most important family in your world. Pay yourself first from every paycheck you receive from this day forward. Save what you must to achieve your goals, *then* pay your bills and enjoy spending the rest. Watching financial goals materialize frees you to spend without guilt. The immediate rewards are increased financial confidence, reduced money worries, and the ability to handle financial surprises. Reward yourself for all the hard work you do. A part of all you earn is yours to keep.

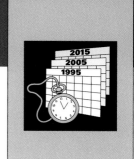

THREE

Harness the Power of Time
Make Your Money Work for You

ou've plotted your course by setting your goals. You've started the engine by learning to pay yourself first. Now we'll share the third secret and give you the solid rocket fuel you need to launch into financial success.

So far, we have only talked about the money you earn by working. Now take a moment and think about all the money you can make *without working*. It isn't illegal. Even the government calls it "unearned income" on your tax return. It is income you haven't actually earned by working. It's the wonderful income your money earns for you.

"Sounds great!" you might be thinking, "But how do I DO that?" With the combined forces of time and compound interest. This is the Third Secret of Financial Success: *harness the power of time to make your money work for you.*

The Time You Have

Procrastination. You know you shouldn't, but you do; we all procrastinate. Each year you finish your taxes at 10:00 PM on April 15. That's a full two hours earlier than a lot of other people and, besides, the sprint to the post office is kind of a thrill. Some cities even hold a tax party, where the postal workers stand in the street and take your returns until midnight.

"Compound interest is the eighth wonder of the world."
– Albert Einstein

21

Beating time at its own game is a challenge only humans are silly enough to confront. Most of the time, the consequences aren't very serious, but when it comes to saving and investing, procrastination destroys your plan. If you'd like to reschedule that visit to your dentist, go right ahead. But putting off saving money beyond today will cost you for the rest of your life.

Procrastination is the number one reason why people *fail* financially. With life expectancy increasing and retirement ages staying the same or getting younger, many retirees spend 15 to 25 years or more living on retirement funds. We must plan to support ourselves for at least one-quarter of our lives without the benefit of regular salaries.

Too many people mistakenly believe the government will support them if they run out of money in retirement. This myth results in sad endings to many life stories. As we mentioned earlier, many surveys indicate that Social Security only accounts for about one-third of a comfortable retirement income. Medicaid has restrictions that often eliminate care for all but the indigent, requiring those who have assets to spend down until they become impoverished. Don't allow yourself to run out of money before you run out of life.

Americans obsess about time. We're constantly racing against it, trying to save it, extend it, or create more of it. This chapter lets you in on the secret: Time is Money's best friend. The two work together like a river and a millwheel to generate amazing results.

In all of our discussions about investments, home equity, and asset allocation, you'll see how these two great friends can work to your advantage. But, Procrastination is their most loathsome enemy, constantly causing delays in their plans for proliferation and success. And Procrastination coupled with Impatience wreaks havoc on financial success. We'll show you how to outsmart these two hoodlums.

Time adds value to money when it is invested.

Once time passes there's no getting it back, and if we don't use it to our advantage, opportunities also pass. Today — right now — is your opportunity to understand that money has a direct and indisputable relationship to time.

The Time Value of Money

When you think about it, a dollar today doesn't have the same value a dollar tomorrow has. For instance, when you invest $100 at 6 percent interest, your $100 isn't worth $100 at the end of the year, it's worth $106. If you had kept the $100 in your dresser drawer for a year, what

FIGURE 3–1

$10,000 Investment Earning a Return of 8%

	Age Invested	Number of Years	Value at Age 65
Trevor	25	40	$ 217,245
Megan	35	30	100,627
Belinda	45	20	46,610
Jeffrey	55	10	21,589

would you have? That's right — $100. The point is the value of your money in any situation is determined by time.

Time, however, only adds value to your dollar when it is invested. Without investing your money, time actually erodes the purchasing power of your dollar through inflation. Investing is the only way you can keep ahead and beat the ravages of inflation.

Compare these two examples:

$3000	at 8% interest for 35 years	=	$44,356
$3000	at 8% interest for 40 years	=	$65,174

The values of the two accounts are the same at the date of investment, but the value of the 40-year account is worth $20,818 more than the 35-year account. The time value of that additional five years was $20,818.

In the real world of money and investing, your money rarely earns simple interest. Instead, it earns *compound interest.* Compounding occurs when the earnings on savings or investments are added back to the principal, or reinvested, which in turn generates additional earnings which are again reinvested, and so forth.

In simple terms, earnings are reinvested to earn more, over and over again. Compound interest picks up speed over time, becoming more dramatic over long periods. It is, indeed, a great way to earn money without lifting a finger. Study the following example.

Assume four friends of ages 25, 35, 45, and 55 each have $10,000 to invest in a relatively conservative account where their money can earn 8 percent annually and accumulate undisturbed. For simplicity, we'll forget about taxes in this example. Take a look at Figure 3–1.

Trevor, the 25-year-old, has twice as much time as Belinda and four times that of Jeffrey. So, logic dictates that Trevor should have,

FIGURE 3–2

$100 per Month Investment Earning a Return of 8%

	Age at Start	Number of Years	Total $ Invested	Value at Age 65
Trevor	25	40	$48,000	$351,428
Megan	35	30	36,000	150,030
Belinda	45	20	24,000	59,295
Jeffrey	55	10	12,000	18,417

respectively, two and four times as much money as his older friends at retirement, correct? No. Let's see why.

Trevor could let his $10,000 work for twice as long as Belinda could, but he didn't end up with twice as much money. He actually earned nearly *five times* more after 40 years than Belinda did after 20 years. And his $10,000 investment is worth more than *ten times* as much as Jeffrey's, in only four times as many years. This is all because of compound interest, the magic synergy between Time and Money.

But how many people have $10,000 to invest, especially when they are only 25? Here's another way of looking at the wonder of compound interest. Let's put our friends on a $100 per month investment plan earning 8 percent with all returns reinvested, as illustrated in Figure 3–2.

Sure, Trevor invested four times as much money as Jeffrey did over the years, but his investment grew to more than 19 times as much. Belinda invested twice the money for twice as long as Jeffrey, but ends up with more than three times as much. As you can see, adding small increments of time and money make an enormous difference with compound interest, regardless of your age.

The Compound Interest Shortcut

"Wow," you might be thinking, "where has compound interest been all my life?" Compound interest *has* been there all your life, all your grandmother's life, and your great, great grandmother's life. They may have known the secret for themselves. Powered by time, compound interest is the ancient secret of exponentially multiplying your investment returns.

Before you scold us for promoting a shortcut when the ink hasn't dried from extolling the virtues of slow wealth accumulation, take note.

This secret "shortcut" is not a free membership to the Millionaire's Club. Actually, there's nothing short about it. Here's another example.

Suppose Morganne's grandparents decide to invest $2,000 a year on behalf of their grandchild, for the four years she is in college (age 18 to 21). See Figure 3–3. Morganne chooses not to make further investments in the account but will allow the money to accumulate until she turns 65. Eight years after college, Morganne's friends, newlyweds Ben and Hailey (now age 30), decide to begin investing for their retirement. Together, they faithfully put $2,000 away each year until retirement.

It is immediately apparent that Morganne's grandparents will invest only $8,000, while Ben and Hailey will contribute $70,000 over 35 years. How do these two investments compare, assuming an annual return of 10 percent?

The two results are not far off in dollars, but there was a substantial difference in the amount invested. Why? Time plus compound interest make the difference. It's so astounding, it boggles the mind. No doubt you're beginning to understand why Albert Einstein proclaimed compound interest "the eighth wonder of the world."

What would have happened if Morganne had continued investing $2,000 a year after she finished college, instead of simply leaving her $8,000 alone? She would have $1,918,345 at retirement. A 12-year head start on Ben and Hailey gives her $1.3 million more. Twelve years is worth a lot with compound interest!

On the other hand, what if Morganne had taken her money at age 30 and used it to purchase a car? Sure, she needed something to drive, but that $24,075 automobile would end up costing her $615,063, or the amount she would have had if she hadn't taken her money out. That's quite a price for an ordinary automobile.

Leave It Alone

Remember Procrastination's best friend Impatience? Did you notice that in all these examples the money was invested over a long period of time and *left there* so compound interest could work its magic? That's Patience at work, the opposite of Impatience. Make a pact with yourself to treat savings income or equity buildup as untouchable money. Be Patient.

Imagine that some great tragedy will befall you, unless you leave it alone. Even a small portion of money withdrawn during the investment period will significantly affect the result. Patience is not only a virtue — it's the key to making compound interest work.

FIGURE 3–3

Morganne and Her Friends

Morganne			Ben and Hailey		
Age	Contributions	Year End Value	Age	Contributions	Year End Value
18	$ 2,000	$ 2,200	18	$ 0	$ 0
19	2,000	4,620	19	0	0
20	2,000	7,282	20	0	0
21	2,000	10,210	21	0	0
22	0	11,231	22	0	0
23	0	12,354	23	0	0
24	0	13,590	24	0	0
25	0	14,949	25	0	0
26	0	16,444	26	0	0
27	0	18,088	27	0	0
28	0	19,897	28	0	0
29	0	21,886	29	0	0
30	0	24,075	30	2,000	2,200
31	0	26,483	31	2,000	4,620
32	0	29,131	32	2,000	7,282
33	0	32,044	33	2,000	10,210
34	0	35,248	34	2,000	13,431
35	0	38,773	35	2,000	16,974
36	0	42,651	36	2,000	20,872
37	0	46,916	37	2,000	25,159
38	0	51,607	38	2,000	29,875
39	0	56,768	39	2,000	35,062
40	0	62,445	40	2,000	40,769
41	0	68,689	41	2,000	47,045
42	0	75,558	42	2,000	53,950
43	0	83,114	43	2,000	61,545
44	0	91,425	44	2,000	69,899
45	0	100,568	45	2,000	79,089
46	0	110,625	46	2,000	89,198
47	0	121,687	47	2,000	100,318
48	0	133,856	48	2,000	112,550
49	0	147,241	49	2,000	126,005
50	0	161,965	50	2,000	140,805
51	0	178,162	51	2,000	157,086
52	0	195,978	52	2,000	174,995
53	0	215,576	53	2,000	194,694
54	0	237,133	54	2,000	216,364
55	0	260,847	55	2,000	240,200
56	0	286,932	56	2,000	266,420
57	0	315,625	57	2,000	295,262
58	0	347,187	58	2,000	326,988
59	0	381,906	59	2,000	361,887
60	0	420,096	60	2,000	400,276
61	0	462,106	61	2,000	442,503
62	0	508,317	62	2,000	488,953
63	0	559,148	63	2,000	540,049
64	0	615,063	64	2,000	596,254
Total at Age 65		**$ 615,063**	**Total at Age 65**		**$ 596,254**

Morganne's Grandparents invest $2,000 a year for four years (Morganne's age 18–21) at 10% interest.

Total Invested: $8,000

Value at Age 65: $615,000

Ben and Hailey invest $2,000 a year for 35 years (age 30 through age 64) at 10% interest.

Total Invested: $70,000

Value at Age 65: $596,254

Figure 3-4

If the Natives Had Financial Advisors...

Where is the most expensive 22½ square miles of real estate in the world? Here's a hint: it's an island near Ellis Island and the Statue of Liberty. *Manhattan Island* is the answer. Do you know how much the Native Americans sold it for? They sold it for the equivalent of 24 dollars in 1626. That 24 dollars could buy the fully developed island back today — in cash — if the Native Americans had invested their $24 in 1626 at 7.2 percent interest. In fact, they could pay cash for every piece of real estate on the island and all the improvements — the Empire State Building, The World Trade Center, Rockefeller Center, Wall Street, Times Square, Trump Tower, everything.

Sound impossible? How does it check out? At 7.2% interest, compounded annually, the investment would double every ten years. So, starting with $24 in 1626, in 1636 it would have been worth $48. In 1646, $96; in 1656, $192 — and in 1986 it would have been worth $1,649,267,441,664 ($1.6 trillion). In 1996 it is worth $3,298,534,883,328 (almost $3.3 trillion).

So if you want your great, great, great, great grandchildren to be really wealthy, invest $24 for them where it will earn a 7.2 percent rate of interest, and then specify that no one touch it for 370 years.

Year	Value of Investment at 7.2% Compounded Annually
1626	24
1636	48
1646	96
1656	192
1666	384
1676	768
1686	1,536
1696	3,072
1706	6,144
1716	12,288
1726	24,576
1736	49,152
1746	98,304
1756	186,608
1766	393,216
1776	786,432
1786	1,572,864
1796	3,145,728
1806	6,291,456
1816	12,582,912
1826	25,165,824
1836	50,331,648
1846	100,663,296
1856	201,326,592
1866	402,653,184
1876	805,306,368
1886	1,610,612,736
1896	3,221,225,472
1906	6,442,450,944
1916	12,884,901,888
1926	25,769,803,776
1936	51,539,607,552
1946	103,079,215,104
1956	206,158,430,208
1966	412,316,860,416
1976	824,633,720,832
1986	1,649,267,441,664
1996	$3,298,534,883,328

Using the Magic of Compound Interest

While not saving money is probably the worst financial mistake we can make, using financial instruments that don't make the most of compound interest is a close second. Even today, at the end of the 20th century, some folks still believe their money is safer under the mattress than in the bank.

While some passbook savings accounts pay little more interest than your mattress, at least your money is earning something, and it is insured up to $100,000 by the FDIC. If a bank savings account is your maximum risk comfort level, by all means, take part. After all, even three or four percent interest is better than none.

Compounding the Difference

Time multiplies the size of your nest egg, no matter what rate of return you realize, but it is doubly amazing when the rate of return is increased by just a few points. Let's go back to the example where Belinda's $10,000 grew to $46,610 after 20 years, and Trevor's $10,000 grew to $217,245 after 40 years, when invested earning 8 percent annually. What would happen if the returns were increased to 10 percent or 12 percent? The results of time and increased return are even more dramatic for our $100 per month investors. Figures 3–5 and 3–6 illustrate the differences.

Don't think that showing you these higher returns means that we want you to run out and put all your money into investments that propose earning high rates of interest. It is also necessary to understand the relationship between risk and reward any time we talk about earnings. We still have four more secrets to share that will help you understand this critical relationship.

No Excuses

Excuses for not saving are like noses; everybody has one. Although it's nearly impossible after the last two chapters, you may still be rationalizing why you can't afford to start saving money right now.

Over the years we've heard it all, and we have discovered the most ingenious excuses. But they don't hold up under the bright light of a thorough understanding of the magic of compound interest. Here's a sampling of the excuses we've heard that prevent too many people from realizing their financial goals.

FIGURE 3–5

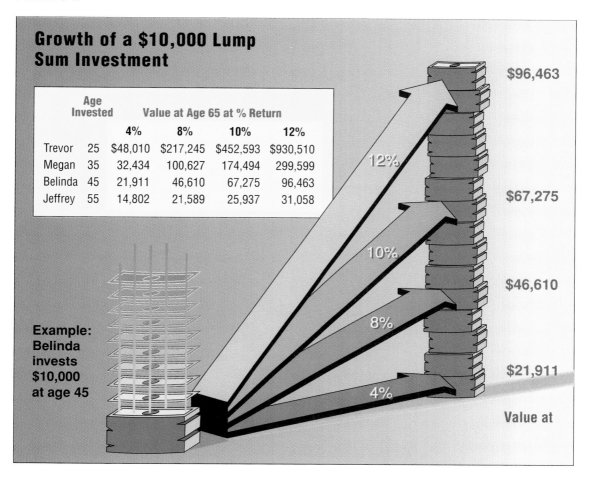

Growth of a $10,000 Lump Sum Investment

	Age Invested	Value at Age 65 at % Return			
		4%	8%	10%	12%
Trevor	25	$48,010	$217,245	$452,593	$930,510
Megan	35	32,434	100,627	174,494	299,599
Belinda	45	21,911	46,610	67,275	96,463
Jeffrey	55	14,802	21,589	25,937	31,058

Example: Belinda invests $10,000 at age 45

12% $96,463

10% $67,275

8% $46,610

4% $21,911

Value at

We're 25. We can't accumulate money now. We're just getting started and we don't make a lot of money yet. We're entitled to a little fun while we're young and, besides, we've got plenty of time.

We're 35. Our family is growing. Our mortgage payments are high. Once the children are older, our expenses will be less. Then we'll begin to invest. We can't put aside one penny now.

We're 45. We have two children in college and it's all we can do to pay their expenses. It seems to be the most expensive time of our lives.

FIGURE 3–6

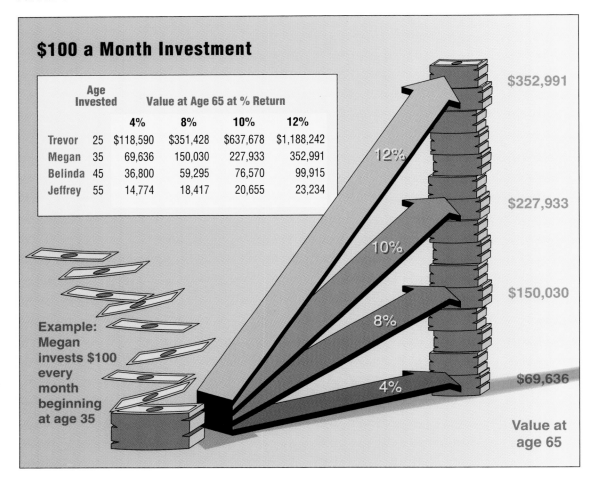

$100 a Month Investment

Age Invested		Value at Age 65 at % Return			
		4%	**8%**	**10%**	**12%**
Trevor	25	$118,590	$351,428	$637,678	$1,188,242
Megan	35	69,636	150,030	227,933	352,991
Belinda	45	36,800	59,295	76,570	99,915
Jeffrey	55	14,774	18,417	20,655	23,234

Example: Megan invests $100 every month beginning at age 35

12% $352,991

10% $227,933

8% $150,030

4% $69,636

Value at age 65

We're 55.   The passing of time is all too evident. We know we should invest, but things aren't breaking for us like they used to. At our age it's tough to start new careers or get a better job. We'll have to sit tight right now and maybe something will break.

We're 65.   Who, us? Sure, investing is a great idea, but we're 65 and Social Security doesn't go very far. We should have started years ago, but it's too late now. Where were you 30 years ago?

Maybe you can come up with a few more reasons why you can't possibly begin financial planning now. Will any of them matter when you're 65 and can't make ends meet, let alone do all the exciting things you planned for during your retirement?

If Only . . .

When is the right time to invest? After looking at the charts which illustrate the magic of compound interest, you are probably thinking the right time to invest was about 20 years ago, correct? Forget it, that's history now.

The best time to begin investing is today — the time you wait is lost forever. Besides, we prevent ourselves from going forward by looking back. You can put off many things in life and emerge unscathed, but time won't wait. Financial success depends on the action you take now, regardless of your age or financial situation. You owe it to yourself to invest now. And it's never too late to begin. Even people who are already retired can use their resources to extend their retirement income.

> **Harness the power of time, and you also harness the remarkable power of compound interest.**

Chances are you'll work 90,000 hours in your lifetime. That's a tremendous amount of time. Will you have anything to show for it? Why not let time work for you? Harness the power of time, and you also harness all the remarkable power of compound interest.

The Rule of 72

The rule of 72 is a quick and easy way to determine how long it takes for a lump sum investment to double in value. You simply divide 72 by the annual interest rate.

For example:

$72 \div 8\% = 9$ years for the investment to double in value

You can also apply this simple equation to see how long it takes for prices to double at a certain inflation rate. Simply use the inflation rate instead of the interest rate.

$72 \div 6\% = 12$ years for prices to double

FIGURE 3–8

Top Ten ~~Budgeting~~ Spending Ideas

1. **Pay yourself first.** Make savings for investments the first item in your monthly budget. If you plan to save what you have left at the end of the month, you will generally find that you have nothing left to save. We recommend that you save a minimum of 10 percent of your income, **before** spending the rest.

2. **Keep track of where you spend your money.** It is often very surprising to discover how much money we spend just 50 cents or a few dollars at a time. Careful attention to your spending patterns will help you develop better spending habits.

3. **Develop and utilize a spending plan.** The word *budget* is a negative one for most people because of the illusion that a budget somehow penalizes us and limits the enjoyment of our money. So, instead of a budget, create a spending plan that you will use to spend your money, after, of course, "spending" 10 percent or more on investments for your future. When you plan your spending, you will discover that you spend more wisely.

4. **Live within your means.** You can probably think of many people who earn less than you, yet still enjoy happy lives. Spending too much is a relative problem; when you live within your means, you aren't spending too much.

5. **Shop for best value and get more for your money.** Take advantage of warehouse stores and buy items in bulk. Buy when things are on sale, especially clothing and furniture. Last year's model car or appliance may be just as functional as this year's, and by next year, no one will notice the difference.

6. **Eat more meals at home.** Restaurants are selling food **and service** and can cost a great deal of money, especially if you include alcoholic beverages.

7. **Look carefully at your transportation costs.** Most households spend a large portion of their income on automobiles and many own more cars than they really need. A good used car will transport you just as well as a new one and will cost much less. The savings in fuel and parking may make public transportation well worth the slight inconvenience.

8. **Minimize your debt.** Some of us spend a ridiculous amount of our income on interest for purchases of items which are long gone before the bill is paid. When you buy something on credit, your future income is already committed.

9. **Look for ways to reduce your housing costs.** Rent a place with fewer amenities — chances are, you are not using most of them anyway. At the outset, home ownership is usually more expensive than renting. However, once you have determined where you will settle, home ownership can be a good investment that gets even better as the years go on.

10. **Set aside a cash reserve fund for emergency expenditures.** Most experts recommend that you should have at least three to six times your monthly income in this fund. Without a cash reserve fund, your spending plan won't last long if you have a sudden illness or major auto repair.

FOUR

Diversify Your Investments
Reduce Your Risk and
Increase Your Earnings

uring the early 1980s, we were licensed with an investment firm headquartered in Southern California. It was not uncommon for spouses to attend certain management meetings, and our CEO would often look at his watch in the early stages of such meetings and say, "My wife should be here soon. Her plane was supposed to land about 30 minutes ago."

After hearing this repeatedly, we asked him why his wife didn't travel with him. He responded, "When we travel without our children, we never fly on the same plane. That way, if one crashes, our kids still have one parent." Our CEO and his wife had worked out a plan to protect their future by managing their risks.

Every investment holds at least some degree of risk. Yet there is no reason to be paralyzed by a black and white image of figures leaping from Wall Street windows, distraught by their losses. The more we understand risk, the more fear dissipates. In the world of finance and investments, risk must be confronted, analyzed, and managed within your level of comfort.

As a general rule, most investments that are quite safe — where you stand little chance of losing the money you invested except to the erosion of inflation — generally earn lower interest rates. As you move to investments that earn higher rates of return, you also move into

"A danger foreseen is half avoided."
– Thomas Fuller

FIGURE 4–1

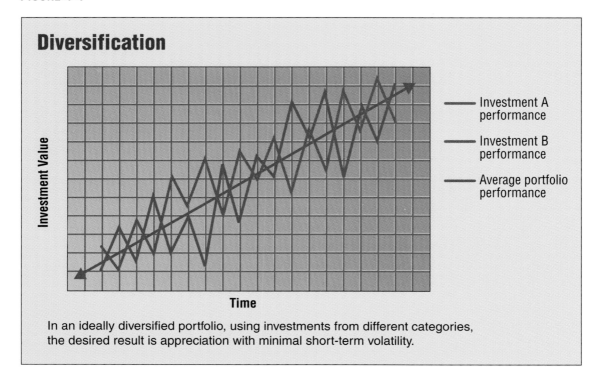

Diversification

Investment Value

Time

Investment A performance

Investment B performance

Average portfolio performance

In an ideally diversified portfolio, using investments from different categories, the desired result is appreciation with minimal short-term volatility.

areas where your money is exposed to increasing risk. The chance of losing part of your principal also increases. There is a direct correlation between risk and reward.

It is necessary, then, to develop a plan of investment which balances money at higher risk and its accompanying potential for greater rewards, with money that is invested in lower yield places to minimize risk. Discovering the fourth secret of financial success reveals the stability and harmony in this balance. Secret Number Four is: diversify your investments. Diversification holds the power of reducing risk over your entire portfolio.

The Diversification Recommendation

In financial terms, diversification means to distribute your money among different investments. Your money should also be distributed among different investment categories. If one category of investments is down, chances are another one will be up. Diversification balances the fluctuation among individual investments to keep the overall portfolio's performance relatively stable, as illustrated in Figure 4–1.

Traditionally, diversification has simply meant "not to put all your eggs in one basket." Today, many financial planners use the term *asset allocation* to describe the process of diversifying your dollars among different investments in different categories. The goal of the asset allocation strategy is to find the ideal balance between investments and investment categories to maximize the expected return relative to an acceptable risk level.

What Can Diversification Do for You?

By spreading the risk, your *portfolio* — which is simply a collection of your assets — gains more potential for higher returns than a portfolio which contains only conservative or only high-risk investments. If your moderate investment takes off and earns a fat 18 percent return and your conservative investment is holding steady at 9 percent, it will be easier to shrug off the 5 percent loss your high-risk investment suffered this year. There will also be times when your moderate investments stay flat, but your aggressive investments take off better than you expected. A well-diversified portfolio simply brings you peace of mind.

Safe Investing

A safe investment is traditionally defined as one in which there is little or no chance of loss. This includes savings accounts, certificates of deposit, and money market funds. At the other end of the spectrum is a speculative investment, which carries a high degree of risk. This category includes certain types of real estate, commodities, options, precious metals, gemstones, and derivatives.

Safe investments carry little risk but only offer low returns. But be aware that the safe investment label used by financial professionals everywhere — bankers in particular — can also be misleading. Let's say you sock away $1,000 for 30 years. Yes, you literally put it in a sock at the bottom of your closet for 30 years. When you take it out what do you have? An investment principal of $1,000. That's pretty safe, isn't it? No, it's really not, because over 30 years, inflation at a rate of 5 percent has diminished its relative purchasing power to just $215.

In essence, a more accurate label for a safe investment would be a stable investment. The $1,000 was very stable; it didn't go down to $900 and then up to $1,200, down to $750 and back up again to $1850 over the years. It remained a stable $1,000, but it wasn't protected from the hungriest predator in the financial environment — inflation. The only way to combat this formidable adversary is to put your money at risk, working in some type of investment.

Many investors make the mistake of thinking that conservative choices are best for long-term investments. Such a strategy offers little or no growth potential and usually leads to a loss of purchasing power when investment returns fail to keep up with inflation. We think long-term investments are precisely the places to stretch a little on risk.

When we analyze both *adverse risk* — the kind that makes us cringe — and the *positive risk* — the pleasing results of higher rates of return — we can begin to understand how to incorporate the balance of diversification. It is the enticing possibility for high returns on investments that makes us willing to brave the adverse side of risk.

Rate of Return

Returns are the lifeblood of investments. Without the incentive for investment returns, there would be no reason to put money at risk.

Look back at Figures 3–5 and 3–6. Then we will take another look at what a difference *rate of return* can mean in the accumulation of wealth. Assume that 20 years ago you invested $10,000. Thinking that equity investments were too risky, you invested the $10,000 in a bank account that averaged 5 percent a year during the holding period.

How much did your $10,000 investment grow? It increased in value by $16,533, for a total account value of $26,533. Not a bad increase, but what happens if the rate of return is increased to 10 percent a year? If the rate of return doubles, will the investment profit double as well?

Actually, it will more than double. If a $10,000 investment grew at a rate of 10 percent annually for 20 years, the account value would be $67,275, resulting in a profit of $57,275 or nearly 3½ times the profit at 5 percent. A few percentage points in the rate of return can make a huge difference.

Types of Risk

We refer to the rapid and unexpected movement of the market as *volatility*. Short-term investments (except money market funds) are especially subject to volatility, because there isn't enough time to ride out a market cycle. Time is the great healer for market volatility. You can probably recall a market cycle in real estate in your area when housing prices fell, but came back within ten years or so.

Secrets or Proven Principles?

FIGURE 4–2

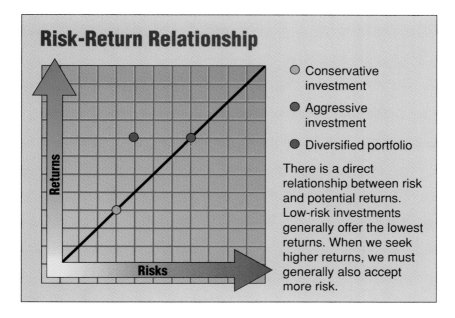

Risk-Return Relationship

○ Conservative investment

● Aggressive investment

● Diversified portfolio

There is a direct relationship between risk and potential returns. Low-risk investments generally offer the lowest returns. When we seek higher returns, we must generally also accept more risk.

Market Risk

What's the first thing that comes to mind when you think of investment risk? The stock market? It is true that stock investments have an inherent risk, yet you'll find us praising this market throughout the book. Why? We like the stock market because it has consistently competed with inflation and generated high returns for investors over its more than 200-year history.

Stock market prices go up and down on a daily basis. It's this dynamic roller coaster effect that has made millionaires and paupers out of high-risk investors. But wise investors in the stock market don't try to catch these waves of volatility. They look at the overall performance of the stock market, note its steady rate of appreciation (an average of 10 percent a year over the last 50 years), and invest for a hedge against inflation. This is not a quick-in, quick-out strategy; it requires investing for the long term and a lot of patience during temporary market swings.

When the market decides to swing down, it's pretty difficult to diversify around it. That is why it is important to diversify into different types of markets. Although there are no guarantees, different asset classes such as domestic stocks, foreign stocks, bonds, tangible assets (precious metals and other collectibles), or real estate rarely all move in the same direction at the same time.

Financial Risk

What about the company that goes bankrupt, leaving you with expensive wallpaper while other bonds appear to be doing just fine? That's a different type of risk known as *financial risk.*

Many Americans have become more aware of this risk over the past 15 years due to such highly publicized financial failures as Washington Public Power Supply, Executive Life Insurance Company, or Mutual Benefit Life Insurance Company.

You always assume a degree of financial risk if your investment return depends on the financial stability of a company, municipality, or other institution. If most of your investment portfolio had been invested in bonds issued by Orange County, California, in December 1994, you would have discovered the value of diversification through bitter experience.

Had those bond holdings been diversified into different municipalities located in different geographical locations, the negative impact would have been lessened considerably. Placing a portion of those bond holdings into domestic stocks, fixed annuities, and tangible assets would not only further reduce financial risk, but market risk as well. Remember our CEO from the beginning of the chapter? Not just different planes, but different airlines!

Inflation Risk

Other risk exposures may not be as obvious as market risk and financial risk. The primary risk people ignore when considering investments is the possibility of losing purchasing power through the effects of

Secrets or Proven Principles?

FIGURE 4–3

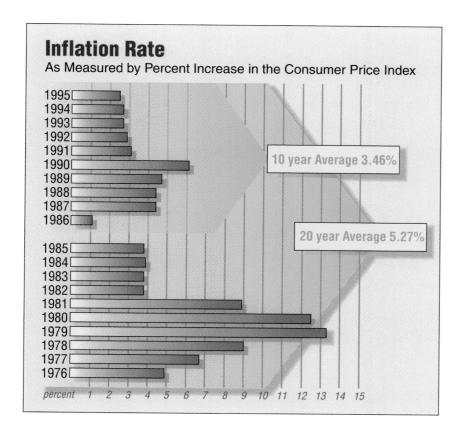

Inflation Rate
As Measured by Percent Increase in the Consumer Price Index

10 year Average 3.46%

20 year Average 5.27%

inflation over time. Inflation is pervasive — remember how it found the $1,000 you had socked away and turned it into $215 in 30 years? Instead of confining yourself to investments that will return your principal, look for investments that will outperform inflation, or at least keep up with it, to increase your purchasing power.

Interest Rate Risk

Changing interest rates are another factor to consider when tallying risks. Some guaranteed, fixed-income investments may pay an attractive yield when purchased, but if interest rates increase after your purchase, you are locked into the lower rates. An investment paying a fixed rate of 8 percent at purchase sounds great — until interest rates go up to 10 percent and you remain locked in at 8 percent.

FIGURE 4–4

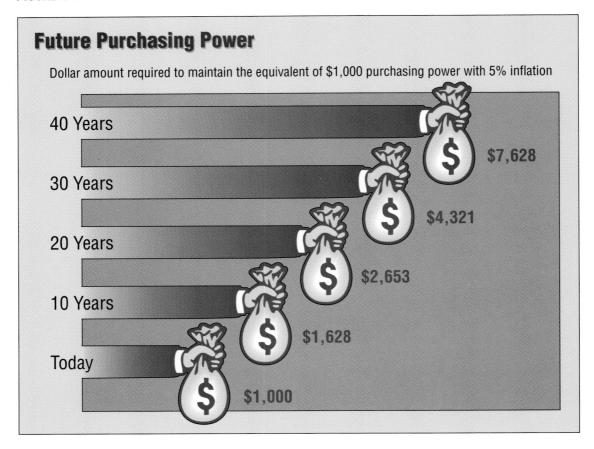

Future Purchasing Power

Dollar amount required to maintain the equivalent of $1,000 purchasing power with 5% inflation

40 Years $7,628

30 Years $4,321

20 Years $2,653

10 Years $1,628

Today $1,000

Diversification Reduces Risk

It's easy to understand that when you spread your money over a variety of investments and one performs poorly, your exposure to the poor performer has been minimized by diversifying. But sometimes it's difficult to remember to diversify when you are convinced that you have found the *perfect* investment.

We were conducting financial planning seminars in Portland, Oregon, during the 1970s. After three evenings of instruction, we felt that we had properly informed those in attendance of the importance of diversification. Yet, at the end of the seminars, people would make comments such as, "This was a very informative class, but I'm putting all my money in rental homes. It's hard to beat their combination of rental income, appreciation, and tax benefits." Our discussions of market cycles, lack of diversification, and marketability fell on deaf ears.

Fast forward to 1982. We were still instructing people on financial planning concepts, but now, we were hearing different comments. "This seminar is great, but we wish we had attended it about five years ago. We could have used the lesson on diversification," they would now say, somewhat dejectedly.

"There is no time like the present to make adjustments," we would respond.

"Yes, but we put all our money into rentals. Now, we can't sell them. It looks like we have assets on paper; we just don't have any money! Until mortgage rates come down, we're stuck," was their all-too-common reply.

They were stuck. They wanted to diversify. They understood the need for liquid cash reserves and marketable (easily converted to cash) investments. They just couldn't do anything about it. They hadn't diversified. And as climbing interest rates and a deteriorating timber economy rocked the housing market in Oregon, the value of their holdings continued to dwindle.

Diversification Increases Return

If your portfolio is typical, not only is it poorly diversified, it's probably invested too conservatively to achieve your financial goals. Adding more aggressive investments adds diversification and increases your chances of improving your rate of return with time.

Diversification Considerations

Don't run out and start buying aggressive investments for the sake of diversification alone. Before you begin to devise your diversification strategy, you will need to understand the marketplace and the enormous variety of choices you face.

Quite simply, there are only three things to do with your money: Hide it in a safe place, loan it to others and hope they repay with interest, or use it to purchase assets.

We've already learned that money stored in a cookie jar or under the mattress does not pay returns. It can't take advantage of compound interest, and it loses purchasing power to inflation at an average annual rate of 5.43 percent for the last 30 years. These facts leave you with two viable options. You can be a lender or you can be an owner.

All of your investment options can be separated into these two categories. Diversifying your portfolio means you will be choosing from each according to what you want to achieve, so you will need to have a basic understanding of how each category functions.

Loanership: Slow Growth Investments

Most people choose to loan their money because it seems to be the safest option. Lending money usually follows some sort of promise to return it in the future. What are your loanership dollars safe from? Certainly not inflation. And there is no opportunity for capital appreciation when you loan your money.

When you loan your money, the best you can expect to receive is the promised interest and a return of all your principal by the agreed-upon date. Your investment grows only by the addition of the earned interest to the principal. When you loan, you are helping an institution work and grow, yet the company is not sharing its success with you. The money you lend could generate thousands of dollars in profits, but you will only see the modest interest returns many loanership investments generate.

"What are you talking about?" you ask. "I'm not loaning my money to anyone. It's on deposit at the local bank." Exactly. You *are* loaning your money when it is in checking and savings accounts, certificates of deposit, and money market mutual funds. Financial institutions borrow your money and loan it out to others. The difference between the rate they pay you and the rate they charge the borrower is the spread, or the profit they earn. Because the government guarantees that the bank will pay you back, you settle for some pretty puny returns.

This may sound like a risk-free investment opportunity, but in reality it is not. Your money is fairly safe from financial risk and market risk, but it is not safe from the erosive effects of inflation. There is no federal guarantee against loss of purchasing power. Other loanership investments such as all types of bonds, fixed annuities, or cash value life insurance are additionally subject to fluctuating interest rates.

When you think about it, loaning your money is giving all the power of what your dollars can achieve through compound interest and time to someone else. In all our experience, people who have truly achieved financial success have accomplished it by using their dollars to own assets and, by doing so, they have maintained command of their potential.

LENDING TO CHRYSLER OR OWNING CHRYSLER

In 1984, Chrysler Corporation offered 12¾ percent notes due in 1992. It was an excellent rate of interest, so Investor Loaner loaned $10,000 to Chrysler in the middle of the year. Loaner would receive half of the interest the first year and $1,275 every year thereafter until 1992, when Loaner would receive the $10,000 principal. Loaner's interest for 8½ years would be $10,837.50. That's pretty good. How could you beat that?

In 1984, Chrysler stock traded between $9.28 and $15 a share. Investor Owner put $10,000 into 833 shares of Chrysler at $12 a share, also in the middle of the year. Dividends that year were $.28 a share, but the first year, Owner only received half of that.

Shares	Year	Dividend/Share	Dividend
833	1984	$.28	$ 233.24
833	1985	.45	374.85
1250	1986	.68	850.00
1874	1987	.98	1,836.52
1874	1988	1.00	1,874.00
1874	1989	1.15	2,155.10
1874	1990	1.20	2,248.80
1874	1991	.75	1,405.50
1874	1992	.60	1,124.40
Total Dividends Received			$12,102.41

Compared to the $10,838 in interest Investor Loaner earned, Investor Owner's dividends of $12,102 look somewhat comparable. But that's only the beginning. By the end of 1992, Chrysler was trading at $32 a share. Investor Owner participated in the growth of Chrysler Corporation and his 833 shares had a three-for-two stock split twice, once in 1986 and again in 1987. By 1992, Investor Owner held not 833 shares, but 1874 shares worth $59,968. Including dividends and capital appreciation, his $10,000 investment had grown to $72,070 in 8½ years. And at the end of 1993, Chrysler stock had moved to over $53 a share!

What does this mean in compound interest rates? The bond earned 12.75 percent. At the end of 1992, the average annual rate of return in the stock was 26.15 percent.

At the end of 1993, if Investor Owner had had the magical foresight not to take the profits and run in 1992, the net gain from the stock, including another year's dividends, computes to an average annual return of 29.08 percent, or $112,999. The irony of this story is that during this 9½ year period, owning Chrysler stock was often considered much more of a risk than owning the bonds!

Ownership Dollars

Ownership, on the other hand, puts you in control. But ownership doesn't carry any promises like loanership does. There is no guarantee that you will receive any return at all, and no guarantee that you will be able to reclaim all of your investment when you want to. Instead, when you use your dollars to purchase assets, your eventual results depend on the performance of those assets.

Remember that feeling of increased independence when you were finally able to move out of an apartment and into a house of your own? Think about your house for a moment. If you are like most people, it was purchased with the help of a mortgage.

The bank or mortgage company loaned you money to purchase a home. Let's say that it was a $100,000 home when you purchased it. What is it worth today? $150,000, $200,000, or more? How much of the increase in value does the bank realize? Zero! They don't own it, you do, so the equity appreciation is yours. That's one of the benefits of ownership.

You are also an owner when you invest in assets such as company stocks, real estate, or tangible assets. Stock ownership represents an ownership interest in the company that issues the stock. When you own stocks or real estate, your investment has the ability to generate profits through earnings (such as dividends or rents) *and* appreciation in value. Tangible assets and collectibles are also ownership or equity investments, but they don't pay dividends or rent. Their only source of profit is in capital appreciation.

Liquidity

There is yet another consideration to add to your diversification equation. Being able to access your money when you need it is referred to as the *liquidity* of an investment. Investments easily converted into cash are more liquid than investments that may take weeks or months to sell. There will be times when liquidity is a primary consideration in the choice of an investment vehicle, and other times when you will be content to let your money stay in one place and grow as long as it takes to achieve optimum returns.

Diversification Strategy

We find it interesting to read *Forbes* magazine's list of the 400 wealthiest Americans each year. Even though the rankings change from year to year, one thing is constant: not one person or family acquired their wealth by lending their money to others. These gurus of finance achieved their successes by making investments in ownership assets.

Our strategy for diversification means deciding what you want your overall portfolio to achieve according to your goals, and then balancing your investments between loanership and ownership positions. Liquidity and safety constraints dictate that a portion of your money

FIGURE 4–5

The Selection of Asset Classes

Loanership		Ownership	
Cash	**Bonds**	**Real Estate**	**Stocks**
Checking accounts	Corporate	Property	Individual issues
Passbook savings	Government	Real Estate	Mutual funds
Money markets	Municipal	Investment	Variable annuities
CDs	Mortgages	Trusts (REITs)	Variable life
Treasuries		Limited partnership	
Cash Values		**Tangible Assets**	
Insurance		Rare coins	
Fixed annuities		Precious metals	
Variable annuities (fixed account)		Diamonds	
Variable life (fixed account)		Collectibles	

will be in loanership investments, but to secure your possibilities for personal wealth, you should move the remainder into ownership positions. *Our motto is: "Own, Don't Loan."*

Within the categories of ownership and loanership, further break down your options and analyze what type of risk each is subject to. Spread your investments among different markets, subject to different types of risk. This strategy is covered in detail in Chapter 23, titled "Implement the 7 Secrets."

Remember not to confuse safety with stability. Because of the federal guarantee, banks hold the edge over equity investments in stability, but inflation will eat your earnings regardless of where money is stored. Loanership investments that seem quite safe also lose purchasing power. Question the ultimate safety of an investment that loses purchasing power and offers no opportunity for substantial growth.

With diversification, you don't have to be so afraid of investing in markets you have previously considered quite risky. It's enough to send you running for the antacid some days, but over the past 40 years the stock market has consistently produced better returns on investments than other, more conservative investments.

The Power of Diversification

When investing, the safest and most reliable way to reduce your risk is through diversification. Regardless of how good an individual investment may seem today, there is bound to be a point in the future when it doesn't perform as well. In the late 1970s, for instance, gold investors thought they had a solid investment. They bought gold at $200 or $400 an ounce (or more) with confidence that it was headed to $1,000 and beyond, especially when it sailed past $800 in 1980. You have to pity the people who put all their money into gold before it bottomed out below $300, early in 1985.

A diversified portfolio is a safer portfolio and smoothes out the bumps from any individual investment. Higher risk investments actually become an excellent way to reduce the overall risk in a portfolio.

Of course, a small portfolio is more susceptible to both economic risks and risks in investing in individual companies. If you invest all your money in one company, you ride every up and down of that one stock. The risk of owning a single company can be lessened by dividing your stock between two companies.

Empirical evidence has shown that as few as five investments can cut risk almost in half. Being diversified into 15 investments offers optimum risk reduction. Market risk cannot be completely eliminated, however. Regardless of how well diversified your portfolio is, your investments will continue to fluctuate with the markets.

The Fruits of Diversification

Assume that Taylor invested $100,000 in a guaranteed investment offering a 7 percent annual return for 25 years. At the end of the 25 years, Taylor's $100,000 has grown to $542,743. That's great; compound interest works again.

But Janet knew $542,743 would not be enough to carry her through retirement. She needed a higher rate of return to get more from her $100,000. Janet's financial advisor explained that she should invest in equity investments that offered no guarantees.

To reduce the overall risk, Janet's $100,000 was diversified among five investments of $20,000 each. However, some of Janet's selections were aggressive investments with high risk and, consequently, had very different performance records. Here's a look at their performances.

Comparing Janet and Taylor (see Figure 4–6 on next page)

Investor Taylor

Amount Invested:	$100,000
Rate of Return:	7%
Years:	25
Future Value:	$542,743

Investor Janet

Investments:	A	B	C	D	E
	20,000	20,000	20,000	20,000	20,000
Rate of Return:	−100%	0%	5%	10%	12%
Years:	25	25	25	25	25
Future Value:	$0	$20,000	$67,727	$ 216,694	$340,001

Total Value of Janet's Portfolio:	$644,422
Difference Between the Two Portfolios:	$101,679

As you can see, Janet's diversified portfolio outperformed Taylor's single investment portfolio by $101,679, even though one of the $20,000 investments was completely lost, and another of the investments earned no return at all.

False Sense of Diversification

Some people only *think* they have diversified their portfolios. When counseling one couple about their lack of diversification, they were quick to point out that we didn't understand. "We own three different rental homes," they said. "We have diversified our money into three different properties."

Unfortunately, this type of diversification would be like our CEO flying in the front half of the plane while his wife is flying in the back half of the plane. If the plane goes down, the kids still lose both their parents. Likewise, when the Portland area real estate market soured, it didn't matter how many rental homes you owned in Portland; they were all subject to the weak market.

Many people have fallen victim to this same false sense of diversification with regard to their holdings in mutual funds. They buy three, four, or five different funds that all invest in common stocks. They don't understand why five different funds with good, long-term performance results all go down in value at the same time. It's because all five are on the same plane!

FIGURE 4–6

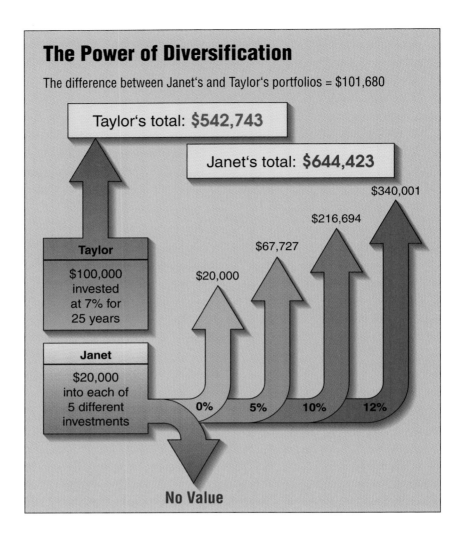

The Power of Diversification

The difference between Janet's and Taylor's portfolios = $101,680

Taylor's total: **$542,743**

Janet's total: **$644,423**

$340,001

$216,694

$67,727

Taylor

$100,000 invested at 7% for 25 years

$20,000

Janet

$20,000 into each of 5 different investments

0%   5%   10%   12%

No Value

Proper diversification would suggest that owning a mutual fund instead of one or two stocks makes good sense. And owning more than one fund is even better if a second, third, or fourth fund would move your money into different types of stocks such as foreign companies, technology, or precious metals mining stocks.

Equally important, however, is that your money must be diversified among various markets. Two or three mutual funds might be great, but money should also be invested in cash reserves and other equity investments, such as real estate, gold, or rare coins. To reduce the ups and downs of investing, dollars should travel on different planes flown by different airlines, not just in different rows of the same plane.

Evaluating Your Diversification

Evaluate any investment in terms of how it relates to your overall portfolio, in addition to judging it by its individual performance. For example, if a financial advisor suggested that a client invest $5,000 in rare coins, you might object because it seems too risky. However, if it was recommended as diversification for a $200,000 portfolio, the $5,000 is only 2.5 percent of the portfolio and is therefore much less of a risk.

Conversely, if a retired individual had only $10,000 to invest, putting $5,000 into tangibles would not be a wise decision. It would represent 50 percent of the portfolio and would not produce income, resulting in unacceptable volatility and liquidity.

Don't get caught in the trap of comparing the performance of different investments in your portfolio every year and wishing you had all your money in the one that did the best. The temptation to sell everything and jump on one investment will result in a lack of diversification and ultimate disappointment. Instead, monitor each investment and calculate the return of your entire portfolio.

The secret of diversification allows you to include investments with higher potential returns in your portfolio while lowering the overall risk. It's the secret of becoming comfortable with investment risk and the secret of increasing your earnings by those few points that make such a tremendous difference.

Long centuries have validated diversification, and it remains a sound contemporary idea. Miguel de Cervantes (1547-1616) wrote about it in *Don Quixote de la Mancha*. As translated in the early 1700s, he said, "Tis part of a wise man to keep himself today for tomorrow, and not venture all his eggs in one basket." Diversification is indispensable to financial success. This secret is now yours.

FIVE

Manage Your Credit Wisely
Good Debt, Bad Debt

O f all the seven secrets, the Fifth Secret to Financial Success may be the most challenging to incorporate into your money management practices. Setting goals, harnessing the power of time, and diversifying are an exploration of concepts that are exciting to add as good habits. Even paying yourself first, which may seem difficult in the beginning, provides an immediate and satisfying sense of accomplishment as you see that first deposit into your personal wealth.

Some of you may have escaped being deluged by debt. If so, congratulations. You already know the fifth secret. You already manage your credit wisely. It's likely you grew up during the Great Depression, or are still suffering the angst of teenage acne and aren't old enough to have established any credit. For the rest of us, the great majority, credit is the American way.

Secret Number Five is: *manage your credit wisely.* Incorporating it may not be a novel idea, but it is often a painful one, for it involves not only adding new habits, but changing and breaking old ones. It involves taking a look backward, confronting the past, and dealing with it. As difficult as it may be, you must realize that it is nearly impossible to move forward when you are shackled by the chains of debt.

Having future income constrained by past events limits your power to make better decisions for that income, and empowerment is what the *Seven Secrets* are all about. Some advisors recommend getting out of debt before they consider any other step. But that philosophy

"Credit buying is much like being drunk. The buzz happens immediately and gives you a lift . . . The hangover comes the day after."
Dr. Joyce Brothers

doesn't recognize the power of time or the psychological value of succeeding. We believe success in paying yourself first and realizing the effect time can have on your money will encourage success in managing credit wisely. We give you the fifth secret as one of seven secrets of empowerment, one of seven tools that are yours to use. The power of your future income is free to work for you when you manage your credit wisely.

Before we go any further, you need to understand that all debt is not necessarily bad, but all debt *is* a double-edged sword. Properly used, credit can be a valuable financial asset. Most people who have accumulated great wealth could not have done so without the use of borrowed money. Credit adds a convenience to our lives that we couldn't envision 20 years ago.

We are literally bombarded by offers of credit from many sources. Banks send unsolicited preapproved offers for credit cards. Retail stores use credit offers as a major selling point in their marketing efforts. You can buy all kinds of goods, such as appliances and electronic equipment, with "nothing down and easy monthly payments." Auto dealers advertise that "they will finance anyone the law allows." Indeed, credit has lured many of us with the promise of enjoying the good life now and paying for it later. And *the abuse of credit is one of the leading causes of financial failure.*

The abuse of credit is one of the leading causes of financial failure.

The primary focus of the fifth secret is the use of *consumer credit* — that credit used for personal needs or wants by individuals or families. It is a major driving force in today's economy, and it gives us a decided advantage if we understand it and use it to help meet our goals. To do so, however, means understanding the difference between good debt and bad debt.

Good Debt

Simply put, good debt is used to purchase *appreciating* assets, to make investments in materials or equipment where an economic gain will result, or when the borrowed money can be invested to produce a gain which exceeds the interest rate. Good debt is especially useful in preparing for the future, such as borrowing to buy rental property, borrowing money to start or grow a business, or using student loans to purchase an education which will greatly enhance your future earning ability.

Good debt may involve the use of *leverage* to purchase an appreciating asset, such as a home, rental property, or commercial property.

FIGURE 5-1

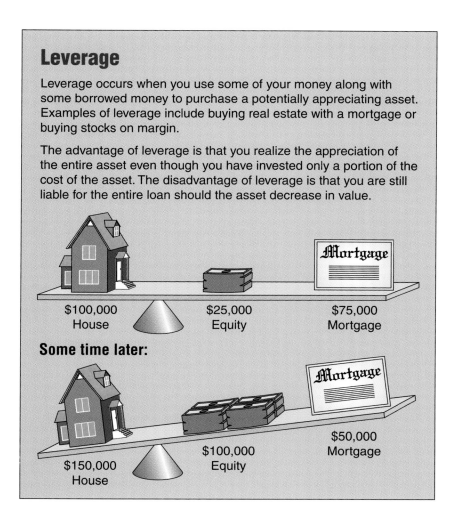

Leverage

Leverage occurs when you use some of your money along with some borrowed money to purchase a potentially appreciating asset. Examples of leverage include buying real estate with a mortgage or buying stocks on margin.

The advantage of leverage is that you realize the appreciation of the entire asset even though you have invested only a portion of the cost of the asset. The disadvantage of leverage is that you are still liable for the entire loan should the asset decrease in value.

$100,000 House	$25,000 Equity	$75,000 Mortgage

Some time later:

$150,000 House	$100,000 Equity	$50,000 Mortgage

Suppose, for example, that you purchase a $100,000 rental house by putting $25,000 down and taking out a mortgage for $75,000. Let's assume that you rent out the house for enough to cover the cost of the monthly payments, taxes, and maintenance, and that the house appreciates at an annual rate of 7 percent per year.

You are able to realize the appreciation on the total value of the home even though you have only $25,000 of your own money invested in the house. So the actual return on your investment in the house is 28 percent. In reality, you are also able to depreciate the home as a business asset, and the interest on the mortgage is tax deductible. Both of these factors will impact the actual return.

We endorse education as one of the best investments that can be made, but many families are not able to afford the costs of sending their children to college. Student loan programs are available at no or low interest rates which can be paid back over several years after graduation and entry into the work force. Educational debt is usually good debt, too.

Advantages of Credit Use

The availability of credit provides useful flexibility and convenience in our personal money management, but only if we can readily differentiate our true needs from our mere wants. Credit can be used to purchase goods and services today which will enhance our quality of life and make us more productive.

Credit can provide emergency funds when cash is low, for essentials such as for medical expenses or car repairs, and it's safer to carry than cash. Just try renting a car without a credit card. It's easier to use a credit card to reserve hotel rooms, to book airline tickets, or to order sports or entertainment tickets. And telephone shopping is a breeze with your credit card.

> **"Credit cards are a convenience for those who have money. They are not an antidote for those who don't."**
>
> Everybody's Mother

It's that "breeze" part that has us worried. A good credit rating is a valuable asset, but credit is so easy to get and so easy to use that sometimes we overuse it. That's where credit can contribute to financial problems, financial headaches, and ultimately, financial failure.

Bad Debt

Recognizing bad debt requires cold-eyed honesty when we are examining our financial situation. Bad debt is used to purchase items with *depreciating* value and no income-producing potential. The use of credit to finance things such as vacations or entertainment with no residual value is bad debt. The use of credit for any purpose to a degree that makes repayment difficult or impossible is bad debt. Feeding an instant gratification tiger is bad debt. The borrow, spend, borrow cycle can eat your financial goals alive.

Disadvantages of Credit

Credit costs money. Even when you are buying appreciating assets, you must always weigh the importance of buying now versus waiting to buy until you can afford to pay cash. The obligation to pay the debt

Secrets or Proven Principles?

FIGURE 5-2

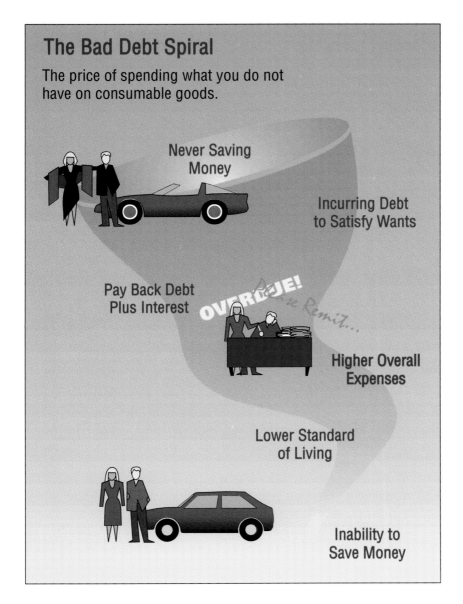

The Bad Debt Spiral

The price of spending what you do not have on consumable goods.

Never Saving Money

Incurring Debt to Satisfy Wants

Pay Back Debt Plus Interest

Higher Overall Expenses

Lower Standard of Living

Inability to Save Money

and the interest ties up future income, so you won't have resources available for savings or investment until you have paid the debt, and by now you know what you lose in terms of the time value of money.

Do you have a heavy consumer debt load? The stress of being in debt may damage your personal and family relationships, may interfere

Wise consumers limit their installment purchases to 10 percent of income, not including a home mortgage payment. When installment payments reach or exceed 20 percent of income, it's a sure sign of trouble.

Most banks today won't consider loans unless total monthly payments, including the mortgage, are less than 35 percent of the borrower's income.

with your job performance, and for some may even lead to alcohol or drug abuse. Here are some tips to help you clean up your financial act without too much pain.

Credit Cards

Americans had more than $257.9 billion in credit card balances in 1991 (up from $80.2 billion in 1980), and that number continues to grow, because Americans love to spend, spend, spend. It's a tough habit to break. By the year 2000, experts estimate that our credit card debt will be over $430 billion.

Credit cards themselves are not evil monsters, but failure to control mounting credit card debt can quickly become an ugly situation. If you hold more than one credit card and find that you use them to pay for everyday items such as food, pay only the minimum amount due every month, and carry large account balances, you are abusing your credit cards.

The interest rates charged on most credit cards are high — from 10 to 21 percent. If you want to hold a credit card for emergencies, fine. But keep the balance low or, better yet, pay it off every month. Don't fall into the trap of holding several cards, each with several hundred or thousands of dollars owing on them. If you must keep a balance, keep it on one card only and don't charge on it again until the balance is paid off. Remember how these interest rates add up. If you can't afford to pay cash for an item, especially a smaller item, then you definitely can't afford to charge it.

Shop around for the best interest rate — some credit cards now offer interest rates under 10 percent. There's no reason to keep an old card charging 18 or 22 percent when other cards are offering 7 to 10 percent. And in spite of familiar advertising, unless you really think you might need it, be sure to leave home without it; sometimes controlling charges might be as easy as not carrying a card in your wallet.

Bank Loans

When shopping for a bank loan, think of it as a long-term relationship. Don't just call a lending institution out of the phone book and ask for a loan. Set up an appointment with a loan officer. Interview the officer as if he or she were going to be a business partner. Ask about the services that come with a loan account. For instance, some banks offer free checking when your payment is automatically deducted from your checking account.

If you're not happy with the interview, look elsewhere until you find someone you feel comfortable with. And look for a competitive interest rate. The interest rates among banks are fairly consistent but you can get good deals occasionally during special promotions.

Home equity loans are fixed-rate loans usually paid over 10 or 15 years. Interest ranges from about 7 to 12 percent, or can be tied to the prime lending rate, depending on the location in the country and the bank. The rate is usually more than a first mortgage rate, but less than an unsecured loan.

Unsecured personal loans are now ranging between 13 and 18 percent or more, because the lender takes more risk without collateral to fall back on. Finance company rates can extend to 19 percent or more.

Consumer Loans

When the 1986 Tax Reform Act was passed, a collective groan was heard across the United States. The act provided for the gradual phase out of tax deductions for consumer credit interest. America — the credit card society — took it on the chin. With 1990 figures of more than $700 billion in outstanding consumer debt, consumers had some rethinking to do. It no longer made sense to finance consumable items such as automobiles, recreational vehicles, and boats.

Before you consider borrowing money for any reason, calculate your actual costs, and know the definition of terms such as annual percentage rate, add-on interest, and the discount method.

Annual Percentage Rate (APR) refers to the rate of interest you pay on funds borrowed, but it doesn't always reflect the actual interest you will be charged; you have to read all the fine print to figure that out. If the annual percentage rate of a loan is 12 percent on a one-year loan of $1,000, at the end of the year you will have paid $120 in interest, right? Not necessarily, unless your loan is an add-on rate (see below).

A **simple interest loan** is a loan where interest is paid only on the balance outstanding. The annual interest rate is divided by the number of days in a year to determine the daily rate. Then the daily

FIGURE 5–3

Don't Cash in Your Investments

Financial advisors will often tell you to pay off all your debts then work on saving. In theory, this seems legitimate; using savings earning 4 or 5 percent to pay off 18 percent credit card debts certainly sounds reasonable.

But this theory doesn't consider two vital points. It doesn't consider the magic of compound interest and the irreparable damage delay causes to long-term investment results. Neither does it consider human nature, subject to the circumstances of fate and the whims of gratification that cannot guarantee a debt-free future. Instead of using your investments to pay off your debts, we recommend the following:

Make an all-out effort to pay off your bills — after you pay yourself first, of course. We believe the only way to get out of debt is to start saving. When you don't have any savings, every time an emergency or an opportunity comes up, you have to go further into debt again. With savings, you can deal with the situation, and sooner than later, the debts disappear.

Borrow against your investments to pay off your credit cards. This is really using debt to pay off bad debt, which only works when the overall cost of the new credit actually reduces the interest cost. A loan secured with mutual funds will have a lower interest rate than the credit card debt, and your money in your mutual fund will continue to work for you. Banks are also usually quite happy to lend up to 80 percent of your savings at a rate 2 to 3 percent higher than what the savings are earning. You still have your savings, and the net cost on the loan is only 2 to 3 percent for its duration.

For example, let's look at Ron and his coworker Kate. Both are age 30 and they each have $5,000 in investments earning 10 percent. They also each have $5,000 in credit card debts at 18 percent that will be paid off in five years at their current repayment rate. Ron decides to cash in his investments and pay off his credit cards, figuring that without credit card payments he can accumulate another $5,000 to invest within five years at age 35. Kate, on the other hand, took our advice, left her $5,000 investment alone, and continued making the minimum payments on her credit cards. Who made the best decision? How would decide if you could look back from retirement?

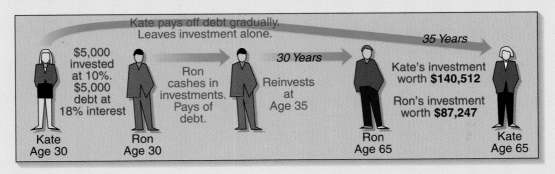

Secrets or Proven Principles?

rate is multiplied by the balance outstanding of the loan for the number of days in the month (31, 30, or 28). In this example, the interest paid at the end of a year would be $66.08.

Some credit card companies figure an average daily balance for the month, and multiply that by a monthly interest rate. Truth in lending laws require that all of this information is available to you, and it is usually clearly printed on the statements. Be sure to read it.

Add-on interest works like this: In borrowing the $1,000 at 12 percent interest, the lender will automatically add the interest ($120) to the principal, making your repayment amount $1,120. That means that you pay interest on the whole loan amount each month, making your annual percentage rate significantly higher. Even though you're repaying $\frac{1}{12}$ of the amount each month, you're still paying interest on the full amount of the loan for the entire term of the loan. You will have paid $120 in interest at the end of one year, at an actual annual percentage rate of 21.46 percent.

The **discount method** may sound good, but beware — this method of figuring loan repayments will actually cost you more than the add-on interest rate method. Here's how it works: The lender figures the interest on the loan (in our scenario, $120), then subtracts that amount from the loan. You receive $880, meaning you're paying the interest up front. And because you don't have use of the money for the length of the loan, your effective interest rate is higher. The annual percentage rate on the discount method for this loan would be 24.28 percent, and you will have paid $136.36 in interest at the end of the year.

As you can see, in both the add-on and discount methods, your annual interest rate was actually about twice what the stated interest rate was. With multi-year loans, your annual percentage rate will be even higher — 27.87 percent for the discount 12 percent loan if the term is two years. If you must take out a consumer loan, be sure you completely understand what the actual interest charges are — before you sign on the dotted line.

Convenient Alternatives to Credit Cards

Debit Cards

A *debit card* looks like a credit card, has all the convenience of a credit card, but it doesn't contribute to indebtedness like a credit card. When you use a debit card, the amount of the purchase is immediately subtracted from your bank account. Reserve your hotel on a debit card, but when it comes time to pay, you need to have the money in your

YOU CAN'T BORROW YOUR WAY OUT OF DEBT

Wrapping up all your debts — the auto loan, the medical bills, the furniture, and the credit cards — in one neat package and paying one easy monthly payment instead of 11 or 12 sounds like the million-dollar answer to your debt headache, doesn't it? And if you use the equity in your home to secure the loan, you get the benefit of the interest deduction, right? Well, yes and no.

The interest on a home equity loan may be deductible, but debt consolidation is often just one more credit trap for the uninformed. Banks, finance companies, and credit unions all offer debt consolidation loans, but you may not always be informed that you are putting your home at risk if you can't make the payments. Neither will anyone be too eager to tell you that you will actually be paying more in the long run. Stretching out the time to keep the payment low may actually increase the cost of borrowing.

Debt consolidation borrowers give up a lot of flexibility. Before consolidation, it remains possible to prioritize, juggle payment dates, and negotiate with certain lenders to reduce the payments or the interest rates. With one loan payment, this flexibility disappears.

It's not good, either, to consolidate non-interest-bearing debts with the rest. Keep paying the doctor's bills and the attorney fees, and don't turn them into interest-bearing debts by consolidating them with high-interest debts. Also, some of the debts may be near the end, when you are paying more principal than interest, and consolidating them would start the interest/principal equation back at the beginning again.

Deciding whether or not to consolidate requires taking a hard look at how you got into debt in the first place. If you were unemployed for a time, or had unexpectedly large medical bills, then consolidation is probably a good idea. But if consolidation will give you such a euphoric feeling that you celebrate by running up all your cards to the limit again, bite the bullet and finish the race instead. You can't borrow your way out of debt, and people shackled with bad debt can't achieve financial success.

account. For credit junkies trying to change bad habits, a debit card might be the perfect answer.

Smart Cards

One answer to increase your future ability to control spending and add incredible convenience to the way you handle your money may lie in the new smart cards. *Smart cards* are credit card-sized pieces of plastic embedded with microprocessors and covered with a substance that can be written on with a laser. They are slightly thicker than a credit card, and like memory cards, their cousins, have a storage capacity equivalent to hundreds of pages of data.

Smart cards can be electronically charged with a certain monetary value which is reduced each time the card is used, and then be discarded. They can be used in the supermarket to pay for your groceries, to collect electronic coupons, and to earn frequent shopper points. They are capable of becoming an "electronic purse," holding health insurance records, frequent flyer records, drivers license and passport information, hotel reservations, and phone cards. Your auto smart card can hold all your warranty and maintenance information, not to mention your complete loan payment records. They can be a bank card, a credit card, and an electronic checkbook, all in one.

If this sounds too futuristic, it will help to know that smart cards aren't all that new. They have been around since the 1970s. More than ten million smart cards are in circulation in France to use in pay telephones that read the card and subtract the price of the call. Italians use them to pay highway tolls and the Japanese have also been on the bandwagon for some time. Americans have lagged behind the rest of the world, primarily because of the millions of dollars invested in readers for the magnetic stripe cards. Industry consultants estimate smart cards will be commonly used by 2006, based on the way Americans adjusted to credit cards.

Tough Choices — Getting out of Debt

Okay, so you understand the theory behind managing your credit, but you're having a tough time applying the theory to your situation because you are swamped with bad debt. For you, the light at the end of the tunnel is a mere flicker, and it nearly goes out every month when you can barely make those minimum payments. When you are completely disabled financially, or when you can see disaster ahead if you don't change something quickly, it's time to make some tough choices about a tough situation.

There are any number of reasons for financial problems: a decrease in income, a change in marital status, or unexpected emergencies can all contribute. But the biggest reason of all remains those credit card accounts that mushroom out of control. When debt becomes overwhelming, some people just try to ignore it, or look for new lines of credit to pay off the old bills. Neither of these attitudes make much progress, in our estimation, and really only make it worse.

Establish a Workable Budget

We think situations like this point to the fact that getting serious about the B word is long overdue. When debt has become a serious problem you simply must figure out a budget. The first tough choices involve identifying nonessential expenditures. Sometimes, you even have to prioritize the essential ones. Then you have to pledge a portion of your income to repayment of debt. If this isn't enough, there are tougher choices ahead.

You may have to renegotiate with creditors. In our experience, simply communicating your problems to your creditors often brings a surprising effort to help. One banker we know told us that he would rather work with clients who have had financial problems and worked through them, because it proved their financial mettle.

Debt Counseling

The good news is: you don't have to do it alone. There are credit counseling services all over the country that are willing to help you for a nominal charge in a nonjudgmental way. Credit Counseling Centers of America are listed in the phone book, as are other nonprofit consumer credit counseling services.

Watch out for the for-profit debt counseling companies and the telephone counseling programs that sometimes charge hundreds of dollars to consolidate your debts. Always look for centers accredited by the National Foundation for Consumer Credit.

You will generally go for a one-hour interview and be charged a one-time fee of about $25, or $5-$10 each for working up the proposals to deal with your creditors. The counselors will help you deal with your creditors, working out payment schedules, eliminating late charges, and stopping those threatening collection calls. Your accounts are flagged AA for agency accounts, to let creditors know that they are being dealt with.

Beware too, of credit repair companies and individuals who offer to fix bad credit reports for an up-front fee. Many of these so called "credit doctors" frequently promise far more than they can deliver. Congress currently has legislation pending to protect the public from the deceptive advertising and business practices of these organizations and individuals.

Second Jobs

One popular radio talk show host always recommends getting a second job to get out of debt, or putting a nonworking spouse to work part-time, and we think there is a lot of good sense in this approach. Moonlighting, whether it is a weekend job or a couple nights a week, can go a long way to getting out of debt fast. It's the tough choice of biting the bullet for a short time to limit long-term agony.

A part-time job 15 hours a week in a fast-food place can bring an additional $100 a week to the budget. In about a year, you could pay

Figure 5–4

Top Ten Ideas to Get Out and Stay Out of Debt

1. **Cancel all your credit cards except one, and pay that one off every month.**

2. **Use a debit card or a charge card instead of a credit card.** Debit cards offer all the convenience of credit cards but money is deducted from your account immediately when the card is used. A charge card requires that you pay your balance in full each month.

3. **Never use credit to purchase consumer goods, depreciating assets, or items with no income-producing potential.** Meals, clothing, and vacations are some good examples.

4. **Never use credit if repayment will strain your finances.** Limit you installment debt (other than your home mortgage) so that monthly payments do not exceed 10 percent of your income.

5. **Always shop carefully to find the lowest interest rates.** Even small differences in interest rates can make a large difference in the total amount of interest you pay over time.

6. **Begin establishing a cash reserve fund immediately.** Without adequate cash reserves, you will have great difficulty getting out of debt, because every time you have an emergency you will be forced to borrow money.

7. **Do not cash in your investments to pay off your debts.** In doing so, you will not be able to realize the long-term value of investing — the time-value of money. Continue making at least the minimum monthly payments on your installment debts, but do not take on additional credit.

8. **Use debt consolidation loans with great care.** You cannot borrow your way out of debt. Debt consolidation loans may allow you to stretch your payments over a longer time period, thereby reducing your total payments each month, but you will lose flexibility in your repayment plan and you may end up paying more interest in the long run.

9. **Use credit as necessary to purchase assets which are likely to appreciate, to start or grow a business, or to purchase education which will enhance your earning ability.**

10. **Understand that the abuse of credit is one of the leading causes of financial failure.**

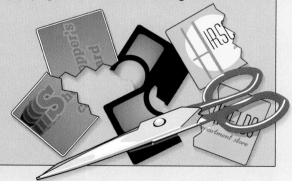

off $5,000 of credit card debt. Add it to what you are paying already, and you might only have to work a few months. One enterprising carpenter we know earned a thousand dollars a weekend by building decks. At that rate, he paid off his debts in a few months, and used his summer weekends for relaxing, free of guilt and worry.

None of this works, of course, unless you *stop borrowing.* Add zero new debt while you are digging yourself out. We have heard that it only takes 26 days to change a habit. But we have also heard that the older we get, the harder it is to make changes, so it only makes sense to do it now, before we get even a day older.

Bankruptcy

As a last resort, there always remains the option of bankruptcy. Bankruptcy has traditionally been a life-wrenching last resort for people impossibly deep in debt, with no other options. Today, people with perfectly good jobs, even two-income families, declare bankruptcy not from dire necessity, but because their debts are making them uncomfortable.

Anyone lured by this seemingly easy way out needs to be aware that lawyers get paid first — up front — and some even accept credit cards for payment. The bankruptcy goes on your credit record for 10 years, and you cannot square things with your creditors later. When that question, "Have you ever declared bankruptcy?" is asked on every credit application for the rest of your life, you have to check the yes box.

There simply isn't an easy way out of debt. The uphill trudge will always be more difficult than sledding down. It's a law of nature. But while you are laboring up the hill, keep your eyes on the goal, and imagine how wonderful the view from the top will be.

Free Yourself

It's not easy in today's world, but managing your credit wisely is a giant step on the road to personal wealth. Owning this Fifth Secret of Financial Success prevents you from robbing yourself of the power of your future income by carrying a burden of consumer debt. The roots of this secret can be traced back through *Poor Richard's Almanac,* the writings of Shakespeare, and beyond. The wisdom remains sound. Keep yourself unencumbered, so you have the freedom to move toward financial success. Manage your credit wisely.

Secrets or Proven Principles?

SIX

Safeguard Your Future
Protect Your Financial Success

"The wise man avoids evil by anticipating it."
– Publilius Syrus

Y ou now hold five of the secrets to creating your personal financial success in your hands. Setting goals and paying yourself first contribute to the creation. Harnessing the power of time and diversification contribute to building on the creation. When you own assets instead of lending your money to others and take charge of your debt, you begin to manage your wealth.

Each, in itself, has been a simple idea; we believe truth is always easy to understand. It is the potent combination, the synergism, that exists among these secrets that generates your financial success. And these alone could almost see you to your goals. Except for the unexpected. Wouldn't it be a tragedy to follow these secrets — to succeed — and then lose it all to a catastrophe? That's why we will give you two more secrets. First, Secret Number Six: *safeguard your future.*

We've talked about market risk and managing it through diversification. But market risk could seem like a mere mishap in the face of a true disaster. As much as we would like to, we can't eliminate risk from our lives. The unpredictability of injuries, illnesses, or natural disasters makes human beings forever vulnerable.

We can't take away the risk of your premature death, but it is possible to manage the financial burden your loss would have upon your loved ones. It is possible to understand the way risk is managed to lessen the financial impact of adversity or disaster. Just as diversification increases your comfort level dealing with market risk, insurance increases your comfort level with life, income, and property risks. Insurance is the secret weapon to safeguarding your future.

How Does Insurance Work?

Insurance is protection. All the millions of insurance policies have one thing in common: to protect against the adverse effects of financial losses. The basic concept of insurance is the transfer of risk from an individual to a larger group of persons. In short, the personal disaster of one contributing individual is paid for by the contributions of many people to lessen the impact of loss to the insured.

This concept goes far back in history, when tribes worked together to replace the belongings or dwellings of families who lost them to fire. The essence of insurance could also be found in the charitable community support to widows and orphans, long before welfare or Social Security.

Insurance companies were formed in the United States during the 1750s. Insurance has since become a major institution, essential to the functioning of virtually all economies. Insurance companies do more than occupy beautiful buildings. They provide a financial safety net for you and your family.

Insurance companies collect sums of money, or *premiums,* from individuals they insure. The premiums are pooled together to pay losses to the insured. Companies provide contracts, or *policies,* that specify the terms and conditions under which losses, or *claims,* are paid.

Insurance is not intended to be a gamble. It is based on probability and the law of large numbers. Insurance companies have kept extensive records for many years, which enables them to determine the probability, or chance, of loss within a large group of policyholders. Actuaries (keepers of the extensive records) calculate the premiums needed to pay claims and cover operational expenses.

Individual policyholders are not meant to profit from buying insurance coverage. Instead, insurance is intended to cover only actual financial loss. Some people feel cheated when a loss doesn't occur and some even feel the premium should be returned if a loss hasn't occurred. But returning premiums would destroy the underlying economic principle of insurance: loss distribution.

Risk Management

Almost everyone needs some sort of insurance coverage. If you are just starting out and have put every extra cent you earn into buying a new car, you'll want to make sure your car will be replaced in the

Secrets or Proven Principles?

FIGURE 6–1

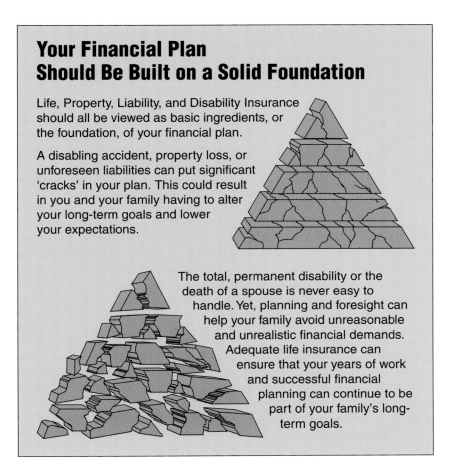

Your Financial Plan Should Be Built on a Solid Foundation

Life, Property, Liability, and Disability Insurance should all be viewed as basic ingredients, or the foundation, of your financial plan.

A disabling accident, property loss, or unforeseen liabilities can put significant 'cracks' in your plan. This could result in you and your family having to alter your long-term goals and lower your expectations.

The total, permanent disability or the death of a spouse is never easy to handle. Yet, planning and foresight can help your family avoid unreasonable and unrealistic financial demands. Adequate life insurance can ensure that your years of work and successful financial planning can continue to be part of your family's long-term goals.

event of a collision; otherwise, the hours you worked to buy that car might as well be considered wasted hours.

Determining that you need insurance is easy. Getting the right kind of coverage at the least cost, however, takes some homework on your part and an understanding of how risk is managed. Anyone who purchases insurance for every risk will soon find themselves broke; unnecessary insurance premiums are costly. Yet those who avoid paying any insurance premiums will find themselves in the same shoes.

Methods for Handling Risk

Risk Acceptance.   Some risks are not very large, so you can decide to accept full responsibility for them. For example, you don't purchase collision insurance for your 1974 Ford pickup truck parked in the garage. If you slide off an icy road and bump into a tree, it will be just another dent in your collection. The economic impact is minimal, so you accept the risk of loss or repairing any damage to the truck.

Risk Transfer. This transfer is done by buying insurance. Risks that you cannot afford to accept are transferred to an insurance company for the price of a premium. Not many of us would be able to write a check for a new house if ours burned to the ground, so we purchase homeowner's insurance.

Risk Sharing or Insurance Deductibles. Risk sharing is a combination strategy where you *accept* a small amount of the risk and *transfer* the majority of the risk to the insurance company. The deductible provision, requiring the policy holder to pay a basic amount before the insurance benefits begin, is the tool with which this is accomplished. You may think that the insurance company should have all the risk; you don't want any of it. But, are you willing to pay the higher premiums necessary for the insurance company to accept all the risk? The more risk the company takes, the higher the premium. Conversely, if you agree to take more of the risk, the premium is lower.

In reality, we find that many people don't use deductibles very well. In most cases, the use of higher deductibles will significantly reduce premiums. When deciding how much the deductible should be, consider what dollar amount of risk you feel comfortable in assuming and the impact that paying more in the event of a loss would have on your financial well being. When you have an emergency fund in place, a loss shouldn't cause undue hardship.

Many people have either reduced their premiums or improved their quality of protection, with little or no additional premium, by increasing the amount of their deductibles on their homeowner's, automobile, and health insurance policies. Special attention to deductibles and their relationship to cost and coverage is a wise application of the sixth Secret of Financial Success.

Risk Avoidance. Some activities present rather large risks which you may not be able to afford to accept. Nobody else wants to accept them, either. Did you ever try to buy collision insurance on the motorcycle your teenage son takes to the motocross track? Don't bother. It's not out there. If you can't afford a wreck, don't go to the track.

Risk Reduction. Can the possibility of loss be minimized by restricting the conditions that can create losses? Certainly. After one person

Secrets or Proven Principles?

FIGURE 6-2

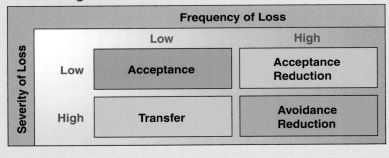

Methods of Handling Risk

1. **Risk Acceptance** – choosing to bear the full financial burden in the event of loss.
2. **The Use of Deductibles** – the sharing of risk, that is, you are responsible for losses incurred up to a specified dollar amount; then the insurance company pays for damages above the deductible amount.
3. **Avoidance** – removing the possibility of loss by deciding not to participate in the risk-creating activity.
4. **Reduction** – minimizing the possibility of loss through restricting the conditions that create loss.
5. **Transfer Risk** – the purchase of insurance to cover any loss incurred.

Risk Management Framework

	Frequency of Loss	
	Low	High
Severity of Loss Low	Acceptance	Acceptance Reduction
High	Transfer	Avoidance Reduction

we know had his car stereo stolen three times, he decided to install an alarm system and be more careful about where he parked his car.

You may be asking how to determine which methods should be used to handle which risks. You can get an idea by using the chart. To be sure, consult a financial advisor.

Planning Your Insurance Program

When planning your insurance needs, ask yourself the following questions: What should be insured? How much should it be insured for? What kinds of insurance do I need? From whom should I purchase the insurance?

Consider the risks you are exposed to and how financial losses would affect you. Carefully examine your potential insurance coverage

FIGURE 6–3

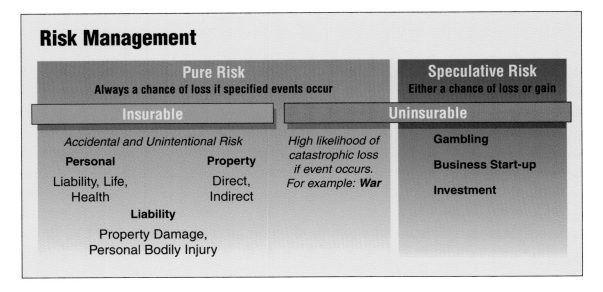

from three perspectives: risk, cost, and benefits. Don't pay for insurance you don't need. Your money is better spent funding investment programs that will serve you in the years ahead.

For instance, a single person with no dependents has minimal, if any, need for life insurance. In this case, the question is, "Who would suffer financially if I died?" Single people need medical and disability insurance because a serious illness or disability could quickly wipe out all their assets. But without dependents, their life insurance needs are few.

Specific insurance needs change throughout life depending on your financial situation, your dependents, your assets, and your exposure to risk. Therefore, it is important to review your coverage regularly. Often, a review will uncover dollars spent on insurance that could be invested elsewhere.

Keep in mind the purpose of insurance. A proper insurance plan should cover all unaffordable losses without spending money on coverage and extras that you don't need. Insurance should be used to protect against losses which would create a serious or catastrophic financial hardship.

In most cases your coverage should include life insurance, disability insurance, medical insurance, homeowner's or renter's insurance, and automobile insurance. Note that homeowner's and automobile

Secrets or Proven Principles?

EXPENSIVE INSURANCE

Extended warranties and repair plans on appliances and electronics are actually insurance policies — usually expensive ones. Defective items will usually indicate their problems quickly and are already covered by a manufacturer's warranty. Repair bills for appliances and electronics can rarely be called a hardship.

The same goes for extended warranties on automobiles. The F&I (Finance and Insurance) person who does the paperwork when closing your new car sale always pushes this insurance. Why? Because it is a high-profit sale for the dealership. It extends coverage beyond the manufacturer's warranty, but doesn't cover routine servicing or things that are most likely to wear out, such as brakes, belts, and hoses. Invest in regular oil changes and other routine maintenance, and chances are your car will outlast the extended warranty.

At first glance, Credit Life and Disability Insurance may seem to be good buys. But compare them to your regular life and disability insurance, and you will see that the cost is extremely high for minimal coverage. Also, these policies cover only the amount owing on the credit contract. The lender benefits far more than the consumer with this coverage. You should have adequate life and disability coverage in your regular insurance plan to protect you.

insurance cover both property loss and potential liability loss. People in their 50s and beyond should also consider long-term health care insurance.

Your Greatest Asset

What do you consider your greatest asset? It's not your investments, it's not your house, and it's probably not even your ability to find where the fish are biting. It's your ability to earn money. Without your earnings or your capacity to support your family, your ability to make investments, make payments, or buy insurance for anything is greatly diminished unless you have disability insurance. Many people would be homeless within several months without an income to pay their mortgage or rent.

Virtually all financial planning experts agree that the total and permanent disability of the family breadwinner is a greater disaster than a premature death because the disabled person remains a consumer but can no longer serve as a provider. Yet, about 75 percent of Americans have no disability insurance. Don't overlook your greatest asset while you are safeguarding your future.

Summary

In our experience, we find that many people carry the wrong types or wrong amounts of insurance and pay too much for inadequate coverage. Some are over-insured while others are grossly under-insured. They associate insurance with the ugly things in life (such as illness, death, and accidents), and would prefer to talk about anything besides insurance.

The secret of safeguarding your future seems to be the most self-evident and logical secret of all. So why don't some people have adequate coverage? Why aren't they making the effort to preserve their financial success? We think it is because most people are worried about being *sold* insurance.

The insurance industry has done a tremendous job of selling insurance, many times to the point where people have purchased policies without understanding why they need them or whether they need them at all. After reading *The Seven Secrets of Financial Success*, you will buy insurance with confidence. We think insurance is vitally important. The secret to overcoming catastrophic obstacles to financial success and maintaining your personal wealth to benefit yourself and posterity is to Safeguard Your Future.

SEVEN

Seek Professional Guidance
Good Advice Is a Great Investment

"Financial planning means managing your own money like a business."

– E. Raymond Pastor, CFP

With six secrets in your pocket, you're probably feeling pretty smart. You can hardly wait to finish this chapter so you can begin to act on these secrets. They are within your power now, and you are saying, "I can do that! I didn't know it was so easy. Why didn't someone teach me these secrets before?"

Our final secret offers a finishing touch — it's the ultimate finesse in building personal wealth. Winston Churchill, a brilliant strategist in his own right once attributed his success to surrounding himself with people who were smarter than he was. We are not demeaning your intelligence, but we think Winston had the right idea. The Seventh Secret of Financial Success, then, is to *seek professional guidance.*

It is almost impossible to go about everyday affairs without seeking professional advice of one kind or another. In matters as important as our financial well-being, it is extremely important to seek out and work with professionals. Most often it takes more than one person to create a financial plan. You will probably need the services of an attorney, accountant, financial planner, and insurance agent.

When we are unfamiliar with a subject, anyone who knows something about it appears to be an expert; however, it is not usually a good idea to take the financial advice of your neighbor — the backyard advisor — regardless of how informed and friendly he or she may seem to be. You wouldn't ask an electrician to landscape your yard or hire a veterinarian to repair your car, would you? Why, then, would you rely on your neighbor or brother-in-law for financial advice? Mix guesswork with haphazard investing, add a dash of ignorance, and you'll end up with hardship and broken dreams.

The field of personal finance and investing is becoming increasingly more complex. There are literally hundreds of financial products to choose from. Which one is best for you? Tax laws change frequently. Sometimes it's difficult for financial professionals — let alone someone who works full-time at another job — to keep up with the field.

That's why good professional financial advisors are worth their weight in platinum. Everyone needs advice about such things as tax planning strategies, how to maximize their investment returns, and how to keep their estates intact for their families. Professionals in the financial planning field can find the best values in your insurance and help you avoid overly risky investments. Good advisors will help you understand your company pension plan and explain how to maximize pension returns upon retirement. They can help you set goals and assist in developing financial plans to meet those goals. In most cases, they can even show you how to invest money you didn't know you had.

The Specialists

Specialists in personal finance provide specific advice and assistance. Identify your needs and seek advice accordingly. When working with more than one professional, you need to coordinate their services — lead your team of advisors — and use them collectively to carry out your financial plan and keep your financial affairs current and in order.

Managing your own income for the greatest benefit and at the least cost is a big job. Ironically, those who don't seem to need professional money management are always the first to seek it anyway. They realize what a great investment it really is to follow the advice of professionals.

Are you wondering whether the time is right to cash in on the stock that rose 40 percent last month? Maybe you want to refinance your house. Sometimes you may find yourself in need of financial advice several times in one week. When you use the services of a good financial planner, advice on these matters is only a phone call away.

Areas of Expertise

Professional financial planners are in the business to help you get your financial house in order. Many planners have areas in which they are especially helpful — and trained. Following are brief explanations of some of the areas where financial planners specialize.

Secrets or Proven Principles?

Retirement Planning. Do you dream of retiring at age 55 or younger? Maybe you have no intention of giving up the job you love just because you turn 65. In either case, a planner can help you take full advantage of your earnings to make the most of your retirement years. Even if you think you have sufficient retirement savings, it is wise to seek a second opinion from a professional.

Investing. A good advisor will get to know you — your likes, your dislikes, your future plans, and your investment comfort zone — before suggesting an investment for you. Because investments are a crucial component of your financial plan, it is especially important to make sure your planner chooses investments that are suitable to your lifestyle, financial objectives, proximity to retirement, and investment comfort level.

Estate Planning. There is no such thing as a simple will. Perhaps you discovered this when a friend or relative died and the estate — which according to the will was left to you — was reduced substantially through administrative costs, probate costs, and estate taxes before you ever touched it. The government has ways of getting a good chunk of your estate when you die, unless you take precautions. A financial advisor will assist you with a plan to ensure that your estate will be dispersed according to your desires. A lawyer will help you with wills, trusts, and other legal questions.

Tax Planning. Reducing the sting of taxes is on everyone's financial wish list. Accountants specialize in tax matters and financial documents. Your accountant should prepare your tax returns to ensure that you are taking full advantage of all allowable deductions. Your financial advisor will help you plan your investment programs to take advantage of any available tax savings strategies. Through good tax planning you may ultimately lower your tax bracket, as well.

Life Insurance. This is perhaps one of the most varied and complex consumer products on the market. In addition to protection, a good life insurance plan can be a good investment and provide tax advantages, but the challenge lies in finding the one most appropriate plan for you. A professional life underwriter is skilled in this area.

Other Services

Other financial services include those of professional money managers. These financial professionals manage large pools of invested money using strategies they believe will provide the greatest benefit to the investors. You can get professional money management through mutual funds or brokers, or by hiring professional money managers who manage large accounts. Some of these services include the following:

Mutual Funds. They are one of today's most popular methods for obtaining professional money management. Mutual fund managers research stocks and bonds, and create a portfolio mix which is continually changing. When you invest in a mutual fund, your money is diversified among numerous stocks, bonds, and other investment vehicles. Mutual funds allow you to invest in stocks or bonds without all the homework associated with picking individual investments. The ease and convenience of mutual fund investing and a history of attractive returns have made mutual funds a favorite among investors.

Stocks and Bonds. When you invest in stocks and bonds, you must enlist the services of a broker. Brokers are available to buy or sell your stock, answer your questions, and provide you with pertinent information. Like mutual fund managers, stock and bond brokers are highly specialized and are not usually the best advisors in other areas of financial planning.

Bank Services. A good working relationship with your banker can yield many benefits over the years. A banker can help you refinance your home or other loans at a lower interest rate, or set up an emergency fund in an easily accessible savings or money market account. An investment banker can help you find the capital to start a business, or increase capital in an existing business.

It's not realistic to expect all these services from one individual. While one advisor could be proficient in several of these areas, it would be difficult for any one person to be competent in every concentration. The longer you accumulate money, the more financial advisors you will need.

Despite their amazing abilities, even the most gifted people need guidance. Athletes, musicians, and actors all need coaching to achieve their goals, to add to their knowledge, and to keep them motivated and disciplined. A financial advisor should be your coach — a trainer who keeps you updated on the latest developments in the financial field. Let's be honest, not everything about money is fun. After all, who wants to think about drawing up a will? Financial advisors can guide you over these hurdles. They will help you avoid costly mistakes.

Secrets or Proven Principles?

Perhaps most important of all, a good financial advisor will help you maintain your discipline and keep on course during setbacks, such as major market declines. People who took our advice and held their mutual fund shares after black Monday, October 19, 1987 recouped their losses within about 18 months and have since continued to reap the benefits of long-term investing in mutual funds. Those people who cashed in their funds and put their money into "safe" investments not only took many years to recoup their losses, but failed to capitalize on the outstanding performance of the market since.

Professional Designations

There are many well-qualified people working in the financial services industry who do not have professional designations, and the designation itself does not make one a good financial advisor. Professional designations cannot guarantee good advice but, for starters, they do ensure that you are dealing with a certified professional who has made the extra effort required to obtain these credentials. Some of the most important designations include CFP, RFC, CPA, CLU, ChFC, and CPCU.

Almost anyone working in the investment business can call themselves a financial planner, but a Certified Financial Planner (CFP) has met the rigorous requirements of the Certified Financial Planner Board of Standards in Denver, Colorado. The CFP licensee has completed an approved education which generally requires passing five examinations over a two-year period, covering insurance, financial markets, tax planning, retirement planning, and estate planning. The CFP

> **"He that refuseth to buy counsel cheap, shall buy repentance dear."**
>
> **Anonymous**

has also taken a rigorous and comprehensive certifying examination, has professional experience in financial planning, and has agreed to adhere to a code of ethics and professional responsibility which is enforced by the CFP board. Continued education is required to maintain the certification.

A Registered Financial Consultant (RFC) has a professional financial planning designation and also meets requirements of experience, professional ethics, and rigid continuing education requirements.

Certified Public Accountants (CPAs) hold an undergraduate degree in accounting, have passed the CPA exam, and have some experience in the field. The title of Personal Financial Specialist goes to CPAs who have three years' experience in personal financial planning and pass a comprehensive exam through the American Institute of Certified Public Accountants. Continuing education is required.

Attorneys (JDs) have an undergraduate degree, a degree from a law school, and have passed the state bar exam. Their services are essential for estate planning issues, such as drawing up wills and trusts. Tax attorneys frequently also hold CPA credentials.

The professional designation of Chartered Life Underwriter (CLU) comes from the American College in Bryn Mawr, Pennsylvania, and requires proficiency in eight areas of insurance and three years of field experience. Continuing education is required to maintain the designation.

A Chartered Financial Consultant (ChFC) has completed an educational program, that includes intensive training in both insurance and financial planning, and has passed certifying exams. A ChFC must also meet experience, ethics, and continuing education requirements.

Finally, Registered Investment Advisors (RIAs) are licensed by the Securities and Exchange Commission to charge a fee for investment advice. This designation merely requires registration with the SEC and has no training or educational requirements.

Professional Associations

Most professional financial advisors will be members of one or more professional associations that provide continuing education and enforce ethical practice requirements. These include the International Association for Financial Planning (IAFP), the Institute of Certified Financial Planners (ICFP), the International Association of Registered Financial Consultants (IARFC), and the American Society of CLU & ChFC (ASCLU). As with the professional designations, membership in professional associations does not guarantee you of an advisor's qualifications or abilities, but at least provides a measure of the individual's professional and ethical commitment.

Choosing the Right Advisor

The types of advisors/planners you choose should depend on your specific needs. Choose an advisor with sufficient experience in the field, and one who is willing to share references with you. Consider recommendations from your other advisors. Qualified people usually like to work with qualified people.

Personal Qualities

In addition to their experience and financial savvy, it is also important to find an advisor whom you feel comfortable working with. Choose a

Secrets or Proven Principles?

FIGURE 7–1

Compensation of Financial Planners

You are probably familiar with the way attorneys and accountants generally charge by the hour or by the case or project. You may not be as familiar with the compensation structure of financial planners. Financial planners may work on a commission-only basis, on a fee-only basis, or some combination of the two.

Commission Based Compensation

Commission-only planners are paid only when you buy financial products or sometimes when selling on your behalf. They do not have an hourly charge, and their financial analysis, advice, and recommendations are "free." However, if you make an investment that warrants a commission, your planner will receive part (or all) of that commission, depending on whether the planner is an independent or what is called a captive planner in a large office (captive planners aren't in cages, they simply work for one company only).

Fee Based Compensation

A fee-only planner charges for their financial planning services but does not sell products. He or she will generally provide you with a complete analysis of your financial situation and recommend future activities. Once your analysis is complete, the planner may refer you to a broker, or you may go to one of your own choosing. You may also continue to work with the financial planner to make specific recommendations for you and you pay an hourly fee for services.

Combination Fee and Commission

Other planners charge a fee for their analysis and financial plan, and then work on commission for specific recommendations.

person who communicates well with you and who takes the time to understand your needs.

Company Affiliation

Ask yourself the following questions before you decide on a planner. What company is your planner affiliated with? Does it have a good reputation? Is it a sound company that has a long-term history of good performance and quality service? A good company carefully investigates the backgrounds of their potential affiliates.

Potential Conflicts of Interest

Some people feel that a financial advisor who is also selling products, from which he or she will receive a commission, has a conflict of interest. We acknowledge that your financial advisor receives a commission when you purchase products from them. However, doesn't your doctor also get paid when you follow his or her recommendations and your mechanic profits only by repairing your car and installing new parts. We could make similar statements regarding your plumber, electrician, dentist, and TV repair person. The point we are getting to is that, if you have carefully selected your advisor, and have thus selected a person with professional ethics and integrity, you can rest assured that he or she will make recommendations with your best interests in mind.

Unfortunately, the financial services business, like all other professions, has its bad apples. We've all heard stories of shysters who have deliberately sold scandalous investments and who bilked unsuspecting investors out of their money. Fortunately these people are easily exposed with a little investigation on your part. They are not employed by quality companies and they do not last long in the business. Nor will they be able to provide any good long-term references. Do not entrust your money to someone you have not thoroughly investigated. The advisors you want to work with will welcome your careful scrutiny.

Just because you're paying for financial advice, you don't have to accept every scenario outlined for you by your financial planner. If you're not happy with a recommendation — for whatever reason — don't implement it. Ask about alternatives to recommendations you are not comfortable with. Everyone has biases, and your financial planner is no exception. Sometimes planners can get hooked on a particular investment strategy and fail to see beyond it. Always remember who's in charge. The planner works for you — not the other way around.

Strictly Business First

An advisor/client relationship should begin as a business partnership. A friend who is a financial planner is not necessarily a good choice for an advisor. The two of you may be less focused on developing a plan and more interested in being buddies. It may be difficult for the planner to see you as a client when you'll be at his or her house to watch the big game on Sunday. And, having your friend as an advisor could

A GOOD FINANCIAL ADVISOR

- Is comfortable talking about money.
- Tells you outright what you will pay, and is up front about fees.
- Always discusses risk.
- Discusses both the pros and cons of any recommendation.
- Compares investment alternatives.

- Offers more than one solution.
- Is pressure-free and gives you plenty of time to think things over.
- Refers you to other professionals.
- Isn't afraid to tell you what you need to hear, instead of what you want to hear.

make it harder for you to disagree with your friend's recommendation. Most important, the combination could be lethal to your friendship if you're disappointed by the results. If, however, your alliance turns into a friendship, go ahead and play golf with him or her. Once the advisor/client roles have been established, they will likely remain the foundation of your relationship.

Even the most astute financial wizards can't always be objective about their own decisions. That's why even financial advisors need financial advisors. As your income and savings build, you will need to seek the advice of a wider variety of financial professionals.

Interviewing Potential Financial Advisors

Interview your potential financial advisor just as you would interview a prospective employee. This is a very important process as you are selecting a person who will help map your entire financial future. Determine whether the person has the qualifications you're looking for and that your personalities are compatible for a productive relationship.

During the interview you will need to discuss many important areas. How will the advisor be compensated for his or her services? What companies are they currently affiliated with? Why have they chosen these companies and how long have they been with them? What special education or qualifications does he or she have? How long has he or she been in the financial services business? Be blunt, ask about their special strengths and weaknesses and whether they are willing to refer you elsewhere for advice in areas in which they are inexperienced or not qualified. What is their general investment philosophy?

Ask about their current clients: How many? What is their income range; their net worth? Ask for references including current clients and other financial advisors they work with. Follow up and contact the references. Generally they will be happy to talk with you.

Ask if your potential advisor/planner conducts any financial seminars. These may provide an excellent opportunity for you to get to know them. And you can also gain some valuable financial information in the process.

What You Get for Your Money

You will receive many benefits from working with your financial advisors, regardless of which financial professional and concentration you choose. A good advisor/planner can provide worthwhile assistance in virtually all aspects of your personal finances.

An advisor will begin your personal financial analysis by evaluating your present situation. Together, you will determine whether or not your assets are properly positioned for the best results within your acceptable risk level and whether your present method of savings and investment makes maximum use of your pretax and after-tax income.

> **"A friendship founded on business is better than a business founded on friendship."**
>
> – John D. Rockefeller, Jr.

Your advisor will show how accepting a little increased risk in well-diversified investments can provide dramatic increases in your overall investment returns. They will help you choose investments that are most suitable for your individual needs and goals and will help monitor the performance of your investment selections. You will discover how to make inflation work for you and how to reduce your taxes through tax advantaged investments.

Your advisor will carefully evaluate your insurance program to be certain that all appropriate risks are covered and will create a balance between your insurance needs and the premiums you pay.

Your advisor will help identify your major financial goals and formulate strategies to achieve them, such as providing for your children's college costs on a tax-favored basis and being certain that you fully understand your retirement planning options. A good retirement plan is vital to avoid ending up like one-third of Americans at retirement — flat broke.

And perhaps most important of all, your advisor will be there to hold your hand; to keep you focused on long-term objectives during setbacks and help you over the mental hurdles that stop so many people from achieving financial success.

Wrap Accounts

Whether the whole investment arena seems totally incomprehensible, or you are quite capable of negotiating the maze but don't have the time to do so, another way to attain professional money management is in the wrap accounts offered by brokerage houses. Wrap accounts manage your money for a flat annual charge, usually a percentage of assets, which includes the management fees and all trading costs.

In theory, your money is turned over to a seasoned professional whose management style has supposedly been matched with your personal risk profile. It's difficult to get hard numbers, but these accounts have between $40 and $90 billion in them now, and predictions extend their popularity to over $1 trillion by the end of the century.

You don't have to be enormously wealthy to qualify for a wrap account anymore. Minimum accounts have come down from $100,000 to $25,000, although accounts under $25,000 may not be considered. Competition has forced the fees down, too; some wrap or asset management accounts charge less than 2 percent of assets.

Getting a valid track record from any investment advisor is tough, because investment advice is inherently an elusive process; there are no firm standards to judge by. A poor investment advisor can honestly report good performance by selecting time periods in specific accounts. We think a better way is to request information on the best account and the worst one, and have the advisor explain the reasons for both.

Beware of managers who suggest only in-house products, that is, those financial products owned by the company you are doing business with. They may be the top performers, but again, they might not be. If you don't like your manager, a change of managers might result in a complete overhaul of your portfolio, bringing on some sticky tax situations, so it's best to gauge your confidence level before going into an arrangement like this. In wrap accounts, as in all professional management situations, you are delegating some responsibility, not abdicating your financial future.

> **One who is not wise himself cannot be well advised.**
>
> Machiavelli
> *The Prince*, XXIII

Stay Involved — It's Your Dollar

Establishing a relationship with an advisor is a gradual process in which you learn to accommodate each other to reach a common goal: furthering your financial success. It takes time to learn to work together and to build trust. On the other hand, don't allow yourself to slip into the role of a subservient consumer, entrusting your financial future to one or more professionals. Continue to take an active role in your finances because no one will ever be as concerned about your personal financial success as you are. Having given you the secret of seeking professional guidance to make the best use of your time and money, we still trust you to continue to take a proactive approach to your financial future.

We don't recommend that you turn your personal financial planning over to an advisor while you sit back passively and watch. Good advisors work closely with you, side by side, to develop plans tailored to your special needs and desires. Good advisors review your plans with you regularly and make suitable changes when necessary.

Additionally, we hope you will continue your financial planning education program. Attend seminars and classes and read publications and articles about personal finance and investing. Advisors will appreciate your interest, and together you can build a mutually rewarding advisor/client relationship.

The Seventh Secret

With this secret of seeking professional guidance, The Seven Secrets of Financial Success are now yours. Their truth has been proven through the ages, and now you can prove them once again. They are yours to use, yours to share with your children, and yours to pass from generation to generation.

The true power of the Seven Secrets is realized when you begin to put them into action. Part II of this book uses our Success Triangle™ to specifically show how your financial future is built, applying the secrets step by step. Part III then shows you exactly how to start putting the pieces together, how to implement and go forward. We think you will find the rest of this book as exciting as learning the best-kept secrets of financial success.

Secrets or Proven Principles?

The Success Triangle
Building Your Portfolio from the Bottom Up

Consider the magic — the power and the aura of transformation — conveyed by the age-old symbol of the triangle. The Egyptians and Mayans buried their dead with their most precious possessions in pyramids, multidimensional triangles, believing the pyramids would channel their souls to the afterlife.

Healers use the triangle to symbolize their power. Magicians use it. And engineers use it because of its solid stability. That's why we chose the triangle as the perfect symbol for building financial success. Our financial Success Triangle™ is a blueprint you can use to bring a powerful transformation into your financial life. It's easy to understand, and we'll deal with each aspect of the Success Triangle in turn to take all the mystery out of your financial decisions.

You already have the Seven Secrets needed to build your financial house. Now, think about the triangle as the place where the time-tested secrets of the ancients meet today's technology and modern financial products. Each of the succeeding chapters is centered around our Success Triangle, and we know from experience that using the triangle guarantees transformation of your financial future. Formerly mysterious things such as financial security and independence magically follow. Your potential for success is truly unlimited.

When architects design a new home for you, they don't show you a plan of the foundation first, do they? No, they show you a plan of the

"Property is the fruit of labor; property is desirable; it is a positive good in the world. That some should be rich shows that others may become rich, and, hence, is just another encouragement to industry and enterprise."

– Abraham Lincoln

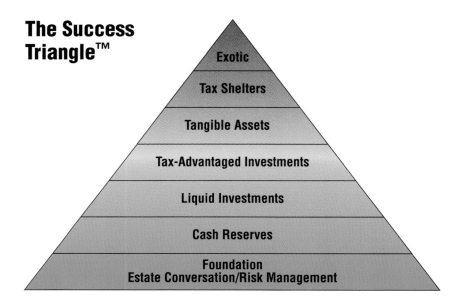

The Success Triangle™

Exotic

Tax Shelters

Tangible Assets

Tax-Advantaged Investments

Liquid Investments

Cash Reserves

Foundation
Estate Conversation/Risk Management

kitchen or the living room so you can visualize how your family will use the dwelling. The truth is, though, the bedrooms could fall into the kitchen if the foundation isn't secure.

There's no shortcut to building your personal wealth, either. With the triangle, we build from the bottom up, laying a secure foundation. If we didn't, the triangle could collapse in disaster. But we also understand that some of the components of your financial foundation are about as interesting as cement blocks. So, although we present the chapters in the order corresponding to a direct ascension up the triangle, you don't have to read them in that order. Start with the chapters that really get your blood pumping. Be sure, though, to read them all. By the time you have the courage to tackle estate planning or insurance decisions, you'll have a clear idea of why they are so important. As a result, protecting all you have worked so hard to achieve will become as exciting as the rest.

Planning your financial future with the Success Triangle, like all other building, is a process rather than a singular event. It involves decisions about investing, saving, taxes, insurance, retirement, estate planning, and, often, special situation decisions for college or starting a business.

It also involves spending: making informed purchases of real estate, insurance, or even consumer products. Spending is making a choice with the understanding that money spent is not available to be spent in any other way.

Most of all, planning your financial future with the Success Triangle involves setting goals: creating clearly defined goals developed with the certainty that nothing can stop your success when you know the secrets.

We don't expect you to go it alone. We absolutely believe in the necessity of professional advice and will always recommend that you consult a personal financial planner. But you must educate yourself to the point where you know whether or not your advisor is giving you good advice. You don't need to know every letter of the tax law, but a working knowledge of how the tax law can impact your financial situation enables you to make informed investment choices.

Don't allow yourself to fall back on old patterns of thinking that rob you of the power to transform your financial position. Procrastination and the failure to establish goals or learn what money must do to accomplish those goals can undermine your foundation. Failure to understand and apply the tax laws and properly prepare for the unexpected put unnecessary burdens on the earning power of your money.

Creating, managing, and building personal wealth is not an easy job. It requires assessing your tax situation, your assets, your financial habits, and your objectives in the current economy. We have provided worksheets in Chapter 23 to help you with this task. It is a rewarding exercise as you see the process taking shape, and you begin to understand just how much can be achieved.

Most important, you must not fail to develop a winning financial attitude. We hold the belief that the only things necessary for financial success are knowledge, discipline, and the confidence that comes from them. You have the Seven Secrets and you have a template for advancement with the Success Triangle, but only *you* can provide the winning attitude.

Ten Investing Ideas for Achieving Financial Success

1. **Start investing as soon as you have an income.** You need to start investing as early as possible, so that you can take maximum advantage of time and compound interest.

2. **Put yourself on a systematic investment program.** Invest a certain amount of money each and every month in a suitable investment vehicle such as mutual funds. Those who lack the self-discipline to do this on their own may elect to have money automatically withdrawn from their checking or savings account, or withheld from their paycheck, and invested for them.

3. **Develop a comprehensive long-term savings and investment strategy.** Look at the big picture and plan accordingly to accomplish the goals that are most important to you. Because of cyclical fluctuations in the markets, short-term investors may be very disappointed and lose sight of their long-term objectives.

4. **Always take full advantage of your employee benefits and company retirement plans.**

5. **Put money in an IRA for you and your spouse every year.**

6. **Invest primarily in ownership vehicles such as stocks, mutual funds, real estate, or your own business.** Loanership investments such as CDs, Treasury bills, and bonds do not generally offer the long-term investment returns that are possible with ownership investments.

7. **Diversify your money into a variety of investments.** Do not put all you eggs into one basket.

8. **Research and completely understand any financial product before you invest your money.**

9. **Utilize the services of qualified investment professionals whom you have carefully selected, to help in your investment planning and selection.**

10. **Be patient.** Do not expect overnight riches. Wealth accumulation requires long-term focus and commitment.

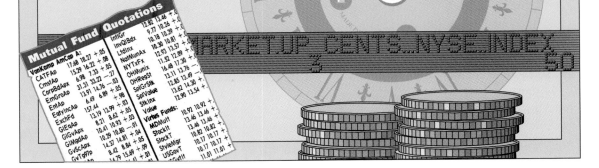

EIGHT

Preparing for the Unexpected
Insure Your Financial Success

otice that the foundation of the Success Triangle is the broadest tier of all. When you begin applying the Seven Secrets to your financial plans, this is something you cannot skip. Shortchanging yourself here undermines everything else you do.

Building a solid foundation by applying the sixth secret — safeguarding your future — gives you room to maneuver all the rest of the way up. It frees you from worry about an unpredictable future. And quite often in our experience, a review of your insurance purchases will uncover dollars spent unnecessarily that can be used more productively in other ways.

If you think insurance isn't very interesting, consider for a moment how interesting life could be trying to survive without 15 months of income if you were injured in an accident. True, insurance isn't the most exciting topic in the world, but trying to figure out whether your policy pays for your family's hotel stay after a tree falls on your house may be more excitement than some of us can stand.

Is there some type of disability insurance with your employer's benefits package? If so, how much is the benefit? How long does it last? More important, how long do you have to wait to begin receiving the benefit?

Sure, you own some life insurance. But is it enough? What does your homeowner's policy cover? The new computer? It pays to discover the answers to these questions before you desperately need to know them.

It is impossible to experience one's death objectively and still carry a tune.

– Woody Allen

Your insurance needs should be taken care of *before* you begin building your investment portfolio, because insurance can shield the rest of your assets from financial disaster and provide long-term security for your family.

Some of the potential risks that could affect your financial security include:

- Loss of family income due to death
- Loss of personal or family income due to disability
- Long-term health care costs (e.g., nursing home costs)
- Personal liability judgments
- Health and medical costs

Let's review the insurance programs designed to protect against these risks.

Life Insurance

It might be more appropriate to call life insurance "death insurance," because the insurance companies are insuring you in the event of your death. On the other hand, if you live long enough for Willard Scott to mention your name on the *Today Show,* many life insurance companies presume you're never going to die and send you a check in the amount of the policy's death benefit.

Life insurance is a sure way to create immediate cash for your family if you are no longer around to support them. It will help your dependents offset the permanent loss of your income and provide for their immediate and future financial needs.

People buy life insurance for two basic purposes: protection and investment. Let's look at each purpose and the types of insurance you might buy for each.

Life Insurance as Protection

The traditional role of life insurance is protection: to provide for dependents in the event of the untimely death of the primary wage earner. Life insurance guarantees dependents the funds to maintain their current standard of living, provide for their educational needs, or pay off the home mortgage if the wage earner dies prematurely. Life insurance may also be purchased to help pay estate taxes or fund charitable contributions upon the death of the insured.

Life Insurance as an Investment

Because of its tax-free, wealth-accumulation properties, more and more people are using life insurance as a tax-free way to build up cash reserves, provide for the stability of principal, earn competitive interest rates, and to take advantage of professional investment management. We'll discuss each of these types of insurance, but first, let's address your foremost question...

How Much Life Insurance Do I Need?

If you have life insurance now, you probably think you already have enough, perhaps too much. It's not that you're against the idea of protecting your loved ones, it's just that the subject of life insurance has some heavy connotations; you'd rather not think about dying, never mind insuring against it.

Nevertheless, we generally find that *most people are significantly underinsured,* rather than overinsured. For instance, consider an individual earning $50,000 a year who owns $100,000 of life insurance. If a spouse, children, or family depend on this person's income for their living, this amount of life insurance would be adequate only if the insured remained dead for no more than two years.

In all seriousness, few people carefully calculate the amount of life insurance needed to replace their income in the event of their death, yet this is the most important purpose of life insurance. Think back to the last time you purchased insurance for your home (or automobile):

"Hello, this is Mary Johnson. My husband and I just bought a new house, so we need to buy some homeowner's insurance," you inform your agent.

"Congratulations on your new home. All I need to know is how much you can afford to pay for your coverage," your agent responds.

You stammer a little, "Well — I'm not sure. I — guess we could afford about — three hundred dollars. How much insurance will that buy us . . . how much would we get if our house burned down?"

The agent quickly answers, "You would receive a check for about $150,000."

"But we just paid $250,000 for the house! That means we would be out $100,000."

"Well, I know it's not all you need, but it's all you can afford," is the consolation you receive from the agent.

Ridiculous to think about, isn't it? Of course. Instead, you determine with the agent how much coverage you need, discuss deductibles, and pay the premium that's quoted to you. We rarely buy homeowner's coverage based on how much we are willing to pay, so why are we willing to buy life insurance using this method? Life insurance should be purchased in the same way you purchase any other insurance. We repeat: Buy enough life insurance to replace your income in the event of your premature death.

To determine exactly how much life insurance you need, sit down with a professional financial advisor and review your family's current and anticipated income needs. You will be considering your other assets, your dependent children, and your future income expectations. You will not be able to decide what type of life insurance is best until you have determined how much you need. You'll have several premium options based on which type(s) of insurance you purchase.

Types of Life Insurance

Just as there are two basic purposes for life insurance — protection and investment. There are two corresponding types of insurance designed for each of them — term insurance for protection and cash value insurance for protection and investment.

Term insurance. Term insurance is suitable for those who only need protection in the event of the insured's death — it provides benefits *only* upon the death of the insured. Term insurance is low cost at first, then the premiums increase over time. The closer the insured is to life expectancy age, the greater the likelihood that the insurance company will have to pay benefits; thus, the higher the premiums.

Term insurance will meet specific short-term needs for life insurance and can provide affordable protection for all or part of your long-term needs. There are three types of term insurance.

- With *annual renewable term* insurance, the death benefit remains level. Premiums increase annually to reflect the increased likelihood of death. This type of insurance is quoted using two different rates: the current rate and the guaranteed rate. The *current rate* will be lower than the *guaranteed rate,* which is the rate the insurance company can increase your premiums to if they find it necessary as a result of adverse mortality experience (actuary talk for "more people are dying than we planned").
- With *level term* insurance, the death benefit and the premiums remain level for a certain period of time, such as 5, 10, or 20

FIGURE 8–1

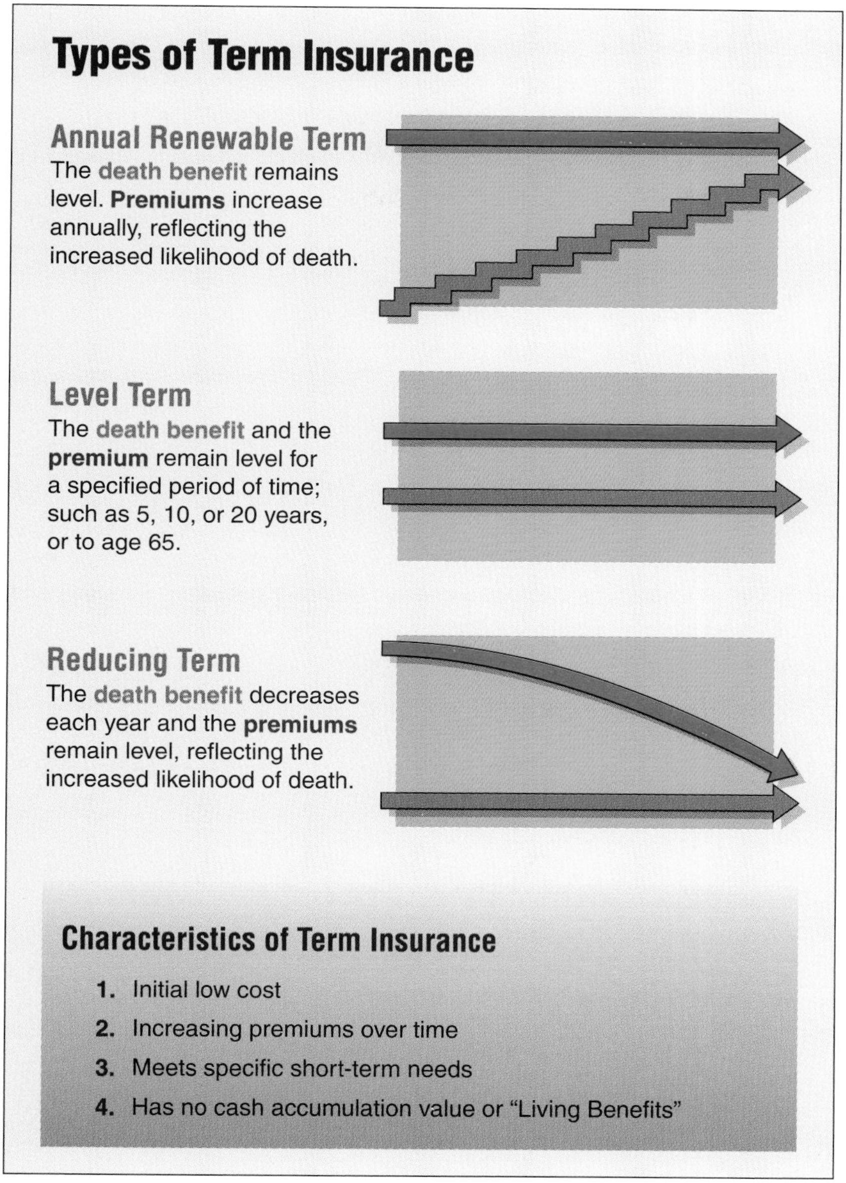

Types of Term Insurance

Annual Renewable Term

The death benefit remains level. Premiums increase annually, reflecting the increased likelihood of death.

Level Term

The death benefit and the premium remain level for a specified period of time; such as 5, 10, or 20 years, or to age 65.

Reducing Term

The death benefit decreases each year and the premiums remain level, reflecting the increased likelihood of death.

Characteristics of Term Insurance

1. Initial low cost
2. Increasing premiums over time
3. Meets specific short-term needs
4. Has no cash accumulation value or "Living Benefits"

years, or until age 65. Some companies offer level term to age 100. Generally, with level term insurance the insurance company "overcharges" you in the early years and "undercharges" you in the later years, providing a consistent premium over time.

- *Reducing term* (also known as decreasing term) insurance premiums remain the same over time, but the death benefit decreases. It is especially suitable coverage to go along with diminishing obligations, such as mortgages. As the mortgage decreases, so does the death benefit, allowing the insured's beneficiary to pay off any remaining loan balance.

Cash Value Insurance. The second type of life insurance is cash value insurance. Unlike term insurance, it provides benefits during the lifetime of the insured *in addition to the death benefit.* While the main objective of cash value life insurance is to create an estate in the event of the insured's death, the cash buildup inside the policy also provides a liquid fund that can be used in emergencies or as supplemental income during retirement.

There are four types of cash value insurance.

- *Whole life* insurance is often referred to as "permanent" or "traditional cash value life insurance." It provides guaranteed death benefits, cash values, level premiums and, occasionally, dividends. Cash values are created when the insurance company invests excess premiums in a long-term portfolio with legal reserve requirements. Whole life purchases insurance on a long-term basis. In its most basic form, a whole life policy is referred to as "ordinary" or "straight" life.
- *Universal life* insurance was created with flexibility in mind. Both premium payments and death benefits may be varied — within certain limits — to meet your needs. As you pay premiums, a portion is used to pay for the pure term insurance rates and the balance is deposited into a side fund that earns interest. If the premium paid is not sufficient to cover the cost of term insurance, the difference is taken out of the side fund. You can vary premiums upward or downward, within limits, and even skip premium payments without losing coverage, if the side fund has enough value to cover the premiums.
- Like universal life, *variable life* has a death benefit created by term insurance with an investment side fund. With variable life, however, the insured may choose the type of investment vehicle used for cash accumulation. The value of the cash accumulation depends on the rate of return of the chosen investment vehicle.
- *Variable universal life* insurance combines the premium flexibility of universal life with the investment flexibility of variable life. Besides the ability to select from various investment funds,

FIGURE 8–2

Cash Value Insurance

Cash value insurance combines insurance protection with a side savings or investment fund called the cash value. The insurance company collects money from you, beyond that required for mortality costs, and it accumulates

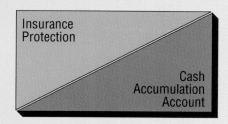

within the policy. This cash value fund can be accessed by the policy holder for emergencies and other needs, or may be used as supplemental retirement income. Many cash value insurance policies pay dividends which are tax-free. Cash value insurance comes in many variations and is known by several names including whole life, permanent life, straight life, and ordinary life.

Benefits of Cash Value Insurance

1. Provides immediate estate in event of death of insured
2. Can provide protection for life or as long as needed
3. Guaranteed premiums
4. Tax-deferred growth of cash accumulations
5. Tax-free dividends
6. Competitive returns on cash values
7. Access to cash values
8. All policy proceeds, including cash value and accumulated earnings, pass to heirs tax-free

the policyholder may also choose to vary the premiums upward or downward, within limits, and may even skip premium payments, if adequate reserves exist.

Which Insurance Is Best for You?

Is your head swimming yet? How can you determine which type is best for you? The answer depends on the reason you are buying life insurance. Is it strictly for the death benefit? If so, you should probably consider term insurance. Will you need to access funds in an emergency, and do you have a difficult time saving money? If these answers are yes, . . . consider cash value insurance.

FIGURE 8–3

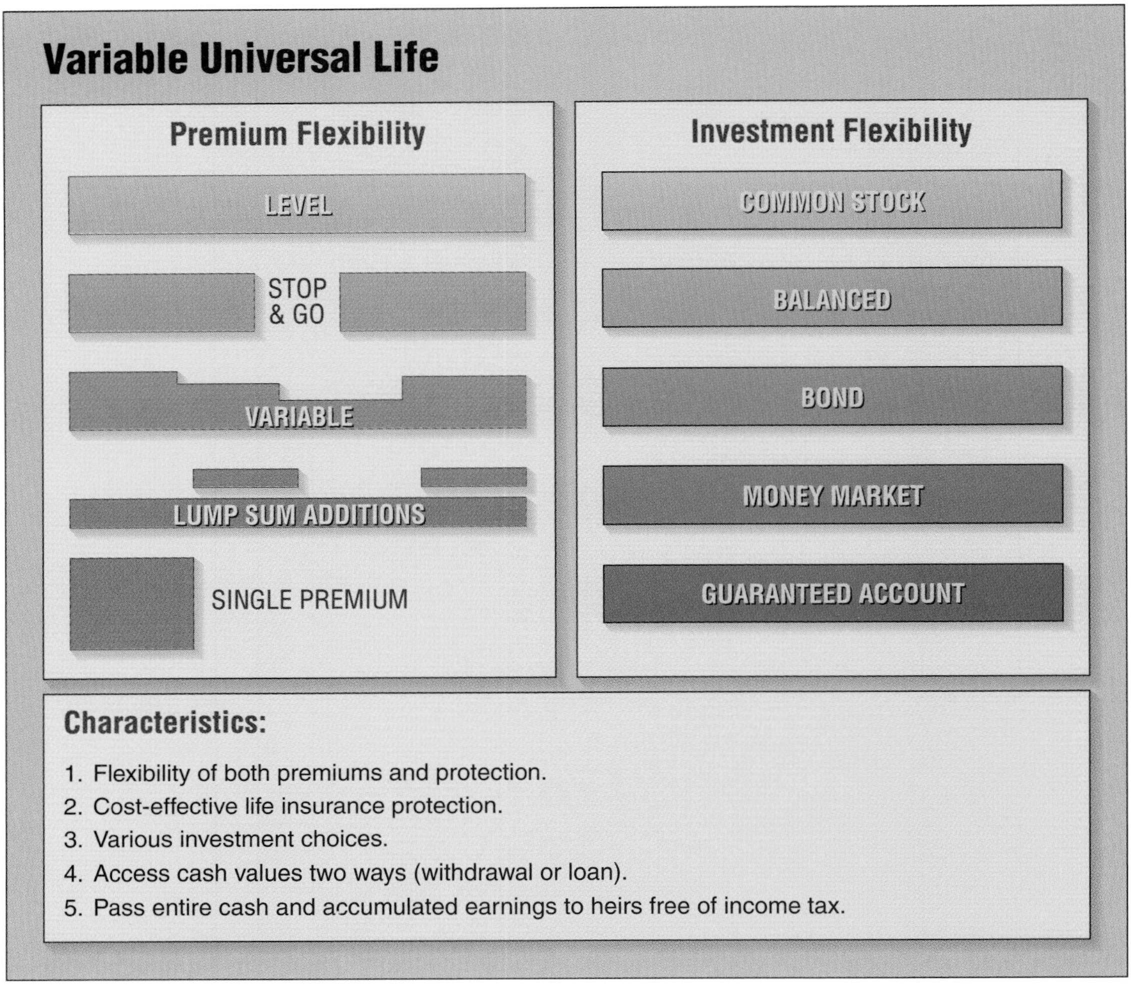

Variable Universal Life

Premium Flexibility

LEVEL

STOP & GO

VARIABLE

LUMP SUM ADDITIONS

SINGLE PREMIUM

Investment Flexibility

COMMON STOCK

BALANCED

BOND

MONEY MARKET

GUARANTEED ACCOUNT

Characteristics:

1. Flexibility of both premiums and protection.
2. Cost-effective life insurance protection.
3. Various investment choices.
4. Access cash values two ways (withdrawal or loan).
5. Pass entire cash and accumulated earnings to heirs free of income tax.

Do you like mutual funds (Chapter 12), but are annoyed with paying taxes on dividends and capital gains distributions? You may be a candidate for variable life or variable universal life. What are your budgetary constraints and your risk tolerance? Do you anticipate needing "extra" cash for your heirs to pay estate taxes? These factors, and many more, should be weighed when considering the type and amount of life insurance that's best for you.

Fortunately, insurance policies exist for almost every situation. Look at Figure 8–4. It can help you learn the features and benefits of

FIGURE 8–4

Comparison of Life Insurance Types

	Term Insurance	Whole Life	Universal Life	Variable Life	Variable Universal Life
Low Initial Cost	X				
Permanent Protection		X	?	X	?
Guaranteed Premiums	X	X		X	
Current Returns			X	X	X
Premium Flexibility			X		X
Choice of Investments				X	X

the different types of life insurance. Next, sit down with a competent financial planner to compare specific policies and companies.

Stability of Insurance Company

Life insurance, whether purchased as an investment or just for protection, should be as risk-free as possible. Before you purchase life insurance from any company, take advantage of the services of one of the well-known rating companies such as A.M. Best, Standard & Poor's, Moody's, Duff & Phelps, or Weiss Research. They will be able to tell you where the company invests its money, its history, and it's current financial stability.

Other Types of Insurance

There are two additional classes of insurance which can provide significant protection against potentially devastating financial conditions. They are long-term disability insurance and long-term health care insurance. Before you think, "It's too soon for me to be worrying about these things," read on to discover why *now* is the perfect time to consider these types of insurance.

Long-Term Disability Insurance

Remember what we mentioned in Chapter 6 as your most valuable asset? That's right — your income. What happens if you're disabled and can't work? Financially speaking, it's worse than dying. Not only do you stop earning income, your family is responsible for your medical and rehabilitation costs.

According to the Health Insurance Association of America, the chances of males becoming disabled increase from slightly over 1 in 100 between the ages of 20 and 30 to over 19 in 100 between the ages of 20 and 60. The rate is lower, 15 in 100, for females between the ages of 20 and 60.

Many financial planners suggest that disability represents a higher risk than death for working Americans, yet only 25 percent of us have purchased individual disability insurance. If you are one of the 75 percent who hasn't, we strongly suggest you consider buying a disability policy. It can ensure that your family will continue to receive the benefits of your income in the event you suffer a disabling injury or prolonged illness. And don't wait too long to buy it; age determines the amount of the premium. Once you purchase a disability policy, premiums should remain the same throughout the life of the policy if it is not cancellable and is guaranteed renewable — usually until age 65.

Don't assume that your employer is taking care of you. Less than half of corporate employees are covered by group long-term disability coverage and in our experience the protection offered is not adequate for most employees. However, you can tailor your individual policy using benefits offered by your employer's group plans to reduce the cost.

Long-Term Health Care Insurance

Contrary to what many people believe, long-term care includes much more than nursing home care for the aged. Today's long-term care refers to a broad range of health care, rehabilitative services, personal care, and social services for people who, due to illness or disability, need special assistance with their daily activities. In addition, because of recent Medicare changes, convalescent nursing-facility care is commonly used to provide continued medical care and rehabilitation therapy after patients leave the hospital. Medicare coverage for this type of care is limited.

The Medicare Myth. A survey conducted by the AARP (American Association of Retired Persons) showed that 79 percent of those

FIGURE 8–5

The Basics of Disability Income

1. Waiting Period
   - ⊃ 60 Days
   - ⊃ 90 Days
   - ⊃ Longer
2. Benefit Period
   - ⊃ Should be a minimum of 5 years
   - ⊃ Preferably to age 65
3. Occupational Classification
   - ⊃ Determines premium
   - ⊃ Determines benefit period
   - Skilled Trade
   - ⊃ 5 Years
   - Professionals
   - ⊃ To age 65
4. Monthly Benefit Amount
   - ⊃ Generally available — Up to 60% of Present income (benefits are tax-free)
   - ⊃ Age determines premium — Once you establish a disability policy, premiums should remain the same throughout life of policy — usually to age 65.

How much would you need if your spouse were unable to earn a living?

To meet basic monthly living expenses:

Expense	Spouse A	Spouse B
Mortgage/Rent	$ 500	$
Food	300	
Utilities	100	
Transportation	200	
Other	200	
Subtotal ❶	$ 1,300	$

To save for your future, educate your children, and prepare for other emergencies:

	Spouse A	Spouse B
Cash Reserves	$ 200	$
College Funds	200	
Retirement Plan	300	
Subtotal ❷	700	
Total (❶ and ❷)	$ 2,000	$

expecting to need nursing home care believed — incorrectly — that Medicare would foot the bill. The reality is that Medicare pays less than 2 percent of total nursing home costs. Medicare will pay for only a limited amount of skilled nursing care, and pays nothing toward intermediate care and custodial nursing care, which constitute the vast majority of nursing home care.

A majority of Americans wrongly believe they will never need long-term care; however, the odds are quite high that people reaching age 65 and over will eventually require it. Two out of every five people will spend some time in a long-term care facility. And most people believe their current health insurance, Medicare, or their Medicare-supplement insurance will take care of them. In nearly all cases, that belief is simply not true.

FIGURE 8–6

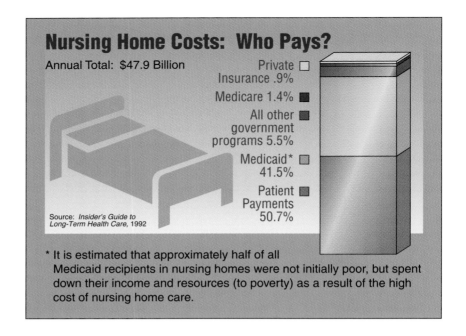

Nursing Home Costs: Who Pays?

Annual Total: $47.9 Billion

Private ☐ Insurance .9%

Medicare 1.4% ■

All other ■ government programs 5.5%

Medicaid* ☐ 41.5%

Patient ■ Payments 50.7%

Source: *Insider's Guide to Long-Term Health Care, 1992*

* It is estimated that approximately half of all Medicaid recipients in nursing homes were not initially poor, but spent down their income and resources (to poverty) as a result of the high cost of nursing home care.

Who Pays for Long-Term Health Care?   Half of the $40.6 billion spent annually on nursing home care comes from direct patient payments — out-of-pocket payments from the patient and family members. Another 40 percent is paid by Medicaid, a welfare program that only kicks in when nearly all of a patient's assets have been exhausted. It is estimated that approximately half of all Medicaid recipients in nursing homes were not poor initially, but spent down their income and resources (to poverty) due to the high cost of nursing home care. This situation eventually made them eligible for Medicaid (welfare). *You or your family do not want to find yourselves in this situation.*

Even if you are a long way from needing long-term health care benefits, consider what would happen if your spouse or parent had to spend an extended amount of time in a nursing home. Many people who *have* considered this possibility purchase long-term health care insurance for their parents to protect their own financial security.

Personal Liability Insurance

Accidents occur at our homes on a fairly routine basis. Most of them are fairly insignificant events — a broken glass, a cut finger, or a spill on the carpet. However, more costly events could happen and a visitor to your home could fall and become disabled as a result. Maybe that tree we mentioned earlier fell on your neighbor's house instead, or your teenager accidentally hits a pedestrian while driving to pick up a younger sibling from dance class.

You could find yourself responsible for the costs arising from any of these or similar type accidents. In most situations, the liability section of your homeowner's or automobile policies will pay for damages, as they typically provide coverage for personal liability up to $100,000.

In the unlikely event that you would find yourself the defendant in a lawsuit for slander, libel, invasion of privacy, or defamation of character, it would be to your benefit to own an umbrella liability policy in the amount of $1 million. Also referred to as *personal catastrophe policies,* they supplement your basic personal liability protection.

Health Insurance

As of this writing, Congress has not passed legislation to change the way health insurance works in the United States. Many of us are fortunate to have employers who offer group health insurance that is either partially of fully paid as an employee benefit. Coverage of spouses and family members may be included or purchased as an add-on to your group policy at a reasonable charge.

The coverage provided by group insurance varies among plans. The amount of protection may be limited, for example, to $250 per day toward a hospital room. If this amount were not adequate for your area you would want to purchase an individual policy to supplement your group insurance protection. You should consult your employer, union, or association to find out exactly how much and what kind of coverage you have. Fortunately, for most people with group insurance coverage, there probably isn't much need to spend time worrying about potential risks in this area. However, if employment is terminated (whether voluntarily or not) or you divorce your insured spouse, you will need to find out how long coverage may be continued and seek replacement coverage.

If you are self-employed or your employer does not offer health insurance, you are put in the unenviable position of needing to purchase an individual health care policy, which covers either one person or family. As you know, it can be fairly expensive. Comprehensive health care policies, covering virtually all potential medical expenses are the most costly, and may not be readily affordable for many families. However, there are some ways you may be able to minimize costs.

Use Higher Deductibles

Remember our discussion in Chapter 6 about using higher deductibles to reduce your insurance premiums? Through the use of deductibles, you agree to accept a small portion of the risk, while still transferring the majority of the risk to the insurance company. Consider this strategy when purchasing your health insurance. The chances of you or a family member suffering a minor illness or injury are relatively high. When you want the insurance company to fully accept this risk, it will charge an appropriate premium to compensate for the risk it has assumed. On the other hand, the chances of you or a family member suffering a major illness or injury are considerably lower, thus the insurance company's risk is lower. By agreeing to pay the first $1,000 or $2,500 of your family's medical bills yourself, through a deductible, you could save hundreds of dollars every year in premiums, while still enjoying the protection from a catastrophic financial loss.

Major Medical Insurance

Imagine yourself with no health insurance. Suppose you or a member of your family suffers from a serious disease and must spend a lot of time in clinics and hospitals and make continual trips to the doctor. The bills steadily climb to $150,000. You see no way out, other than to file bankruptcy.

Now let's assume that you receive a call from your attorney. He says that if you can get a $5,000 check to his office by the end of next week, an anonymous person will pay the remaining $145,000. How would you feel? Relieved, of course. Could you come up with $5,000? If so, think about a major medical policy that pays for the expenses of long illnesses and serious injuries.

Many Americans have become accustomed to having an insurance plan where even the most routine medical care is paid by the insurance company. Although the benefits are great, they are also very expensive. Since major medical policies don't pay for routine care, the premiums are much more affordable. In addition, they usually contain co-insurance clauses, which means you share certain costs up to a specified annual maximum. Your share would typically be 20 percent, up to a maximum of from $2,500 to $5,000 in any one year.

If you are in the position where you are without employer-provided health insurance, carefully weigh your options with an experienced health insurance agent. Virtually everyone needs health insurance. You do not want to be in a position where an illness or injury could deplete your assets and destroy your financial security.

Property Insurance

Now let's look at the second category of potential risks: damage to property. Potential property risks include:

- Home
- Personal Property
- Automobiles

What risks are you exposed to as an owner of a home, car, or personal property? Obviously, it is difficult to imagine a loss of property that could be as financially devastating as a personal loss (death, disability, or major medical expenses). Nonetheless, significant losses could occur and ruin your hopes for financial security.

Risks Associated with Home Ownership

Many American homes and the personal property within them are underinsured, primarily because they are insured for the amount you paid for them, rather than the cost to replace them. As the home increases in value over the years, the owners are assuming more and more financial risk.

Many policies purchased in recent years include some sort of inflation rider, and you might think that's all you need. Regardless of this fact, if the value of your home has increased over the past several years, review your policy to make sure that your home is properly covered.

Risks Associated with Personal Property

One of the most frequent complaints we hear from people regarding their insurance companies is "they only paid a fraction of what it cost me to replace my furniture (or stereo, appliances, etc.)."

Why do so many people have the same complaint? Most often they are unfamiliar with the specifics of their policies. Your homeowner's policy will provide for settlement of claims for loss of personal property using one of two methods: actual cash value or replacement value.

Actual Cash Value (ACV).   People are confused by this term. Many mistakenly believe it means they will receive the actual amount it takes to replace their stolen or damaged property. Unfortunately for them, the actual cash value method will take the actual cost to replace the property, less depreciation for the number of years you owned the original item.

You may have paid $800 for an item three years ago that now costs $1,000 to replace. If the property in question has an estimated life of five years, the company will pay you $400 ($1,000 ÷ 5 years = $200 per year; $200 × 3 years = $600; $1,000 – $600 = $400). If you don't want to get stuck forking over $600 to replace an item (probably quite a bit more, if more than one item was stolen or damaged), check your policy to make sure that it pays claims based on replacement value.

Replacement Value. This is the method most people assume all policies use to pay claims, but make sure you check yours before it's too late. Policies that settle claims based on the replacement value will usually replace your property with no cost to you (exclusive of any deductibles).

However, there may be a cap on the replacement value, based as a percentage of actual cash value. Typically, a policy may state that the insurance company will pay actual replacement value, not to exceed 400 percent of actual cash value. Based on our ACV example above ($400 × 400% = $1,600), the insureds would not have had a problem getting their property replaced.

Risks Associated with Automobiles

This subject doesn't appear to be complicated — we all seem to be familiar with automobile accidents; however, most people associate this risk with fixing a fender along with some new paint or, in a worst-case scenario, replacing the car. Although repair work or a new car can cost plenty, automobile insurance companies spend even more on medical expenses, legal fees, and injury lawsuits.

A majority of states require that you purchase automobile liability insurance but many financial experts believe that state minimums are not sufficient to protect motorists from the large costs associated with bodily injury liability (people injured that were not in your car) and medical payments (people in your car). If you are not sure about your coverage limits, review your policy with your agent.

Summary

Laying a firm foundation through risk management is a prerequisite to all other financial planning on the Success Triangle. Protecting your assets through insurance applies the Sixth Secret of Financial Success: Safeguard Your Future.

Consider how your family would cope financially with the following situations:

- A reduced standard of living for your family as a result of your premature death.
- A reduced standard of living for you and your family as a result of your disability.
- Large medical bills incurred as a result of serious illness or injury.
- The huge cost of long-term care, if necessary, for you or other family members (parents).
- Liability judgments.
- Damage to or loss of home or automobiles.

Identify each of the types of risk to which you might be exposed. Then decide whether you want to accept the risk, transfer the risk, share the risk through the use of deductibles, avoid the risk, reduce the risk, or by some combination of the above.

Once you have made decisions about managing your financial risks, a professional financial advisor can work with you to create a program that will balance your insurance needs, your income, and your assets. With the foundation in place, you're free to apply the other secrets to building your personal wealth.

SECRETS IN ACTION

Adam Tucker, a marketing executive, and Julie Tucker, an accountant, earn $150,000 a year, affording them and their three teenage children a comfortable lifestyle in the northwest Chicago suburbs.

They have been diligent savers, frugal enough to make a $75,000 down payment on their $300,000 home in Arlington Heights. They have accumulated $25,000 in a tax-free money market fund and have added $500 a month to Adam's 401(k) plan at work every month for nearly five years.

Julie started an Individual Retirement Account five years ago after they bought the house, and adds $2,000 every year now. She is interested in stocks, and has enjoyed watching her three mutual funds grow to more than $18,000.

Besides the $225,000 mortgage on their home, the only other debt the Tuckers have is a $7,000 car loan. The Tuckers aren't wealthy, but they learned to live within their means when they were saving for their home, and they like the freedom of keeping their debts under control. Adam feels very secure about their financial situation. Julie doesn't.

College education is important to Julie. Adam has two whole life insurance policies with combined death benefits of $275,000, but if Adam were to die, Julie wants to pay off the mortgage. She feels that the remaining $50,000 and her $40,000 annual income might not be enough to pay for her children's college. Liquidating their savings would mean the loss of retirement funds, leaving Julie doubly vulnerable.

Julie and Adam met with an insurance agent, and found they could purchase an additional $300,000 of level term life insurance on Adam for only $1,200 a year. When their children are educated, they can cancel the policy, but until then, they consider the monthly cost a small price to pay to safeguard their future.

The Success Triangle

NINE

You Can't Take It with You...

...but you can determine who gets it and who doesn't!

The foundation of your Success Triangle is based on risk management, but it isn't complete until you deal with one other eventuality: you won't always be around to manage your money. As unthinkable as this may be, there is freedom and power in knowing that your estate planning is in place. You can extend wise financial management for the benefit of those you love beyond your personal supervision. You are freed by estate planning and risk management to go forward and make decisions to build your personal wealth with confidence.

Before you say, "I don't have much money. Estate planning isn't for me," think again. Without proper estate planning, you may be giving the government more than its share of the wealth you worked so hard to accumulate. What if your estate isn't that large (yet)? Even people with small estates may find there's no such thing as a "simple will." What assets do you own? Who do you want to receive them upon your death? How do you want to transfer your assets? Your household may be the result of a second or subsequent marriage (or no marriage at all). While you are applying the principles of building personal wealth, it is imperative to review your intention for the disposal of your assets and to make sure you have a plan that reflects your wishes.

"In this world nothing can be said to be certain, except death and taxes."
– Benjamin Franklin

How is your estate defined? For purposes of taxation, it consists of all your *tangible* and intangible assets. Your share of any item in which you retain ownership interest is generally considered part of your estate at its fair market value at the time of your death. These assets include your house, other real estate, automobiles, jewelry, precious metals, and personal property. Your estate also includes your share of *intangible* assets such as bank accounts, annuities, stocks, bonds, mutual fund shares, limited partnership interests, retirement plan proceeds, pension plans, profit sharing plans, Keogh plans, IRAs, and possibly even life insurance.

Objectives of Estate Planning

What can you accomplish with proper estate planning, besides keeping the legal profession in business? A visit to the estate planning attorney's office can be time well spent when you discover all the advantages of estate planning. There are several, really. Among other things, you will be able to:

- Determine who receives your assets.
- Place restrictions on heirs. You can specify when and in what form individual heirs will receive property.
- Avoid probate.
- Reduce estate transfer costs.
- Minimize the taxes your heirs must pay.
- Appoint an executor(s) (personal representative).
- Appoint a guardian(s) for minor children.
- Establish living or testamentary trusts and durable powers of attorney.
- Determine plans for lifetime giving.

Estate planning also provides for the management of your affairs in the event you become incapacitated, and probate can be avoided, if appropriate.

Assessing Your Finances

The first thing to do when assessing your own estate planning needs is to examine your balance sheet, a listing of your assets and liabilities, which helps you determine the size of your estate. For this purpose, use the *fair market values* of your assets — the price agreed upon between a willing buyer and a willing seller. It is the highest price that

FIGURE 9–1

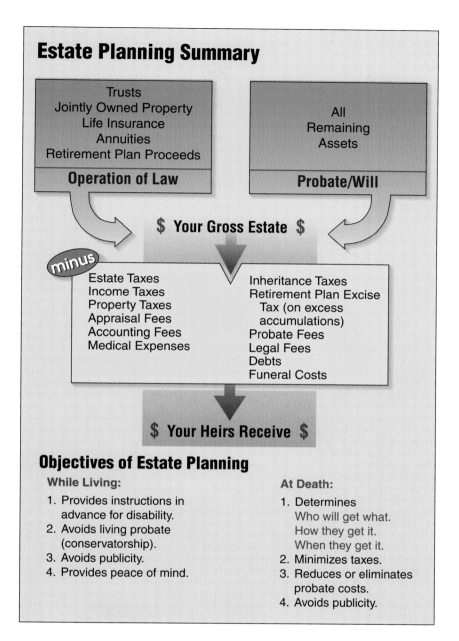

Estate Planning Summary

Trusts
Jointly Owned Property
Life Insurance
Annuities
Retirement Plan Proceeds

Operation of Law

All
Remaining
Assets

Probate/Will

$ Your Gross Estate $

minus

Estate Taxes
Income Taxes
Property Taxes
Appraisal Fees
Accounting Fees
Medical Expenses

Inheritance Taxes
Retirement Plan Excise
Tax (on excess
accumulations)
Probate Fees
Legal Fees
Debts
Funeral Costs

$ Your Heirs Receive $

Objectives of Estate Planning

While Living:

1. Provides instructions in advance for disability.
2. Avoids living probate (conservatorship).
3. Avoids publicity.
4. Provides peace of mind.

At Death:

1. Determines
   Who will get what.
   How they get it.
   When they get it.
2. Minimizes taxes.
3. Reduces or eliminates probate costs.
4. Avoids publicity.

you could reasonably expect to receive for an asset if it were sold. The primary tax payable upon death is the federal estate tax that is imposed upon the net fair market value of your estate.

Your financial statement also includes a list of liabilities so your estate planner will be aware of any creditors who need to be paid before the estate can be settled.

Your estate planner will help choose which of the three methods of distributing your remaining assets is best in your situation.

1. Probate (with or without a will)
2. Operation of law (e.g. joint tenancy, beneficiary designations)
3. Trusts

Probate

The word *probate* is derived from the Latin word *probase,* which means "to prove." Thus *probate* is the *legal process* through which your executor and beneficiaries prove to the court that they are acting according to your will. In the absence of a will, the probate process follows established state laws. Probate is used to accomplish the following objectives:

- To determine the validity of and interpret the intent of the will.
- To transfer legal title.
- To make sure all creditors are paid.

Is it always desirable to avoid probate? No, there are instances where it works very well. Consider the following example of probate in action.

Joe Smith dies with a simple will. The will specifies that his brother Ron is to receive his car, and his wife Mary is to receive the remainder of his property. At first glance, it seems like a very simple will; a will no one could get into an argument over. However, it turns out that Joe had two cars registered in his name: one an old Volkswagen and the other a new Mercedes. Joe's will does not specify which car Ron is to receive, the Mercedes or the Volkswagen. Ron thinks the will means he receives the Mercedes, but Joe's wife generously offers him the Volkswagen.

From our example, probate seems like a good thing, doesn't it? Some process is needed to determine the intent of Joe's will. The legal process must decide issues such as whether Ron gets the Mercedes or the Volkswagen, and put it to rest. Probate also limits the time in which creditors can come forth with debts to the estate. After probate is closed, the estate is free of further obligations.

FIGURE 9–2

Understanding Probate

Probate is the legal process of distributing your property to your survivors after your death. If you have no will, the assets that are subject to probate will be distributed as the court believes you would have, had you bothered to write a will. This may or may not be in accordance with your wishes. If you have a will, the function of probate is to execute the instructions of your will.

Advantages of Probate

1. Provides for the distribution of assets according to your wishes (assuming you leave a valid will).
2. Usually limits the amount of time during which the will can be challenged.
3. Generally limits the amount of time in which creditors can make claim on the estate.
4. Executor's activities are supervised by the court.

Disadvantages of Probate

1. Survivors do not have access to most of the property or assets during the probate period, which can last 18 months or longer.
2. The cost of court fees, attorney fees, executor fees, accounting fees, and appraisals may cost from 3 to 7 percent of the value of the estate in some cases.
3. Probate files are open to the public in most cases.

Source: *It's Easy to Avoid Probate and Guardianships,* by Barbara Stock

Probate Costs

Probate costs vary by state. Texas is an inexpensive state to die in, with large estates settled for $1,500 to $2,000. In New York, on the other hand, combined fees for attorney and executor start at $10,000 for a $100,000 estate, and go to $68,000 for an estate of a million dollars. California is about average for most states, settling $100,000 estates for $6,300 and $1,000,000 estates for $42,300.

It is nearly impossible to predict final estate costs; until it is settled, almost anything can raise the price. In most probates, the attorney and executor will ask for additional fees, especially for extenuating circum-stances. Filing and appraisal fees, bonds or publication fees, and additional legal fees if the will is contested can increase the cost of the probate process.

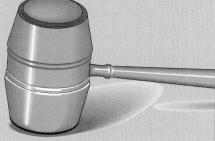

Why do many people want to avoid probate? First of all, the probate process can take a lot of time — usually from six months to a year and as much as two to five years in some cases. And it can be expensive. Generally, probate and all its associated costs (attorney fees, court fees, executor fees) can cost from a few thousand dollars to as much as three to seven percent of the value of the estate. The longer and more complicated the probate process is, the greater the expense. Also, in most states the files are open to the public. Many people don't relish the idea of their estate being a matter of public record.

The decision of whether or not to avoid probate is an individual one. If you're an 80-year-old widow and want to divide your modest estate equally among your three children, then it's a simple choice. No useful purpose can be served by going through the probate process. But, if you're 25 years old with a modest estate and expect to live another 60 to 70 years, it's probably not necessary to go to great lengths now to avoid probate in the distant future.

Wills

What can a will accomplish? Keep in mind that the probate court interprets the intent of a will. If most of your assets will pass via operation of law or trusts, your will isn't worth much. We'll address this problem later in this chapter.

Despite its limitations, a will is an extremely important part of your financial planning. Without one, probated assets will pass according to the laws of intestacy (dying without a will) in your state. The court's distribution of your assets might not be the same as yours would have been if you had taken the time to write a will. With a written will, you can accomplish the following:

- Designate who receives your assets.
- Place limitations on when and how an individual will receive your assets.
- Designate a guardian(s) for minor children.
- Name an executor or personal representative (the person or entity responsible for the affairs of your estate).

Operation of Law

A second and very simple way to transfer assets at your death is through *operation of law,* such as holding the title to property in joint tenancy. If you're married and hold property in both your and your spouse's name, you have *joint tenancy with right of survivorship.* While both of you are alive, each of you has an undivided 50 percent interest in the property. Upon the death of either of you, the survivor immediately acquires a 100 percent interest in the entire property through operation of law.

Designating beneficiaries on insurance and retirement plans works the same way. Since the entire property automatically passes to the survivor, it does not pass through probate.

This situation sounds great, right? It's an easy thing to do: simply register bank accounts, deeds, and titles in both names. But what can go wrong? Suppose you have children from a previous marriage. Your will stipulates that half of your estate goes to your children. If you are remarried and own all of your property in joint tenancy with right of survivorship, you have just cut your children out of your estate. Regardless of what your will states, operation of law takes precedence. All the property will pass directly to your current spouse, who may or may not be inclined to share it with children from your previous marriage. Let's look at another example where joint tenancy doesn't work the way it was intended.

Remember the 80-year-old widow we mentioned earlier who wanted to leave everything equally to her three children? Let's call her Mildred Johnson, and let's see what happened to her estate. Rather than place all three children's names on each asset (resulting in cumbersome paperwork and difficulties if she should want to sell an asset), Mildred decided

> **Regardless of what your will states, operation of law takes precedence.**

to place all of her property in joint tenancy with her eldest child, Myrna. Mildred stipulated in her will that everything would be shared equally among her three children.

When Mildred died, even though her will stated she wanted her children to enjoy the benefits of her estate equally, her estate basically vanished. Myrna, holding joint tenancy with right of survivorship, now owned everything. When Myrna's siblings pointed out that their mother's will specified they should receive equal shares, Myrna said, "Sorry. The will says we share everything that passes through probate. This property went to me by operation of law; it's mine, and the will has no affect on property that passes by way of joint tenancy."

Myrna was right. By placing all of her property in joint tenancy with her eldest child, Mildred unknowingly disinherited her two other children.

Obviously, using joint tenancy with one child requires a lot of trust and faith that your child will honor your wishes. It is ironic that people always have a tough time deciding what other people's wishes were — especially where money is involved.

You can't put limitations or restrictions on the survivor, and you could create a potential gift tax liability. Used incorrectly, joint tenancy frustrates estate planning, making it difficult to minimize taxes.

Trusts

The third method of distributing assets at your death is through a trust. A *trust* is a legal relationship whereby one person, called the *trustor,* grantor, or settlor (the creator of the trust) transfers property to a second person, known as the *trustee.* The trustee has legal title to the property, but is required to manage and administer the property for the benefit of a third person, called the *beneficiary.* A trust is not limited to these three people, either; you could have one settlor, one trustee and 150 beneficiaries if you wanted. Or the trustee and the beneficiary could be the same person. In fact, all three positions can be filled by the same person.

Regardless of who fills each role, a trust is an arrangement whereby title of the property is given to the trustee for the benefit of the trust beneficiaries. The trustee is held to some strict legal requirements as to how the property is administered. In other words when managing the assets of the trust, the trustee must, by law, fulfill certain *fiduciary obligations* arising from this special relationship of trust, confidence, and responsibility to the beneficiaries. The terms of the trust are established by the originator of the trust.

Why would you want to establish a trust? Assets owned by a trust can be managed and distributed exactly as you wish, in addition to avoiding probate. Your assets can pass directly to specified heirs at your death or may remain in the trust for distribution over a period of time. Perhaps you would prefer that your 19-year-old son not receive $50,000 in cash all at once. You can specify that he receive some money now, if it's used for college, and receive the balance when he reaches age 30.

Estate Taxes

One area that estate planning should address is liquidity. Suppose you leave a $750,000 home to your children at your death. A portion of the value of your home will be subject to estate tax. Where will your children find the money to pay the taxes? If they don't have the cash available, they will either have to sell the house — possibly at a fire-sale price — or borrow the money, resulting in interest due.

Many people use life insurance in estate planning to provide for the needed cash to pay estate-transfer costs. If owned properly, such as through an irrevocable life insurance trust, the proceeds can be excluded from your estate, and there will be no income tax or capital gains tax payable on the proceeds.

Why are we so interested in reducing estate taxes? We hate to see your hard-earned money disappear when it can be so easily avoided. And how bad are estate taxes, anyway? If the value of your estate is less than $600,000 you have, in effect, no estate taxes payable. A unified tax credit of $192,800 is applied against all estate taxes, which is the amount of tax on the first $600,000.

In other words, if you died with a $600,000 estate, the tax would be $192,800, but there would also be a credit of $192,800, so there would be no tax to pay. If you don't think you have much to worry about because your estate's not worth nearly $600,000, remember, your estate includes all of your assets: your investments, your home, retirement plan assets, and possibly your life insurance.

With inflation and compound interest, your estate can very easily double in value over a 10-year time period. You don't have to be extremely wealthy to be concerned about estate taxes. Once your estate exceeds $600,000, the estate taxes take a big bite, starting at 37 percent. The first dollar above $600,000 is taxed at 37 percent, and that rate increases rather rapidly to 55 percent.

Many people think, "Well, if I leave everything to my spouse, won't I avoid paying taxes?" The answer is yes — and no. You are entitled to the deduction available to every married couple, the *unlimited marital deduction*. If one of you dies and leaves property to the other, that property can be included in the estate, and there is a 100 percent marital deduction for it.

If you die and leave a multi-million dollar estate to your spouse, your estate receives a marital deduction equal to the value of the estate and there is no estate tax to pay. But, remember that the marital deduction is only a temporary solution — estate taxes will be fully assessed at the death of your spouse.

Credit Shelter Trusts (Bypass Trusts)

How can you use a *bypass trust* to reduce estate taxes? Consider the following example.

Gordon Camp and David Michaels are each 50 percent owners of the fictitious American Business Ventures Corporation, worth $2.4

FIGURE 9–3

Unified Tax Credit

A valuable estate planning tool, the unified credit allows an individual to distribute up to $600,000 to heirs other than a spouse without paying estate taxes on the bequest. A Unified Tax Credit of $192,800 is applied directly to the tax owed. The net effect being that no estate or gift taxes are due on cumulative taxable transfers of $600,000 or less.

Many people, though, are unaware that the unified credit is reduced by gift taxes owed on taxable lifetime gifts. Annual gifts to any one individual are limited to $10,000 ($20,000 if a spouse joins you in making the gift) without being subject to gift taxes. Gifts above the annual limitation are subject to gift taxes at the same rate estates are taxed. No gift taxes are actually paid on taxable lifetime gifts until the $600,000 unified credit has been exhausted, but, any portion of the credit used during one's lifetime is not available to his or her estate.

Planning opportunities are immediately apparent. Assume that an individual wishes to bequeath interest in a business which is rapidly appreciating in value to a child. The business owner knows there will be even larger estate taxes as the business increases in value so gives away an interest in the business today, removing future appreciation from future estate tax exposure.

If the gift is valued at $500,000, no gift taxes are payable as the unified credit would be applied against the amount owed. Should this business interest increase in value to $1,000,000 before the death of the prior owner, it is easy to see that the strategy resulted in substantial estate tax savings. Using the unified credit during one's lifetime can leverage its tax-reducing capabilities. In this example, had the interest been transferred at death, an extra $500,000 would have been subject to estate taxation.

There may be situations where it is desirable to pay gift taxes when the gift is given to preserve the unified tax credit for the estate.

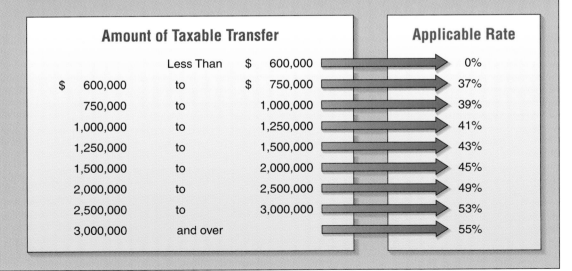

Amount of Taxable Transfer			Applicable Rate
	Less Than	$ 600,000	0%
$ 600,000	to	$ 750,000	37%
750,000	to	1,000,000	39%
1,000,000	to	1,250,000	41%
1,250,000	to	1,500,000	43%
1,500,000	to	2,000,000	45%
2,000,000	to	2,500,000	49%
2,500,000	to	3,000,000	53%
3,000,000	and over		55%

million. Both men die in a plane crash while traveling to a customer site, leaving estates worth $1.2 million each. Shortly afterward, their wives also die, leaving everything to their children. The Camp children receive $1.2 million. And the Michaels' children receive — $965,000. Why the disparity?

The Michaels' relied on the unlimited marital deduction for transfer of their assets. When David Michaels died, his wife inherited $1.2 million. Because of the unlimited marital deduction, no taxes were payable. However, at his death she was no longer married; therefore, when she died, the unlimited marital deduction did not apply. The unified tax credit applies against the first $600,000, but the remaining $600,000 is fully taxable. When the $235,000 of taxes is applied (which is payable in cash, in full, within nine months after the second death), the result is a net inheritance for the children of $965,000.

The Camps, on the other hand, set up their wills so that upon the first death (in this case, Gordon's), the $1.2 million was split into two parts. The first $600,000 went to a *credit shelter trust,* also called a by-pass trust. It goes into the trust tax-free and uses up Gordon's $600,000 exemption equivalent. Incidentally, the $600,000 is not an accidental amount; if Gordon's estate had been worth more, the trust would still have had a specified value of $600,000 to take advantage of the exemption equivalent.

Everything in excess of $600,000 passed to Gordon's surviving spouse. Since the estate is worth $1.2 million, it is divided exactly in half. The $600,000 that went to the surviving spouse qualified for the marital deduction and resulted in zero estate tax.

What happened to the $600,000 in the trust? In most cases, the trustee is required by law or terms of the trust, to manage the assets, invest them to generate a reasonable rate of return, and make distributions of the trust income to the surviving spouse during her lifetime. The trustee can distribute a portion of the principle to the surviving spouse to maintain the same standard of living the couple enjoyed while both of them were living, within the limit of $5,000 annually or 5 percent of the principal. The $600,000 in the trust does not have to be cash; it can be in whatever form that is most economical to manage.

What happened at the death of Mrs. Camp? The trust continues to work. At her death, whatever property has not been used up passes to the children. Prior to Mrs. Camp's death, the $1.2 million was already split into two shares. The $600,000 that passed directly to Mrs. Camp from her husband is included in her estate because she owns it. The $600,000 that went into the credit shelter trust was not included in her estate because she did not own those assets.

FIGURE 9–4

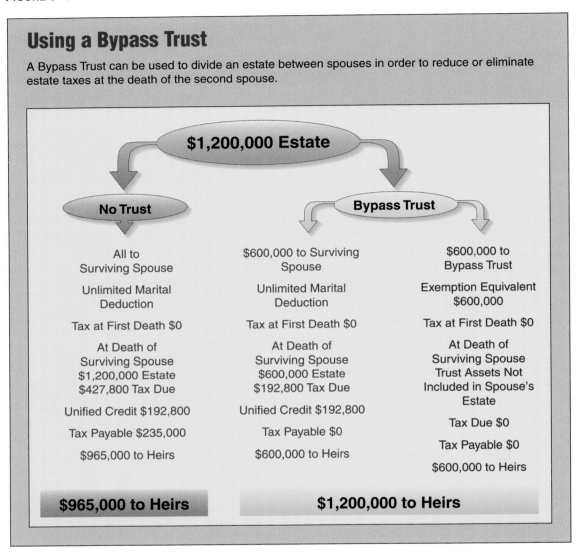

Using a Bypass Trust

A Bypass Trust can be used to divide an estate between spouses in order to reduce or eliminate estate taxes at the death of the second spouse.

$1,200,000 Estate

No Trust

All to
Surviving Spouse

Unlimited Marital
Deduction

Tax at First Death $0

At Death of
Surviving Spouse
$1,200,000 Estate
$427,800 Tax Due

Unified Credit $192,800

Tax Payable $235,000

$965,000 to Heirs

$965,000 to Heirs

Bypass Trust

$600,000 to Surviving
Spouse

Unlimited Marital
Deduction

Tax at First Death $0

At Death of
Surviving Spouse
$600,000 Estate
$192,800 Tax Due

Unified Credit $192,800

Tax Payable $0

$600,000 to Heirs

$600,000 to
Bypass Trust

Exemption Equivalent
$600,000

Tax at First Death $0

At Death of
Surviving Spouse
Trust Assets Not
Included in Spouse's
Estate

Tax Due $0

Tax Payable $0

$600,000 to Heirs

$1,200,000 to Heirs

Mrs. Camp's estate is only worth $600,000 and is eligible to receive the unified credit of $192,800, which allows the entire $600,000 to pass tax-free to her heirs. The property in trust passes to the children, and they are able to receive $1.2 million without any estate tax due. They saved $235,000 in estate taxes through proper estate planning.

SECOND-TO-DIE POLICIES

The Economic Recovery Act of 1981 (ERTA) had a significant impact on estate planning by creating an unlimited marital deduction. This was good news for spouses and estate planners, but bad news for the children of parents who relied too heavily on the deduction.

As discussed earlier, individuals may leave their entire estate to a surviving spouse regardless of its value and there will be no estate tax to pay. However, when the surviving spouse dies, the entire estate may be subject to estate taxes with only the $600,000 exemption equivalent available (if part or all of it has not already been used). Even when appropriate estate planning techniques have been implemented, there is often a taxable estate at the death of the surviving spouse.

If a significant portion of the estate consists of nonliquid assets, life insurance can provide the needed funds for the payment of estate taxes. *Survivorship life insurance* can be an attractive alternative to traditional life insurance policies. Also known as second-to-die life insurance, it pays a benefit at the death of the surviving spouse. This means that the benefit will become available when it is actually needed. Because benefits are paid only on the person living longest, the premiums are less expensive than policies covering one life.

Although paying premiums is never enjoyable, survivorship life insurance is a lot less expensive than paying estate taxes. Even those estates with enough liquid assets to pay the estate taxes, can significantly reduce the financial impact of estate taxes by paying them with proceeds from life insurance. In addition, having survivorship life in place may keep the heirs from having to liquidate an asset that the deceased had desired to keep in the family, such as a family residence.

Revocable Living Trust

The credit shelter trust worked well for the Camps because the estate consisted of one item that was in Gordon Camp's name: his business ownership. But suppose Henry Miller owns all property jointly with his spouse, Wilma. At the death of the first spouse, all of the jointly owned property passes to the second spouse, even though they set up a credit shelter trust. Why? Because operation of law takes precedence, whether or not there is a will or trust. Clearly, a credit shelter trust won't work with jointly-owned property.

What's needed in this case is a *revocable living trust.* Let's say that Henry and Wilma set up a revocable living trust. They both transfer all their property to the trust. Each names themselves as both the trustee and the beneficiary during their lifetimes. They reserve the right to change the trusts, to revoke them, to add property to them, or to take property away. They can deal with the property exactly as if it were their own; for tax purposes it's as though they didn't transfer the property at all. For legal purposes, the trustee or settlor owns the property and holds it pursuant to the terms of the trusts, which happen to be revocable while they're alive.

Why should anyone go to all this trouble? Because the terms of the trust also provide that at the death of the trustee, a spouse (or anyone else the trustee may choose) becomes the successor trustee. The successor trustee has legal title to all of the property, and the trust terms instruct the successor trustee to divide the property into the credit shelter trust portion and the marital portion.

These instructions accomplish the same results as in our previous example. The $600,000 stays in trust for the benefit of the spouse, and the rest of the property passes outright to him or her. The trust avoids probate entirely and, since it still owns the property and causes the property to be divided, only what is distributed to the surviving spouse can be included in that spouse's estate. Both estate taxes and probate are avoided.

Warning: This example only works with respect to property that is actually transferred to the trust during your lifetime. For practical purposes, you will not get every last penny into a trust. If you forget to transfer property to the trust, it will pass through probate. To tie down the loose ends, you can write a "pour over" will with instructions that any property passing through probate be added to the trust and divided under the terms of the trust.

Planning for Incapacity

Just as you can direct the trust to transfer trustee status upon your death, you can also direct it to a successor trustee if you become incapacitated. The successor trustee takes over and manages the property for your benefit during the rest of your lifetime. Upon your death, assets are distributed as directed in the trust.

Durable Power of Attorney

In the event a person becomes incapacitated, his or her spouse can manage the assets if a durable power of attorney was previously established.

A *durable power of attorney* is a written instrument that is used by a person (the principal) to appoint another person as his or her attorney-in-fact (agent). It can become effective immediately (with the

GROUCHO MARX

"Love flies out the door when money comes innuendo."

– Monkey Business

The press labeled it a show the Marx Brothers would have appreciated, but the star, at 86, didn't seem to be enjoying it. Confined to a wheelchair by hip surgery that refused to mend and several ailments that stole his memory and his speech, Groucho Marx sat through the famous 1977 court battle that determined the guardianship of his estate. He had no words to say with a voice reduced to low static. There was no comedic look in his sunken face. The sardonic owlish eyes were void of mischief, but often full of tears.

The California Supreme Court heard the case of Arthur Marx, who wanted Groucho's seven year companion, Erin Flemming, removed as secretary and manager of his father's three million dollar estate. Although Zeppo had come forward and labeled Flemming "the greatest girl in the world," Groucho's nurses testified that Flemming shrieked at him, calling him a "pig" and a "vegetable," and forced him to take tranquilizers.

On April 22, 1977, Supreme Court Justice Edward Rafeedie appointed gag writer Nat Perrin as the conservator of Groucho's estate. The last fracas of the great comedian's life was no *Duck Soup*. It was a real-life circus. Was it love or money that motivated Flemming? Groucho couldn't say. There were no schizophrenic insults, no logic to the lunacy, or no lunacy to combat the proceedings. "All that is left of Groucho Marx," the papers said, "is money."

understanding that it won't be used unless the principal becomes incapacitated) or upon the incapacity of the principal (referred to as a "springing" durable power of attorney).

The agent can be granted power to transfer the principal's assets into an already existing living revocable trust. This approach can add ease and flexibility to managing the affairs of the incapacitated.

Summary

Preserving your estate and distributing your assets as you wish is a concern to anyone who has built personal wealth. Taking full advantage of estate planning gives you the power to provide for the proper distribution of your assets, avoid probate if desired, and reduce or eliminate estate taxes. Estate planning works in concert with risk management to solidify the foundation of the Success Triangle.

Upon your death, assets are distributed through probate, operation of the law (depending on if the property is held in joint tenancy), or through trusts (credit shelter, irrevocable, or revocable living trusts).

Because estate taxes must be paid in cash within nine months of death, liquidity within the estate is an important consideration. One way to ensure that your estate has the liquidity needed is to purchase life insurance specifically for this purpose. Life insurance is not taxable to the beneficiary, but will be included in the value of the estate when calculating estate taxes if the policy holder retains any incident of ownership in the policy.

Trusts require some time and money to establish, but are desirable because they offer options not otherwise available. Trusts can also be a way to deal with special circumstances such as second marriages or incapacitation. Besides minimizing taxes, the peace of mind it produces is well worth the time and effort it takes to set up a trust.

SECRETS IN ACTION

Gerry and Jill Andrew were both previously married. Gerry has two boys from his first marriage, and Jill has an 11-year old daughter, Hillary, who lives with them. Gerry's boys visit every other weekend, and Gerry and Jill are extremely happy.

Jill's employer sponsors an estate planning seminar every year, but she thought it would be quite boring and didn't ever think of attending until Gerry saw it advertised. They agreed they didn't know much about estate planning, and decided to attend.

Gerry was shocked to learn that his current will would not accomplish what he really intended. He had updated his will after his marriage to Jill, thinking he was dividing his estate between Jill and his sons. But he hadn't considered the unintended consequence of putting all of their assets (about $800,000) in joint ownership.

The attorney at the seminar certainly got Gerry's attention. He explained that all joint ownership property would pass to Jill. Gerry's boys wouldn't get anything! Gerry

loved Jill and Hillary, but he certainly didn't wish to disinherit his sons.

Jill understood Gerry's wishes, and after much discussion with an estate planning attorney, they divided a large portion of their assets and placed them into separate revocable living trusts.

This allowed each of them to control their own property while living, and upon their deaths, the property in the trusts would be distributed without passing through probate. Gerry's sons would receive approximately half of his estate.

The Andrew's estate planning enabled both of them to assure their respective children an appropriate portion of their assets after their deaths, reduced potential estate tax liabilities, and provided trusts that could be changed, if necessary.

"We are free to enjoy of new family now," Gerry told the other fathers at Little League, "we took steps to safeguard the future of our children."

TEN

Rainy Day Money
Cash Reserves

The telephone rings as you walk in the door from work.

"Hello, Mrs. Smith. This is Don at the repair shop, and I'm afraid I have some bad news for you. We're going to have to replace the transmission." The newsflash immediately makes you wonder where you'll get the money to pay for the job.

While attempting to sound as though you are just wondering which checking account to use to pay the bill, you ask, "How much is it going to cost?" The check you just wrote at the grocery store took your balance down to $129.47, and payday is four days away.

"Unfortunately... it's going to run about $2,200. I wish I had better news for you," Don replies apologetically. "The good news is that we can have it done in two days," he boasts. "Shall we go ahead and get started?"

"Yes... sure, go ahead. I'll be there to pick it up on Wednesday." After hanging up the phone, you run upstairs and shuffle through the bills on your desk until you find the VISA statement. Ripping open the statement you immediately slump into a nearby chair as the bad news jumps out. Available credit: $1,400.

There is only one remaining option. You invested $8,000 in a mutual fund earlier in the year. When your spouse walks in the door you tell him the bad news and proceed to ask him for the name of the broker who sold him the mutual fund.

> *"More people should learn to tell their dollars where to go instead of asking where they went."*
>
> –Roger W. Babson

Unfortunately, he doesn't agree with your strategy and feels entitled to give his opinion. "Oh no — we can't do that, the fund is down about four percent since we bought it. We'll be forced to take a loss if we liquidate any shares now," he says. "Besides, we started that fund so that we could send our kids to college."

This scene, or something similar, takes place more often than most people care to admit. It's simply impossible to plan for the unpredictable. Liquid cash reserves are needed for those "rainy days." This is the reason the Success Triangle™ is arranged as it is. Without the foundation of estate conservation and risk management, and the next layer of maintaining adequate cash reserves, it's impossible to effectively create and build personal wealth.

Emergencies come up, as do opportunities. When they do, you don't want to be forced to use a credit card (assuming credit is available), or be forced to sell securities during one of those "dips" in the market. Either option will increase your stress level, reduce your financial peace of mind, and move you farther away from achieving your financial goals.

Plan for the Unplanned

Cash reserves are an important part of financial planning. They consist of the liquid investments people hold in anticipation of planned or unplanned expenses. As shown in the Success Triangle™ at the beginning of this section, cash reserves are the first layer added to your portfolio after the foundation has been established.

By definition, *cash reserve vehicles* offer full liquidity (access to money with no delay or cost) with no market risk (price fluctuation). We call these unrestricted cash reserves. Examples include checking accounts, savings accounts, money market accounts, and money market funds.

Most financial consultants suggest keeping the equivalent of three- to six-months of living expenses readily available in highly liquid investments. How *much* money you decide to keep in cash reserves depends on your particular situation and financial temperament. For example, someone in a cyclic or seasonal business such as construction or a commissioned salesperson should plan on keeping a higher proportion in cash reserves than someone with more predictable income, such as a school teacher or physician. Use the following worksheet (Figures 10–1A and 10–1B) to determine whether your cash reserves are adequate to meet your needs.

If you have a cash reserve deficit, you need to increase your savings. The most painless way to accomplish this task is through a payroll deduction into a savings account, credit union account, or money market fund. Don't wait for extra money to come along before beginning to build your cash reserves. There is no such thing as extra money.

If you have saved so well that you have a cash reserve surplus — congratulations — but please consider investing the extra dollars where they can work harder for you. Remember, cash reserve dollars are loanership dollars. As we will discuss in the following chapters, we are big fans of ownership investments such as stocks or mutual funds, which provide growth of your investment principal.

The only way to fund your cash reserve account and keep part of what you earn for any investment is to do it systematically by paying yourself *first*. Remember the second secret of financial success is this: *Pay yourself first.* Instead of spending what you need to spend and saving what's left over, try saving what you need to save and spend what's left over. Most people have a significant amount of their income they can't readily account for, and could easily set aside $50 to $100 a month. If you can set aside more than that amount, so much the better. The important thing is to get started. But don't worry — at the end of the month you'll *still* run out of money two days before payday, but at least you will have begun a systematic savings program.

> **Instead of spending what you need to spend and saving what's left over, try saving what you need to save and spend what's left over.**

Other Considerations

Is the three- to six-months of living expenses guideline "carved in stone?" Absolutely not! It serves as a starting point when evaluating your portfolio. The objectives are to make sure you have an adequate supply of money to pay both planned and unplanned expenses and prevent a build-up of excess cash that won't keep up with inflation on an after-tax basis. Here are some issues to consider as you determine how much to keep in cash reserves.

The Sleep Factor

No, this isn't what the critics suggested we name this book! It describes the personal level of comfort an individual or couple has with the amount of money they keep in cash reserves.

As an example, assume that a couple has monthly living expenses of $3,000. This would suggest they keep $9,000 to $18,000 in cash reserves. Currently, their money market fund has a balance of $50,000, indicating a substantial surplus. Their financial advisor told them about

FIGURE 10–1A

Determining Your Cash Reserve Needs

Current Cash Reserves

Unrestricted Cash Reserves

These investments offer the highest degree of liquidity and safety and are held in anticipation of emergencies or special opportunities. The interest rates, minimum deposit requirements, and liquidity provisions will vary depending on the specific program selected.

	EXAMPLE		Yours
Checking Accounts	checking	$1,200	$
Passbook Savings	passbook savings	2,300	$
Money Market Accounts	money mkt. acct.	0	$
Money Market Funds	money mkt. funds	1,800	$
Credit Union Share Draft Accounts	credit union share draft acct.	0	$
Treasury Bills	T-bills	$0	$
Total Unrestricted Cash Reserves	Total	$5,300	$

Restricted Cash Reserves

These investments offer investors a high degree of safety and stability, but penalties, market value adjustments, or restrictions may apply to some or all withdrawals, especially during the first several years of the program. If an investor has a significant amount of money in these types of investment programs, the amount of money required in liquid cash reserves could be adjusted downward.

	EXAMPLE		Yours
Certificates of Deposit	CDs	$2,000	$
Life Insurance Cash Values	life insurance cash values	3,500	$
Series EE and HH Bonds	series EE and HH bonds	0	$
Fixed Annuities	fixed annuities	1,200	$
Total Restricted Cash Reserves	Total	6,700	$
Total Current Cash Reserves	Unrestricted + Restricted Total	$5,300 +6,700 $12,000	$

The Success Triangle

FIGURE 10–1B

Liquidity Needs

Monthly Living Expenses

EXAMPLE

Yours

Rent or Mortgage	rent/mortgage $1,100	$
Food	food 600	$
Utilities	utilities 350	$
Auto Expense	auto expenses 800	$
Insurance	insurance 200	$
Taxes	taxes 200	$
Installment Debt	installment debt 550	$
Other	other 300	$
Total Monthly Living Expenses	Total $4,100	$

Calculating Your Liquidity Needs

$4,100 $4,100
x 3   x 6
$12,300 $24,600

Monthly Living Expenses x 3 = $

Monthly Living Expenses x 6 = $

Total Liquidity Needs
$12,300 to $24,600

Calculate Your Cash Reserve Deficit or Surplus

We generally recommend keeping three times your monthly living expenses in unrestricted cash reserves. If you have a deficit, you may be in a precarious position. You need to build your unrestricted cash reserve investments through increased monthly savings in suitable vehicles or by liquidating some of your less liquid assets.

Total Restricted Cash Reserves $ _____

— 3 Months Liquidity Needs $ _____

= $ _____

Total unrestricted
cash reserves $6,700

3 months
liquidity needs   – $12,300

DEFICIT!!!   – $5,600

Some people feel the need to keep up to 6 months' living expenses in cash reserves. If your situation or temperament warrants keeping more than 3 months living expenses in cash reserves, we suggest that the amount beyond 3 months living expenses be kept in restricted cash reserves that maintain liquidity plus the benefit of higher returns on savings. Again, if you have a deficit, build your cash reserves. If you currently have more than 6 months living expenses in cash reserves, consider investing your surplus dollars for long-term growth.

Total cash
reserves $12,000

6 months
living expenses   – $24,600

DEFICIT!!!   – $12,600

Total Cash Reserves $ _____

— Your Liquidity Needs $ _____

= $ _____

the three- to six-month rule and suggested that their amount of money held in cash reserves be reduced.

Being an experienced professional, the advisor realized the couple was not comfortable with the suggestion and asked how they would feel if their money market fund statement were to show a balance of $18,000. The reply was that they would not be able to sleep well with only an $18,000 balance.

The advisor continued the exercise by increasing the amount until both the husband and wife agreed that they would be comfortable with a balance of $30,000, which represents six months of their gross income. No rule of thumb can compete with the sleep factor. Our example couple's sleep factor was $30,000, leaving them a surplus of $20,000 in cash reserves.

Did you arrive at a significant surplus after completing the cash reserve calculation? Did you react by thinking, "That wouldn't be enough; I couldn't take all that money out and invest it somewhere else!" That's the sleep factor at work. Conversely, you may think that you don't need to keep as much in savings as the calculation indicates. Some people sleep better than others.

Restricted Cash Reserves

There are some investment vehicles that, for one reason or another, do not fit neatly into the cash reserve section of the Success Triangle. We refer to them as *restricted cash reserves*. If you own these types of investments, any dollars accumulated could reduce the actual amount you need to keep in cash reserves. Restricted cash reserves include:

- Certificates of deposit
- Treasury bills
- Series EE and HH bonds
- Life insurance cash values
- Fixed annuities

We have classified these vehicles as *restricted cash reserves* because an unplanned withdrawal from them could result in withdrawal fees, premature distribution penalties, or other costs.

Restricted cash reserves can play an important role for those who have problems in the *sleep factor* area. Over the years, our mission has been to help people reposition their money to obtain a higher rate of return and realize their financial goals more quickly. These efforts meet with resistance at times because some people worry about not having enough cash if "something comes up." These people frequently had from $100,000 to $250,000 in cash reserves and their monthly living expenses were $3,000 to $4,000. We haven't seen a transmission that costs $100,000!

These situations present a dilemma. There is an excessive amount of money in cash reserves, yet the sleep factor prevents these people from putting their money into more productive, long-term investments. We point out that money in restricted cash reserves is safe, and is readily available if something drastic happens. Until it is needed, it is generating higher returns than are generally obtainable in unrestricted cash reserve vehicles.

Lines of Credit

The availability of lines of credit is more prevalent today than ever before. It is not unusual for consumers to have credit cards with credit limits of $5,000 to $15,000 or more. In special circumstances these lines of credit could affect the amount you keep in cash reserves. The lines of credit are available if an emergency or other need arises.

We've also worked with people who hated keeping money in cash reserves because they were losing purchasing power on an after-tax basis. With annual incomes in excess of $100,000, large credit lines were easily available. Many felt that if an emergency came along, they could tap into these lines of credit to pay unplanned expenses. This aggressive strategy is appropriate only if you have a high income and little or no debt.

Assume that a family has an annual household income of $120,000 ($10,000 a month). With no consumer debt, family expenses total about $3,500 a month. If a new transmission is needed, they can use part of their $10,000 credit line. When the statement arrives, they will pay it from their monthly cash flow. If the expense is larger it can be paid off over two or three months.

Is there a flaw in this strategy? Not if you can sleep with it. Many would argue, however, that it provides no cushion if you lost your job. We couldn't agree more. Even if there are other investments that could be liquidated in the event of an emergency, the timing could be very poor.

Where to Keep Your Cash Reserves

Over the years, banks, savings and loans, and credit unions have offered products used by many people for investment dollars designated as cash reserves. The popularity of these institutions has been a result of convenient branch locations, insured principal (within certain limits), and in the case of many of their products, fixed interest rates. In addition other financial institutions such as life insurance companies, investment companies, and brokers also offer products which are good vehicles for investing cash reserve dollars. Let's take a look at some of them.

Checking Accounts

Checking accounts aren't used just to pay your bills, anymore. They have many features and offer options to fit nearly every need.

Basic Accounts. Basic checking accounts are usually available for small monthly fees ($8 to $10), which are often waived with minimum account balances of $100 to $500. Services such as free checks or no charge for the first 10 or 15 checks written each month may also be offered. Before you decide on a checking account, carefully examine how you will use it. If your account consistently falls below the minimum balance requirement, you may be paying as much as $120 per year in fees.

Preferred Customer Accounts. Preferred customer accounts require larger minimum balances ($1,000 to $1,500). You pay no fees and sometimes earn interest on the money in the account. Preferred customer accounts often offer other perks such as no-fee credit cards and higher ATM withdrawal limits

NOW (Negotiable Order of Withdrawal) Accounts. NOW accounts offer adjustable rates of interest, but charge a monthly maintenance fee and a fee for each check written.

Share Draft Accounts. These are the credit union version of checking accounts. Unlimited check writing and competitive interest rates, referred to as dividends, make share draft accounts very attractive alternatives to checking accounts offered by banks. Are these accounts a good place for rainy day cash? Sure; just be careful not to spend it.

Savings Accounts

Money Market or Current Interest Accounts. These accounts were created by banks and savings and loan associations so that they would be able to compete favorably with money market mutual funds. Money market accounts pay current short-term interest rates which

FIGURE 10–2

Cash Reserve Institutions and Vehicles

	Unrestricted Cash Reserves		Restricted Cash Reserves	
Available Funds (additions, as necessary)	Fully Liquid No Restrictions on Withdrawals No Price Fluctuation		Readily Convertible Into Cash Penalty for Early Withdrawal Minimal Market Risk	
Bank	Checking Accounts Passbook Savings Money Market Accounts	FDIC Insured	Certificates of Deposit US Savings Bonds	FDIC Insured
Savings and Loan	Checking Accounts Savings Accounts Money Market Accounts	FDIC Insured	Certificates of Deposit	FDIC Insured
Credit Union	Share Draft Accounts Share Accounts		Certificates of Deposit	
Brokerage	Treasury Bills Cash Mgmt. Accounts		Certificates of Deposit US Savings Bonds	
Investment Company	Money Market Funds			
Life Insurance Company			Fixed Annuities* Cash Values	

*Appropriate only for investors age 59½ or older due to possible IRS withdrawal penalties prior to that age.

may fluctuate. Savers are allowed to write a limited number of checks each month and may have unlimited ATM access. Penalties may also be imposed if the balance drops below minimum account requirements. Money market accounts are quite safe because they are covered by the federal deposit insurance.

FEATURES OF MONEY MARKET FUNDS INCLUDE:

- **Competitive Short-Term Yields.** Money market funds pay current market rates, and dividends are declared daily.

- **Liquidity.** Money market funds generally provide free check writing of $100 or more, and allow access to your funds by mail or phone.

- **Records and Information.** You will receive written confirmation of every transaction, deposits, withdrawals, and payment of dividends. For income tax purposes you will receive monthly statements and a year-end summary.

Passbook Savings. When people think of a "savings account," they typically envision the traditional passbook type of account. These were so named because there was a time when withdrawals, deposits, and interest earned were recorded in a passbook that had to be presented by the account holder when making a transaction. We still meet people who have virtually all of their savings, frequently tens of thousands of dollars, in passbook savings accounts. The problem is that savings accounts pay relatively low interest rates and you can't justify keeping more than a small portion of your cash reserves in them.

Share Accounts. These are the credit union's version of a passbook savings account. Technically, they are not deposits, but rather ownership shares in the credit union that provide you with voting rights. Share accounts are ideally suited for the cash reserve portion of the Success Triangle because they pay a competitive rate of interest and provide full liquidity.

Certificates of Deposit. A certificate of deposit (CD) is a savings plan that requires that you deposit a certain amount of money for a specified time period to earn a specified interest rate. The time period may range from 30 days to 10 or more years. CDs offer attractive interest rates when compared to other savings accounts. The longer the time period, the higher the interest rate you will receive. CDs are available from banks, savings and loans, credit unions, and investment brokers.

But beware: money in CDs cannot usually be accessed prior to maturity without early withdrawal penalties. Furthermore, if interest rates go up after you invest, your CD is locked in at its specified rate of interest until the term is completed. An exception is the jump-rate CD offered by some institutions. Although specific features may vary, these certificates typically offer one opportunity for the yield to increase prior to maturity.

Because of the restrictions and penalties for early withdrawal, we put them in the restricted cash reserve category, and recommend that you don't use CDs to meet all your cash reserve requirements. If you need the money for that transmission, you'll have to pay the penalty.

Should CDs, then, be used for longer-term investing? Probably not. When inflation and taxes are factored in, you may find that you're losing money in the loanership business.

Money Market Mutual Funds

Money market mutual funds (money market funds) offer an excellent alternative to regular checking and savings accounts for cash reserves. Unlike the money market accounts, offered by banks and savings and loans, money market funds are not insured. However, because money market funds invest primarily in government securities and the securities of the most creditworthy companies, they are considered quite safe. Many money market funds typically pay higher rates of return than regular checking and savings accounts and many will allow you to open an account with as little as $500 or even less.

Money market funds pool the resources of many individuals, enabling them to invest in a variety of money market instruments which are otherwise available only to large investors such as institutions and the very wealthy. Examples of the short-term investments money market fund managers can select from include jumbo Certificates of Deposit, U.S. Treasury- and government-backed obligations, and commercial paper. Many life insurance companies, banks, and large corporations invest in these same instruments when they do not want to tie up cash for long periods, but want to earn high interest.

Tax-free money market funds invest in *tax anticipation notes* which is short-term municipal paper. As the name suggests, these funds offer the features and benefits normally offered by traditional money market funds, with the added benefit that you earn interest on which you pay no federal income taxes.

Sounds good. Shouldn't everyone own these instead of the regular money market funds? No. The yield on tax-free money market funds was nearly 39 percent less than taxable funds at the time of this writing.

How do you know which is better? Simply divide the tax-free yield by the complement (100% minus your marginal tax rate) of your marginal tax rate to calculate the equivalent taxable yield. Let's assume the yield from tax-free money market funds is 3 percent and that you are in the 31 percent federal income tax bracket.

Tax-Free Yield ÷ [100% – marginal tax rate] = Equivalent Taxable Yield

3.00% ÷ (1 – .31) = Equivalent Taxable Yield

3.00% ÷ .69 = 4.35%

If taxable money market funds were yielding less than 4.35 percent in this example, you should put your money in the tax-free money fund. Conversely, if taxable money market funds are yielding more than 4.35 percent, go with the taxable funds.

Treasury Bills

Treasury bills are short-term government securities. They do not offer the instant liquidity of cash, but we include them as cash reserve investments because they are readily converted into cash, if necessary. There is no state income tax on T-bill interest, and they are guaranteed by the federal government.

T-bills are issued by the government in minimum denominations of $10,000 (with incremental increases of $5,000) with three-month, six-month, and twelve-month maturities. They are offered to investors through competitive bidding or noncompetitive sale, in which case the investor pays the average of the acceptable competitive prices. Investors buy the bills at a discount with the price dependent on face amount, time to maturity, and current interest rates. For example, you might pay $9,500 for a $10,000 T-bill with a 12-month maturity. If held to maturity your T-bill is worth its face amount of $10,000 and your profit would be $500; a return of 5.26% ([$500 ÷ $9,500] × 100%).

Treasury bills are available directly from the Federal Reserve Banks and their branches (with no transaction fee) or through stockbrokers and banks (with a transaction fee). T-bills are actively traded in the secondary market prior to maturity, and their values fluctuate in response to changes in current interest rates and time to maturity.

Summary

Cash reserves build a base for financial security, providing readily available cash to deal with unexpected needs. Cash reserve vehicles include checking accounts that pay interest, savings accounts, or money market

CREDIT UNIONS

Credit unions are user-owned, nonprofit, cooperative financial institutions. They may seem like a company- or organization-owned bank but share account holders are the owners of credit unions. Credit unions are usually located in the same vicinity as their affiliated "sponsor," and many times the credit union's name includes part or all of the company's or organization's name. The sponsors have no control over credit unions; they only provide the customers.

Historically, in order to receive a charter, the credit union's members needed a common bond such as an employer, union, church, or community. If you weren't a member of the group, you couldn't become a member of the credit union unless a relative was already a member. This common bond restriction has been relaxed in recent years. It has been our observation that almost anyone can find a credit union to join with a little effort. And millions have.

What's the attraction? For employees of large corporations with on-site credit unions, convenience is often reason enough to become a member. And even if it isn't located near their place of employment, some would argue that credit unions are worth the drive because they offer better or more personalized service than banks.

Others cite the fact that credit unions offer slightly higher interest rates on deposits and slightly lower rates on loans than banks.

Many people feel that credit unions offer more personalized service than other financial institutions. Since they don't have any big corporate customers, they don't snub the "little guy" in favor of large business accounts. Everyone receives equal treatment.

Additionally, because credit unions are owned by their members, who do not require dividends, and have a board of directors made up of volunteers, they can preserve cash that commercial banks must disperse. Probably the most significant advantage credit unions have over banks is that they don't pay taxes (remember, they are nonprofit organizations) which means that their costs of doing business are reduced.

Should you close all of your accounts at the local bank and move them to a credit union? Not necessarily. As attractive as credit unions may be, there are certain services they don't offer that may be available at a bank. Evaluate the services you use, or plan to use in the future at your bank. Are they available at the credit union? If not, you may want to do business at both.

funds. Money market funds typically carry advantages of a higher rate of interest, the necessary liquidity, and ease of record keeping.

We recommend keeping a minimum of three months of living expenses in unrestricted cash reserves, which have maximum liquidity. Many people, depending on their individual situations, should keep up to an additional three months' living expenses in restricted cash reserve vehicles, such as CDs, life insurance cash reserves, or fixed annuities, which provide a better return on your investments.

We favor money market funds or accounts for holding your rainy day dollars. You can get the most mileage, in terms of attractive current returns, checking privileges, and no withdrawal penalties, when your cash reserves are invested in money market vehicles.

SECRETS IN ACTION

Christine and Kevin Burgess are tired of always being broke. No matter how hard they try, they can't get out of debt.

"It's so frustrating," Christine told their financial advisor. "We overspent during the first few years of our marriage, and now we owe almost $8,000 on four different credit cards. We just get to the point where we can make more than the minimum payment on one of the cards, then the washing machine breaks down. We have to use a card to pay the bill. It's one step forward and two steps back. What can we do?"

Their financial advisor took a careful inventory of the Burgess' finances. Working together, they determined it was possible to arrange their expenditures to come up with $200 a month more than the minimum payments on the four credit cards.

"Shall we pay the $200 to one card at a time, or divide it between them?" Kevin asked.

"Neither," their advisor answered, expecting their puzzled glances. "You have $120 in a share account at your credit union. Have $100 deducted from your paycheck twice a month and automatically deposited into your share account. Keep paying the minimum payments on your cards for now."

"You will never be able to get out of debt until you start building some savings," their advisor explained. "Then, when an unexpected repair bill comes in, you can use your savings to pay it and avoid increasing your credit card balances. It will be a three to four year process, but you will see a steady decline in your credit card balances and a steady increase in your savings."

"It's amazing," Christine told Kevin on the way home. "It's such a simple plan, but it makes sense. By paying ourselves first, we can better manage our debt."

ELEVEN

Share in the Wealth
Growth Investments — Stocks

Playing the Market

D o you agree or disagree with the following opinion? The wealth of America belongs to the opportunists, the Wall Street *players* who have rigged the system to make millions of dollars, leaving the rest of us with no chance to make any money.

If you disagree, you're right — it's not true! A few people have crossed over the line of fair play and accumulated fortunes, often at the expense of others. Many of these big-time cheaters such as Ivan Boesky and Michael Milken have been caught and punished, too. Yet all the while, thousands of Americans have legitimately earned double-digit annual returns on their stock portfolios and mutual fund holdings.

After you have established your solid foundation and accumulated enough cash reserves to meet emergencies, it's time to look at investment vehicles that will increase the earning power of your dollars. On this level of the Success Triangle, you will be examining investments that are liquid. This category of investments can be purchased on short notice and can be sold within a few days, if necessary.

Investors put their money in the stock market to increase their yields, participate in capital appreciation, and share in the corporate wealth of America, as well as companies worldwide.

When people laughingly refer to *playing* the market, you might get the wrong idea. The successful investors we have known are actually dead serious. They aren't swayed by hot stock tips from the guy selling magazines on the corner or fantastic get-rich-quick flukes. Like those

"Back in graduate school I learned the market goes up 9 percent a year, and since then it's never gone up 9 percent in a year, and I've yet to find a reliable source to inform me how much it will go up, or simply whether it will go up or down. All the major advances and declines have been surprises to me."
– Peter Lynch, from his book, *One Up on Wall Street*

successful investors, our attitude toward playing the market is to establish a plan for investing, and stick to it over a long period of time. The market fluctuates like crazy in the short run, but over time, those gyrations average out and long-term trends show that double-digit returns are possible.

If you're thinking you have to devote a lot of time to investing in order to achieve those types of returns, you're right. That's why we usually recommend mutual funds to our clients who don't want to take the time to pick their own stocks. As we will discuss in the next chapter, mutual funds are an investment vehicle in which you invest your money with the mutual fund company that in turn uses expert managers and analysts to invest in the stock market. By simply investing in Vanguard's Standard & Poor's 500 stock index mutual fund, for example, you would have averaged 14.58 percent a year over the 10-year period ending December 31, 1996 and 14.44 percent for the 15-year period ending the same date.

However, you just might want to put your financial genius up against the best financial minds in the country and see how you do. Or you may wish to buy and sell stocks for the sheer joy of the experience. The market is exciting and fun. If you and your financial planner decide that it is appropriate for your position in the financial life cycle, and you have the dollars to invest, this chapter will show you how to get started as a serious player in the market.

"But aren't stocks speculative?" you ask. Obviously, there is a degree of risk in any investment, even in certificates of deposit and money market funds. Stock investments are exposed to a different kind of risk, called *market risk;* however, if you consider the potentially erosive power of inflation which diminishes purchasing power over the long term, it is often riskier *not* to invest in common stock. The returns on many more conservative, so-called "safe" investments fail to keep pace with inflation. The important point to remember with this kind of investment is that some stocks — and stock strategies — are riskier than others.

We have already discussed why your money needs to work harder for you in the Seven Secrets. Now in this chapter we will suggest a very conservative, time-tested strategy for investing — and sharing — in the corporate wealth of the world.

We will review the rather attractive rates of return that investors have earned over the years by investing in common stock. You'll see that investing in the stock market has been well worth the risk for thousands of people. So go ahead, take the plunge, and dispel the myth that Wall Street is nothing more than a grand casino in which the house always wins.

Figure 11–1

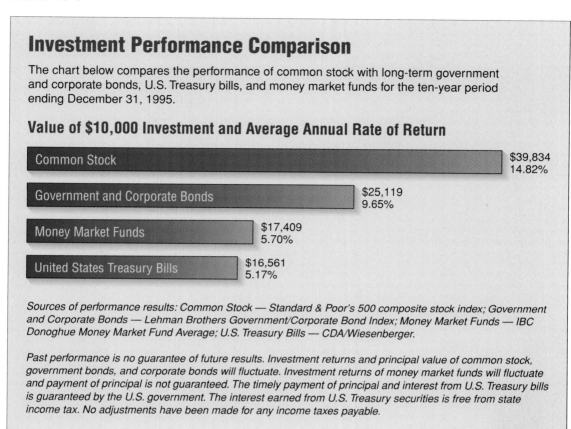

Investment Performance Comparison

The chart below compares the performance of common stock with long-term government and corporate bonds, U.S. Treasury bills, and money market funds for the ten-year period ending December 31, 1995.

Value of $10,000 Investment and Average Annual Rate of Return

Common Stock	$39,834 / 14.82%
Government and Corporate Bonds	$25,119 / 9.65%
Money Market Funds	$17,409 / 5.70%
United States Treasury Bills	$16,561 / 5.17%

Sources of performance results: Common Stock — Standard & Poor's 500 composite stock index; Government and Corporate Bonds — Lehman Brothers Government/Corporate Bond Index; Money Market Funds — IBC Donoghue Money Market Fund Average; U.S. Treasury Bills — CDA/Wiesenberger.

Past performance is no guarantee of future results. Investment returns and principal value of common stock, government bonds, and corporate bonds will fluctuate. Investment returns of money market funds will fluctuate and payment of principal is not guaranteed. The timely payment of principal and interest from U.S. Treasury bills is guaranteed by the U.S. government. The interest earned from U.S. Treasury securities is free from state income tax. No adjustments have been made for any income taxes payable.

Stock Ownership Is Business Ownership

Have you ever thought about owning a business? Stock ownership *is* business ownership — and by owning stock you participate in the free enterprise system. Despite some problems, the United States has made capitalism work better than any other country in the world, including Japan and Germany. The reason capitalism works better here than anywhere else is simple: capital is available for business development and growth. This money comes from the stock market. And the stock market is us — Americans who have been willing to invest their money in the stock of many corporations.

When you purchase stock in a company, it allows you to go into business without having to start from scratch; instead you purchase

FIGURE 11–2

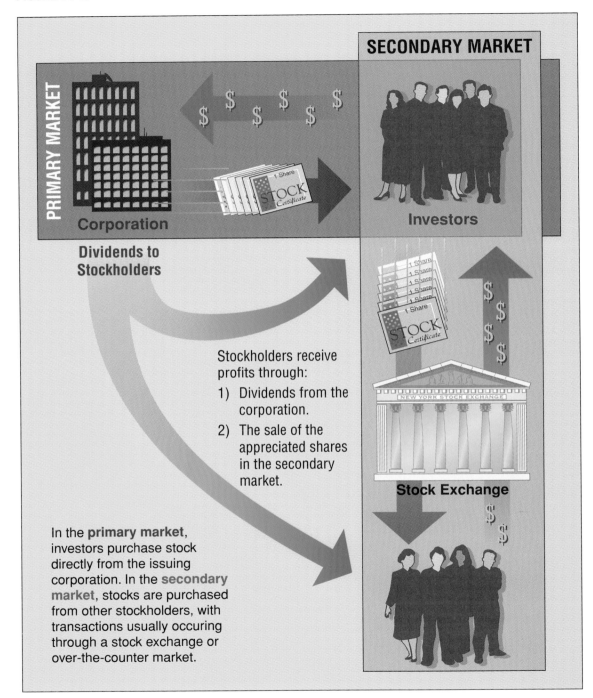

PRIMARY MARKET

Corporation

Dividends to
Stockholders

SECONDARY MARKET

Investors

STOCK Certificate

NEW YORK STOCK EXCHANGE

Stock Exchange

Stockholders receive
profits through:

1) Dividends from the
corporation.

2) The sale of the
appreciated shares
in the secondary
market.

In the **primary market**,
investors purchase stock
directly from the issuing
corporation. In the **secondary
market**, stocks are purchased
from other stockholders, with
transactions usually occuring
through a stock exchange or
over-the-counter market.

a piece of an existing company. Buy shares of stock and you will own part of a business without any of the financial obligations associated with starting one yourself. You may even vote on various decisions affecting the company, including whether to sell or merge with another company, and you can vote when it comes time to elect the board of directors.

Sources of Profit

When investing your cash reserves in a money market fund, your dollars work in one way. A dollar earning 5 percent a year will earn a nickel every year, but at the end of 5 or 10 years, what is your dollar worth? A dollar. Less, really, if you consider the erosion inflation has inflicted on your principal.

Investing in the stock market, on the other hand, gives you the opportunity to earn in another way, *capital appreciation.* The potential for capital appreciation is the reason most people invest in stocks. Investors earn profit from stocks in two ways: income dividends and share value appreciation. When your dollar is at work in a stock investment, it can earn dividends every year, and there is also the possibility that it will be worth two or three or five dollars in five or ten years because of capital appreciation.

Income Dividends

Going back to *Business Basics 101,* you'll recall that companies are in business for one reason: to make money. On Wall Street, this money is referred to as *earnings.* One of the things a company can do with its earnings is pay them out to the owners, or stockholders, of the company in the form of income dividends.

What happens to the earnings that aren't paid out as dividends? They are used to keep the company competitive by investing in research and development, new product introductions, expansion, marketing, acquisitions, or other areas that will contribute to its growth.

Some people will tell you the big money to be made in stocks is not in dividends, but in potential share price appreciation. That may be true, but some interesting studies have shown that companies with a history of steadily increasing dividends have also experienced steadily increasing share prices as well. So, don't discount dividends as something only retired people are interested in.

Share Value Appreciation

Few things offer more potential for people to realize their financial goals and achieve financial security than the growth potential of common stocks. We've all heard the stories about the lucky guy who bought Wal-Mart at $4 a share and sold it at $40. We've also heard the horror stories (or experienced them ourselves) from someone we know who bought IBM at $100 (because it was cheap) and watched it head straight to $50. A 50 percent loss is not what anyone would call building personal wealth. We could spend all day discussing individual successes and failures in the stock market. That's not our purpose.

Historically, stock prices have been steadily increasing even though they retreat every now and then. That's why it is important to follow the principles of the Success Triangle. When you have a solid foundation with risk management and cash reserves to fall back on, you have the financial resources to weather whatever storms hit the market.

Handling Stock Market Volatility

A lot of people are frightened away from the stock market because stock prices can change dramatically within a short time. Sweaty palms and heart palpitations set in when people think back to "Black Monday," October 19, 1987, when the Dow Jones Industrial Average dropped more than 500 points in one day. Stock market volatility is commonplace — although not often of this magnitude — and goes hand-in-hand with *marketability* (the ability to buy and sell on a daily basis).

Think about those sharp declines in stock prices for a moment. Can the actual financial strength and future economic outlook for all companies change so significantly in one day? No, they can't. But human emotions can!

There may be a sound reason for one company's stock to rise or fall 5 or 10 percent in one day. Sales, profitability, and competitiveness (or the outlook for them) could suddenly change. However, the financial outlook for thousands of companies just doesn't change overnight. So, why does the Dow Jones Industrial Average increase or decrease so many points in one day?

Investor optimism (or pessimism) can shift quickly when influenced by a new government statistic, a market prediction by a well-known financial analyst, or even a well-spread rumor. Like frightened cattle, investors run to their phones and place sell orders. And what happens when everyone wants to sell at the same time?

FIGURE 11-3

The Bulls and the Bears

The stock market goes through recurrent cycles of upward trends and downward trends. Bulls attack throwing their horns upward. Bears attack with their claws downward. Thus, a rising market cycle is called a bull market and a falling period is called a bear market.

The Bulls are the market optimists who drive the prices up. The Bears, on the other hand, are the pessimists who retreat from the market as prices fall. For the astute investor, there are profit opportunities in both bull and bear markets.

Because the market operates on supply and demand, it becomes a buyer's market, with those desiring to sell far outnumbering those wanting to buy. Prices have to drop in order to induce buyers to step in and buy shares that everyone seems to want to sell. Eventually, good sense finds its way back into investors' heads and they begin buying again, pushing share prices back to their previous levels and beyond. Remember: it did not take the market long to recover from its October 1987 decline. In fact, those investors who held their shares saw the market return to its previous level within two years and investors who bought shares on October 20, 1987, realized large gains by the end of that year.

When daily marketability and constant pricing changes are mixed with human emotion, volatility occurs in the stock market. It's a fact everyone must learn to live with. To understand why you should ignore short-term price fluctuations, let's take a look at an investment closer to home — your house. You may be justifiably proud of the great investment your house represents. Suppose you paid $50,000 for your house and could sell it today for $200,000. That's a great investment, right? But could you sell it immediately and collect your cash next week? Probably not. It might take weeks or months to sell and several more weeks after that to close the sale. Why does it take so long to sell a house? Because unlike stocks, real estate is not readily marketable.

The House Market

Let's suppose there was a giant house market just like the stock market. Every day, prospective buyers would call in bids on houses and each homeowner would call in the price at which he or she would be willing to sell. What would the result of this increased marketability be? Greatly increased price volatility. An asset, then — such as your house — is only worth what someone is willing to pay for it at a given time.

Fortunately, we don't have to sit around worrying about the values of our homes every day. If they are located in desirable areas and have good long-term potential for appreciation, we don't even think about their actual values for months or even years at a time. But when it comes time to sell, what kind of bid would we get during a blizzard in January?

Nobody wants to come out and look at your house during a snow-storm. However, if you dropped your asking price low enough, the word would get around among real estate agents and pretty soon some-body would show up at your door with a ridiculously low offer. Would you panic and sell at that price? Of course not! You would say, "I know there aren't many buyers out there today; however, I believe my house is worth a lot more than your offer. I'll wait until the weather gets bet-ter. Prices will be better then."

Stocks should be purchased the same way. Select stocks of well-managed companies that are in desirable industries and have good long-term potential. You know the secret of harnessing the power of time, so you're in this adventure for the long haul. Don't worry about their daily prices. It may be great fun to check them every day, but it won't improve your results one bit.

"What if a bad news story knocks the price down?" By that time, it's too late, anyway. The price has already fallen. You should treat an investment in common stock like you would treat an investment in your home, with the added comfort of knowing that the stock can be converted to cash much more quickly, if necessary.

The Success Triangle

Figure 11-4

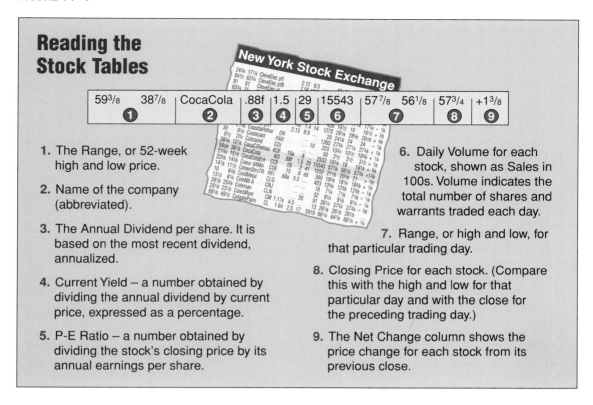

Reading the Stock Tables

New York Stock Exchange

| 59³/₈ | 38⁷/₈ | CocaCola | .88f | 1.5 | 29 | 15543 | 57⁷/₈ | 56¹/₈ | 57³/₄ | +1³/₈ |
| (1) | (2) | (3) | (4) | (5) | (6) | (7) | (8) | (9) |

1. The Range, or 52-week high and low price.

2. Name of the company (abbreviated).

3. The Annual Dividend per share. It is based on the most recent dividend, annualized.

4. Current Yield – a number obtained by dividing the annual dividend by current price, expressed as a percentage.

5. P-E Ratio – a number obtained by dividing the stock's closing price by its annual earnings per share.

6. Daily Volume for each stock, shown as Sales in 100s. Volume indicates the total number of shares and warrants traded each day.

7. Range, or high and low, for that particular trading day.

8. Closing Price for each stock. (Compare this with the high and low for that particular day and with the close for the preceding trading day.)

9. The Net Change column shows the price change for each stock from its previous close.

Your Stock Investment Strategy: Increasing Dividends

Once you understand and accept the fact that stocks will fluctuate in value, you are ready to build a stock portfolio and become an active investor in the world of finance and investments. But where do you start?

Since some stocks make money and some don't, how do you decide which company or companies you want to own? This is not the time to rely on guesswork or hot stock tips. Your chances for big gains using this "random abandon" strategy are worse than lottery odds. The best way to select stocks is by using a sound strategy for investing.

The increasing dividends strategy we suggest is a conservative method that has generated profitable results over the years. It is neither secret nor exotic; in fact, it is fairly straightforward and several mutual funds state in their literature that they use this method (or a similar one). By its very name, the increasing dividends strategy is not designed to find young companies that could offer great profit (or loss) potential, but rather to seek out well-established companies that have demonstrated profitability over many years. Of course, other investment strategies exist, which could be better or worse for you than this one. We profile this method because it is relatively easy to explain and understand, and it provides good profit potential with minimal risk.

How Do You Examine a Potential Company?

We will simplify the process of choosing a stock by asking you to look at stock investment the way you might look at buying a small, privately held company in your local community. Imagine that you are considering purchasing the Oakdale Lumber Company. What would you want to know about the company before buying it? First, and most important, you should be interested in — and optimistic about — the type of business it conducts. Are you interested in the lumber business? If you don't like or understand that type of business, look at another business. The first rule, then, is to choose a company you know, understand, and are interested in.

If the Oakdale Lumber Company passes this initial test, look at its entire industry group. How is the lumber industry doing? What is this group's potential for growth compared with other industries? Have you come across any articles or information that say the lumber industry is depressed? Did you read that it is poised for a great recovery? If you are satisfied with these answers, then it is time to begin evaluating the financial health of the company.

How much annual revenue does the company generate and how does it compare with prior years? Is the revenue increasing? If it isn't, try to find out why and whether there is reason to believe a more positive trend can be established. How does the company's revenue growth compare with other companies in the industry? Next, find out what portion of the company's revenue consists of profits (earnings).

How much is the seller asking for the business? Is the price a good value based on its current earnings and anticipated future earnings? What have other buyers paid for similar companies based on their earnings? If the seller is asking a price that is 20 times earnings and similar companies have recently sold for 15 times earnings, you may be looking at a company that is overpriced. You need to justify why this company is worth more than other similar companies.

You can use the same exercise and apply the same criteria when choosing stock in publicly owned companies. There are more than 8,000 companies traded publicly, and there is an amazing amount of information about these businesses readily available. Most newspapers

The Success Triangle

list the P/E ratios (see below) of the stocks they cover in their business section along with the dividends and the trading price.

You can find more information on the company you are investigating at the library, in *The Value Line Investment Survey,* or *Standard & Poor's Stock Guide.* In addition, you may want to call or write the company and ask them to mail you a copy of their past several annual reports. If you're going to be a part-owner in the business, you should find out as much about it as you can.

Examine the company's *price-to-earnings ratio (P/E ratio)* — the relationship between the share price and its earnings per share. Let's say that a company's stock sells for $50 a share and its annual earnings (the prior 12 months) are $5 per share. In this case, its P/E ratio is 10, or 10 times earnings. The per-share price of its stock is 10 times its per-share earnings—so we say its P/E ratio is 10. If similar companies are selling for 15 times earnings, you may have discovered a bargain. Or you may have discovered a clunker. You don't know yet. Investment decisions based solely on P/E ratios or any other single criterion are not only too simplistic, they are investment suicide. But, it is important to understand what P/E ratios are and how they can be used to make comparisons during the stock selection process.

Next, explore the company's recent and anticipated performance to see whether it might be a bargain or will continue selling at low multiples for some time to come. Don't be intimidated — this information is actually easy to research. Most stock indexes are organized by industry group, and it's easier reading than you might suspect at first glance.

We feel that companies worthy of your attention should offer a 10-year history with earnings growing at an average rate of at least 6 percent a year. The earnings should also be increasing consistently. Look for companies with earnings that have increased in at least 7 of the past 10 years.

Be aware, though, that some money managers call earnings a "figment of an accountant's imagination." That is because earnings retained by the company for investment in research and development, marketing, or plant expansion may eventually make the stock worth more, but these earnings are not available for the shareholders' immediate use. With that in mind, let's look at something more tangible: income dividends. Dividends aren't a figment of anyone's imagination — they're immediately spendable. (Although your net worth will increase more rapidly if they aren't spent, but reinvested instead.)

Increases in annual dividends paid by the company should have at least kept pace with inflation over the past 10 years. Preferably, they have doubled during the decade and, like earnings growth, the increases should be consistent. We believe, as many money managers who follow the increasing dividends strategy do, that a good stock choice will include a dividend increase in at least 8 of the last 10 years.

Now let's compare the earnings with the dividends. You should be reasonably sure that a company can afford to keep paying dividends. Be certain it is not spending all its earnings on dividends, leaving nothing for future growth. Every company needs to reinvest some portion of its earnings on market research, product development, marketing, and so on, so that it will remain competitive. Look for companies that retain at least 30 percent of their earnings for growth, using no more than 70 percent for the payment of stock dividends. Some advisors even recommend a 35 or even 40 percent earnings retention rate.

> **"Investment is not a science. It is a matter of human judgment."**
>
> Massachusetts Investment Trust manager,
> Dwight Parker Robinson

If you follow these guidelines, you will eliminate a lot of good companies from consideration. It is important to remember that this is a strategy for building a conservative portfolio — and we have not finished establishing our criteria yet.

You will eliminate even more companies from consideration by selecting only those companies with modest amounts of long-term debt. This debt should not exceed 25 to 30 percent of a corporation's total market capitalization. To find this number, simply multiply the number of outstanding shares times the price per share to find the market capitalization of a company. You can find the short- and long-term debt figures in the annual reports.

Additional Criteria

A company may pass all of the above tests, but may not be fairly valued. You can eliminate companies that are overpriced by considering only those with a price-to-earnings ratio below their median P/E ratio for the past 10 years. Suppose that a stock sold at a low P/E ratio of 9 times earnings and sold as high as 17 times earnings. Ideally, you would only purchase it if it was selling at 13 times earnings or less.

Of course, there will be times when you need to bend the rules a little. For example, you might find a company that meets the criteria for earnings, dividend, debt, and P/E ratio, but decide not to buy it because you feel its industry group will be facing turbulent times during the next couple of years. Indeed, some stock market performance studies suggest that being in the right *industries* is more important than being in the right *companies*.

The Success Triangle

We believe, however, that the increasing dividends strategy we have suggested will direct you to companies that are so attractively priced it won't matter which industry they are in. When they pass all our tests, it's likely they can stand on their own merits. We aren't exactly original thinkers here. Peter Lynch, one of the best mutual fund managers the industry has ever known, has emphasized that investors should focus on individual companies rather than industry groups.

As you become more experienced, you may want to modify, expand, or change your strategy for selecting companies. That's fine; our conservative approach might not be aggressive enough for some. But remember, once you pick a sound strategy, stick with it! Don't abandon a legitimate strategy because it underperforms the market for a short time period. If it's worked successfully for years, it will more than likely keep working on a long-term basis.

Purchasing Stock

In order to buy your first stocks, you have to open a brokerage account. Accounts can be opened at a full-service brokerage firm, a discount broker, or through a financial planner who is also securities-licensed.

If you want help with stock selection, consider a full-service broker or a financial planner who provides such services. If you will be doing your own research, a discount broker will execute your purchases and sales at a reduced cost. But, if you are using the services of a financial planner, ask him or her about the possibility of executing

FIGURE 11–5

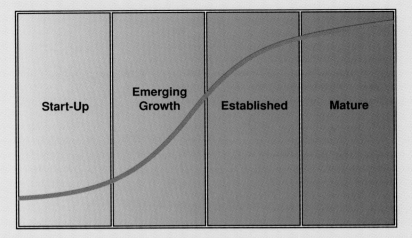

Risk Factors

| Start-Up | Emerging Growth | Established | Mature |

One underlying factor that determines the risk level and volatility of a stock is the point in the business cycle the company is in at the time of purchase.

Investors seeking maximum capital gains should target the stocks of emerging growth companies whose return will come from growth in share value rather than from dividends. Conversely, individuals seeking income or a combination of growth and income should buy stocks of established or mature companies. These stocks provide a total return from both income dividends and capital gains.

In general, the higher the dividend yield the lower the risk and volatility. Likewise, the lower the dividend yield, the higher the risk and capital gains potential.

trades for you at a discounted rate, particularly if you are using that person's services for other purposes.

Be sure to ask what the commission will be before placing your order. With smaller investments the difference between full-service and discount houses may not be much. Discount brokers often have minimum commission charges of $30 to $50.

Caution: When working with a full-service broker, explain the investment strategy you are going to use (whether it is the one we discussed or another one) and get a commitment from your broker to recommend only those companies that meet the described criteria. When a company is recommended to you, ask for the financial data showing that it meets your standards.

Do not let your broker talk you into purchasing a stock just because it is a "fantastic opportunity only available today." It may be a wonderful opportunity, but if you get into the habit of deviating from your strategy you'll end up with a portfolio that is not accomplishing the desired results. *Your plan won't work if you don't work the plan.*

In other words, if your broker is committed to your investment strategy, he or she can keep you on the straight and narrow and help you avoid distractions. Sometimes it can get very lonely sticking with a strategy that temporarily underperforms the market. A good broker can help you remain disciplined and stick to that strategy.

You must feel comfortable with your brokerage arrangement before you place your first trade (purchase order). As in all financial decisions, change this arrangement if you *don't* feel comfortable with it.

Selling Stock

Assuming you buy a stock using the strategy just described, you will eventually be faced with an even more difficult question: "When should I sell?"

The decision to sell is a difficult one, because it often involves human emotion. First, you have carefully screened a company based on a disciplined strategy and have purchased its shares based on your findings. But after completing your objective research, you hop on an emotional roller coaster. You are elated when the price of your stock goes up and discouraged when the price tumbles.

When prices rise, you don't know whether to sell, sit tight, or buy more. If prices drop quickly, panic may lead you to sell before you lose your shirt.

The best solution, in this case, is to get off the emotional roller coaster and go back to your numbers. It doesn't matter whether a stock's price has risen or fallen. Apply the same test to a company today that you did when you purchased it. Ask yourself these questions:

1. Have the earnings and dividends continued to grow at the appropriate rate over the past 10 years?
2. Is the company's debt still at an appropriate level?
3. Do the current earnings exceed the dividend payout by an acceptable level?
4. Is the P/E ratio still at an acceptable level?
5. Is the company's potential for increasing earnings still positive?

AVERAGING DOWN

Joseph Stearns bought 300 shares of Mousetraps, Inc., for $22 a share. Within six months, the price had fallen to $12. Through his research, Joseph discovered the company recalled several million of their 340XL mousetraps because they were defective. It also revealed that a new mousetrap, the 360XL, was in the research and development stage and was a great improvement over the 340XL.

Joseph believed the company's past earnings and dividend history indicated the company was worthy of his continued participation. He decided to buy 300 more shares at $12 and average down his purchase. After five years, Mousetraps has recovered, and the success of the 360XL carried the share price to $30.

If Joseph had kept his original 300 shares for the five years, his initial investment of $6,600 would now be worth $9,000, a 36 percent increase in value. But because he averaged down, he now owns 600 shares of Mousetrap at an average price of $17 per share. His Mousetrap shares are worth $18,000, and he paid $10,200 for them, or a 76 percent increase in value.

If the answer to even one of these questions is no, try to find out why. If there are two or more no answers, it is probably a good time to sell the stock. If all the answers are yes, it's a keeper. If all the answers are yes after a decline in value, it may be a good time to buy more shares and reduce your average cost per share. This process is referred to as *averaging down.*

In short, pretend that you don't own the stock and have some money to invest. Would you buy it today? If the answer is yes, keep it. If the answer is no, sell it!

Eliminating Losers

Over the last several years we have heard many investors say, "As soon as this stock gets back to the price I paid for it, I am going to sell." If you find yourself using this excuse, give up! You're letting your ego cloud your judgment. Everyone picks an occasional loser — even the best of managers. If your research (or your broker's) suggests it's time to move your money somewhere else, do it.

No one likes to lose money. But once a stock has dropped in value, the loss has already occurred. There are often unforeseen reasons why the financial condition of a company can reverse. Don't hang on to a stock all the way down — satisfying your ego isn't worth it. There's no rule that says you have to make your money back in the same stock you lost it.

When Not to Buy

What if you can't find a company that fits your criteria when you have cash to invest? Unless your criteria are too stringent (which is rarely the case), the market is probably overheated. In other words, investors' expectations are ahead of actual earnings growth. This situation results in unusually high P/E ratios. Very often, the best approach is to sit tight and wait for a downward trend in prices to bring companies back within your criteria. Move your cash into a money market fund if this situation happens. It may cause you to miss the tail end of a bull market (rising prices), but more often it will simply reduce your exposure to a down market.

Where Is the Market Headed?

Far too much time is spent worrying about the short-term direction of stock prices. In our 50+ years of combined experience in the financial services industry, we have never met anyone who can accurately predict the direction of stock prices for any significant length of time.

We believe that investors who select companies meeting our suggested investment criteria (or other sound methods) will be rewarded with attractive returns over the long term. And we have witnessed the superior results that people have achieved by simply concentrating on good companies and ignoring which way the market is going. These people are the well-known mutual fund managers John Templeton (Templeton Growth Fund), Peter Lynch (Fidelity Magellan), and Charles Albers (Guardian Park Avenue).

A Word on Taxes

Don't make the mistake of letting taxes influence your decision-making process. It's better to take a gain and pay the tax than sit tight and watch your gain melt away; so don't stick with a stock just because you want to avoid paying capital gains taxes. If you think you'll have a problem in this area, consider buying your stocks within a qualified retirement plan or Individual Retirement Account (IRA), where payment of taxes won't be an issue.

Summary

Investors look to the stock market for increased rates of return, the potential for capital appreciation, and to keep up with the rate of inflation. Stocks are liquid investments, the first level of the Success Triangle where you begin to put your dollars to work. An investment in stocks is an investment in the growth of the corporate world.

There are two ways to make money with stocks: earnings, known as dividends, and increase in share value, also referred to as capital appreciation. The volatility of the market is closely tied to the marketability and liquidity of these investment vehicles. We recommend a long-term approach to buying stocks within conservative guidelines.

The stock market has an excellent history of being a hedge against inflation over long periods of time. To become a wise investor, you must know the basics of the market and the principles of investing, even when you use the services of an investment advisor.

SECRETS IN ACTION

Yvonne worked hard as marketing manager for a small software company. But after eight years, she was concerned that she had nothing to show for her efforts besides her condominium and a money market fund of $7,000.

She decided that her money had to work harder if she was ever going to go forward, but she didn't know whether she had the courage to pick stocks.

She was strolling through a mall when she spotted a new Bagel Break. She loved their variety of bagels and the coffee was excellent. She was excited to see one open up on this side of town. Apparently, other people were, too. There was quite a line, but she didn't mind waiting.

As Yvonne enjoyed her bagel and coffee, she noted a table tent listing seven Bagel Breaks in town and stores in two adjacent states. Yvonne wished she owned a business like this. Was it possible to purchase Bagel Break stock?

She spoke with the manager and found that Bagel Break owned 24 stores in state and 12 more regionally. The manager told her the company had plans to open another twenty stores in the next year. To top it all off, Bagel Break went public last year at $6 per share and was currently selling for $9.50.

Yvonne told the manager she was intrigued by their business. He gave her the name and phone number of the assistant financial officer. "Give Greg Abrams a call. He will answer any questions you have," he said.

When Yvonne called Abrams, he told her that company revenues had grown over 60 percent a year for the past three years and that earnings had been increasing 43 percent annually. He discussed their plans to steadily expand throughout seven western states and sent her an annual report and other corporate information. She was impressed with the company's prospects.

However, she was still nervous about buying her first stocks. She stopped by the Bagel Break and it was more crowded than the week before. She thought, "Business is booming, earnings are increasing, and they are expanding. I love this place. I have to buy their stock."

She purchased 300 shares at $9.75 a share. Two years later the stock was selling for $21.50 a share. She sold 200 shares at that price and purchased two other stocks. She felt that Bagel Break would continue to grow over time, but also thought it prudent to diversify.

TWELVE

Buying Time
Investing for Growth in Mutual Funds

e haven't actually met a single person who invested in mutual funds 10 years ago as a poor person who became a millionaire as a result. Mutual funds aren't miracle funds, and you know from reading the book this far that 10 years isn't enough time. But the assets of mutual funds have soared, growing from a relatively small $137 billion just over a decade ago to about $2 trillion today. Obviously, Americans must see some value in this investment vehicle. What is the main attraction?

Mutual funds hold potential. It's the same inflation-beating potential, the same capital appreciation potential, and the same participation in the corporate wealth of the world that we talked about with stocks in the previous chapter. Yet mutual funds have the added advantage of diversification, and they minimize risk and worry.

Mutual funds fit on the same plane of the Success Triangle™ that stocks do. They are liquid; you can get your money in a few days when you want to sell. For many of us, mutual funds are our best ticket to financial independence. It's no coincidence that some people *have* actually become multimillionaires by investing in them.

Most of our clients share one problem: time — or the lack of it, really. Who has it? Commuting to and from work, 10-hour workdays, getting the kids to dance lessons and soccer practice, and various household responsibilities seem to fill each day. Just makes you want to cuddle up with some annual reports and *The Wall Street Journal* before nodding off to sleep, doesn't it? Maybe not.

"The entire essence of America is the hope to first make money — then make money with money — then make lots of money with lots of money."
— Paul Erdman

If you're like us, you think it would be kind of fun and interesting to sniff out the Microsoft of tomorrow. But without a reasonable amount of time to devote to investing in common stock, you're likely to do more harm than good to your future financial security.

As you proceed through this chapter, think of mutual funds as a way to buy time. After all, the primary difference between a mutual fund manager and you is that they have all day to pick stocks.

In the Beginning...

Massachusetts Investors Trust, the nation's first mutual fund, was introduced to the public in 1924 in Boston. It was a new idea that startled the financial world and set the pattern for all that followed. They offered to sell shares to anyone who wanted to buy and redeem them anytime anyone wanted to sell, spawning the *open-end* fund concept.

The fund was so well received that after the first year they had 200 investors. In the market crash of 1929, Massachusetts Investors Trust rode out the storm. They shunned the quick profits and concentrated on long-term gains, and investor confidence survived the debacle. They opened their books and portfolios to the public, and made only minor grammatical changes to their bylaws to comply with the Investment Company Act of 1940.

The founders of this fund, with their original assets of $63,629, could never have imagined the enormous impact it would have on the future of investing. At the end of December 1995, there were 73,572 Massachusetts Investors Trust investors who held shares worth almost $1.81 billion. Today, there are more than 7,000 mutual funds to choose from. Mutual funds are household words and appropriate financial vehicles for investors from all walks of life.

What Is a Mutual Fund?

First, let's look at the basics. A mutual fund is an investment vehicle in which investors, large and small, put their money together into a large pool which the mutual fund company then invests in various stocks, bonds, or other assets. Small investors who can only set aside $20 to $50 or more a month realize the same benefits of professional management, wide portfolio selection, and diversification as "big-timers" investing $5,000, $25,000, even $1 million or more. Any given fund may have total assets ranging anywhere from several million to billions of dollars.

The Success Triangle

Types of Mutual Funds

All mutual funds are not alike. They are offered with a wide variety of portfolio holdings, each designed to meet the fund's specified investment objective(s). The mutual fund prospectus will specify which of the four major objectives the fund has targeted: Income, Long-Term Growth, Growth and Income, or a Balanced investment strategy. Each fund tries to achieve its stated objectives by establishing a portfolio of investments carefully selected from a wide range of investment opportunities. Funds may be classified by either their investment objective or by their portfolio holdings. Here are some examples of the types of funds you might consider investing in.

Stock funds, also called *equity funds*, invest primarily in stocks, *bond funds* (see Chapter 14) invest in various types of bonds, and *balanced funds* will include both stocks and bonds, shifting the balance according to market changes. *Money market funds* (see Chapter 10) invest in instruments with short-term maturities with the objectives of 100% stability of principal and favorable interest rates.

Growth funds concentrate on stocks expected to provide long-term capital appreciation with little consideration given to current dividends or income. *Aggressive growth funds* will take more risk in seeking the greatest long-term growth.

Income funds emphasize high yielding stocks, so they pay dividends. As a result they are favored by retired people.

Global funds or *international funds* invest your money outside the national marketplace to participate in companies all over the world.

Sector funds will specialize in stocks of a particular industry or portion of the economy. *Speciality funds* have been created for almost any investment need. These include *precious metals mining funds*, *mortgage funds*, and *socially conscious funds*. You can even invest in a *mutual funds fund*, that is, a mutual fund that invests in the shares or other mutual funds.

Informed investors choose funds with objectives and portfolio mixtures that are compatible with their own attitudes and goals.

Advantages of Mutual Funds

Why should you invest in a mutual fund rather than make your own stock purchases? We've touched on these briefly but they bear repeating. Essentially, there are three reasons: economies of scale, diversification, and professional management.

FIGURE 12–1

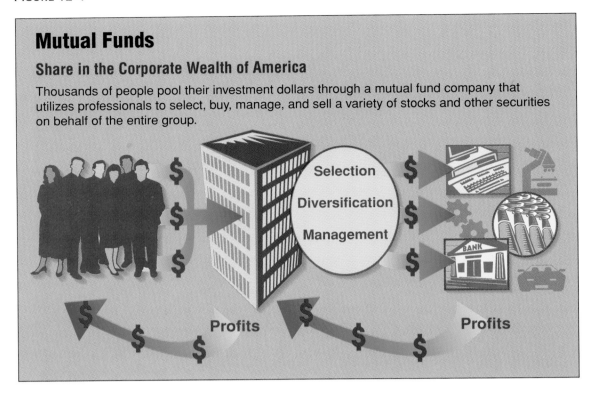

Mutual Funds

Share in the Corporate Wealth of America

Thousands of people pool their investment dollars through a mutual fund company that utilizes professionals to select, buy, manage, and sell a variety of stocks and other securities on behalf of the entire group.

Economies of Scale

First, certain economies of scale are achieved with mutual funds. Large pools of investment capital enable the fund to trade in large volumes with exceptional buying power. Many Americans do not have enough money to hire professional money managers, but mutual funds allow investors to take advantage of their expertise at a low cost. Many funds pay a management fee of as little as 0.5 to 1.0 percent of their assets per year to an investment advisory firm. In comparison, individual investors historically pay 1.5 to 2.5 percent a year for private management of their portfolios, and most programs require minimum account sizes of $50,000 or more.

Instant Diversification

Mutual funds also provide instant diversification across a number of companies and industries regardless of the amount invested. It is not unusual to find your investment split among 50 to 200 or more compa-

The Success Triangle

nies at any given time. This diversification reduces the risk associated with having all of your eggs in one basket. If you tried to achieve the same kind of diversification by investing on your own, you might need $100,000 or more, a figure initially beyond the reach of most investors.

Professional Management

Investors who do have large sums of money to invest have asked, "Why would I want to invest in a mutual fund if I can establish a diversified portfolio on my own?" Because mutual funds provide more than just diversification — they also provide the financial expertise of professional advisors who can add a lot of value in terms of portfolio selection and management.

Some mutual funds are managed by one person while other funds employ two or more managers. In larger mutual fund families, the manager evaluates data compiled by an entire department of research analysts. Each of them is responsible for companies within a limited number of industry groups. Depending on the fund's size and the experience of the analyst, some of them evaluate only one industry group while others evaluate as many as three or four industries.

Of course, individual investors can do a good job of gathering corporate financial information on their own, but this data rarely reaches the depth or breadth of analysis that fund managers and their analysts develop. True, individual investors read the same annual reports and the same pages of *Value Line* or *Standard & Poor's,* but how many of them interview a company's chief financial officer, chief executive officer or, for that matter, their competitors, vendors, and clients? How many times do investors actually visit a company's headquarters before deciding whether to purchase their shares? They probably never do, so fund managers and analysts offer investors a unique opportunity to gain in-depth knowledge of a corporation without any of the hassles.

What happens after the mutual fund research analyst performs this in-depth research? First, the analyst compares the company with others in the same industry group. If all the data looks attractive, the analyst then presents it to the fund manager as a possible purchase. The fund manager evaluates the analyst's assessment at that point and decides whether the company's shares should be purchased.

Mutual fund managers may also employ economists to advise them about the overall economy and which industry groups to consider or to avoid. They also receive institutional research reports from some of the top analysts at major and regional brokerage firms because these managers buy and sell large blocks of stock.

Does all of this research keep fund managers from making mistakes? Of course not. After all, they are human and surprises happen. There are always unforeseen events that can negatively impact a company and no one is immune to these kinds of events, including the fund managers. Overall, however, the thorough research performed by the professional fund manager's analysts improves the odds that more winners — and fewer losers — will find their way into your portfolio.

Fund managers have the time to do the research — it's their job. So, mutual funds eliminate the need for individual investors to spend the extra time. Of course, there are some investors who want to obtain diversification on their own *and* benefit from mutual fund managers' investment expertise. They invest some of their money in mutual funds and manage their own stock portfolio at the same time.

How Profit Is Earned through Mutual Funds

Mutual fund profits are earned in much the same way as stock profits. As with stocks, mutual fund investors expect the value of their funds will appreciate over time and expect to receive their portion of the dividends the fund receives from its holdings. Unlike stocks, mutual funds provide a third avenue of profits, capital gains distributions, which are the profits the fund realizes when shares of stock from its portfolio are sold.

Appreciation in Share Value

When shares of the companies owned by the fund are increasing in value, the assets of the fund increase accordingly. At the close of each business day, the assets of the fund are totaled and divided by the number of outstanding shares to determine the closing price per share. This price is called the *net asset value per share,* or *bid price,* and is the price at which a shareholder can sell shares back to the fund.

When you sell shares for more than you paid for them, the profit is taxable as capital gains income. On the other hand, if you hold shares which are valued at more than you paid for them, you have *unrealized gains* which is the amount of appreciation in share value. The gains remain unrealized until the shares are sold and are thus not subject to current income tax.

The value of mutual fund shares will fluctuate just like the values of the investments in their portfolios. If share prices decline over a given period of time, the value of your shares in the fund will decline as well. Shares of mutual funds investing in the stock market are subject to the same market risk.

FIGURE 12–2

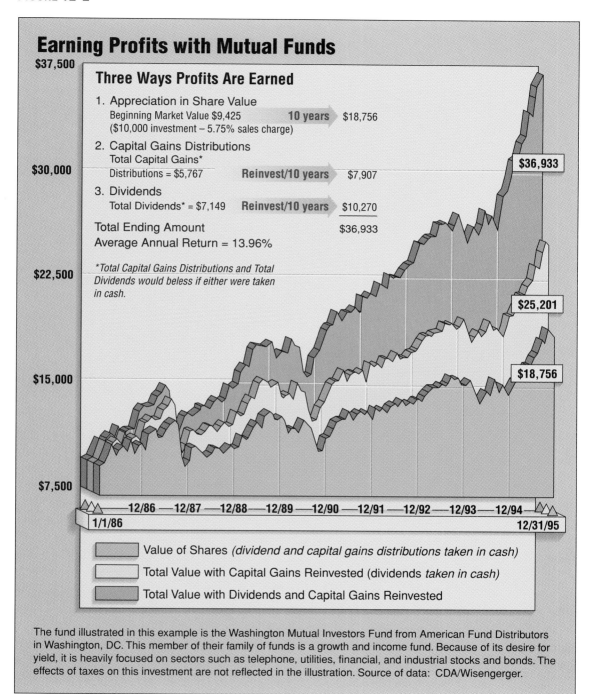

Earning Profits with Mutual Funds

Three Ways Profits Are Earned

1. Appreciation in Share Value
   Beginning Market Value $9,425   **10 years** $18,756
   ($10,000 investment – 5.75% sales charge)

2. Capital Gains Distributions
   Total Capital Gains*
   Distributions = $5,767   **Reinvest/10 years** $7,907

3. Dividends
   Total Dividends* = $7,149   **Reinvest/10 years** $10,270

Total Ending Amount $36,933
Average Annual Return = 13.96%

*Total Capital Gains Distributions and Total Dividends would beless if either were taken in cash.

$37,500
$30,000
$22,500
$15,000
$7,500

$36,933
$25,201
$18,756

1/1/86   12/86 — 12/87 — 12/88 — 12/89 — 12/90 — 12/91 — 12/92 — 12/93 — 12/94   12/31/95

Value of Shares *(dividend and capital gains distributions taken in cash)*
Total Value with Capital Gains Reinvested (dividends *taken in cash*)
Total Value with Dividends and Capital Gains Reinvested

The fund illustrated in this example is the Washington Mutual Investors Fund from American Fund Distributors in Washington, DC. This member of their family of funds is a growth and income fund. Because of its desire for yield, it is heavily focused on sectors such as telephone, utilities, financial, and industrial stocks and bonds. The effects of taxes on this investment are not reflected in the illustration. Source of data: CDA/Wisengerger.

Dividends

In our discussion of stocks, we talked about corporate earnings and how an individual company can retain its earnings for future growth or pay a portion of them to the shareholders as dividends. Mutual funds receive dividends from the many companies they own shares in and then redistribute the dividends to their shareholders through the fund. Mutual funds investing in common stock typically distribute dividends quarterly, semiannually, or annually. (The fund's prospectus will tell you when dividends are declared.)

As a shareholder in a mutual fund, you may choose to receive the dividends in cash or have them automatically reinvested.

When your stock pays dividends, you get a check in the mail. To apply the seven secrets, and take advantage of compounding you know that your dividends should be reinvested right away. But dividend checks may not amount to enough for a stock purchase; you might have to accumulate them for awhile. Then, you must make a separate purchase to reinvest.

Mutual funds offer investors the option of automatic reinvestment, a real time-saver. As dividends are declared in the fund, you are paid in additional shares or partial shares of the fund. Even when it seems that the net asset value per share is not increasing, you will have more shares. The share price multiplied by the number of shares you own is what your investment is worth.

Capital Gains Distributions

During the course of business, the fund manager sells shares of companies he or she feels no longer suit the fund's objectives or needs. When shares are sold at a higher price than the original purchase price, capital gains are generated. Generally at the end of each year, the manager adds up any gains realized during the prior 12 months and subtracts any realized losses (shares sold at prices less than the original purchase price) to determine the net capital gains. These gains are then paid to the fund shareholders, or as with dividends, they may be reinvested in additional shares.

How Much Profit Can You Expect?

We cannot predict or guarantee the future dividends, capital gains distributions, or increases in share value for any fund. Nor can Registered Representatives licensed to sell securities tell you what they will be, either. Not only do they lack a crystal ball, the National Association of

FIGURE 12–3

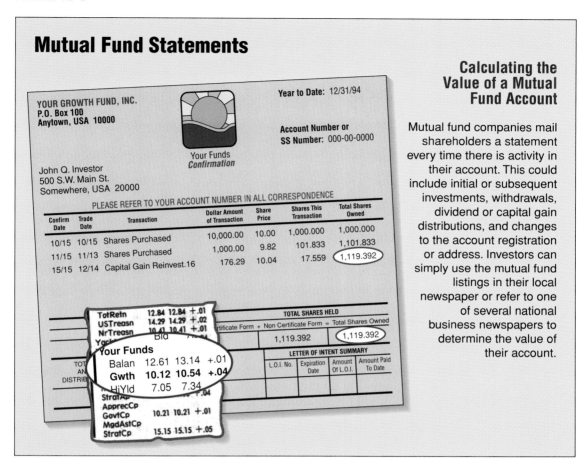

Mutual Fund Statements

Calculating the Value of a Mutual Fund Account

Mutual fund companies mail shareholders a statement every time there is activity in their account. This could include initial or subsequent investments, withdrawals, dividend or capital gain distributions, and changes to the account registration or address. Investors can simply use the mutual fund listings in their local newspaper or refer to one of several national business newspapers to determine the value of their account.

Securities Dealers (NASD) strictly prohibits them from making such claims. Avoid representatives who try to tell you how well your mutual fund will perform in the future.

"Why should I invest in a stock or mutual fund if I don't know how much money I will make?" We have heard this question often over the years. First, a mutual fund should be a long-term investment program of 5, 10, 15 years, or more. As a point of comparison, consider that many people are willing to put their money in the bank for indefinite periods of time, but don't stop to think that bankers have never promised how much they will pay over the next 10- or 15-year time period.

Second, while we cannot predict how a mutual fund will perform in the future, we can review its past performance and compare it with the results of alternative investments during the same time period.

For illustration purposes, let's compare investments made by brothers Adam and Tristan for the same 10-year period ending December 31, 1995. The results of these investments are summarized in Figure 12–4. Assume that Adam deposited $10,000 in a savings account on January 1, 1986, and left it in the account until the end of December 1995. Let's also assume that Adam received an average annual interest rate of 6 percent (which is a pretty generous assumption for that time period), and that he spent the interest earned rather than letting it compound. Thus, during the ten years, Adam's $10,000 investment paid him a total of $6,000 in interest. Doesn't seem too bad!

Now, let's assume that his brother Tristan was more astute. Tristan realized that he would have to put his $10,000 in an equity investment in order to make a profit on an inflation-adjusted, after-tax basis. Because he did not have a lot of time to devote to managing a stock portfolio, Tristan consulted his financial planner who, because of Tristan's desire for current income as well as growth of equity, recommended a growth and income mutual fund.

During the 10-year period, the fund paid Tristan $4,909 in dividends. But that is not all. In addition, the fund also paid him $3,923 in capital gains distributions. In total, Tristan received $8,832 to spend on whatever he desired, compared to the $6,000 Adam received from the bank. That's a difference of $2,832, or 47.2 percent more money to spend.

One of the features of investing in a bank savings account, however, was that Adam's principal was fully insured up to $100,000. It was guaranteed never to go down in value. On the other hand, it was also guaranteed never to go up.

Conversely, Tristan's investment in the mutual fund was not guaranteed against a decline in value. In fact, it did decline during three calendar years during the decade and during many shorter term periods. To offset this risk, however, the fund shares offered the potential to increase in value, something the bank account couldn't do. And increase they did.

In our example, after spending all of his dividends and capital gains distributions, Tristan could have liquidated his account at the end of the ten years for $18,756. His original investment was $10,000, so the increase in share value was $8,756. When added to the $8,832 Tristan spent over the years, he had a total investment profit of $17,588. That's $11,588 more than Adam was able to earn at the bank.

FIGURE 12–4

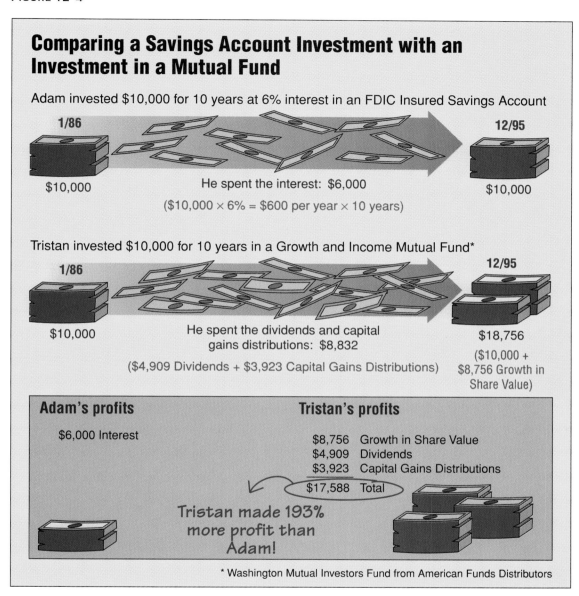

Comparing a Savings Account Investment with an Investment in a Mutual Fund

Adam invested $10,000 for 10 years at 6% interest in an FDIC Insured Savings Account

1/86   **12/95**

$10,000

He spent the interest: $6,000

($10,000 × 6% = $600 per year × 10 years)

$10,000

Tristan invested $10,000 for 10 years in a Growth and Income Mutual Fund*

1/86   **12/95**

$10,000

He spent the dividends and capital gains distributions: $8,832

($4,909 Dividends + $3,923 Capital Gains Distributions)

$18,756

($10,000 + $8,756 Growth in Share Value)

Adam's profits	**Tristan's profits**
$6,000 Interest	$8,756 Growth in Share Value
	$4,909 Dividends
	$3,923 Capital Gains Distributions
	$17,588 Total

Tristan made 193% more profit than Adam!

* Washington Mutual Investors Fund from American Funds Distributors

Tristan's investment profits were 193 percent larger than Adam's. In comparison, Adam's investment wasn't all that good.

Of course, many bank depositors and most investors in common stock mutual funds don't receive their interest or dividends and capital gains distributions in cash; they harness the power of time and let them accumulate and compound instead. Adam's $10,000 invested at 6 percent for 10 years would compound on an annual basis to $17,908. The $10,000 in the same mutual fund we profiled above, with all dividends and capital gains reinvested, would have grown to $36,933. That's equivalent to an average annual compounded return of 13.96 percent.

We are not suggesting that you take all of your money out of the bank or money market fund and invest it in growth mutual funds. But if you have established adequate savings and cash reserves, do not let any excess reserves lie around gathering dust. Put them to work in the corporate world. Let business and industry finance your children's college education and let the free enterprise system build your retirement nest egg. Typically, any long-term goal can be met using common stock, common stock mutual funds, or both.

Which brings us to our next point: Do not use growth funds to accumulate capital for short-term goals. Historically, there have been three years out of every decade when share prices have generally declined. It would not be wise to plan a mutual fund investment for just one year, because it could turn out to be a declining year.

Time — Not Timing — Is Everything

It is critical to understand the importance of time when investing in common stock mutual funds. The goal of those who practice market timing is to invest their money in the stock market when it is rising and move their money out of the market when it is falling. In principle, market timing seems like a good idea. In practice, it is very difficult to execute with any degree of precision.

As we mentioned earlier, no one has accurately predicted the highs and lows of the market over long periods of time — even the finest professionals are often profoundly wrong in their market predictions. The biggest risk is that market timers may find themselves out of the market when the bulls suddenly stampede. History demonstrates that missing just a few bull markets can negate the long-term return advantage that stock market investing provides.

Obviously, investing close to a market peak is not the best timing. But time is much more important than timing. Time is also a great cure for bad timing, as you will see in the following illustration.

Let's say that an individual planning to retire in 15 years made a $100,000 investment on January 1, 1973, in a growth and income fund. In case your memory is a little rusty, let us remind you that the largest stock market decline, other than the Great Depression, occurred during

1973 and 1974. By the end of 1974 the value of our investor's account had dropped 35 percent to only $65,000. What terrible timing that was!

Our investor decided to stick with the fund anyway, because retirement wasn't due for another 13 years. When we add 13 years to 1974, we reach 1987. Once again, this time period turned out to be bad timing. Our investor was planning to use the proceeds from this mutual fund account for retirement. But retirement occurred only a couple of months after October 19, 1987, the worst single day in the history of the stock market. It was on this day that the Dow Jones Industrial Average declined 508 points (a decrease of 22.6 percent).

Our investor did everything wrong: bought at the wrong time and sold at the wrong time. Yet, despite this bad timing, the original $100,000 investment had an ending value of $478,984 on December 31, 1987 — an average compounded rate of return of slightly more than 11 percent a year. Most people would agree that an 11 percent annual return over 15 years is pretty impressive. Given the timing choices in this illustration, it is outstanding!

Monthly Investing in Mutual Funds

Not everyone has $10,000, $50,000, or even $5,000 to invest. Some people are just beginning to accumulate assets, and mutual fund investing offers another important advantage: many mutual funds will accept minimum monthly investments of as little as $25, $50, or $100. As a result, even small investors can start moving toward financial success through participation in the stock market.

For example, let's look at George Rogers, who began investing $200 per month for his retirement in a growth and income fund in January 1954 at age 45. Recall that this type of fund invests in high-quality common stocks that usually pay higher-than-average dividends. Although growth and income funds tend to be slightly less volatile than growth funds, their total returns are, concomitantly, frequently lower over longer periods of time as well.

The performance of George's fund wasn't all that great, but his $200 invested on the first day of every month from January 1954 through December 1973 grew to $90,691 by December 31, 1973. This was an average compounded annual return rate of slightly less than 6 percent. At that time, George, age 65, retired, stopped investing, and began withdrawing $600 per month instead. He continued to do so for the next 20 years. During the 20-year period the fund had an average compounded annual return rate of about 9.6 percent. On December 31, 1993, at age 85 George's account had grown to $176,230.

Because he systematically invested $200 per month for the last 20 years of his working life, George was able to draw steady monthly income from his fund while the bulk of his principal continued to grow. During the 20 years of retirement, the $600 could have been increased if needed, to compensate for inflation.

Dollar-Cost Averaging

Mutual funds are an ideal vehicle for a dynamic investing theory called *dollar-cost averaging* — a strategy that employs systematic, fixed amount investments, regardless of fluctuations in share prices. We prefer regular monthly purchases to take full advantage of price swings rather than attempting to predict the ups and downs of the market.

We can tell you exactly what the market is going to do — it will fluctuate. Dollar-cost averaging gives you a tremendous edge in your strategy, because it works when the market goes up or down. Instead of bemoaning the eccentricities of the market, put this volatility to work. Historically, dollar-cost averaging usually provides better returns than buying a fixed number of shares at one time, because the average cost you pay is always less than the average share price for the period.

Fixed, periodic investments allow you to purchase more shares when prices are lower and fewer shares when prices are higher. The result is that your average cost per share is reduced. To understand how dollar-cost averaging works, see the accompanying illustration.

What is the average price per share? When you add $25 and $20 and $30 together and divide by three, the answer is $25. But what is the average cost paid per share in the above example? When $300 is divided by 12⅓ shares it is $24.33 per share. This illustration covers only three months. But no matter how far you extend these calculations, in a fluctuating market the average amount you pay for each share will be less than the average price per share for that period. This phenomenon occurs because, when investing the same dollar amount each month, more shares are purchased when prices are lower and fewer shares are purchased when prices are higher.

Dollar-cost averaging is not just effective for monthly investors. People with lump sums to invest can take advantage of this strategy, too. One method is to invest dollars targeted for common stock funds in a more conservative bond fund and reinvest the monthly dividends in a growth fund. This strategy takes advantage of dollar-cost averaging, but never places the original principal in the growth fund.

A second strategy calls for an investor to systematically withdraw 5 percent (or some other predetermined amount) every month from a

FIGURE 12–5

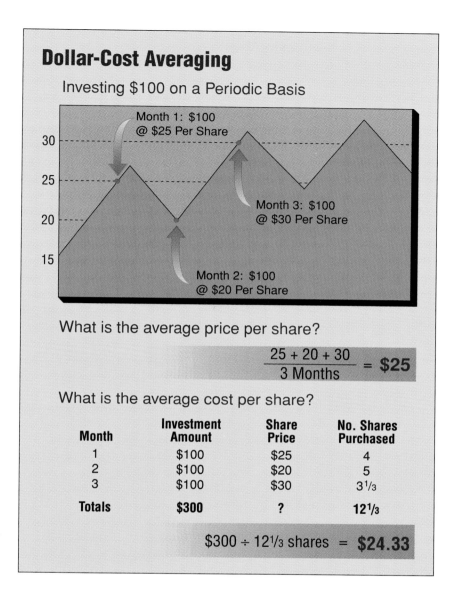

Dollar-Cost Averaging

Investing $100 on a Periodic Basis

Month 1: $100
@ $25 Per Share

Month 3: $100
@ $30 Per Share

Month 2: $100
@ $20 Per Share

What is the average price per share?

$$\frac{25 + 20 + 30}{3 \text{ Months}} = \$25$$

What is the average cost per share?

Month	Investment Amount	Share Price	No. Shares Purchased
1	$100	$25	4
2	$100	$20	5
3	$100	$30	3 1/3
Totals	**$300**	**?**	**12 1/3**

$$\$300 \div 12\,1/3 \text{ shares } = \$24.33$$

money market fund or bond fund and automatically invest it in a stock fund. This strategy keeps investors from fretting about the timing of their investment, but allows them to invest their entire principal in equity funds in around two years while benefiting from dollar-cost averaging.

Dollar-cost averaging, through systematic monthly investing in mutual funds, is a great way to apply several of the secrets of financial success. Set a goal to pay yourself a specified amount of money every month; continue the practice over a long time period, and diversify your investment in a variety of stocks through mutual funds. Systematic investing can be easily accomplished. You simply set up an automatic bank draft through a mutual fund company to authorize the transfer of a specified amount from your checking or savings account to your mutual fund account, on a certain day each month.

Load Funds versus No-Load Funds

Whenever the subject of mutual funds comes up, you'll inevitably hear the debate between load funds and no-load funds. In a nutshell the load is a sales charge, which is a sales commission. Thus, *load funds* are those that assess a sales charge, or load, whenever shares are purchased. *No-load funds* are generally considered those that do not levy a sales charge when shares are purchased. We use the word generally because several major mutual fund companies are usually classified as no-load fund groups even though many of their funds do charge a modest load.

Even though one of us owns a diverse mix of load funds and the other has purchased a portfolio of no-load funds, we both agree the load cost of a mutual fund is not the most critical issue. Some authors of investment guides and books on personal financial planning suggest you avoid paying a sales charge at any cost.

Newsletters and publications do cost money and — more important for many people — require time to read. And many people find such information boring or confusing. If you try to put into practice all of the recommendations in publications, you may suffer from "analysis paralysis," a condition that leaves you searching for the best fund, but never quite finding it. However, they also recommend you subscribe to mutual fund newsletters and read publications such as *Money, Barron's,* and so on. And we don't disagree with these suggestions, either.

The most important point we make here is that you should own some common stock mutual funds — period. Invest in one whose stated objective matches your goals and risk tolerance. Furthermore, we feel that criteria such as long-term performance, consistency of management, and exchange flexibility are all more important than fund costs and expenses.

Having stated these points, it should follow that when you are comparing two funds with similar investment objectives and performance histories, the least expensive fund would be the obvious choice.

But cost is not always easy to determine. Let's take a look at some of the different ways funds may charge investors. They include:

- Front-end load (sales charge)
- Investment advisory fees (management fees)
- Fund operating expenses (brokerage commissions, administrative costs, etc.)
- 12b-1 charges (fund marketing expenses)
- Back-end loads (redemption charges)

Every fund manager is in business to earn management fees, and it is impossible to manage a fund without incurring operating expenses. The other charges are optional, although it is important to note that some funds which assess both front-end loads and nominal 12b-1 charges end up being less expensive over time than funds that don't. Keep in mind, however, that there is no hard and fast rule here.

If you have the time and the desire to carefully select funds for investment (those that match your own objectives and risk tolerance), then no-load funds are a viable option for you. After all, if you are going to take the time to perform the research, you should reap the savings by avoiding commissions.

We have often compared the debate between no-load funds and load funds to the decision of how to get the oil changed in your car. Some people have time to work on their cars and really enjoy spending time under the hood. They buy oil by the case whenever they find it on sale, do the work themselves, and spend under $15 per oil change. But other people don't choose to spend the time to work on their cars. They prefer to take their cars to one of those 10-minute oil change specialists. It may cost $30 instead of $15, but it gets the job done when they don't have the time or the desire to do it themselves.

That is how it works when investing in mutual funds. If you enjoy reading financial publications and mutual fund newsletters, and want to spend time evaluating mutual funds to find those that most closely match your objectives, then saving money with no-load funds makes sense. But if you are pressed for time and have little desire to read financial publications, then load funds are probably a better option. With load funds, you can consult with a broker or financial planner and follow that person's recommendations.

The bottom line is that it's more important to invest in a fund that meets your overall objectives than it is to worry about the actual charge structure. It can also be more important than the annual rate of return.

Comparing Annual Rates of Return

Let's assume that you have decided to add mutual funds to your investment portfolio. After reading a little bit about them you decided on a no-load fund, and call the toll-free numbers of four mutual fund companies that were advertised in a financial publication. A few days later you received the first packet of information. We will call it Fund A. In compliance with securities regulations, the fund publishes the average annual rate of return for the past 10 years. According to the literature, Fund A has earned a rate of return of 11 percent a year. You said to your spouse, with enthusiasm, "Honey, look at this. Eleven percent a year. That is more than three times what the bank is offering! I think we should invest in this fund."

The next day, a prospectus from Fund B arrived in the mail. You anxiously opened the envelope to see whether there is any possibility that this fund could have performed as well as Fund A. To your delight, you discovered that the 10-year average rate of return for Fund B was 13 percent a year. You yell to your spouse, "Come here and look at this mutual fund. It's better than the one we got yesterday. Thirteen percent a year! I think we should invest the money from our CD that's maturing in this fund."

Your spouse reminded you that you were ready to invest in Fund A yesterday and said, "Why don't we wait until we receive the information on the other two funds?" You reluctantly agreed, as you restrained yourself from filling out the application.

The packet from Fund C arrived a couple of days later. You already had a negative attitude toward it because the literature was slower to arrive than that for the first two funds. But your attitude did a complete about-face when you discovered that Fund C generated an annual rate of return in excess of 15 percent a year! "I don't want to wait any longer; let's send our money in to this company," you pleaded with your spouse.

"There is one more packet yet to come," was the calm reply.

Sure enough, the Fund D packet arrived two days later. "Anyone who takes this long to mail out their brochures probably doesn't manage money very well, either," you grumbled while opening the envelope.

"Oh, my gosh!" you exclaim to your spouse. "I can't believe it. Twenty-one percent a year! Let's cash in our savings bonds, too."

Knowing nothing more about these funds but their past performance, which one would you choose?

Fund	Annual Return
A	11%
B	13%
C	15%
D	21%

Not surprisingly, every person we have ever presented this choice to selected Fund D. Why not? Twenty-one percent a year sounds pretty good, doesn't it? Unfortunately, this is a classic case of comparing apples and oranges. You see, we've just compared funds with *different objectives* and *investment types* — and thus, *varying degrees of risk*. Let's take a closer look at the funds.

Fund	Objective	Investments	Risk Level
A	Income	Corporate Bonds	Low
B	Total Return	Bonds & High-Quality Stock	Moderate
C	Growth	Common Stock	Moderately High
D	Aggressive Growth	Small Company Shares	High

For some investors, Fund A may be the appropriate fund. For others it might be Fund B or Fund C. Investors should choose mutual funds that most closely match their own goals, objectives, and risk tolerance. Sometimes, Fund D is the answer, but often it is not.

The problem with type D funds is that they are subject to the sharpest declines in value when stock prices are retreating. And a large decline in value may cause conservative investors to liquidate their accounts and put their money back into cash reserves. This decision can be costly.

Be Cautious in Accepting Recommendations

Not all brokers or planners are qualified to make mutual fund recommendations. Unfortunately, there is no easy way to tell whether you are receiving proper guidance, so here are some other things you should consider after receiving a recommendation to purchase a specific fund or funds:

Selection Process

Ask why that fund was selected and listen carefully to the answer. Ask to see where the prospectus states the objective of the fund. The broker or planner should not just tell you that the fund is a good fund, but also why the fund is a good match for your goals, risk tolerance level, need for diversification, and tax situation. You should feel comfortable with the answers.

Fund Expenses

Ask the broker or planner to show you the annual expenses listed in the prospectus, and ask whether there are similar funds with lower expenses. If they don't know the answer, ask them to find out. Funds with total expenses exceeding two percent a year should usually be avoided unless considering international or global funds. Funds with total expenses less than one percent a year are exceptional.

Percentage of Front-End Load

Find out the amount (percentage) of the front-end load. Again, ask if similar funds offer lower sales charges. A four or five percent load is typical. Investments of $25,000 or more may reach breakpoints that result in reduced charges.

Why a Proprietary Fund?

Proceed carefully when you are asked to purchase a *proprietary fund* (a fund managed by the same firm selling it). One example would be a representative licensed with XYZ Company telling you to invest in XYZ funds. We would not exclude a proprietary purchase on this basis alone, but independent funds reduce the chance for conflicts of interest.

Fund Manager

Question the broker or planner about the fund manager and the manager's investment strategy. They should know who the manager is and how the fund is managed. The current manager(s) should have been managing the fund for at least five years, to make any of its past performance relevant.

Long-Term Performance Record

Of course, you will want to know the long-term performance of the fund. The last 5 to 10 years are the most important part of its record.

The Success Triangle

There are too many well-managed funds that have been around for more than 10 years for you to risk investing your money in a new fund. A fund history longer than 10 years is nice to have, but it isn't critical; it may even be irrelevant unless the current manager has been there the entire time.

Service

Finally, you should ask about the quality of service the fund management company provides. Inquire about difficulties other clients have had working with the shareholders' service department.

If you feel comfortable with your broker's or planner's answers to these questions, the fund(s) should be a good home for your money.

In the past, many traditional load funds assessed maximum sales charges of 8.5 percent of the amount invested. Now, most of them are 5 percent or less. Many traditional no-load funds now levy sales charges ranging from 1 to 3 percent of the amount invested. The distinction between the two has blurred, making the load versus no-load decision less important than it used to be.

We want to make one last important point about load versus no-load funds: If the only criteria for fund selection were no sales charge, many people would have missed out on the top performing fund of the 1980s, Fidelity Magellan. Furthermore, you might want to know that the funds we used as examples in this chapter were load funds, and the results shown are net, after all charges and expenses.

On the other hand, for those of you who want to conduct your own research and select mutual funds on your own, you should limit your choices to those funds that truly are no-load funds. Why pay 3 to 5 percent unnecessarily?

Families of Funds

When selecting mutual funds, look for one that is part of a *family of funds*. A mutual fund family consists of anywhere from three or four funds to as many as 60 or more that are managed by the same fund company. Various funds offer differing investment objectives so that, as investors' objectives change, they can exchange their shares in one fund for those of another. These exchanges offer individuals a lot of flexibility over the years.

Most fund families will allow you to make exchanges for $10 or less, and some offer the service at no charge. Most exchanges are as easy as placing a toll-free telephone call. Keep in mind, however, that

FIGURE 12–6

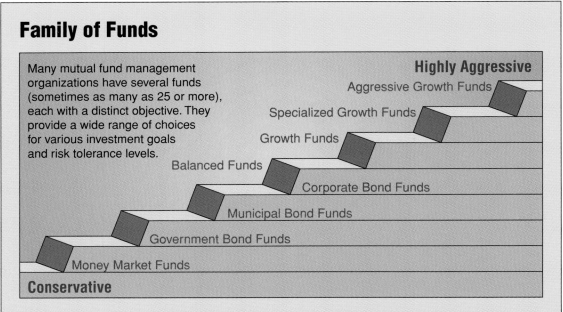

Family of Funds

Many mutual fund management organizations have several funds (sometimes as many as 25 or more), each with a distinct objective. They provide a wide range of choices for various investment goals and risk tolerance levels.

Highly Aggressive

Aggressive Growth Funds

Specialized Growth Funds

Growth Funds

Balanced Funds

Corporate Bond Funds

Municipal Bond Funds

Government Bond Funds

Money Market Funds

Conservative

When purchasing within a family of funds, investors have the privilege of transferring from one fund to another as their needs or objectives change. It enables shareholders to choose the fund they feel is most appropriate at a given time — a growth fund as they accumulate money for long-term goals, a bond fund when their need is current income. A small service fee may be charged to exchange from one fund to another.

exchanges between funds are taxable events. Choose your timing carefully when you switch funds, and be prepared to pay taxes on your earnings.

One idea that has worked well for many people over the years is opening a money market fund account with the same fund family as your growth funds. When you need to liquidate part or all of your account, you can simply transfer the desired amount into your money market fund and access the funds with your money market checks. Buying new mutual fund shares is a simple transfer.

Summary

Mutual funds offer both large and small investors the opportunity to build a portfolio of assets at minimum risk and minimum cost. As we've seen, mutual funds are a great way to diversify your portfolio

SECRETS IN ACTION

Kendall paid little attention to mutual funds until the day a brainstorming session at work turned into an investment discussion.

"I keep my retirement funds in Steady Growth Mutual Fund," one coworker said. "I made 9 percent last year."

"I invest in Income Plus," another said, "I'm getting over $100 a month in dividends."

"I'm in Adventure Technologies," a young engineer told the group, "Last year I made 46 percent."

"Wow," thought Kendall, "that's the one for me," and asked the name of his financial advisor.

Kendall was surprised to learn, though, that Mrs. Landon, the engineer's advisor, wanted to meet with Kendall before he invested in mutual funds.

At the interview the next week, Mrs. Landon asked Kendall pointed questions that made Kendall impatient. "Look, he finally said, "just put me in Adventure Technologies."

"What will happen if the fund loses 34 percent this year, like it did two years ago?" Mrs. Landon asked.

"I can't afford to lose money," Kendall blurted.

Mrs. Landon showed Kendall that Adventure Technologies was an aggressive mutual fund that invested in a small number of emerging technology companies with uncertain futures. Over the last ten years, the fund had shown solid returns, but in several years it had sustained large losses too. It was best suited to people who understood financial risk and were able to leave their money in their investments for a long time.

Since Kendall's savings goals were retirement and a down payment on a house, Mrs. Landon recommended that Kendall split his money into more than one mutual fund, investing some in Adventure Technologies and the rest into a mutual fund with growth potential, but less risk.

"In the long run, you'll be happier with a more diversified approach," Mrs. Landon predicted. "We'll let time and diversification power your investments."

and achieve very good rates of return over the long haul. Mutual funds are professionally managed and allow investors to take advantage of dollar-cost averaging, that is, purchasing fewer shares when prices are high and more shares when prices are low.

Because of their minimal investment requirements and the variety of funds available, there's sure to be a mutual fund that is right for you. Provided you choose a fund that matches your objectives, a mutual fund can be a very smart investment for your future.

THIRTEEN

Fixing Your Income
Income Investments — Bonds

Y ou and your spouse just inherited $5,000 from your spouse's aunt. It's a great windfall, but you have never had money to invest before and really don't know what to do with it. While talking about it, you remember that you are playing golf with your boss the next day. "I'll ask her what she does with her money," you promise.

Your boss is in good form on the fairways. You bring up the subject of investing and finally ask her outright. "Where do you invest your money?"

"I put it all in municipal bonds," she says as she swings her golf club for a long drive.

She's a multimillionaire. If that's where she puts her money, then that's the place for you, you think. Right? Probably not.

For years, people have associated wealth with large bond portfolios as if bonds were a golden investment. The truth is, over time bonds can rarely compete with the money-making potential of stocks and stock mutual funds. They never have and they never will.

Remember our discussion in Chapter Four about ownership and loanership? Stocks are equity *ownership*. Bonds, on the other hand, are a *loanership* investment. When you purchase bonds, you are loaning money to corporations, municipalities, and government agencies.

"There are three great friends: an old wife, an old dog, and ready money."
– Benjamin Franklin

Bonds Defined

Bonds are simply IOUs — a promise to repay your money with interest. These IOUs are issued by corporations, municipalities, or government agencies with stated maturity dates. The *maturity date* is the date the issuer promises to repay the face value, technically called the *par value,* of the bond.

The issuer of the bond also promises to pay the bondholder a stated (fixed) annual interest rate during the holding period, or until maturity. As a result, bonds are often referred to as fixed-income securities. Once purchased, you will receive a fixed income, usually paid on a semi-annual basis.

First the Good News

Bonds, like stocks, fall within the Liquid Investments segment of the Success Triangle™. Municipal bonds have the added bonus of being a tax-advantaged investment. Bonds are traded on the exchanges just like stocks; some are also available from banks or the Federal Reserve banks and branches. We think bonds have a place in investment portfolios, but they must be purchased for the right reasons. Bonds are suitable if your objectives include investment income, portfolio diversification, protection against deflation, or tax-free dividends.

Investment Income

Bonds provide an opportunity for those dependent on investment income to earn yields that are generally more attractive than those paid by savings accounts, certificates of deposit, and money market funds. In addition, bonds have historically been considered a much more stable investment than common stock. This notion has changed somewhat in recent years as interest rates have become more volatile, but high-quality bonds can still be relied upon to provide a steady income stream for investors.

How have bonds performed during recent times? Assuming reinvestment of interest over the 15-year time period ending December 31, 1995, the Lehman Brothers Corporate Bond Index averaged a total return of 12.85 percent a year. The Lehman Brothers Government Bond Index did slightly better, averaging 10.76 percent on an annual basis. These are outstanding returns, and we should caution you not to expect this type of return over the next 15 years. At the time of this writing, current yields are between 6 and 8 percent.

FIGURE 13–1

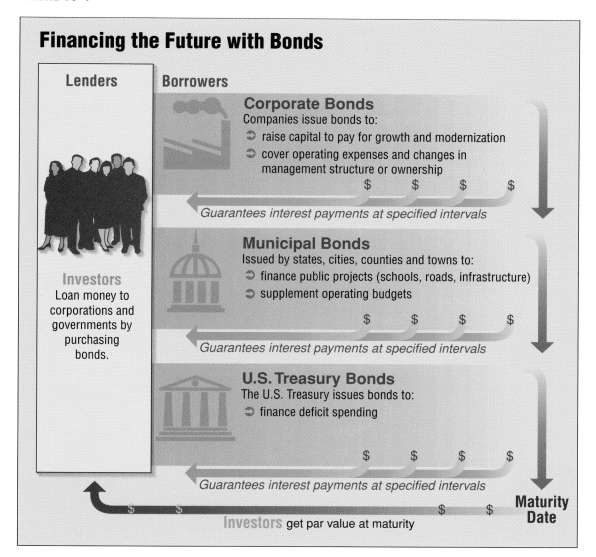

Financing the Future with Bonds

Lenders

Borrowers

Investors
Loan money to corporations and governments by purchasing bonds.

Corporate Bonds
Companies issue bonds to:
- ➲ raise capital to pay for growth and modernization
- ➲ cover operating expenses and changes in management structure or ownership

$ $ $ $

Guarantees interest payments at specified intervals

Municipal Bonds
Issued by states, cities, counties and towns to:
- ➲ finance public projects (schools, roads, infrastructure)
- ➲ supplement operating budgets

$ $ $ $

Guarantees interest payments at specified intervals

U.S. Treasury Bonds
The U.S. Treasury issues bonds to:
- ➲ finance deficit spending

$ $ $ $

Guarantees interest payments at specified intervals

Maturity Date

Investors get par value at maturity

Portfolio Diversification

You know common stock has generated attractive rates of return for investors over long time periods, and that these returns have not been earned without occasional downward price movements. Bonds are traded on the national and international exchanges so they are subject to some market risk, but the value of bonds is not necessarily tied to the stock market. For example, on October 19, 1987, when the Dow Jones Industrial Average declined more than 22 percent, the Dow Jones Bond Index declined only slightly more than 1 percent — and then actually gained more than 2 percent that same week.

Generally, bonds offer less risk than stocks but also offer lower total returns over long periods of time. An exception to this rule was in the early 1980s when long-term U.S. Treasury bonds offered double-digit yields as high as 16 percent. Those bonds outperformed the stock market with as little risk as possible. A lot of us would like to go back in time and have one more chance to buy those bonds.

Even though we can't buy 16 percent bonds today, adding bonds to an investment portfolio offers some potential to reduce its volatility while generating attractive yields.

Protection against Deflation

When investing, it is always best to expect the unexpected. Deflation may show up when you least expect it, and most likely when you least want it. Too much deflation for too long a period of time leads to a depression.

Unlike stocks, high-grade bonds tend to perform well during times of deflation. When economic activity is so slow that interest rates fall to extremely low levels, prices increase for bonds that have not defaulted. Treasury bonds and high-quality corporate and municipal bonds do especially well in this climate.

Thus, bonds can be used as a hedge against declining stock prices brought on by a deflationary economy. Don't go overboard on bond purchasing, however. Younger investors, for example, may want to invest only 10 percent of their portfolios in bonds as a portfolio hedge. As you get closer to retirement, though, you should increase bond holdings to further minimize the volatility of your portfolio. Interest earned from the bonds can also be invested in stock or stock mutual funds to take advantage of dollar-cost averaging.

Tax-Free Capital Building

Buying bonds to diversify your portfolio or protect against deflation are both *defensive* strategies — "just in case" something goes wrong with stocks on either a short-term or long-term basis. But, a bond-investing strategy can also be used *offensively* to accumulate capital.

Municipal bonds generate income that can be compounded free from federal income taxes. Assuming that all interest income was reinvested, municipal bonds (as measured by *Lehman Brothers Municipals,* a municipal bond index) earned an average annual rate of return of 10.36 percent a year for the 15-year time period ending December 31, 1995. This rate easily surpassed the 3.94 percent rate of inflation (as measured by the Consumer Price Index) during the same time period.

In short, you can diversify and accumulate capital at the same time by purchasing municipal bonds. Because reinvesting the income may not always be practical due to the small amount of interest earned, municipal bond mutual funds can be a more efficient way to compound the tax-free dividends. We will discuss them in the next chapter.

Of course, you may not be interested in the protective or capital-building possibilities of bond investing. You may want income right now. Later, we will detail a strategy for bond investing that can reduce risk, but first we want to help you understand what these risks are.

Now the Bad News

Bonds are looking like pretty good investments because of their stability, aren't they? However, during the lifetime, or term, of bonds they are subject to market risk, interest rate risk, and credit risk. In addition, if you purchase bonds at par value and hold them to maturity, you aren't offered any opportunity for growth or protection from inflation, thus bonds are also subject to inflation risk. As a result of these risk factors, an investment that was once considered very conservative and suitable for timid investors has become more speculative.

Market Risk

Bonds are liquid investments because they can be readily sold in the secondary market through the exchanges. However, you won't necessarily be able to sell your bonds for their face amount. Prior to maturity, the value of bonds — the price at which they are bought or sold — fluctuates in response to many factors such as changes in interest rates, the credit rating of the issuer, how the interest is paid (*payment terms*), and the time to maturity. Even though you may lose or gain principal when selling prior to maturity, price volatility is of no consequence when bonds are held to maturity. At maturity, assuming that the issuer remains credit worthy, the issuer redeems the bond at its face amount from the current owner.

Interest Rate Risk

Suppose that you went into the local bank and asked what interest rates were available on certificates of deposit. Your banker may reply, "The rates are kind of low on our short-term certificates, but we have new 10-year CDs paying 8.7 percent interest!"

You reply, "Thanks, but no thanks. I wouldn't dream of tying up my money that long. What if interest rates go up? I would be stuck at 8.7 percent and couldn't get out without paying a penalty!"

The same scenario can happen if interest rates go up while you own bonds. If you redeem them prior to the maturity date, you will incur a penalty — and probably a larger one than with the CDs because the value of your investment goes down. How does this happen, you ask? We'll explain.

Let's assume that you bought a $10,000 bond at par ($10,000) paying 9 percent interest. That's $900 a year of interest income, which sounds pretty good, right? However, two years later, similar bonds are being issued that pay 10 percent interest. You are a little bothered by the fact that your bond isn't generating as much income as the new ones, but accept the fact that it is part of the risk of investing.

Your slight disappointment turns into extreme frustration a little while later, however, because a brokerage statement reports that your bond is now worth only $9,000. "How can this bond be worth only $9,000?" you ask your broker. "I thought it was a triple-A rated issue. You told me it was a conservative investment. Now, my investment has lost 10 percent of its value."

How can this happen? It's really quite simple. If investors can select from new bonds paying 10 percent interest, why would they want to buy your bond, which is only paying 9 percent interest? In order to sell your bond, you must discount its price to a level that would cause the $900 of annual interest to equal 10 percent ($9,000).

Now you know why bonds decline in value when interest rates increase. But, the converse is also true: the value of your bond will *increase* if interest rates decline. Let's assume that bonds similar to yours are now being issued with 8 percent yields. Theoretically, your bond would be worth $11,225 because an investment of $11,225 yielding $900 would be equal to 8 percent.

In reality, it isn't quite so simple as selling a 9 percent bond for $9,000 if interest rates increase to 10 percent. A mathematical equation is used by bond investors to calculate *yield to maturity*. This calculation results in a value that is actually more than $9,000. For this example let's look at the flip side and assume that we are now bond buyers. It

FIGURE 13–2

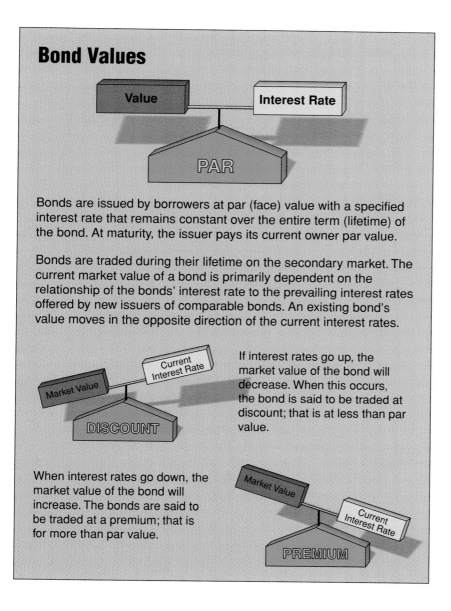

Bond Values

Bonds are issued by borrowers at par (face) value with a specified interest rate that remains constant over the entire term (lifetime) of the bond. At maturity, the issuer pays its current owner par value.

Bonds are traded during their lifetime on the secondary market. The current market value of a bond is primarily dependent on the relationship of the bonds' interest rate to the prevailing interest rates offered by new issuers of comparable bonds. An existing bond's value moves in the opposite direction of the current interest rates.

If interest rates go up, the market value of the bond will decrease. When this occurs, the bond is said to be traded at discount; that is at less than par value.

When interest rates go down, the market value of the bond will increase. The bonds are said to be traded at a premium; that is for more than par value.

makes sense that if we bought a bond for $9,000 that was paying $900, we would be receiving a 10 percent return.

If we hold the bond for 8 years until it matures for $10,000, we would also receive a $1,000 capital gain in addition to our annual interest. To factor both the gain and the interest into a yield figure, we use

YIELD TO MATURITY CALCULATION

The yield to maturity calculation allows us to compare the yield between bonds and other investment alternatives. It takes into account the relationship between a bond's maturity value, the time to maturity, its current price, and the dollar amount of annual interest.

$$\text{Yield to Maturity} = \frac{\text{Interest Amount (\$)} + \dfrac{\text{Face Value} - \text{Market Value}}{\text{Number of Periods to Maturity}}}{\dfrac{\text{Face Value} + \text{Market Value}}{2}}$$

This equation looks complicated, but it's not all that difficult when you work the numbers. To illustrate, assume that a $10,000 bond earning 9 percent was purchased for $9,000. The bond will mature in eight years. The yield to maturity considers both the interest income and the capital gain realized at maturity. This is especially useful when comparing bonds to other investment vehicles. For example:

$$\text{Yield to Maturity} = \frac{\$900 + \dfrac{\$10,000 - \$9,000}{8}}{\dfrac{\$10,000 + \$9,000}{2}}$$

$$= \frac{\$1,025}{\$9,500}$$

$$= .108, \text{ or } 10.8 \text{ percent yield to maturity}$$

the yield-to-maturity calculation. It determines the discounted value for a bond based on its annual income plus its average annual appreciation if held to maturity.

Credit Risk

In addition to fluctuation in value prior to maturity, another risk for bondholders may be the financial condition of the borrower. When you borrow money from a bank, they check your credit history thoroughly and compare your present earnings with current debt obligations to determine whether you are a good credit risk, right?

You should do the same when you purchase a bond. You are lending money, so doesn't it make sense to check the creditworthiness of the borrower? Of course! But how can you check the creditworthiness of a bond issuer?

The Success Triangle

FIGURE 13–3

Bond Ratings

Investment Quality	Standard & Poor's	Moody's
Highest Quality Issuers Extremely Stable, Minimal Risk	AAA	Aaa
High Quality Slight Degree of Long-Term Risk	AA	Aa
High-Medium Quality Strong Attributes, Somewhat Vulnerable over Long Term	A	A
Medium Quality Investment Grade, but Unreliable over Long Term	BBB	Baa
Below Investment Grade Somewhat Speculative	BB	Ba
Speculative Future Default Risk	B	B
Poor Quality Clear Risk of Default	CCC	Caa
Highly Speculative Quality Often Already in Default	CC	Ca
No Real Investment Potential Income Bonds Not Paying Interest	C	C
Bonds in Default	D	

Investment Grade Bonds

Junk Bonds

Fortunately, services are available to help you. The two most respected rating agencies in the bond market are *Standard & Poor's* and *Moody's*. Both of these agencies evaluate the financial health of large corporations and municipalities and assign letter ratings to them, illustrated in Figure 13–3.

Conservative investors should only consider purchasing bonds in the three highest categories, concentrating on the two highest ratings. Keep in mind that higher-rated bonds will pay less interest and lower-rated bonds will pay more interest. Lower-rated companies have to sweeten the yield to attract investors. Unless you devote a lot of time to the bond market, the increased peace of mind is usually worth the reduced interest offered by quality bond issuers.

Unfortunately, selecting only high-grade bonds doesn't guarantee investment success. We once had a client who lost his job a month after his new $500,000 home was completed. Just as the creditworthiness of a consumer can change because of a job loss, the creditworthiness of a corporation or municipality can also change with circumstances. A bond that is rated AA today can be rated A two years from now.

The downgrade of a company's bond rating causes a decline in the value of their bonds. With the rapid changes in the financial condition of many American corporations, investors should spend as much time, if not more, managing a bond portfolio as they do a stock portfolio.

One way to eliminate credit risk is to purchase U.S. Treasury bonds and avoid corporate bonds altogether. Of course, the yields on Treasury securities are lower than those earned from corporate bonds, because they are guaranteed by the full faith and credit of the United States government. When you really need that extra income, but don't want to worry about the credit risk, consider a corporate bond mutual fund. They will be covered in the next chapter.

The Smart Way to Invest in Bonds

Have we scared you away from investing in bonds completely? That wasn't *necessarily* our intention. It *is* possible to reap the income-generating benefits of bonds while minimizing the risks associated with bond investment (devaluation or default). These risks can be minimized by choosing only high-quality bonds and staggering the maturity dates.

However, don't be lulled into a false sense of security by believing that you can establish a portfolio and forget about it. Credit rating downgrades have cost bondholders, who sold their bonds prior to maturity, plenty of money during recent years. In fact, some studies have shown that downgrades are a larger risk for bond investors than defaults. California municipal bonds, for example, were rated AAA in the late 1980s, but were downgraded to single A by July of 1994. Investors saw a drop in value after the downgrade, proving once again that you can't buy AAA bonds and forget about them.

Lower-grade bonds, otherwise known as high-yield or junk bonds (those rated BB or Ba and lower), have earned a fairly attractive average annual rate of return over the past 10 years. And at any given time, their yields may be 2 to 6 percent higher than high-grade bonds. However, it goes without saying that investors in these types of bonds expose themselves to substantially more risk.

Choose Quality

Generally, we suggest that most people stay away from junk bonds for two reasons. First, many more defaults have occurred in the high-yield sector of the bond market. Second, the price of junk bonds is more significantly affected by changes in the direction of stock prices.

Earlier in this chapter, we mentioned that high-grade bonds performed quite well during the stock market crash in October 1987. Junk bonds, on the other hand, took a nose-dive in value. Junk bond prices tend to follow stock values; they don't provide a lot of hedging opportunities for stock investors. Invest in a high-yield mutual fund if you can't overcome the fascination of junk bonds. That way, diversification can reduce the impact of a default.

Stagger Maturity Dates

You now know that bonds usually decline in value as interest rates rise. The closer a bond is to maturity, however, the smaller the decline. When buyers know that a bond is going to mature in one year, they don't require much of a discount, even if your bond is paying interest at below-market levels. You also know that longer-term bonds pay a higher rate of interest than short-term bonds during most economic cycles.

The solution is to own bonds with different maturity dates. In the financial planning world this is also known as "laddering." The chart below suggests one possible maturity date strategy.

Percentage of Bond Portfolio	Years until Maturity
15% to 30%	3 to 7
30% to 65%	8 to 15
20% to 40%	16 to 30

Staggering maturity dates will not eliminate principal fluctuation or prevent you from earning below-market rates at times, but it will allow you to adjust your portfolio much more often than if you buy only 30-year bonds. This strategy reduces the potential volatility of owning a portfolio full of bonds with the same maturity date. The current yield will probably be less, but a Sanford Bernstein study showed that the total return would still be 80 to 90 percent of a portfolio full of 30-year bonds. Yes, we're sacrificing a little yield for peace of mind.

Types of Bonds

Purchasing bonds is especially difficult. There is an incredible array of bonds from which to choose, and we are not going to attempt to explain the specific features of each and every type of fixed-income security. The particulars of each would not only become confusing, but also quite boring. We'll give you a brief overview of each category.

Before continuing, we should mention that in order to achieve adequate diversification in a bond portfolio you should have $50,000 or more, even though bonds can be purchased for as little as $1,000 to $10,000.

Wait! Don't skip the rest of this chapter just because you have less than $50,000 to invest in bonds. Each category of bond is available through bond mutual funds. You can combine the information that follows with the information in the next chapter to determine the type of bond fund(s) that is most appropriate, based on your goals and objectives.

Taxable Bonds

First, let's look at the different types of taxable bonds, including corporate bonds, treasury securities, mortgage-backed bonds, and collateralized mortgage options (CMOs). The taxable bond market is larger and more active than the market in nontaxable bonds, which we'll discuss next.

Corporate Bonds. When Cascade Chocolate, a young, emerging company needs money to finance its growth, Frank Cascade, the owner, obtains the needed capital by selling shares of stock. Raising capital by issuing common stock costs Frank part of his ownership, but costs the corporation nothing.

As time moves on, Cascade Chocolate continues to grow, but at a somewhat slower pace. Frank and the board of directors decide to build their own corporate headquarters to include a research and development facility.

The company needs to borrow money to finance the project. The trouble is, their bank is willing to lend money to finance the project,

FIGURE 13-4

Types of Bonds

Taxable	**Corporate**	**Debentures** Backed by the full faith and credit of the issuing corporation. These bonds represent unsecured borrowing with no collateral or any other security.	**Secured Bonds** Backed by collateral of real or personal property. May be secured by real estate (mortgage bond) or equipment (equipment trust certificates).	**Convertible Bonds** Bondholders have the right to convert these issues into shares of the company's common stock, if the stock reaches a predetermined "trigger" price.
Taxable	**Mortgage- Backed**	**Government National Mortgage Association (GNMA)** *Ginnie Maes* consist of pools of mortgages insured by the FHA and the VA.	**Federal Home Loan Mortgage Corporation (FHLMC)** *Freddie Macs* invest in conventional mortgages rather than those guaranteed by the FHA or VA.	**Federal National Mortgage Association (FNMA)** *Fannie Maes* invest in conventional mortgages.
Taxable	**Federal Government**	**Treasury Bills** Mature in one year or less and require minimum investments of $10,000 with subsequent investments available in $5,000 increments.	**Treasury Notes** Mature in 1-10 years. $1,000 and $5,000 denominations. **Treasury Bonds** Mature in ten years or longer. $1,000 and $5,000 denominations.	**Savings Bonds (series EE)** Issued with specified maturity values of $50 to $10,000. Sold at half of their maturity value and mature at face value.
Nontaxable	**Municipal (Munis)**	**General Obligation Bonds** A bond that is backed by the full faith, credit, and taxing power of the issuing state or local government agency.	**Revenue Bonds** Bonds that are repaid from the income of the project that was financed; for example, toll bridges or public utilities.	

but at interest rates and terms Frank and the board find unacceptable. They consider selling more stock, but are advised by their investment banker that because the stock market has been weak lately, it would be difficult to get a reasonable price. The solution: raise the money by borrowing it from the investing public on terms that are more favorable than those offered by their bankers. The Cascade Chocolate board of directors decides to float a bond issue.

Their investment banker recommends selling bonds to investors for $1,000 each, with a minimum purchase of ten bonds, or $10,000. Cascade will pay the bondholders interest semi-annually for 30 years. At the end of 30 years, Cascade Chocolate will pay the bondholders their original investment of $1,000 per bond, along with a pound of chocolate.

There are three major ways Cascade can borrow money by issuing bonds: debentures, secured bonds, and convertible bonds.

Debentures are corporate bonds backed by the full faith and credit of the issuing corporation. These bonds represent unsecured borrowing with no collateral or any other security. The investors buying debentures have no physical security, so they expect a higher interest rate than on other types of bonds.

Secured bonds are corporate bonds that are backed by collateral of real or personal property. Typically, they are secured by real estate (mortgage bond) or equipment such as aircraft or trains (equipment trust certificates). The interest rate is usually lower on these types of bonds than on debentures.

Convertible bonds are corporate bonds that pay a still lower rate of interest because bondholders have the right to convert these issues into shares of the company's common stock, if the stock reaches a predetermined "trigger" price, which is generally from 20 to 30 percent more than the current share price.

Now, how does this information help you as a potential bond buyer? First of all, you should not blindly buy a bond without doing some homework. You should know whether it is a debenture or a secured bond. Or, if it is a convertible bond, at what price can you convert it? And how has the company's stock been doing?

You do not want to be enticed into a debenture bond with an extremely high yield (junk bond), only to have it default and then discover there are only enough assets to return 30 cents for every dollar you invested. It may be preferable to look for secured bonds when considering those paying high yields. Remember: the higher the interest, the greater the risk.

Treasury Securities

Treasury bonds are often an attractive alternative. As with corporate bonds, their values will fluctuate inversely to interest rates, but the timely payment of principal and interest is backed by the full faith and credit of the U.S. government. You don't have to worry about *Standard & Poor's* or *Moody's* rating these securities; they are all AAA-rated.

All you need to decide is what interest rate you want and how much volatility you will accept. During a normal interest rate environment, bonds with longer maturities pay more interest than those with shorter maturity dates. The trade-off is that the value of the bonds with longer maturities will fluctuate more as interest rates increase and decrease.

Treasury securities can be divided into three categories: bonds, notes, and bills (or long-, medium-, and short-term). *Treasury bonds* are those debt obligations that mature in 10 years or longer. Thirty-year Treasury bonds are used as a benchmark for what's going on in the bond market. They can be purchased in minimum denominations of $1,000 and $5,000. *Treasury notes* are issued with maturity dates of one to ten years, and they are also sold in $1,000 and $5,000 denominations.

Treasury bills are short-term zero coupon bonds. They were mentioned in the discussion of cash reserves in Chapter 10. They mature in one year or less and require minimum investments of $10,000, with subsequent investments available in $5,000 increments.

When choosing between the higher-yielding corporate bonds and Treasury bonds, remember that there is no credit risk with Treasury securities, and all interest paid is free from state and local income taxes, which in many states could increase your after-tax rate of return by 5 to 10 percent.

Mortgage-Backed Bonds

"I don't know what to do," you may say. "I need income and like the peace of mind I have from knowing that the government is backing my bond portfolio. But the yields just aren't high enough. On the other hand, corporate bonds seem too risky for me." This is a statement investors often make to us. The trade-off between risk and return is the toughest part of building an investment portfolio.

Mortgage-backed securities compromise between the safety of Treasury securities and corporate bonds. Investors buy into pools of residential mortgages, which is where the complexity comes in. When you finance a home with a mortgage, you know that a portion of each monthly payment is applied toward principal reduction and the remainder is applied toward interest.

Similarly, when you invest in mortgage-backed securities, a portion of each monthly check is a return of your original principal and the remainder is interest. If you fail to reinvest your principal, your investment will eventually deplete. This can be an advantage if you need current income but is a major disadvantage if you need to preserve principal.

Types of Mortgage-Backed Securities. The three major types of mortgage-backed securities are called by rather strange-sounding names: Ginnie Maes, Freddie Macs, and Fannie Maes.

Government National Mortgage Association (GNMA) Bonds. Called
Ginnie Maes, these issues are backed by the full faith and credit of the U.S. government. Ginnie Mae pools consist of mortgages insured by the Federal Housing Administration (FHA) and the Veterans Administration (VA). These issues typically pay one to two percentage points higher than long-term Treasury bonds.

A mortgage-backed security is classified as a fixed-income vehicle, even though the returns fluctuate because home sales and refinancings alter the planned flow of investment return. Investors subsequently receive a higher yield from these securities, even though they are backed by the U.S. government, because of the uncertainty as to when the principal will be repaid. A 30-year Treasury bond pays back the principal in 30 years while a GNMA pool could completely refund your entire principal in only a few years, especially if interest rates decline dramatically. This occurs because mortgage loans are paid back when homes sell or when homeowners refinance.

Ginnie Maes often require a minimum investment of $25,000. However, existing pools may be purchased for considerably less after some of the mortgages in the pool have been paid off, or you may consider investing in a mutual fund that invests in Ginnie Maes. Of course, the remaining portion could pay down more quickly than when buying a new issue.

Federal Home Loan Mortgage Corporation (FHLMC). Also refer-
red to as Freddie Macs, these issues invest in conventional mortgages rather than those guaranteed by the FHA or VA. Because of this difference, they are not backed by the full faith and credit of the U.S. government; however, they are rated AAA by Standard & Poor's. Because of the slight difference in credit quality, they may pay about a half percent more than Ginnie Maes.

Freddie Macs are sold in minimum units as low as $1,000, making them more affordable for smaller investors.

Federal National Mortgage Association (FNMA) Bonds. Called Fannie Maes, these issues are quite similar to Freddie Macs. They invest in conventional mortgages and have received a AAA rating from Standard and Poor's. They will also pay about a half percent more than Ginnie Maes. They can also be purchased in units as small as $1,000.

Reinvestment Risk. In addition to the principal depletion we mentioned earlier, there is another major drawback to investing in mortgage-backed securities — reinvestment risk. This occurs when an investment matures or otherwise returns part or all of your principal, and you are forced to reinvest it at a lower interest rate. This is a big problem with mortgage-backed issues because borrowers refinance their mortgages as interest rates decline and investors receive large returns of principal at the least desirable times.

Because of the possibility of principal depletion and reinvestment risk, mortgage-backed issues pay yields that are more attractive than Treasury securities, and many offer equal or nearly equal credit quality.

Risk of Devaluation. Many investors in mortgage-backed securities have been disappointed by the results of their investments. Aggressive brokers have promoted them as being safe investments with yields higher than Treasury securities. In the case of Ginnie Maes, their pitch goes something like this:

"Do I have the perfect investment for you! You have invested in Treasury bonds in the past because you like the fact that they are backed by the government. We'll move your money to Ginnie Maes. The beauty of these securities is that they yield about one-and-a-half points more than 30-year Treasuries and they offer the same credit quality. Better yet, you will receive a check every month instead of every six months. I'll put you down for $50,000."

If the situation were as simple as this sales pitch, it would be almost too good to be true. Unfortunately, the broker forgot to tell the investor that even though Ginnie Maes are backed by the federal government, these securities can go down in value when interest rates rise. And when interest rates decline, the investor's principal may be sent back in rather large chunks. When this occurs, the investor could be forced to reinvest the principal at lower rates instead of realizing the principal appreciation that would occur with other bonds. In addition, the investor would receive some principal each month regardless of what happens to interest rates as a result of normal mortgage amortization.

Mortgage-backed securities are complex investments, and it can be difficult to predict how they will react in a given interest-rate scenario.

We caution against using them unless you are working with a broker or financial planner who specializes in these issues and fully explains to you the potential outcome when interest rates rise or fall. Even fairly sophisticated investors have been surprised by the results of their mortgage-backed holdings.

Here again, if this area interests you but sounds too complicated for you to go it alone, there are mutual funds that specialize in mortgage-backed issues.

Collateralized Mortgage Obligations (CMO)

The final category of taxable bonds, collateralized mortgage obligations are debt securities backed by cash flow from a pool of mortgages. The difference between CMOs and the mortgage-backed securities discussed above is that CMOs are split up into several classes, or *tranches,* with differing maturity dates. You are able to pick the tranche that best suits your needs. The cash flow from the mortgages is used to pay one tranche at a time, reducing the prepayment risk associated with other mortgage-backed instruments. Like other mortgage-backed securities, CMOs are exposed to interest rate swings and uncertain maturity date risks.

CMOs are one of many types of investments that are known as *derivative securities.* These issues generally receive a AAA rating from Standard & Poor's and are sold in minimum units of $10,000.

Tax-Free Bonds: Municipal Bonds

In our experience, few investments have attracted as much misguided interest from investors as municipal bonds. Many have pursued the tax savings strategies of municipal bonds to such an extreme that it has cost them money. Because they are one of the few tax-advantaged investments remaining after the tax reform of the 1980s, municipal bonds have attracted money from investors even when they might have been better off investing in Treasury bonds.

If you are going to invest in bonds, it is quite easy to determine whether tax-free municipal bonds or taxable (corporate or Treasury) bonds deserve your consideration. Just as we showed in our discussion of tax-free money market funds in Chapter 10, all you need to do is calculate the equivalent taxable yield by dividing the tax-free yield of the municipal bond by the difference between one and your tax bracket (expressed as a decimal).

FIGURE 13–5

Tax-Exempt versus Taxable Yields

Use this table to determine the rates of return you must earn from taxable yields to equal tax-exempt yields.

1995 Taxable Income			A Tax-Exempt Yield of			
Single Return	Joint Return	Tax Bracket	4%	5%	6%	7%
			Is Equivalent to a Taxable Yield of			
$0 - 23,350	$0 - 39,000	15.0%	4.7	5.9	7.1	8.2
23,350 - 56,550	39,000 - 94,250	28.0%	5.6	6.9	8.3	9.7
56,550 - 117,950	94,250 - 143,600	31.0%	5.8	7.2	8.7	10.1
117,950 - 256,500	143,600 - 256,500	36.0%	6.3	7.8	9.4	10.9
over 256,500	over 256,500	39.6%	6.6	8.3	9.9	11.6

Assume that you are trying to decide between a tax-free municipal bond that is paying 5 percent interest and a Treasury bond paying 7 percent. You are in the 15 percent tax bracket. Which is the better deal?

Five percent (municipal bond yield) divided by (1 – 0.15, or 0.85) = 0.059, or **5.9 percent** equivalent taxable yield.

In this case, the 5 percent municipal bond is not nearly as attractive as the taxable Treasury bond yielding 7 percent. But it's a different story when the tax bracket is 31 percent.

Five percent divided by (1 – 0.31, or 0.69) = 0.073, or **7.3 percent** equivalent taxable yield.

In this case, the 5 percent municipal bond yield is somewhat more attractive than the 7 percent taxable yield of the Treasury bond.

The yield spread between taxable bonds and tax-free bonds widens and narrows as market conditions change. Keep an eye on your tax bracket from one year to the next as your incomes change or as tax brackets are changed by Congress.

Types of Municipal Bonds

Municipal bonds are also classified by the purpose for which they have been issued and by the source from which interest and principal will be repaid. The two principal types are general obligation bonds and revenue bonds.

General obligation bonds are those for which the timely payment of principal and interest is backed by the full faith and credit of the issuer. As a result, the bondholders have a legal claim to the unencumbered revenues received by the municipalities. These types of municipal bonds are considered a safer type of issue than other municipal bonds.

Revenue bonds provide money for the construction of specific facilities such as toll bridges, sewer projects, or convention centers. The bondholders are repaid only from the revenue generated from the project that was constructed with the proceeds. Revenue bonds are not a general liability of the municipality, so bondholders have no recourse beyond the facility itself. For this reason, revenue bonds can pose a greater risk to investors than general obligation bonds if revenues from the project should decline.

Types of revenue bonds include hospital revenue bonds, housing revenue bonds, industrial revenue bonds, and public utility bonds. It should be noted that interest earned from industrial revenue bonds may be subject to the alternative minimum tax (AMT). The AMT usually affects people with extremely large municipal bond portfolios or other tax preference items. The AMT was designed by the IRS to make sure that those who receive tax breaks also pay a fair share of taxes.

Additional Tax Savings

Obviously, the most important feature of municipal bonds is that the interest they pay is free from federal income taxes. The interest they pay is also exempt from state and local income taxes if purchased by residents of the same state as the issuer. These issues are referred to as double-exempt (federal and state) and triple-exempt (federal, state, and local).

However, don't forgo geographic diversity entirely in favor of double- or triple-exempt issues. An economic downturn in a particular region could negatively impact the ratings of local issues, resulting in reduced bond values.

Insured Municipal Bonds

Municipal bonds are generally considered to be second only to U.S. Treasuries in their ability to make timely payments of interest and principal. Even so, there is some credit risk involved when investing in tax-free bonds. Insured municipal bonds can alleviate concerns about possible defaults.

To make municipal bonds more marketable, some issuers purchase insurance on their bonds from the Municipal Bond Insurance

Association or the American Municipal Bond Assurance Company. These companies insure the timely payment of interest and principal of the issuer's bond. This insurance will result in an AAA credit rating from Standard & Poor's even if the issue would have earned a lower rating without the insurance.

Municipal bonds trade in the open market, similar to Treasury and corporate bonds. However, smaller investors may find themselves subject to slightly larger spreads (the difference between the bid and ask price) in the municipal bond market.

Summary

Bonds can provide a reliable source of income and appreciation in a declining interest rate environment, and are one of the best investments to own during a depression. On the other hand, bonds provide no inflation hedge and little long-term growth potential. They carry the risk of downgrades, defaults, and prepayments. In addition, their prices can be volatile during interest rate swings.

We recommend building a bond portfolio with diversification of maturity dates by owning short-, medium-, and long-term bonds to allow more frequent rollovers within your portfolio to current rate bonds. Diversification in interest rates and bond qualities also adds stability to the portfolio. For most investors, we believe that bonds should make up only a relatively small portion of their investment portfolio.

The decision of whether to purchase taxable or tax-free bonds depends on the calculation of an equivalent taxable yield. Once it is determined, issues regarding both quality and yield must also be considered. If you have not invested in bonds before, but would like to own individual bonds rather than bond mutual funds or unit investment trusts (next chapter) we recommend that you seek the advice of a broker or financial advisor who specializes in fixed-income securities. In our experience, it can be much less risky picking your own stocks than selecting bonds.

SECRETS IN ACTION

Edwards Canning Company specializes in canning premium quality fruits and vegetables grown locally and then sells them primarily under private labels of local supermarkets. Founded on a shoestring budget by Al and Ruby Edwards 19 years ago, the company successfully went public, eight years ago. Today, the Edwardses and their three children retain over 60 percent of the company's stock and all serve on the company's board of directors.

Soon after going public, the company landed the exclusive account of a major regional supermarket chain and expanded their plant to increase production capacity. Following early success as a publicly owned company, Edwards Canning soon found themselves at a major crossroads. Their large supermarket chain customer was building several new stores every year and expanding into neighboring states. Edwards Canning found it impossible to keep up with their growing demand, as the plant was already producing at maximum capacity. In order to keep their best customer, Edwards Canning subcontracted many orders to other canneries.

The company had, prior to this time, experienced steady growth. However, their facility's size and outdated and inefficient equipment limited further growth. Even though the previous year's sales exceeded $43 million, profit margins were at their lowest since Edwards Canning went public. It became clearly apparent that the company needed to act quickly if they hoped to maintain a viable position in the market.

During weeks of meetings and work with outside consultants, the directors established some ambitious goals for the company and formulated a plan to enlarge and modernize their plant. They could increase production immediately to meet present demand and provide space for expected continued growth with a $12 million investment. The problem was that the company simply did not have the resources to finance the needed expansion. With their declining profit margins, another stock offering seemed a poor choice. Even though the company has impeccable credit, they found lending institutions reluctant to finance their project and interest rates were at a ten-year high.

One consultant, citing the company's high profile in the community and its excellent reputation with suppliers and customers, suggested that a bond offering would be a good choice to finance the plant expansion and modernization project. A local stock brokerage assisted with the bond issue and sales. Bond sales were brisk, with just five weeks needed to complete the financing. Thanks to a mild winter and a good construction team, the entire project was completed in time for the first early summer harvests.

Production in that season met all goals. The company's expansion allowed them to exceed the previous year's output by over 40 percent. Over the next few years production and sales continued to increase, rising to over $80 million in just the fourth year after the bond issue. Edwards Canning has become their city's largest employer, profit margins have increased substantially, and its stock price has followed. Bonds played a vital role in the success of Edwards Canning Company and in the success of their entire community.

The Success Triangle

FOURTEEN

Coupons and Shock Absorbers
Bond Mutual Funds

"*T*heir growth has been little short of phenomenal — from a half billion dollars in 1941 to nearly $60 billion in 1972 ..." So said Louis Engel about mutual funds in the sixth edition of his book, *How to Buy Stocks.* Mr. Engel would have laughed us right out of his office if we could have told him then that 20 years later there would be over $2 trillion invested in mutual funds!

What do mutual funds mean to you? Most people, hearing of the impressive returns of the aggressive growth stock funds, think mutual funds are only equity funds. In truth, stock, or equity, funds account for only 25 percent of all the assets invested in mutual funds. While bond funds account for more than 38 percent. The other 37 percent is comprised of money market funds.

"I used to think that money was the most important thing in life. Now that I'm old, I know it is."
– Oscar Wilde

What Are Bond Funds?

Bond funds are simply mutual funds that invest in bonds. Like bonds, bond funds produce regular income. However, unlike bonds, you are buying shares in a mutual fund which in turn owns the bonds. Subsequently, bond funds have no maturity date and no guaranteed repayment of principal. You can opt to have your dividends reinvested to purchase additional shares in the fund, thereby increasing your principal.

Like equity mutual funds, bond funds come in several varieties, with different objectives to suit individual investor preferences. Some bond funds purchase only high-grade corporate bonds; others specialize in riskier high-yield junk bonds; some invest in short- or long-term treasuries; some purchase mortgage-backed securities; and still others invest only in tax-free municipal bonds.

Government income, Ginnie Mae, municipal, high-yield, and global bond funds were not available for investment in 1972, yet they have been more responsible for the spectacular growth of the mutual fund industry than stock funds. But their investment returns have historically trailed equity funds. How then, can we account for their popularity? The answer is income yield, liquidity, and diversification. As we mentioned in the last chapter, an individual investor would need $50,000 or more to achieve adequate diversification with individual bonds. Bond funds will achieve the diversification for you with minimum investment requirements of $1,000 or less.

Who's Investing in Bond Funds?

As interest rates declined during the past few years, investors in several areas switched to bond mutual funds for their income yield potential. These investment areas included:

- Maturing certificates of deposit
- Money market funds
- IRA contributions
- 401(k) contributions

However, we think bond funds have been purchased for all the wrong reasons. Many investors purchase income-oriented bond funds when their goal is actually long-term growth. Before considering bond mutual funds, take time to carefully define your investment objectives. To find a fund that matches your investment objectives, review the fund's prospectus, which clearly spells out the objectives of the fund.

Here's another important suggestion: Don't switch to bond funds just because your broker recommended it. Just as investors often choose bond funds for the wrong reasons, brokers often recommend bond funds for the wrong reasons, too.

Who *Should* Invest in Bond Funds?

Investors should choose bond funds as an investment for the same reasons they would choose individual bonds. Specifically, bond funds usually provide an opportunity for retirees and others dependent on

WHY BROKERS LIKE TO SELL BOND FUNDS

1. It's easy to compare the yield of a bond fund with a CD or money market fund yield.
2. It's more difficult to explain growth to an investor than it is to explain yield.
3. Bond fund values fluctuate less than stock fund values — so client concerns are reduced.
4. Government securities funds *sound* like they are guaranteed investments.

investment income to earn yields that are more attractive than those available with savings accounts, certificates of deposit, and money market funds. Younger investors will choose bond funds for diversification, hedging, and tax-free capital building.

Bond funds allow investors to achieve these investment objectives without taking the time to select individual bonds on their own — and they allow diversification for investors with even small amounts of money.

If a stock collapses in price due to corporate mismanagement, the potential exists to make the money back in another company's stock. However, if a bond collapses in price due to financial weakness of the issuing corporation, it is generally quite difficult to make up the losses in another bond since bonds don't offer appreciation potential unless they are selling at deep discounts. But deep discounts should be carefully scrutinized: Is the issuing company in the same financial distress as the one that issued the bond you just sold?

Unit Investment Trusts

Unit investment trusts allow investors to create an instant bond portfolio with as little as $5,000. They differ from bond mutual funds in that they are not actively managed (they are a *fixed portfolio*), they have a finite life, and the yields of unit investment trusts tend to be higher as a result of charging only an annual surveillance fee of about one-tenth of one percent. Unit trusts issue a predetermined number of shares, or units, at which point the trust is closed to investors. However, units may be sold or redeemed like shares in a mutual fund.

Unit investment trusts offer the following features:

- Professional selection of bonds
- Diversification

- Predetermined, specified portfolio of bonds
- Fixed interest payments (monthly, quarterly, or semi-annually)
- Return of principal as each bond matures or is called (exposes investors to reinvestment risk)

Many bond investors have divided the income-generating portion of their portfolio between bond funds and unit trusts in order to receive the benefits of both types of investments. It should be noted that bond funds that are performing well have demonstrated an ability to increase dividends during a period of rising interest rates, while unit trusts have no ability to increase interest payments. On the other hand, if interest rates continue to rise indefinitely, the value of a bond fund could continue to fall, while the value of a unit trust will eventually return to par value at maturity.

Advantages of Bond Funds

Bond funds provide investors with several conveniences: monthly dividends, ease of reinvestment, cross reinvestment, increased liquidity, and exchange privileges.

Monthly dividends. Bond fund dividends are distributed to investors on a monthly basis, while individual bonds generally provide only semi-annual interest payments. (Of course, we recommend reinvesting your monthly dividends to take advantage of compounding.)

Ease of reinvestment. Dividends in odd and small amounts may be automatically reinvested in additional shares, which solves the problem of what to do with small interest checks from individual bonds, and allows for dollar-cost averaging within the bond market. Reinvested dividends will purchase more shares of bonds as their value rises and falls inversely to interest rate changes.

Cross reinvestment. Monthly dividends may be reinvested in shares of a growth or balanced fund within the same family of funds. This allows for hedging and automatic dollar-cost averaging into the stock market.

Increased liquidity. If an investor tries to sell small amounts of bonds or thinly traded issues on the open market, it can be disappointing. The spreads between bid (sell) and ask (buy) prices seem to widen dramatically if dealers are not interested in purchasing the bonds you want to sell. Owning bond funds generally eliminates this problem.

FIGURE 14–1

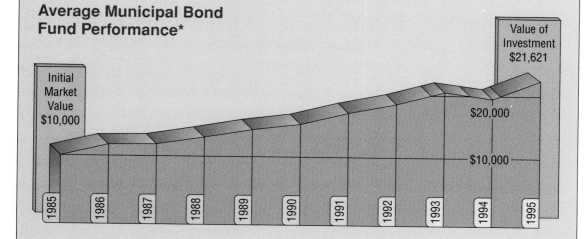

Municipal and Corporate Bond Funds

$10,000 Hypothetical Investment
for the 10-year period ending December 31, 1995

Average Municipal Bond Fund Performance*

Value of Investment $21,621

Initial Market Value $10,000

$20,000

$10,000

1985 1986 1987 1988 1989 1990 1991 1992 1993 1994 1995

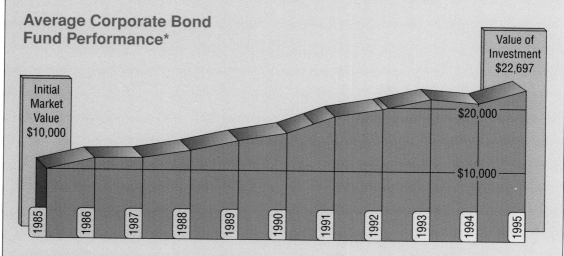

Average Corporate Bond Fund Performance*

Value of Investment $22,697

Initial Market Value $10,000

$20,000

$10,000

1985 1986 1987 1988 1989 1990 1991 1992 1993 1994 1995

*The results shown above represent the composite performance of all municipal and corporate bond funds monitored by CDA/Wiesenberger since 1985 and are not intended to relate to a specific fund. Past performance is no guarantee of future results. Investment return and principal value will fluctuate. No adjustment has been made for any income taxes payable. Ending value assumes the reinvestment of all dividends and capital gains distributions.

Exchange privileges. Most fund families allow investors to exchange shares of one fund for shares of another. Exchanges offer investors the opportunity to change their portfolio at no cost, or in some cases, for small fees. This feature may be important if your personal financial situation changes, or as tax laws or the market changes.

For example, *if your tax rate increases* due to rising income or new tax legislation, you may want to switch from a government securities fund or a corporate bond fund to a municipal bond fund. *If your tax rate decreases* as a result of retiring, it may be to your advantage to switch from a municipal bond fund to a government or corporate fund.

The spread between yields on high-quality corporate bonds and Treasury bonds may become so wide that it is worth the risk to transfer from a government securities fund to a corporate bond fund. Of course, the reverse could also be true.

Whatever the reason, you can make adjustments in your bond mutual fund without incurring costs or without suffering losses — adjustments that may cause a loss of 1 or 2 percent or more when buying and selling individual bonds.

Disadvantages of Bond Funds

Unfortunately, not all the news is good. It wouldn't be fair if we didn't also tell you the disadvantages of these funds.

No maturity date. Individual bonds, if held to maturity, offer the opportunity for the return of the original investment (par value) regardless of interest rate changes. During a rising interest rate environment, bond funds do not offer this feature.

Uncertain dividend. Barring default, most bonds offer a fixed-interest payment that you can depend on, on a semi-annual basis. The monthly dividends from a bond fund, however, may increase or decrease over time as interest rates rise and fall.

Lower yields. The income stream from a bond fund will usually be less than individual bonds of the same type and maturity for two reasons: management fees of the fund, and the fact that most funds keep a small portion of their assets in money market instruments in order to facilitate redemption or exchange requests.

TYPES OF BOND FUNDS

- *Government securities funds* — U.S. Treasury bonds.
- *Mortgage-backed securities funds* — Ginnie Maes, Fannie Maes, and Freddie Macs.
- *Investment-quality corporate bond funds* — BBB rating or better corporate bonds.
- *High-yield (junk) corporate bond funds* — BB rating or lower corporate bonds.
- *Investment-quality municipal bond funds* — BBB rating or better municipal bond funds.
- *High-yield municipal bond funds* — lower rated or unrated municipal bonds.
- *Global/International bond funds* — government or corporate bonds issued in countries outside the United States.

Differences in Bond Funds

Each category of bond mutual funds listed in the Sidebar, will differ by such factors as:

Average maturity dates. Bond funds purchase bonds with short-term, medium-term, and long-term maturity dates.

Quality. One investment-grade fund might concentrate on AA and AAA funds while another emphasizes A and BBB funds.

Option writing. This is the technique of writing (selling) call options against a portion of the portfolio to increase income. An option is a type of *derivative* investment (not representing actual stock or bond ownership), where investors purchase the right to buy or sell assets at a predetermined price during a specified time period. This method often reduces the potential for price appreciation should interest rates decline, because of the costs incurred in purchasing the option. Option writing is most common among government securities funds. As a result, the actual distribution rate (income paid to shareholders) can vary widely from one government fund to another. The total return (income and share price appreciation or depreciation) from those funds that write options has generally been poor because option writing is a market timing technique — a bet that the option writer can properly predict the magnitude and direction of future interest rate movements.

Management style. Many bond fund managers tend to buy bonds and sit on them unless they anticipate a change in their credit rating or if yield spreads change among specific types of bonds (for example, revenue bonds offer unwarranted yield advantages over general obligation municipal bonds). Other fund managers may shift from long-term bonds to short- and medium-term bonds if they anticipate interest rate increases and vice versa. A better total return may occur if they anticipate correctly more often than incorrectly, but the current income yield may not be as high as with other funds. Which outcome is more important to you?

Commissions and Expenses

If you have not read Chapter 12, titled Buying Time, turn to it now and review the section where we compared load and no-load funds. Most of the points made in Chapter 12 apply to bond mutual funds as well; only the investment objective is changed. Because a growth mutual fund (stock) may be able to generate gross annual returns well into the double-digit category, annual expenses exceeding industry averages may not be critically important. If the 10-year net annual return of a particular growth fund was 16 percent a year, you may not worry about the fact that your fund manager was paid 0.5 percent more than the manager of another growth fund which returned a smaller amount.

On the other hand, a retired individual or couple who invests in an income fund (bond) and takes the monthly dividends in cash to supplement their Social Security checks would be well advised to search for funds with below-average annual expenses. An extra one-half percent in annual expenses could cost $250 of annual income on a $50,000 investment.

All things being equal (which they rarely are), select the fund with lower expenses. After all, bonds are bonds, and there is not that much you can do to make them perform better to offset higher fees.

Which Bond Fund Is Best?

The type of bond fund or unit investment trust that is most appropriate for you can best be determined by asking what type of *bond* is best. As with individual bonds, first determine whether you want to invest in taxable or tax-free bonds using the formula we discussed in Chapter 13.

When performing the after-tax calculation, don't forget to add your state income tax rate to your federal income tax bracket if double-exempt municipal bond funds and unit trusts are available. Residents of many states can purchase mutual funds and unit trusts that invest solely or primarily in issues of their state of residence. This option allows them to avoid income taxes at both the state and federal level and increases the equivalent taxable yield. Some funds are triple-exempt, meaning they are not only exempt from state and federal taxes, but also exempt from local (city) income taxes as well. New York City has triple-exempt funds available, as an example. It is also worth remembering that Treasury interest is exempt from state and local taxes even though it is fully taxable at the federal level.

Once you have calculated the equivalent taxable yield, you will be able to compare a tax-free fund with taxable alternatives. Be sure that you are not comparing apples and oranges. Don't compare a municipal bond fund that invests in AA and AAA bonds with a corporate bond fund that invests in junk bonds. This comparison is not valid. Also, don't compare a long-term municipal bond fund with an intermediate-term Treasury fund. Different maturities mean different yields and different degrees of risk.

Portfolio of Funds

Just as with buying individual bonds, conservative investors may want to consider buying bond mutual funds/unit investment trusts with different maturity objectives. Dividing your investment between short-, intermediate-, and long-term municipal bond funds or trusts will result in better interest-rate risk protection.

If the equivalent taxable yield is low enough to suggest that you own taxable bond funds, you may want to diversify not only by maturity objectives, but by type as well. A mix of Treasury obligations, mortgage-backed securities, and corporate bond funds can provide added diversification and potentially soften overall volatility.

Summary

Despite some inherent disadvantages, bond funds offer investors attractive income without having to worry about individual bond credit analysis or diversification. In fact, bond mutual funds and unit investment trusts can achieve diversification that could only be accomplished by individual bond investments of extremely wealthy investors.

In addition, bond fund shareholders have the opportunity to exchange one type of fund for another without cost (or at a nominal cost), and take advantage of the ease of reinvestment if current income is not needed. The added feature of monthly income is attractive for those relying on investment income to supplement other income sources.

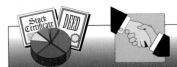

SECRETS IN ACTION

Jean Winston retired with a modest nest egg. Her lifestyle was also modest, but she realized her savings would have to earn the maximum yields to supplement her Social Security. She spoke to her nephew, who suggested bond mutual funds as an appropriate investment.

She compared yield figures provided by her nephew and found that bond funds were currently yielding between 6 and 8.6 percent. Jean telephoned a mutual fund company and they sent her several prospectuses for bond funds, but Jean filed them without reading them. She chose the fund with the highest yield and invested her $75,000 in the Bedraggled Bond Fund.

Jean's dividend checks arrived regularly, and she was content until she read an article in *The Wall Street Journal* that mentioned Bedraggled. Several of their bonds had investment grades that were being rated down. "Ratings?" thought Jean, "What are those?"

Jean dug through her old files and read the fund prospectuses. She realized that Bedraggled Bonds invested in only low grade bonds. Her nest egg wasn't invested as conservatively as she thought.

Fortunately for Jean, her mutual fund family held other bond funds. Jean met with a financial planner who sat down with her and explained ratings and yields. She transferred her assets to three other bond funds: a corporate bond fund investing in only the highest grade bonds, a government-backed mortgage bond, and a corporate bond fund investing in medium grade bonds.

Jean's mistake was in basing her investment decision on yield alone. She suffered a small loss of principal and her earnings weren't quite as high; but she decreased her level of risk, gained a more balanced portfolio, and learned an invaluable lesson. Investing is a compromise between risk and reward.

FIFTEEN

Reducing Your Taxes
Tax Planning and Tax-Saving Tips

Probably nothing irks Americans more than having to pay — *and pay* — *and pay* — taxes. We all understand that taxes are vital to our society; they provide funds for beneficial public services and programs and other important government activities. But we also like to do everything we can (legally) to keep what we've earned. Fortunately, Congress has allowed us many ways of reducing our tax liability as incentives for individuals and businesses to spend their money in ways they believe will ultimately benefit society.

Use this chapter to be your reference guide for tips on reducing your taxes. Let's face it, every dollar diverted from taxable income will save you a minimum of 15 cents and, for a lot of us, 28 to almost 40 cents! And that's not counting state income tax savings! Now how many investments can offer returns of 15 to 39.6 percent and more, on a consistent basis? Use your tax savings to spend as you please or to invest for your future.

In considering tax reduction strategies it is important to differentiate between *tax avoidance,* which involves taking advantage of the legitimate methods available to reduce taxes, and *tax evasion,* which involves using illegal means to avoid paying taxes. Tax avoidance is good planning; tax evasion is criminal. Tax avoiders can use their savings to vacation in Hawaii; tax evaders go to Leavenworth!

In planning tax reduction strategies this rule of thumb is important to remember: *It's usually best to put off paying taxes for as long as*

> *"Collecting more taxes than is absolutely necessary is legalized robbery."*
> – *Calvin Coolidge*

possible. The value of money invested increases over time; because of the opportunity to earn a return, one dollar today will be worth more than one dollar a year from now. There's also the possibility that you will be in a lower tax bracket the following year. Even if you're not, you have had the use and earning power of money that would otherwise have gone to Uncle Sam.

It's difficult to recover tax dollars after you have paid them. Many people pay more taxes than necessary because they don't understand the tax system and fail to fully utilize the deductions legally available to them. A dollar sent to Uncle Sam doesn't earn any investment returns. Your money can't work for you if it is used to pay unnecessary taxes now. The bottom line is, keep those dollars, invest them, and put them to work for you.

Some Tax Don'ts

Let's start with a few tax-saving strategies you *don't* want to use.

Don't give Uncle Sam an interest-free loan. If you are receiving a large tax refund, you have overpaid your taxes. You are having too much withheld from your paycheck and should reduce it; otherwise, you are simply letting the government use your money interest free.

Don't let tax savings rule your investment strategy. Our aim is to reduce the *amount* of taxes you have to pay, not to eliminate them altogether. But don't make a common mistake and resent paying taxes so much that it keeps you from earning money on your investments. Keep in mind that the taxes you pay are only a percentage of the money you've *earned*. Don't limit your earning potential simply because you'll have to pay more taxes.

Don't become obsessed with your income tax rate. If you can reduce it, fine, but if you skip into the next higher tax bracket, don't panic. You'll only be taxed at the higher rate on the amount that spills into the next tax bracket.

Don't cheat. We certainly believe that we all should pay the taxes we owe. There are enough legal ways to save money on your taxes without resorting to illegal means to avoid them. You never want to face an IRS audit with anything less than a "squeaky-clean" return.

FIGURE 15–1

Income Tax Information

Personal Exemptions

The Tax Reform Act established the personal exemption amount at $2,000 in 1989.

This figure has been adjusted annually for inflation. In 1995, the personal exemption will be $2,500.

The 1990 tax law phased out personal exemptions for high-income taxpayers. Personal exemptions are reduced by 2 percent for every $2,500 (or fraction thereof) that adjusted gross income exceeds the "threshold amount." The threshold amounts are $172,050 for married couples filing jointly, $114,700 for single taxpayers, and $143,350 for heads of household.

Social Security Wage Base

The Social Security wage base increased to $61,200 in 1995. However, the Medicare portion of the Social Security Tax (1.45 percent) is assessed on all income beginning in 1994.

Itemized Deductions

The tax law enacted in 1990 disallows a certain percentage of many itemized deductions for taxpayers with adjusted gross income in excess of $114,700 ($57,350 for married filing separately). Except for investment interest, casualty and theft losses, and medical expenses, allowable deductions are reduced by 3 percent of excess AGI. However, the deductions will not be reduced by more than 80 percent.

Standard Deductions

The standard deductions for nonitemizers are shown in the chart below. They were determined in 1989 and have been adjusted annually for inflation.

	1995	1996
Married, Filing Jointly	$6,550	$6,700
Single Taxpayers	3,900	4,000
Heads of Household	5,570	5,900

The standard deduction is not built into the rate tables, but is subtracted from income before calculating taxes for nonitemizers.

Long-Term Capital Gains

The tax on capital gains was limited to 28 percent in 1991. This limitation provides a benefit for taxpayers in the top three tax brackets.

Alternative Minimum Tax

Taxpayers subject to the alternative minimum tax (AMT) experienced a rate increase from 24 percent in 1992 to 26 percent on AMT income up to $175,000 and 28 percent on amounts larger than $175,000.

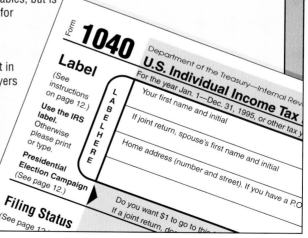

Some Tax Dos

Now how about some strategies you *do* want to consider.

Do use a professional tax preparer. If you itemize deductions, pay for the services of a professional tax specialist. Find someone you're comfortable with who will make it their mission in life (at least for the time spent preparing your return) to find all the deductions you're entitled to.

Do take advantage of every tax deduction and tax deferral plan you're eligible for. We've listed several of these suggestions below, but your accountant may be able to suggest others. Out aim is to provide an easy reference, but you may find that we've only scratched the surface in some areas. You'll find more detailed information in the chapters we'll reference in these sections.

Do keep good records. Accurate records are your best friends in the event of a tax audit. There are now several good software products, such as Simply Money™, Managing Your Money®, Quicken®, and Microsoft Money® that make your record keeping easy and even fun.

Tax Reduction Strategies

There are many investments and strategies that individuals can use to reduce or postpone taxes. In the remainder of this chapter, we will briefly survey some of the basic tax-planning strategies. When appropriate, you will be referred to other chapters of this book where many of the strategies are discussed in greater detail.

For best results, tax planning should be an ongoing activity. When it comes time to prepare last year's return, it is too late to take advantage of most tax savings strategies. As we have repeated over and over again, utilizing the services of professional advisors is almost always a good investment. In the area of tax-planning, this is especially critical because of the complexities and frequent changes of our tax laws.

Retirement Plans

You'll find detailed information on retirement plan options in Chapter 18, but we've listed them here, too, because they are one of the best ways to reduce your tax liability and accumulate tax-deferred funds. IRAs, tax sheltered annuities, 401(k)s, SEPs, and Keogh plans are all used to defer taxes. They not only reduce your tax liability by generally

FIGURE 15–2

Tax-Free versus Tax-Deferred

Tax-free (also called tax-exempt) means that there is no tax due now or in the future. Interest paid on municipal bonds is tax-free at the federal level and may also be free from state and local taxes if you reside in the state or locality where the bonds were issued. Interest on Treasury securities is tax-free at state and local levels. Within certain limits, many fringe benefits such as accident and health insurance, group term life insurance plans, dependent care plans, and education assistance plans are tax-free. Practically all of your other income and employment compensation is taxable.

IRS

No Taxes Now...

IRS

...or in the Future

Tax-deferred, on the other hand, means that there are no current taxes due on earnings, but will be payable in the future when money is withdrawn or assets are sold. Examples of tax-deferred investments include qualified retirement plans, IRAs, investments within life insurance policies, EE bonds, deferred compensation plans, and most annuities. The concept behind tax deferral is that your earnings will be reinvested and compound instead of being used to pay taxes, and that you can expect to be in a lower tax bracket after retirement when you use the income. You will ultimately be taxed less than if you paid taxes along the way.

IRS

No Taxes Now...

IRS

...but Pay at Time of Withthdrawal/Sale

Unrealized appreciation of an asset such as stocks, real estate, or collectibles may also be considered tax-deferred, because you don't owe taxes until the asset is sold and you receive the money in excess of what you paid for the asset. The IRS allows, within specified guidelines and limits, "like-kind exchanges" which are tax-free exchanges for assets similar to those which you have sold. For example, let's say you purchased a rental house 10 years ago for $50,000 and sell it for $100,000. You will be liable for taxes on your $50,000 gain. But if you reinvest your proceeds into another piece of rental property within a specified time limit, you won't owe any taxes. You may repeat the process over and over until you finally sell your property and don't reinvest your cumulative proceeds. When you sell without reinvesting, you will owe capital gains taxes on the cumulative gain you have realized. In reality, then, a tax-free exchange is a means of tax-deferral. But, if an appreciated asset or an asset acquired in a tax-free exchange is held until death, the heirs receive a stepped-up basis, and the unrealized gain escapes income tax forever.

allowing you to contribute pretax dollars, in most cases, and your earnings accumulate at a faster pace without being slowed by the tax bite.

It is important to remember that these plans are designed for *retirement*. Misunderstanding their use destroys their advantage because substantial penalties can be incurred for withdrawing the funds before retirement age. Besides their tax-deferment advantages, some retirement plans also offer *employer-matching contributions* that will substantially increase the rate at which you accumulate wealth.

If you don't remember any anything else we say about taxes and retirement planning, remember this general advice: *In most cases, contribute the maximum to your company's qualified plan before investing in any other retirement plans.* It is one of the best ways to accumulate wealth.

And here's an equally important warning: Don't plan to withdraw funds from retirement plans until retirement. Early withdrawals will not only be subject to federal, state, and local taxes, they are also subject to a 10 percent penalty — altogether, the taxes can wipe out 50 percent or more of your savings.

Success Tax Avoidance

Congress has levied a special tax applicable to those who have been "too successful" at accumulating money in retirement plans. If you withdraw more than $150,000 in any one year from a retirement plan (pension, profit sharing, 401(k), IRA, and so forth), an excise tax of 15 percent may be levied. For example, if you are age 64 and withdraw $200,000 from your 401(k) plan. The penalty would be $7,500 (15% of the amount over $150,000, in this case .15 × $50,000). In the case of early withdrawals (see Chapter 18) this tax is in addition to premature withdrawal penalties.

In the case of lump sum distributions from qualified plans, those born before 1936 may be able to take advantage of 5- or 10-year forward income averaging, in which case they may receive up to $750,000 before the excise tax is applicable. The laws relating to this situation are fairly complex and thus we recommend that you consult your tax advisor for specifics.

Distributions can also be rolled over into IRA accounts or other qualified retirement plans to delay receiving money until age 70½, if you don't need the income sooner. Of course, any amounts withdrawn from retirement plans are added to taxable income in the year withdrawn.

In addition to the fact that you will have to pay the excise tax if you take out too much from your retirement plan while you are alive, your estate will owe the surtax if there is a lot left in your retirement plans when you die (retirement plan funds may pass to a spouse without tax consequences). This surtax, assessed in addition to any estate or income taxes payable could add up to a severe bite for your heirs.

Strategies to avoid the success tax include *not* accumulating funds in a pension plan *during* retirement, and not waiting until you are over 70 to begin withdrawing from the plan. If you are accumulating large amounts of money in your retirement plans obtain professional tax help to evaluate both the impact of potential estate tax liabilities and excess accumulation penalties on withdrawals, from your plans.

Nondeductible IRAs

If either you or your spouse participates in an employer or self-employed qualified retirement plan, the amount of your IRA contribution that is deductible may be reduced or eliminated, depending on your combined family income. The IRS utilizes a phase out schedule in determining IRA deductibility when your combined modified adjusted gross income is between $40,000 and $50,000 ($25,000 and $35,000 for single taxpayers) and no deduction is allowed if this level is exceeded.

However, you may still find it advantageous to contribute to a nondeductible IRA because of the tax-deferred accumulation of earnings on investments within the IRA. Generally a nondeductible IRA should be considered if you plan to leave the funds alone until retirement. One disadvantage is that withdrawals from a nondeductible IRA before age 59½ could have unintended tax consequences if you also have a deductible IRA.

Life Insurance

More and more people are using life insurance as a tax-advantaged way to build cash reserves and, in some policies, take advantage of a variety of multiple investment options to earn competitive rates of return. Life insurance contract earnings accumulate tax-deferred, and certain strategies may allow tax-free access to cash values. They also ensure peace of mind for you and your family by providing a cash benefit upon the death of the insured. Life insurance proceeds are not taxable at the death of the insured and are not considered part of the

FIGURE 15–3

Comparison of Tax Benefits Offered by Investments

Tax-Deferred Earnings

Allows taxpayers to delay income taxes on investment earnings until such time as earnings are withdrawn.

		Example
Investment	$ _____	$5,000
Annual Return	_____	10%
Deferred Earnings	_____	$500
Marginal Tax Bracket	_____	28%
Taxes Deferred	_____	$140

Tax Deduction

Allows taxpayers to reduce their taxable income by the amount of their deductions.

Investment	$ _____	$5,000
Deduction	_____	$5,000
Marginal Tax Bracket	_____	28%
Taxes Saved	_____	$1,400

Tax Credit

Offers a dollar-for-dollar reduction in the amount of taxes owed.

Investment	$ _____	$5,000
Tax Credit Rate	_____	10%
Amount of Credit	_____	$500
Taxes Saved	_____	$500

deceased person's estate unless the deceased was the owner of the policy or retained "incidence" of ownership. A good life insurance policy can be a major component in building your financial portfolio. Chapter 8 has more information on this important financial instrument.

Income-Splitting Advantage

Each additional dollar of ordinary income you receive, such as dividends, interest, or rents, will be taxed at your highest marginal tax bracket. If such income is transferred to children or other dependent relatives (other than a spouse), the income may be taxed at their lower tax rate, and in some cases is not taxed at all. Income splitting strategies can result in less overall taxes for your family.

However, to split income you must transfer actual ownership of the income producing asset. The income can't be assigned to the child unless the child owns the asset. Earned income may not be split under any circumstances.

Income splitting can involve gifts, trusts, and custodian accounts. The "kiddie tax" rules have reduced the advantages of income splitting for children under age 14, in which case all income over $1,200 (1995) received by the child is taxed at the parents highest tax bracket.

Gifts of up to $10,000 are allowed each year ($20,000 for both you and your spouse) per person receiving the gift, without having to pay a gift tax. For example, if you gifted a mutual fund account worth $10,000 or less to your child, there is no tax on the gift. Future income generated by the fund is then taxed at the child's rate, and the child may use the income to purchase things you would otherwise be purchasing.

Custodian accounts may be set up through a bank, mutual fund company, or brokerage firm. The *custodian* — the person who manages the account for the child — may be a parent, relative, or in some states an unrelated adult, bank, or trust company. Income from the account may be used by the child or reinvested; however earnings must be used to pay expenses that are not legally required (and therefore not seen as being used for the support of your child). Custodian accounts are most frequently used to pay for college costs, although they might also be used to pay for summer camp fees, music lessons, auto expenses, and so on. Kiddie tax rules apply to custodial accounts.

Irrevocable trusts may be used in income splitting but revocable trusts may not be. With revocable trusts the IRS considers that the property was not completely transferred and trust income is thus taxed at the grantor's (the person who established the trust) highest tax bracket. See Chapter 9 for more information on trusts.

Charitable Giving

Giving money to charity is a very personal decision. Quite often it seems to be something we do without a lot of enthusiasm. Instead, it's that nagging phone call, reappearing letter, or knock on the door that produces enough guilt to write a check to a certain charity. (After all, we might just help find a cure for a disease, feed a starving child, or provide other kinds of much needed humanitarian support.) Even though it is for a good cause, and the donation may be *100 percent deductible,* it often doesn't always make the exercise easier.

If you can relate to these feelings, you're probably not alone. Charitable giving as a tax savings or retirement planning technique requires one very important motive: a desire on your part to contribute money to one or more charitable organizations. If that motive exists and you are planning to make contributions via your will or trust, there might be good reasons to make your contribution while living. Lifetime charitable gifts can provide:

- A current year tax deduction
- A way to convert low yielding, appreciated property to a higher income-producing asset, without paying capital gains taxes
- A continuing source of income to the donor or named beneficiaries or both throughout their lifetimes
- Access to your gift by the charity prior to your death
- The enjoyment of being able to help a worthy cause while living

There are many popular forms of charitable giving.

Bequests. Assets willed to a charity reduce the taxable estate.

Charitable Remainder Trusts. The property is donated to a charity and, in return, the donor or other named beneficiary or both receive an annual income for a specified number of years or for life. In addition, the donor receives an immediate tax deduction based on actuarial tables and the amount of annual income received. The charity keeps the remainder of the assets after the donor (or donor and donor's spouse or other beneficiary) dies or the specified number of years have expired.

Wealth Replacement Trusts. When a donor places assets in a charitable remainder trust, they are not available to heirs. In order to compensate for this, the donor gives part of the trust income to heirs, who in turn buy a life insurance policy on the donor. The policy proceeds replace the assets in the trust and pass outside the estate of the donor.

Charitable Lead Trusts. When donors are not in need of current income and have assets that they would like to leave to certain heirs, they can use a charitable lead trust. The charity receives the income from the trust and may use part of it to buy a life insurance policy on the donor(s). At the death of the donor, the trust will distribute the property to the heirs outside the donor's estate, and the charity will receive the life insurance proceeds to replace the property.

Life Insurance Trusts. The donor gives the charity a current life insurance policy, or the charity buys a new policy on the donor. The donor makes a tax-deductible contribution to the charity in the amount of the premium. This procedure ensures the charity of a rather large donation and allows donors with limited amounts of money to make larger donations than would be possible with outright gifts.

Gifts of Appreciated Property. This technique turns a large capital gain asset into an income stream, without paying capital gains taxes. In addition, donors receive a current year write-off and reduce their taxable estate.

Estate Planning

An estate planning attorney who has worked with us for many years says that *estate taxes are voluntary.* It is true. There will be no taxes to pay on the estates of many who have done proper estate planning. With this in mind, please refer to Chapter 9 to learn the essentials of estate planning.

Purchasing a Home

Obtaining a home mortgage is an effective way to reduce taxes. Investing in a home allows you to write off interest paid (substantial in the early years of the mortgage, declining with each passing year) and deduct property taxes (renters indirectly pay property taxes within their rent, but have no deductions.)

Your home can also prove to be an appreciating asset that you can defer taxes on the gain until a later date. When you sell and move to another house the gain may be deferred, and the process can repeat over and over again from house to house. If you or your spouse are age 55 or older you may elect to receive a one-time tax exemption on up to $125,000 ($62,500 each for married persons filing separately) of the profits from the sale of your principle residence.

New home buyers shouldn't forget the deductions associated with the closing process, either. Points, for example, are generally deductible if paid at closing, as are prorated property taxes.

Home Equity Loans

Because consumer loan interest is no longer deductible, home equity loans have become a very attractive way to get your hands on some cash, while writing off the interest paid on the loan at the same time. Since interest paid on a home equity loan is usually tax-deductible (consult your tax advisor), always consider a home equity loan *before* a consumer loan. For example, interest on a car purchased for personal use is not tax deductible. So instead of financing the car, pay for it with a home equity loan and deduct the interest. We'll discuss making effective use of your home equity in Chapter 21.

Municipal Bonds

Municipal bonds are one of the few tax-advantaged investments that remain after the tax reforms of the 1980s. The interest received from them is free from federal income taxes. If these bonds are purchased by residents in the same state as the issuer, the interest is usually exempt from state and may be exempt from local income taxes, too. Municipal bond issues are referred to as double-exempt (federal and state tax-free) and triple-exempt (federal, state, and local tax-free) issues. See Chapter 13.

Treasury Securities

As we discussed in Chapter 13, there is little credit risk in investing in Treasury securities, and all interest paid to you is free from state and local income taxes. This tax-free interest could increase your after-tax rate of return by 5 to 10 percent in many states. But, also remember there is market risk in owning treasuries; the market value of the bonds fluctuates with changing interest rates prior to maturity. See Chapter 13 for further discussion of Treasury securities.

Fixed and Variable Annuities

Investing in a tax-deferred annuity may save thousands of dollars in current income taxes and accumulate wealth which otherwise would have been paid to the IRS. For example, let's say that you are in the 28 percent tax bracket and have a $50,000 investment returning 10 percent annually. The taxes on your $5,000 return would be $1,400. If you move the money to an annuity, the $1,400 would not be paid out in taxes. It would be reinvested and earn future returns which makes your investment grow that much faster.

Not only does an annuity allow investment on a tax-deferred basis, tax-advantaged retirement income can be distributed from it. Whether it is a fixed or variable annuity, a portion of each distribution is considered a tax-free return of principal when the proceeds from an annuity contract are received under one of the annuity options mentioned earlier. For more information on annuities, see Chapter 16.

Tax-Sheltered Limited Partnerships

Despite the scorn aroused among some at the mere mention of the words, a *tax shelter* is simply a legal means by which taxes due on certain income may be decreased, deferred, or in some cases, eliminated altogether. Even though many investments (IRAs and other retirement plans, annuities, and certain types of life insurance) are technically tax shelters, the term *tax shelter* has become synonymous with limited partnerships among many investors and financial services sales people.

With a limited partnership investment, any income received is offset by part of the expenses incurred in maintaining the investment, thereby reducing the amount of income subject to taxes. That is what makes limited partnerships tax shelters. When the investment is later sold, however, some taxes may be due.

A *limited partnership* is similar to a mutual fund in that individual investors pool their investment dollars together in order to obtain professional management, large-scale purchasing power, and perhaps diversification. Unlike mutual funds, limited partnerships are not open ended, investments are in less liquid assets, and your shares cannot be easily sold. Through limited partnerships, you can participate in the growth and income of multi-million-dollar projects with an investment as low as a few thousand dollars. Limited partnerships use pools of investors' money to purchase holdings as diverse as office buildings, shopping malls, low-income housing, oil wells, equipment leases, or cable television stations.

Every limited partnership is made up of one or more general partners (GPs) and limited partners (the investors). The general partner may be one or more individuals, a corporation, or a partnership, and has the responsibility for managing the business activities of the partnership and keeping the limited partners informed of partnership operations.

Now what does the word *limited* mean in limited partnerships? It means that your liability is limited to the amount of your investment. If a tenant is severely injured in a fall because of a loose railing and wins a million dollar judgment, the investors (limited partners) are not liable for anything more than the amount of their original investment. That is, investors have no responsibility for liability claims. Who, then,

FIGURE 15–4

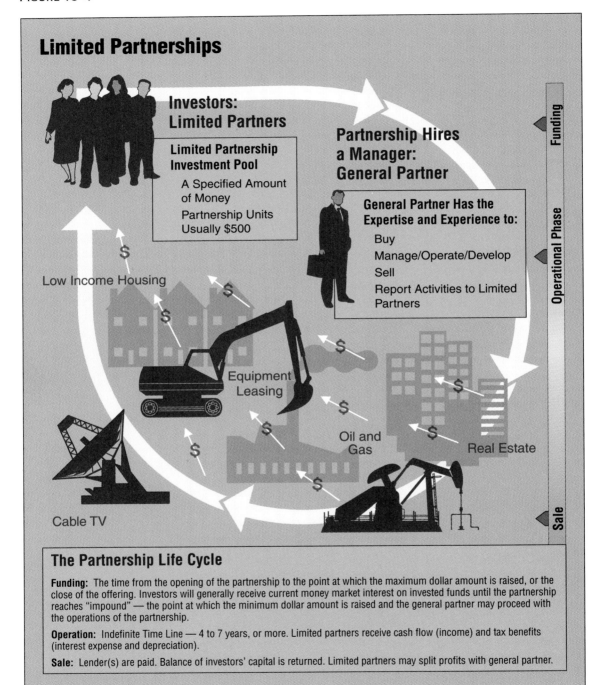

Limited Partnerships

Investors:
Limited Partners

Limited Partnership Investment Pool

A Specified Amount of Money

Partnership Units Usually $500

Partnership Hires a Manager:
General Partner

General Partner Has the Expertise and Experience to:

Buy

Manage/Operate/Develop

Sell

Report Activities to Limited Partners

Funding

Operational Phase

Sale

Low Income Housing

Equipment Leasing

Oil and Gas

Real Estate

Cable TV

The Partnership Life Cycle

Funding: The time from the opening of the partnership to the point at which the maximum dollar amount is raised, or the close of the offering. Investors will generally receive current money market interest on invested funds until the partnership reaches "impound" — the point at which the minimum dollar amount is raised and the general partner may proceed with the operations of the partnership.

Operation: Indefinite Time Line — 4 to 7 years, or more. Limited partners receive cash flow (income) and tax benefits (interest expense and depreciation).

Sale: Lender(s) are paid. Balance of investors' capital is returned. Limited partners may split profits with general partner.

is reponsible? You guessed it — the general partner, who accepts personal, unlimited liability on behalf of the operations. The trade-off for this limiting of liability is that you really don't have anything to say about how the investment is run.

The investment life of the limited partnership is generally several years or more, and even if specified in the offering prospectus the time-frame is not enforceable and could be much longer. The partnership ends when the GP sells the properties and distributes the proceeds. Limited partnerships are meant to be illiquid, long-term investments. Also, there is limited marketability for partnership units. They can be sold, but you must locate a buyer. And when you find a buyer, you generally sell at a loss because your shares are discounted to the value of the underlying assets.

Many partnerships also have up-front fees and commissions, which come out of your original investment, and continuing management fees, which are a percentage of partnership revenues. In spite of the disadvantages, people invest in them because of their potential for high earnings and tax advantages.

Limited partnerships typically offer diversification within the program (invested capital is spread over several investments) and an alternative to conventional investments such as the stock market. Whenever revenues, such as rents, exceed operating costs and debt service, the partnership generates cash distributions. If the general partner can increase the revenues over time, the assets will tend to increase in value; the appreciation is realized by the limited partners at sale.

All or a portion of the cash distributions may be sheltered from taxation by passive losses. Passive losses generated through operations or depreciation may not be used to reduce other taxable income, but they can be carried forward to offset capital gains when partnership assets are sold. Distributions receive long-term capital gains treatment when partnership assets are sold.

The Rise of Tax-Sheltered Limited Partnership Investments

Over the years, high-income Americans have sought various ways to reduce their tax liability. After taking advantage of all available deductions and deferral techniques (mortgage interest, exemptions, retirement plans, and so on), they continued to search for other tax-advantaged investments. Their search eventually led them to higher-risk tax shelters packaged in the form of limited partnerships.

For these investors, the tax benefits of some investments helped offset the risks involved. For example, a $10,000 investment that generated a 100 percent deduction for a taxpayer in the 50 percent tax bracket resulted in a $5,000 tax savings. So, an investor could offset the risk of loss of their investment by 50 percent due to the tax savings alone.

The Fall of Tax-Sheltered Limited Partnership Investments

In the early to mid 1980s tax-sheltered investments were very popular — in reality, too popular. The high demand for these investments resulted in everyone and their friends forming and selling limited partnerships. Many poorly managed, highly leveraged, and in some cases even bogus limited partnerships reached the marketplace. However, just as there are good and bad in other investment categories, there are good limited partnerships and some bad ones, too.

Tax law changes in the late 1980s significantly reduced the advantages of limited partnership investments. Because the maximum tax rate was reduced to 31 percent, the risk of these investments was no longer offset by a significant tax savings. And, under the new tax structure, many tax deductions were either reduced, eliminated, or reclassified as passive losses and can no longer be used to reduce taxable earned income, but they can be used to offset passive gains.

Deflationary pressures on real estate and energy prices resulted in a decline in asset values. As a result, many partnerships failed to make their promised income distributions and few were able to return investors' principal. This declining performance, along with changes in the tax code, ultimately led to the fall in popularity of these investments.

No one can predict whether or not tax-sheltered limited partnerships will become popular investments again. We do know that Congress is never happy with the status quo when it comes to taxes. The limited partnerships that remain today are more mature, better managed, and not over leveraged. For some, limited partnerships may still be worthwhile investments.

Low-Income Housing

When Congress created tax credits to stimulate investment in low-income housing in 1986, investors in limited partnerships designed to facilitate low-income housing development received one of the best tax shelters available today. Why? Whereas many tax shelters merely reduce taxable income, *tax credits* directly offset the amount of taxes owed — in any tax bracket. Low-income housing tax credits directly reduce taxes, dollar-for-dollar against the investor's tax liability, within the specified limits.

Low-income housing limited partnerships, buy, build, or rehabilitate housing for low-income renters and the tax credits are passed in annual installments over a 10-year period from the partnership to the

FIGURE 15–5

Low-Income Housing Limited Partnerships

1. Partnerships build or purchase affordable housing for low-income renters, mainly the elderly.
2. The Low-Income Housing Tax Credit (LIHTC) program is a permanent part of the tax code.
3. Directly reduces taxes through dollar-for-dollar credits against investor's tax liability.
4. Investors can potentially recoup 100 to 160 percent of their investment by receiving tax credits over a 10-year period.
5. Provide worthwhile social value by filling demand for desperately needed low-income housing.

How Many Tax Credits Can You Use?

Tax Bracket	Ordinary Income	Maximum Credits*
15.0%	$ 25,000	$ 3,750
28.0	25,000	7,000
31.0	25,000	7,750
36.0	25,000	9,000
39.6	25,000	9,900

*Credits only allowable to reduce federal income tax down to Alternative Minimum Tax level.

investors in the partnership. Due to a nationwide shortage of affordable housing, the federal government has made this program a permanent part of the tax code.

Investors can potentially recoup 100 to 160 percent of their investment through tax credits over a 10-year time period. They are allowed an annual maximum tax credit equivalent to the taxes due on $25,000 of taxable income in their tax bracket. For example, an investor in the 28 percent tax bracket would have a tax liability of $7,000 due on $25,000 of taxable income. Therefore the maximum tax credit they may use is $7,000. Since paying some taxes is mandatory, the tax credits may only be used to reduce federal taxes down to the alternative minimum tax (AMT) level. Actual tax credits allowed will depend on factors such as the occupancy rate and performance of the partnership.

Don't forget, most limited partnerships are high risk and highly illiquid investments. The reason tax benefits existed, and still remain for low-income housing investors, is that Congress believed that tax savings would encourage more people to invest. All the rules that we have given you for other investments apply to limited partnerships. Consider them on an economic basis first and don't invest your hard-earned money solely for tax-motivated reasons. Ask yourself: If the tax benefits were not a part of this investment opportunity, would I still consider it a viable option? If the answer is *no*, don't invest. If the answer is yes, take your tax benefits and smile.

Self-Employment

Be careful if you are self-employed! The IRS is becoming more stringent than ever about what it will accept as business and home office deductions. Self-employment is not the be-all and end-all solution to tax savings you may wish. For instance, if you enjoy painting and once sold a painting for $10 to your Aunt Ethel, you're not considered self-employed. If you do run a legitimate business, either part-time or as your only source of income, there are plenty of deductions you may be eligible for. Some of them include business mileage, a percentage of your house payment (if office space is used strictly for your business venture), interest on your car payment (if you use your car principally for business), entertainment, and travel related to the business. However, if your expenses consistently exceed your income, the IRS will qualify your business as a *hobby* and will not accept these deductions.

Employing Family Members

When you own your own business and use your minor children to perform simple work tasks such as copying or cleaning at a reasonable wage, you could pay them up to almost $6,000 each, annually, without the child incurring a tax liability -— after taking the allowed standard deduction (maximum of $3,900 in 1995) and a $2,000 IRA deduction. Plan these deductions carefully with a qualified tax accountant to be sure you'll qualify under IRS regulations.

Rental Income

You may be able to receive a certain amount of income generated by your vacation home tax free. If you rent it out for *fewer than 15 days* during the year, none of the rental income has to be included in your gross income, But, none of the business expenses attributable to the rental are deductible either (no rental income, no business deductions).

The Success Triangle

If your vacation home is rented out for *more than 14 days* a year you are allowed to deduct the full amount of expenses up to the limits for passive losses on rentals. To do so, however, you may not make personal use of the home for more than 14 days during the year or for more than 10 percent of the number of days during the year you rent the home, whichever period is greater.

You can deduct the mortgage interest and taxes of a second home even if you don't rent it. This option is only available on a second (not a third or fourth) home. Some restrictions, such as the value of your home, apply.

Deferring Income, Accelerating Deductions

Remember what we said about postponing paying taxes as long as possible because of the increasing value of money over time? Here are two areas where you can put that suggestion to work. First, by *deferring income* you postpone paying taxes by pushing the income into later years. Examples of income deferment include taking a bonus check in January rather than December, or contributing a portion of your earnings to a qualified retirement plan.

Second, by *accelerating deductions* you can take the tax write-off a year earlier, which gives you the use of those tax dollars for another year. For instance, you might purchase a tax-deductible item (such as a computer for business use) in December rather than January or pay your property taxes for the next year in December.

NOTE: This strategy may not be advisable if your tax rate will be higher next year than this year. Consult your tax advisor before making a determination.

Taking a Loss

Perhaps one of the more painful ways of reducing your taxes is by realizing a financial loss — whether it is in the sale of a stock or other investment. Look at a loss objectively, however; it's better to take one when it can do you some good (save money in taxes) than when it can't. Using losses to offset gains can actually be a wise strategy.

Suppose a particular investment has dropped in value from your original purchase price. The best time to take a capital loss from this investment is when you will be realizing capital gains from another investment, a bonus at work, or the distribution of your retirement benefits. Timing the sale of an investment that took a nose dive to coincide with a gain realized in another area can reduce your net loss by your marginal tax bracket percentage — that is, the amount of money you won't have to pay in taxes! Losses are never fun, but they can be scheduled to become a little less painful.

Summary

It is important for you to take advantage of tax deductions and tax deferrals whenever possible. Have a professional tax preparer help find them and have more dollars to invest, as a result. Of course, you need to keep in mind that tax deferrals help postpone, not avoid, paying taxes later on. Every dollar your taxable income is reduced by means a percentage return equal to your tax bracket.

Among the many legitimate ways to reduce your tax liability and defer paying taxes are retirement plans, self-employment deductions, income deferment, and accelerated deductions, Retirement plans allow you to contribute before-tax dollars and accumulate earnings tax-deferred.

Tax-sheltered investments in the form of limited partnerships offer the benefits of pooled investing, along with special tax advantages such as the tax credits from low-income housing. No investment should be considered on the merits of tax advantages alone; each should be examined with the same criteria used in all wise financial decisions.

Whichever strategies you use to reduce your taxable income, keep accurate records to substantiate your deductions in the event of an IRS audit.

SECRETS IN ACTION

Sam and Edie Bradford hate paying taxes. Three years ago Edward Sneaker, their neighbor, told them about a limited partnership that could shelter a significant portion of their income from taxes. "That's for us," they decided, and jumped in with an investment of $25,000.

Sam and Edie figured the savings in taxes would more than offset any loss, even if the investment lost 10 percent. At the end of the first year, they received a check for $2,000. "See, Sam," Edie said, "you don't need to worry anymore." When their accountant filed their taxes in April, sure enough, most of the income was sheltered through depreciation of the assets. It was the same the second year.

Then in October of the third year, the Bradfords got a letter from the limited partnership. The investment didn't lose 10 percent — it lost everything. So did Sam and Edie — every cent of their investment.

Sam and Edie sat around the kitchen table with Edward and read the prospectus for the first time. Their money had been invested in resort condos in a "developing" (also known as "run-down") area. Now, it sounded speculative. They realized a professional financial advisor would have pointed out the unsuccessful prior history of the general partners.

The three neighbors asked themselves the $25,000 questions: "Would we have made this investment if it had not been for the tax benefits associated with it?" Their answer was an unequivocal "No."

The partnership sounded like a quick way to beat the IRS, and they had focused their decision on the tax advantages alone. They hadn't done the normal research. They hadn't even read the prospectus. "From now on," they decided, "we will make out investment decisions based on the soundness of the investment, not on the tax savings alone."

SIXTEEN

You Won't Run out of Money

You Can Also Defer Taxes with Annuities

What is an annuity? Everybody has heard the word, but we'll bet that most people can't tell you what it means. By definition, an annuity is a series of payments made at regular intervals over a certain period of time. This meaning leads many investors to ask, "If that's true, then what's the difference between an annuity and my car payment?" The difference is that *an annuity pays you.* In the real world, an annuity is a financial product purchased from a life insurance company which provides a guaranteed income for life or for a specified time period. We think the following terms accurately reflect the character of an annuity.

- Certificate of tax-deferred accrual
- Deferred-taxation savings plan
- Insured retirement income account
- Private pension accumulator
- Retirement savings certificate

How did life insurance companies get into the act? Let's think about that for a minute. As we learned in Chapter 8, life insurance is really death insurance. It insures that your beneficiaries will be financially protected in the event of your death — your life insurance pays

"The size of sums of money appears to vary in a remarkable way according to whether they are being paid in or paid out."

– Julian Huxley

them when you die. Annuities, on the other hand, can provide an income that you cannot outlive. Annuities pay when you live. Like life insurance, annuities are actuarially based using life expectancy tables. Financially speaking, you can use annuities to protect yourself from living too long — longer than your income lasts. We think this insures you against life. Therefore, annuities are rightly connected to life insurance.

Annuities are placed in the level of Tax-Advantaged Investments on the Success Triangle™. Having established a broad base of the fundamentals, established liquid cash reserves, and added investments that put your money to work for you, it's time to consider those financial products that layer benefits.

Before we begin looking at the various types of deferred and immediate annuities that are available, we'd like to make one point very clear. *Before you invest in any annuity, make maximum contributions to available qualified retirement plans, such as 401(k) plans, 403(b) plans, Keoghs, and deductible IRA accounts.* These plans are wiser investments than annuities because, unlike annuities, the contributions themselves are tax-deductible. Both qualified retirement plans and annuities offer tax-deferred accumulation of investment earnings. Refer to Chapter 18 for more information on tax-deductible retirement plan investments.

Annuities are divided into two basic types, each of which is generally considered appropriate for investors in different age groups. The first, an *immediate annuity,* is appropriate for people of retirement age, who are ready to begin receiving income from their investment. When you purchase this type of annuity you give the insurance company a lump sum and, in return, they guarantee you an income for life or an otherwise specified time period.

The second type, a *deferred annuity,* is an investment vehicle where the earnings will accumulate (compound) free of current income tax. Deferred annuities are generally used to save money for retirement. The actual payments are deferred until a later date. This provides some interesting tax benefits which we will discuss later in the chapter.

Immediate Annuities

An immediate annuity is a contract where the investor (usually the annuitant/owner/beneficiary, although it could be someone other than the actual annuitant/owner/beneficiary) deposits a single, lump sum of money (known as a *premium*) with a life insurance company. The company promises to make a series of payments to the beneficiary, which begin within one year, at most, of the deposit. The payments are usually made monthly, although they could be made quarterly, semi-annually, or annually. The amount of money the beneficiary receives in each payment depends upon the age of the annuitant, current market interest rates, and how often the payments are to be made. The length of time payments continue depends on the payment option selected by the owner of the contract.

These annuities are actually true life insurance, yet, are often described as the opposite of traditional life insurance. When we buy a "traditional" life insurance policy we are, in essence, betting the life insurance company that we are going to die and they are betting that we will live. If they know we are dying of cancer, they won't insure us, will they? They want us to live.

When we purchase an immediate annuity, on the other hand, we are betting that we are going to live and the insurance company is betting that we are going to die. Annuities protect us from running out of money if we "live too long."

Once the beneficiary begins receiving payments, it is similar to receiving a check from a pension plan. In most cases, the amount of the check never changes. It stays the same throughout the lifetime of the annuitant or for the specified time period. But also like a pension benefit, all financial obligations of the insurance company could end at the annuitant's death with no proceeds payable to the heirs of the beneficiary. The situation depends on the particular annuity option selected.

In a sense, when you purchase an annuity you are buying your own personal pension plan. You deposit an amount of money in return for a monthly payment that you cannot outlive. You could live to be 120 years old or more and the insurance company would still be paying you a monthly income. The only exception to this would be if you specifically choose to receive payments for a specified time period.

Annuity Options

Several payment options are available on annuities. These options include:

Life annuity. Benefits payable for the life of the annuitant only.

Life annuity with period certain. Benefits are payable for the life of the annuitant, with the benefit paid to a named beneficiary should the annuitant die before the end of the designated time period. Typical time periods are 10 and 20 years.

Refund annuity. Should the annuitant die before total payments equal the amount of the premium (deposit), the insurance company will pay the balance to the beneficiary either in a lump sum (cash refund) or by continuing the monthly payments (installment refund).

Joint and survivor. Payments made over the life of the annuitant and survivor (typically spouse). At the death of the survivor, all benefits cease.

Annuity certain. Payments are made to the beneficiary for a specified number of years.

Other options are available, but they tend to be some combination of the above. The more flexible the payment option, the smaller the actual payment amount will be.

Deferred Annuities

A deferred annuity is the more popular type of annuity being purchased by investors today. It is called deferred because any benefit payments are deferred to a later point in time. This type of annuity is used to accumulate money for the future and is a popular vehicle for building retirement savings.

Features of Deferred Annuities

The most important feature of deferred annuities is that all earnings accumulate free of current income tax. This means that 100 percent of your earnings are reinvested to work for you. Figure 16–1 illustrates the profound difference the tax-deferral feature can make in the growth of your investment principal.

Should the investor die during the accumulation period, the total amount of principal invested is guaranteed by the life insurance company and will be paid to the designated beneficiaries. In the case of variable annuities, this applies even if the investment has dropped in value. In addition, many annuity contracts include step-up provisions where the guaranteed amount is periodically increased to reflect increases in the value of the investments.

A minimum interest rate, typically of 3½ to 4 percent, is guaranteed by the life insurance company on a fixed annuity or the fixed account option of a variable annuity contract. Excess interest earned on the investment may be paid at the discretion of the board of directors of the insurance company or in some cases increases in interest rates may be tied to an index.

FIGURE 16–1

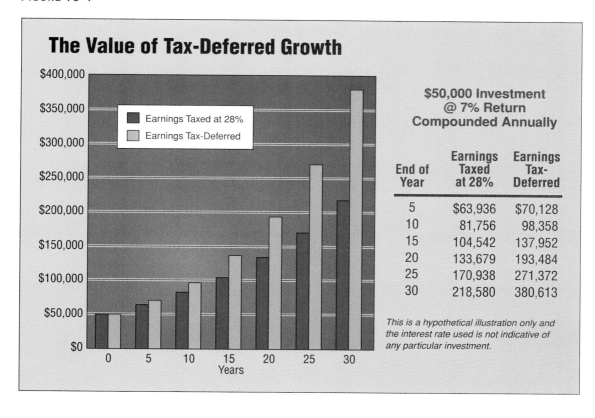

The Value of Tax-Deferred Growth

$50,000 Investment @ 7% Return Compounded Annually

End of Year	Earnings Taxed at 28%	Earnings Tax-Deferred
5	$63,936	$70,128
10	81,756	98,358
15	104,542	137,952
20	133,679	193,484
25	170,938	271,372
30	218,580	380,613

This is a hypothetical illustration only and the interest rate used is not indicative of any particular investment.

Annuities are sold without a commission or sales charge being deducted from the investment at purchase. However, withdrawals exceeding 10 percent of the invested amount (may vary depending on company) during any of the early years of the contract may be subject to contingent-deferred charges.

Deferred Annuities versus Certificates of Deposit

An investment in a deferred annuity should be considered a long-term investment because of penalties and surrender charges that may be applicable to withdrawals made within the early years. Therefore, it should not be considered an alternative to a savings account or a money market fund. Like your investments in certificates of deposit, annuities could reduce the amount that you need to maintain in cash reserves. As we discussed in Chapter 10, we refer to annuities and CDs as *restricted cash reserves.*

If you like the idea of investing in CDs (for purposes other than cash reserves), we believe you should consider deferred annuities as an alternative for at least a portion of those dollars. Deferred annuities usually offer higher returns than CDs, your returns can accumulate in the annuity without current taxes due, and annuities offer more flexibility than CDs (for example, you can make a partial withdrawal from an annuity). Even though they are not insured by the FDIC or FSLIC, annuities are considered safe investments.

For many people, the features of an annuity make it more attractive than a certificate of deposit. Yet, others can't sleep at night unless they have money in their local branch bank — it "feels" more liquid if they can drive by the bank building. If you desire more liquidity but would still like to consider an annuity, ask your insurance agent or planner about an *annuity with liquidation by draft,* which is similar to a money market fund. This feature allows easy access to the money without penalty if it is within the 10 percent limitation during the early years of the contract. During the later years, the entire account balance can be accessed via draft without penalty. Now what CD offers this flexibility?

The Caveat

"This deferred annuity sounds a little too good to be true. What's the catch?" The catch is that deferred annuities are designed and best suited for retirement savings. Congress has stipulated that you must leave your money in these programs until age 59½. If any interest or investment earnings are withdrawn prior to age 59½ they are subject to a 10 percent penalty. And deferred annuities are subject to last-in, first-out (LIFO) accounting. This means that partial withdrawals are considered interest until the remaining balance is equal to or less than the original investment. For these reasons, deferred annuities should be considered as cash reserves only by those who are close to or are already 59½ years of age.

Fixed Deferred Annuities

Fixed deferred annuities (usually just called *fixed annuities*) guarantee a fixed rate of interest for a specified period of time. They are well-suited for conservative investors who are saving for retirement and don't need current income. Since they are designed to provide retirement income, investors shouldn't expect to use these funds until at least age 59½.

A fixed annuity might be a better deal than a CD, because the earnings will accumulate tax-deferred. But if you find yourself with most of your savings in a fixed annuity, and have no other source of funds for ready cash, you should go back and establish adequate cash reserves (refer to Chapter 10) elsewhere for emergencies and other expenses.

Variable Deferred Annuities

If taxes are a concern and you love investing in mutual funds as much as we do, consider a *variable deferred annuity* (usually just called variable annuities), which is basically a tax-deferred mutual fund. The Securities Exchange Commission (SEC) and the National Association of Securities Dealers (NASD) don't like the financial industry using the words *mutual funds* when discussing variable annuities; therefore, companies that sell variable annuities call the investments within them *funds* or *sub-accounts,* not *mutual funds.* However, if it looks like a duck, waddles like a duck, and quacks like a duck, chances are it is a duck, even though some people refuse to call it a duck.

Variable annuities are popular investments that provide the same features as fixed annuities, except that the investor selects one or more funds within a family of (mutual) funds. All dividends, capital gains, and interest accumulate on a tax-deferred basis. Most also allow unlimited contributions.

Even though all variable annuities offer tax deferral, not every one is alike. Investors should look for a broad range of investment choices, particularly a good selection of stock funds. And the funds should also have superior track records, going back three years or longer.

It is important to point out that tax laws prevent you from purchasing well-known mutual funds inside variable annuities. Variable annuity contracts must be purchased from life insurance companies, which in turn contract with mutual fund companies that create separate funds managed exclusively for variable annuity products. These funds are described as *separate accounts* in the variable annuity prospectus. A particular variable annuity product may or may not offer a fund with similar objectives (or managers) as one or more of the investment advisor's stellar performing mutual funds. Be sure you investigate the available options closely as to their objectives, past performance, and portfolio managers.

Guaranteed Death Benefit

An added benefit of variable annuities is the *guaranteed death benefit.* This benefit stipulates that in the event of the death of the investor prior to annuitizing the contract, the beneficiary will receive the value of the account or the amount invested, whichever is greater. This death

FIGURE 16–2

Tax-Deferred Variable Annuities

Investment Management on a Tax-Deferred Basis

Tax-deferred variable annuities allow investors to accumulate money for retirement using professionally managed investment portfolios. Although contributions are not deductible, all investment earnings accumulate tax-deferred until such times as they are withdrawn.

Variable annuities offer investors the ability to select one or more professionally managed separate accounts*. Each separate account offers a specific investment objective.

Because a withdrawal of money prior to age 59½ may result in a 10 percent tax penalty, variable annuities should be used only for those dollars earmarked for retirement.

IRS

Variable Annuity

Corporate Bond Portfolio

Money Market Portfolio

Guaranteed or Fixed Account

Total Return Portfolio

Growth Portfolio

Government Securities Portfolio

Investment Options

Variable annuities offer investors multiple investment options to meet various investment objectives.

As investors' objectives change, they may switch from one portfolio to another.

1. **Tax-Deferred Accumulation of Earnings**
2. **Tax-Free Exchanges among Portfolios**
3. **Tax-Advantaged Income at Retirement**

Variable annuities may have mortality and expense fees associated with them.

benefit will typically be "stepped-up" every five to seven years, depending on the specific company.

To illustrate, let's say that you invested $25,000 in a variable annuity. Due to a decline in stock prices, the value of the account dropped to $23,000. But, if you died, your beneficiary would still receive $25,000, the amount of your original investment, because the amount was guaranteed.

To take another example, let's assume that death did not occur and seven years later the account is worth $50,000, and as stated in the contract the death benefit is "stepped-up" to its current market value (if it is more than the original investment). Then following a severe decline in prices, the value dropped to $38,000. If you died at that time, your beneficiary would receive $50,000, the stepped-up value of your account.

Some variable annuity contracts offer variations of the death benefit. Check the prospectus for details.

Retirement Income that Can Keep Up with Inflation

At annuitization, a variable annuity contract owner may elect to receive a monthly check, as with a fixed annuity. However, instead of receiving a fixed amount of money each month, the annuitant might choose to receive the proceeds from the redemption of a fixed amount of *units* (fund shares in the annuity) each month. The value of the units will change based on the performance of the underlying fund(s) that the investor selected.

This process allows retirees to establish an income stream that cannot be outlived, while at the same time providing a potential hedge against inflation. The contract owner can switch from one fund portfolio to another even after beginning to receive monthly payments under one of the lifetime or term-certain income options.

Mortality Charges and Expenses

Like fixed annuities, variable contracts are issued by life insurance companies. The actual funds available for investment may be managed by a subsidiary company or by independent investment advisors. In either case, the investment portfolio will pay an advisory fee to the fund manager for their services. In addition, the insurance company receives *mortality charges* in return for providing the guaranteed death benefit and the guarantee that expenses will never increase.

Most variable annuities charge annual fees to cover mortality risks and expenses at the rate of one to one-and-a-half percent a year. As with portfolio management fees, these expenses are deducted from fund assets before the share price is calculated, so investors do not see the charges.

Some financial planners might argue that the extra expenses make variable annuities less attractive than purchasing shares directly from a mutual fund and paying taxes on dividends and capital gains as they are earned. We disagree. Although we feel the size of the fees are questionable in some cases, careful planning can allow investors to accumulate wealth more quickly using variable annuities than through traditional mutual funds. Investors (or their advisors) need to carefully calculate the advantage of tax deferral versus the increased management cost. We are assuming that it is the investor's objective to leave the money in the account until at least age 59½ because the penalties for early withdrawals will impact net investment returns.

Net Worth Acceleration

As with other tax-saving strategies, variable annuities are an even more attractive alternative if the tax savings are reinvested. What do we mean? Let's assume that you invested $100,000 in a variable annuity. If the account increased in value by 15 percent the first year, we would assume that you avoided paying tax on $15,000. It follows that if you are in the 31 percent tax bracket, you just saved $4,650 in federal income taxes. Had this money been in another type of investment not offering tax-deferral of earnings, you would have had to pay the $4,650 to the IRS. Instead, we suggest you add this amount to your variable annuity. That is *net worth acceleration*. Adding tax savings to investments will help you reach your financial goals much more rapidly!

Of course, if the annuity contract owner were to liquidate the account, income taxes would be due on any profits at the time of redemption, and capital gains taxes would be due on previously unrealized gains in the mutual fund account. However, as a long-term accumulation vehicle, tax-deferred variable annuities can outperform mutual funds.

Tax-Advantaged Distributions

Annuities not only allow you to defer paying taxes on investment returns, tax advantages also apply to distributions. Whether fixed or variable, when the proceeds from an annuity contract are received under one of the annuity options mentioned earlier in the chapter, a portion of each distribution is considered to be a tax-free return of principal.

The percentage used to classify a portion of the benefit as principal is called the *exclusion ratio*. It is determined by dividing the amount invested by the expected total return from the contract. The amount invested is easy to obtain, while the expected return is the result of multiplying the annual payment (under the annuity option) times the annuitant's life expectancy (number of years), which is based on IRS tables. A sample calculation is shown below:

Amount invested	$100,000
Age	70
Life expectancy (from IRS tables)	16 years
Annuity option	Straight life
Annual payment	$13,000

$$\frac{Premium}{Annual\ Annuity\ Payment \times Life\ Expectancy} = Exclusion\ Ratio$$

$$\$100,000 \div (\$13,000 \times 16) = Exclusion\ Ratio$$

$$\$100,000 \div \$208,000 = 48.07\ percent$$

In this example, almost half of all income (48.07 percent) received from the annuity contract under an annuity option would be considered a tax-free return of principal. The remainder of the income would be taxed as ordinary income.

It is important to mention that initial annuity payments to annuitants may be more or less for variable annuities than fixed annuities because the variable payout will fluctuate based on underlying fund performance. However, over the long-term, variable annuity payouts have demonstrated an ability to surpass the fixed annuity payouts (over the long term, ownership investments usually outperform loanership investments).

How to Purchase Annuities

Where you purchase an annuity may depend on the type of annuity you wish to purchase.

Purchasing Fixed Annuities

Fixed annuities (whether deferred or immediate) are purchased from licensed life insurance agents. These usually include traditional life insurance agents, most financial planners, and many stockbrokers.

When purchasing a fixed annuity it is important to know the financial strength of the issuing life insurance company, since they are the entity offering guarantees on the safety of your principal and minimum interest rate guarantees. When you are entrusting a company to manage a lot of your money for many decades, you need to demand tough standards. Insurance companies are rated by Standard & Poor's, A.M. Best Company, Moody's, and Weiss Research (see Chapter 8 for more detail). Avoid those companies that do not receive the higher ratings from each rating service. Among the rating companies, Weiss Research has the toughest standards.

Purchasing Variable Annuities

Individuals must have both a life insurance license and a securities license to sell variable annuities. The list of qualified agents is the same as that for fixed annuities, with the exception of some traditional life agents who are not licensed to sell variable products. Likewise, some stockbrokers are not licensed to sell either fixed or variable annuities.

When purchasing variable annuities, the issuing life insurance company is not as important as the manager of the funds. Many variable annuity portfolios are managed by well-known mutual fund companies. As with mutual funds, select variable annuities where the current manager has at least a three-year performance record with the fund.

Also, don't assume that just because a well-known company is involved, it is a good investment fund. Find out who the individual managers of the specific fund(s) within the variable annuity are. This information is available in the prospectus for variable annuities as it is for mutual funds. A good financial planner, broker, or agent who is familiar with these products will be able to make recommendations and help you select good products.

Penalty Charges

Most annuities are offered without up-front charges or commissions. In addition, many of the contracts allow you to withdraw 10 percent of the amount invested each year after the first year without charge. Withdrawals in excess of 10 percent during the early years will typically result in a penalty, referred to in the contract as a *contingent-deferred sales charge*. An example of a contingent-deferred sales charge schedule is listed below.

The Success Triangle

Sample Contingent-Deferred Sales Charge Schedule

For Withdrawals in	Deferred Sales Charge
Year 1	6%
Year 2	5%
Year 3	4%
Year 4	3%
Year 5	2%
Year 6	1%
Year 7+	0%

Charges typically apply to withdrawals of principal only and are assessed only for those amounts exceeding the 10 percent annual limitation.

The length of these schedules typically varies from 5 to 10 years. We believe you should only consider those products in which the contingent charges vanish after 7 years or less. Why pay a penalty for a withdrawal in year 8, 9, or 10 when it is not necessary?

No-Load Annuities

Although publicity for these products has been nearly nonexistent, there are some variable annuities available that don't apply a deferred sales charge. Because there are more details associated with no-load variable annuities than with mutual funds, they have not been wildly successful at attracting money from investors.

It is important to note that if annuities are used as they were designed, very few contract owners should be making large withdrawals from them in the early years. Doing so reduces the attraction of a no-load product for most people. The same rules of selection apply here as they do for mutual funds (see Chapter 12, Load Funds versus No-Load Funds).

Summary

Annuities are financial products offered by insurance companies which guarantee the beneficiaries an income for life or other specified time period. Annuities are tax-advantaged investments that are primarily used to accumulate savings for retirement.

Investing in a deferred annuity allows you to save thousands of dollars while accumulating wealth that otherwise would have been paid to the IRS. To build wealth at the most rapid rate, the annual tax savings should be reinvested in the annuity or other investment programs.

Fixed annuities should be considered an alternative for some of the dollars that are continually rolled over from one certificate of deposit to the next with no intention of using the money.

Variable annuities should be considered a way to diversify some of those dollars that otherwise might be invested in mutual funds. One potential drawback to mutual funds is that during any one year, capital gains and dividend distributions could create a large tax liability for some investors.

Immediate annuities offer a retirement income that cannot be outlived; however, inflation can reduce the attractiveness of the income from a fixed annuity over a period of years. Immediate variable annuities offer an income that cannot be outlived and the potential to keep pace with inflation.

Because of the intricacies involved in an annuity investment, expert advice should be obtained when deciding which annuity (and which option) is best for you. Select an annuity based on its performance, not on gimmicks or fancy features in the annuity. And most important, remember that annuities should supplement, not replace, your 401(k) or IRA savings.

SECRETS IN ACTION

Bill and April Wilson are over fifty. Contrary to the advice of their financial planner (and the authors of this book!), they kept an unusually large portion of their assets in certificates of deposit. "I don't see much reason to change. I've never lost a dime in a CD," Bill responded to the planner's recommendation to move more of their money into equity investments back in 1991.

The Wilson's became concerned as interest rates continued to drop the next two years. They realized their planner had been right about CDs. However, April felt stock market investments required too much time, and were too risky. Despite her fears, Bill called their planner.

Bill admitted they should have listened to his suggestions and that they didn't know what to do about the low interest rates on their CDs. "We just don't want a roller coaster ride in the stock market," Bill instructed.

After talking with the Wilsons, their planner pinpointed the real problem. Bill wanted to invest in stocks; but April didn't want to deal with them if something happened to Bill.

Bill and April were genuinely excited about a product that their planner proposed. He suggested that Bill and April split their CD money between fixed and variable annuities. Bill liked earning more interest in the fixed annuity and the opportunity to participate in stocks in the variable annuity. Since April didn't want to be bothered with managing money, she was thrilled to learn the investment would guarantee her an income for life. In addition, she liked the fact that the variable annuity would pay at least the amount of their investment should something happen to Bill.

"By the way," the planner added, "you don't have to pay any taxes on the interest or investment earnings until the money is withdrawn."

SEVENTEEN

An Investment... or Just a Dream?

Homes and Other Real Estate Investments

T o many people, home ownership is the most important component of the American Dream.

What is it that attracts Americans to home ownership? No doubt it is that same spirit of individualism and independence that filled the ship's passenger list on the Mayflower. We like a space to call our own. We like a place where we set our own rules. We seek a place to set our roots. Home ownership is viewed as a symbol of status and success. It provides a special sense of emotional fulfillment through pride of ownership, and feelings of security, privacy, and independence.

"If I were asked to name the chief benefit of the house, I should say: the house shelters day-dreaming, the house protects the dreamer, the house allows one to dream in peace."

– Gaston Bachelard

A Place Called Home

Throughout history, home ownership has been a vital economic and social element in America. Yet, in a strange way, the story of home ownership in America is not the story of people staying at home but, paradoxically, the story of pioneering, internal migrations, and times of significant population shifts. The first exodus that gave birth to a new nation evolved into waves of migrations that settled the country, then populated it. At the beginning of this century, a largely agricultural population had found a place called home in rural America.

Then, in tune with the industrialization of America, the first World War, and the Great Depression, Americans were forced into the cities to find work and a new way of life. The cities were hard pressed to house the influx and for many, housing deteriorated to tenements and tent cities. For nearly two decades, during the Depression and the Second World War, few new homes were constructed.

In the aftermath of World War II, 3.5 million ex-soldiers seeking housing, waited in lines with thousands of others to buy homes. But, there were few houses to buy in 1946. That is, until the Levitt family bought a potato field 30 miles east of New York City, and began the largest housing project ever assembled by a single builder. Employing the principles of mass production they built Levittown, constructing over 17,000 homes between 1947 and 1951 in their planned community. This marked the beginning of the suburbanization of America. Today, urban renewal projects may be signaling a shift back to the cities. We don't know how far this influence will reach, but we do know that this place Americans call home is continually changing.

Since the end of World War II, our government has implemented a number of programs utilizing tax incentives and subsidies to encourage home ownership. The success of these programs is evidenced by the fact that from 1940 to 1980 the percentage of owner-occupied homes increased from 40 percent to 65 percent, and remains at about that level today.

Escalating prices and high interest rates have made the prospects of home ownership seem out of reach for many. However, in the case of home ownership, America is still the land of opportunity. With the wide variety of financing options and government programs available, home ownership can become a reality for almost anyone who is willing to put forth a little extra effort and make some small personal sacrifices.

Quite often, home ownership may lead to financial gain but there are two faces to home ownership. Here we depart a little from our usual cold-eyed critical assessment of your investment portfolio. You must first look at your home as a comfortable dwelling for yourself and your family. We think it is impossible to assign a dollar value to the emotional aspects of home ownership, the place where our children have grown up, or the good times we have shared in our homes with our friends. We accent the emotional side of home ownership because we realize that most home buyers are not buying an investment, but rather a place to call home.

The Success Triangle

FIGURE 17–1

Reasons for Buying a Home

Most Americans purchase a home to fulfill various needs, some of which include: gaining privacy, establishing a sense of belonging, and investing in their future.

The chart below expresses the results obtained from a survey conducted by the National Association of Realtors®.

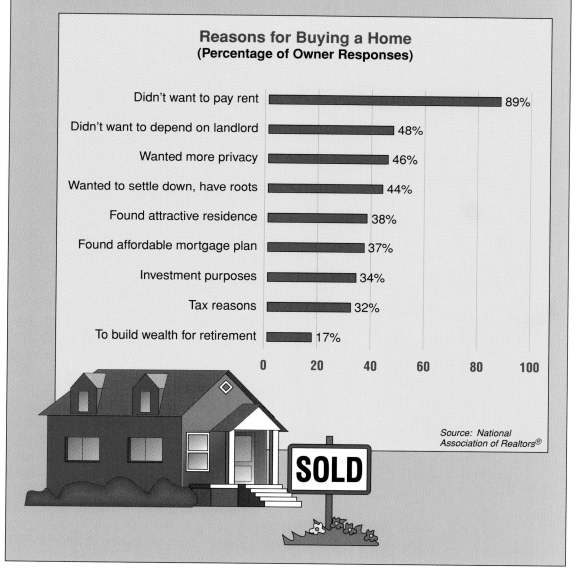

Reasons for Buying a Home
(Percentage of Owner Responses)

Didn't want to pay rent	89%
Didn't want to depend on landlord	48%
Wanted more privacy	46%
Wanted to settle down, have roots	44%
Found attractive residence	38%
Found affordable mortgage plan	37%
Investment purposes	34%
Tax reasons	32%
To build wealth for retirement	17%

Source: National Association of Realtors®

Yet, buying a home is the largest investment most people will ever make and for most Americans home ownership will play a major role in their financial progress over the course of their lifetimes. During the early working years, the accumulation of money for a down payment and closing costs on the first home will be of primary importance. Then, as families grow and incomes increase, many will seek to upgrade their lifestyle by purchasing larger and more luxurious homes. In the later years, home equity may provide the foundation for a financially secure retirement. In fact, the home remains the largest asset that most Americans own at retirement, with home equity representing two-thirds of the average net worth of people age 65.

Is Home Ownership an Investment?

We've all heard a boast that goes something like this: "You can have all the stocks you want. There's no stock that has done as well as my house. It has been a fantastic investment. I paid $30,000 for it back in 1968. Today it's worth $225,000. Try beating that!"

Sound familiar? Sure it does. Could you have beat it? Sure you could have. You should be getting pretty familiar with compound interest by now. You could have purchased some stocks or stock mutual funds back in 1968. They could be below-average performers and still beat the 7.75 percent annual rate of increase on the house described above. That's right. The boaster wasn't such an investment wizard after all.

About 20 years ago, people started noticing an unprecedented increase in the value of their homes. Fueled by an inflationary economy, we started buying homes as an investment, almost a failproof money scheme, until this thinking became so ingrained we ceased to question its validity. But several sharp declines in regional pockets around the country have reeducated us to the sharp reality that housing prices do return to equilibrium.

Most observers agree that houses won't be the gold mines we thought they were in the last decade. They expect appreciation to return to the traditional rate of inflation plus one or two percentage points. Hardly anyone will say that owning a home is going to make you rich anymore. But we agree that home values will continue a slow, steady growth.

And actually that's good news, because we prefer slow, solid growth over get-rich-quick schemes any day. It is only when we take the blinders off and assess our home investments realistically that we begin to see how home ownership benefits our financial plans.

FIGURE 17–2

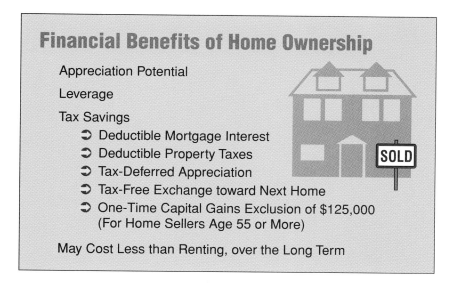

Financial Benefits of Home Ownership

Appreciation Potential

Leverage

Tax Savings
- ➲ Deductible Mortgage Interest
- ➲ Deductible Property Taxes
- ➲ Tax-Deferred Appreciation
- ➲ Tax-Free Exchange toward Next Home
- ➲ One-Time Capital Gains Exclusion of $125,000
  (For Home Sellers Age 55 or More)

May Cost Less than Renting, over the Long Term

Financial Benefits of Home Ownership

The real reason behind your love affair with your home investment is that you are using the Seven Secrets, probably without even realizing it. Every time you sit down at the beginning of the month and pay your mortgage payment first, you are in essence paying yourself first. And you chose an ownership position when you chose to own a home. You didn't buy it to move out next month, so without thinking much about it, you harnessed the power of time. And it worked. The power of the Seven Secrets is proven once again. It's absolutely no surprise to us that your home has appreciated over time.

Home ownership is the most common method of using leverage to control a larger investment than you could otherwise afford to own. Leverage comes into play when you put $10,000 down to buy a $60,000 home. In five years, when your home has appreciated to $80,000, it is an annual rate of 5.9 percent. But you didn't invest $60,000 in the home; you only invested the down payment. When you add the appreciation to the down payment, your $10,000 has actually grown at an annual rate of 24.57 percent a year.

Unfortunately, the picture is not that simple. Scenarios like this illustrate the beauty of using leverage, but they don't reflect a true picture until all the mortgage payments are added to the cost of repairs and maintenance, and the tax deduction you received for interest is accounted for. In the end, however, even though the startling rate of return on your down payment is greatly reduced, the use of leverage continues to be an excellent advantage in owning real estate.

With the phase-out of consumer interest deductions in the Tax Reform Act of 1986, about the only "good debt" left for tax purposes is the home mortgage. To take advantage of the tax savings available though, you have to have a mortgage; otherwise, no debt, no deductible interest. The deductibility of mortgage interest remains a significant incentive to home ownership. In our chapter on Home Equity as a Source of Money (Chapter 20), we tell you why mortgages are a sound financial bet — perhaps the best debt you can buy.

Disadvantages of Home Investments

With so many advantages wrapped up in one pile of bricks and boards, are there any disadvantages? Of course. You already know that real estate is a tax-advantaged investment on the Success Triangle™. In the continual compromise between reward and risk, remember that moving up on the Success Triangle means lessening liquidity and increasing risk.

Most of us think that our home investment is the safest investment possible. But there are people in Southern California who could tell you stories about selling their homes for 60 percent of their original purchase price. The market will revive again; it nearly always does, if you have the time to wait it out. Survivors of hurricanes in Florida could tell you a little about risk, too. We talk more about this risk in Chapter 20, Home Equity as a Source of Money.

We should also mention again that money invested in real estate has a very low level of liquidity. Access to your investment cash isn't as easy as with marketable securities. In fact, it's just plain difficult. It usually takes three to six months to close a real estate transaction after listing a house for sale. A flat market in any sector of the marketplace could push that out to nine months or longer. Don't ever count on retrieving your real estate investment cash in a tight time frame.

Renting versus Owning

Typically, families start out living in rental housing with the idea that it will be a temporary situation until careers become more settled and money is accumulated for a down payment.

In many situations renting makes more sense than owning a home. Renters enjoy a mobility that home-owners don't have because they aren't tied down by the responsibility of a mortgage and the need to sell before they move on. In exchange for this freedom, renters forgo the tax advantages of home ownership, and they often have restrictions on what they can do in their homes in terms of decorating, owning pets, or how loudly the stereo can be played.

Renting often requires putting up a security deposit to insure against property damage, but renters don't have to pay a large down payment. Neither are they responsible for maintenance or repairs on the property. Often, people who need more room than apartments offer can rent single family homes. In addition, apartment complexes often offer extensive recreational facilities and other amenities at no extra cost, a definite lifestyle advantage.

In the early years home ownership is usually more costly than renting but, because of inflation, as the years go by home ownership becomes less costly than renting. See Figure 17–3.

Deciding between renting and owning is both a lifestyle and a financial decision. Our advice is to rent until you plan to stay at least three to five years in one place. When you are starting out, and career decisions mean frequent moves, it is much easier to move if you are renting.

Buying Your Dream Home

When you are ready to settle for a while, purchasing a home makes more sense than renting, for many people. Instead of watching your housing dollars evaporate in rent payments, home ownership provides a vehicle to begin accumulating equity. Once you have determined that home ownership is right for you, searching for exactly the right home for your family can be both a frustrating experience and a rewarding adventure.

The home buying process has many variables to consider and requires that many decisions be made. All of your life's savings, credit, and even some degree of your freedom will be at stake. But if you first educate yourself about the process through reading or seminars, many of the uncertainties can be eliminated and you'll save both time and money. A good real estate agent can be very helpful, especially for inexperienced home buyers. Although we realize that emotions play a large part in home ownership, you must plan your home purchase carefully and proceed with caution to assure that the whole process is a rewarding experience with a happy ending.

We have compiled a few guidelines to help you buy a home easily and painlessly.

FIGURE 17–3

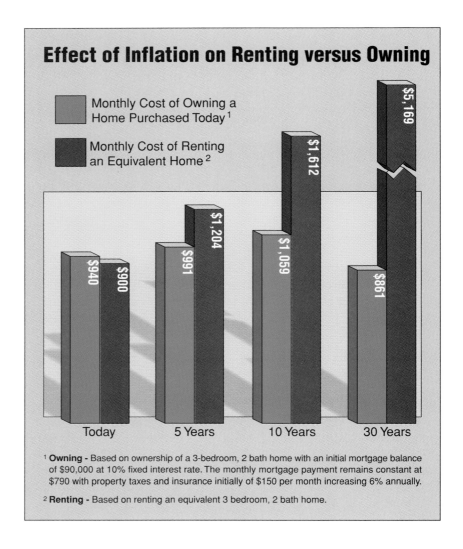

Effect of Inflation on Renting versus Owning

Monthly Cost of Owning a Home Purchased Today [1]

Monthly Cost of Renting an Equivalent Home [2]

	Today	5 Years	10 Years	30 Years
Owning	$940	$991	$1,059	$861
Renting	$900	$1,204	$1,612	$5,169

[1] **Owning** - Based on ownership of a 3-bedroom, 2 bath home with an initial mortgage balance of $90,000 at 10% fixed interest rate. The monthly mortgage payment remains constant at $790 with property taxes and insurance initially of $150 per month increasing 6% annually.

[2] **Renting** - Based on renting an equivalent 3 bedroom, 2 bath home.

Determine How Much You Can Afford

For most of us, the home of our dreams has to be tempered by the reality of the house we can afford. Many people become very disappointed when they find a home they want and then find out they cannot obtain enough financing to buy it. Deciding exactly how much you can or should pay for a house involves looking at your income, your job security, your living expenses and liabilities, and how much money you have accumulated for a down payment.

Down Payments

The leading reason (cited by over 70 percent of the respondents to a National Association of Realtors® survey) that prospective home buyers postpone their home purchase is that they do not have enough money for a down payment rather than by insufficient income to make the monthly payments.

Down payment requirements will typically range from 5 to 20 percent of the purchase price depending on your income level, the term of the loan, the type of the loan, whether the loan will be insured, and your previous credit history. In some situations, little or no down payment may be required.

Most first-time home buyers use personal savings for their down payment while most repeat buyers use equity from their previous home. Other down payment sources include life insurance cash values, gifts from family members, or the proceeds from refinancing other real estate.

Qualifying for a Mortgage Loan

Certain qualification guidelines are imposed by most mortgage lenders. Prequalification, prior to getting serious about house hunting, will determine the approximate amount you can borrow and thus how much you can afford to pay for a home. A real estate agent can give you a quick estimate for the purposes of house hunting, but we encourage you to meet with a mortgage banker or broker who will take you through the steps to prequalify. You'll also know whether the lender will consider "sweat equity" as part of your down payment. Sweat equity is credit for work that must be done on the home. Banks are more willing to do it if you can give them a good reason to trust you to do the work.

In the qualifying process, two rule of thumb tests are used by real estate agents and by many lenders: the Housing Expense Test and the Debt Repayment Test. Both of them use gross monthly income to determine the eligibility of a borrower.

Housing Expense Test.   In this test, the total monthly housing costs (principal, interest, mortgage insurance, property taxes, home owner's insurance, and association dues) may not exceed 28 percent of your gross monthly income. For example, if your gross monthly income is $4,000, your housing expenses should not add up to more than $1,120 ($4,000 × .28 = $1,120).

FIGURE 17–4

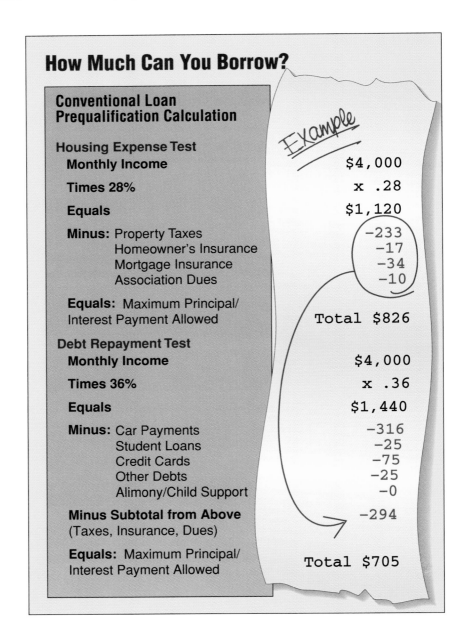

How Much Can You Borrow?

**Conventional Loan
Prequalification Calculation**

Example

Housing Expense Test
 Monthly Income — $4,000

 Times 28% — x .28

 Equals — $1,120

 Minus: Property Taxes — −233
 Homeowner's Insurance — −17
 Mortgage Insurance — −34
 Association Dues — −10

 Equals: Maximum Principal/
 Interest Payment Allowed — Total $826

Debt Repayment Test
 Monthly Income — $4,000

 Times 36% — x .36

 Equals — $1,440

 Minus: Car Payments — −316
 Student Loans — −25
 Credit Cards — −75
 Other Debts — −25
 Alimony/Child Support — −0

 Minus Subtotal from Above — −294
 (Taxes, Insurance, Dues)

 Equals: Maximum Principal/
 Interest Payment Allowed — Total $705

Debt Repayment Test.   Using the Debt Repayment Test, the total
monthly payments for all your debts (total monthly housing costs from
the Housing Expense Test plus automobile payments, credit card
payments, student loan payments, alimony/child support payments, and
any other loan payments) may not exceed 36 percent of your gross

monthly income. This is also known as the debt-to-income ratio. For example, if your gross monthly income is $4,000, your combined expenses (all of the above) cannot exceed $1,440 ($4,000 × .36 = $1,440). A person with a low debt-to-income ratio will find it easier to qualify for a loan than someone with the same income but more debts.

After determining the loan amount you qualify for, consider the amount of cash you have for a down payment. With these two figures in mind, you will know the price range to work within when shopping for a home. A rough estimate is that you can usually afford a house worth about 2½ times your annual income.

If you are a first-time home buyer, be aware of an important point concerning the down payment. Lenders will not allow anyone to loan you all or part of the down payment. But, they will allow someone to "give" you the funds, provided they furnish a written statement to that effect for the lender's records.

Buy to Sell

A famous Wall Street trader said that he never went into a deal without a plan for getting out of it. You usually buy a home with long-term holding in mind, but we think his advice holds true for real estate, too. Always look at property with the idea that you will be selling it to someone else. Characteristics that make a house especially appealing will also help it appreciate at a rate above the local average.

Therefore, after your price range is set, think about other things that are important to you. How far away from your work do you want to live? Do you have school-age children? Make a list of your criteria before you go house hunting.

Location, location, location. If everyone has heard of the old location adage, why would anyone purchase a piece of real estate in a bad location? We can't think of any good reasons except an especially low price or planned urban renewal. Otherwise, stick to real estate in good locations. Is there development in the area? Development brings jobs, and access to jobs means rising property values.

Are there good schools in the area? Is it easy to access highways or mass transportation? What about the shopping and entertainment? Does the lot offer a view? Taken one by one, these attributes create a good location. When they overlap, they create an environment where other people will also want to live, where resale will be easy, and where you can expect good appreciation.

The trick is to try to identify tomorrow's hot spots early, and get in on the ground floor. Do your homework. Monitor city council meetings for large development projects. Watch local papers for news of major companies moving in or expanding.

When you have honed in on the neighborhoods you want to consider, drive around and look at the condition of the homes. Ask your real estate agent about recent sales. How long did the homes sit on the market? Homes that move quickly mean buying demand is strong.

Also ask, how far apart were the asking and selling prices? Sellers often list their houses at a higher price than they expect to receive so they have room to negotiate. When the selling and purchase prices are close together, that also indicates a heavy demand area. There's no way to see into the future, but it is possible to collect enough information about a neighborhood to confirm your decision at the time.

Even in sagging real estate markets, properties with a picturesque view will outperform other real estate. Waterfront locations are perennial winners, too. Neighborhood amenities such as restaurants, theaters, and recreational facilities also shore up property prices. Since you are buying a house anyway, you might as well look for features to maximize appreciation on your investment.

Home Inspections

Home inspections determine the condition of the entire building structure and property. The use of professional inspectors can reduce the chance of an unexpected major expense after the purchase of a home.

A general home inspection is very common in today's marketplace. The inspector will check the entire property, considering all potential problems. The property's condition is summarized in a written report which describes any deficiencies such as termite damage, defective wiring or a leaky roof, and may suggest possible remedies. If the home inspector concludes that a detailed pest or structural inspection is called for, he or she will suggest that the appropriate specialist be consulted.

Laws requiring disclosure of property defects vary from state to state, but you can rest a little easier if you are willing to spend the money for a home inspection. Many lending institutions now require a home inspection before closing on a mortgage. We wouldn't advise buying a house without one.

Terms: Earnest Money, Contingencies, and Settlement Dates

After finding a house you wish to buy, an offer is generally made through your real estate agent, who takes care of all negotiations. An offer to purchase is a sophisticated method of doing some old-fashioned bargaining, and can extend to counter offers and counter offers to the counter offer. Offers to purchase are binding contracts that tell the seller how much you are willing to pay for the house, and generally are submitted with *earnest money* which is deposited in a special account to demonstrate that your offer is made in good faith. Although local custom varies, earnest money deposits can be anywhere from $1,000 to $5,000 or more.

The larger the earnest money deposit, the stronger the message is that you are serious about the purchase. From a seller's standpoint, an earnest money check for $15,000 clipped to an offer is a pretty strong incentive. If you are feeling your way with a lowball offer, put up the $1,000, but if this house is THE ONE, be prepared to ante up.

An offer can be written with any number of contingencies, or provisions. It could be contingent upon your selling your current home or upon the seller repairing the roof or septic system, or any number of things. But remember, the fewer contingencies in the offer, the more likely it is that your offer will be accepted. Finally, while price is a big factor, things such as settlement date also translate into money. Forty-five to sixty days usually allows enough time to get the financing and title insurance arranged, as well as other details that need to be taken care of.

The Financing Package

In a perfect world, we would all have the cash to plunk down for our houses, and none of us would care about a tax deduction for interest because we wouldn't be paying interest. Instead, most of us have to go the route of securing financing for our dream houses. When it's time to actually go for that home loan, you'll probably be faced with two different types of loans: fixed-rate loans and adjustable-rate loans, and a field of variations of these themes. Let's look at some of the options.

Fixed-Rate Mortgage Loans

A fixed-rate mortgage loan is the old 30-year standard, and until recently, the preferred way for most buyers. With this type of loan, the buyer agrees to pay interest on the loan at a fixed interest rate, determined at the time of closing. Fifteen-year fixed rate loans are available too, but you might want to read the Home Equity chapter before you decide on one.

The fixed-rate loan is the no-surprises loan. You know what your payment will be from beginning to end. They are usually the best bet for buyers who plan to stay in their homes more than a few years.

FIGURE 17–5

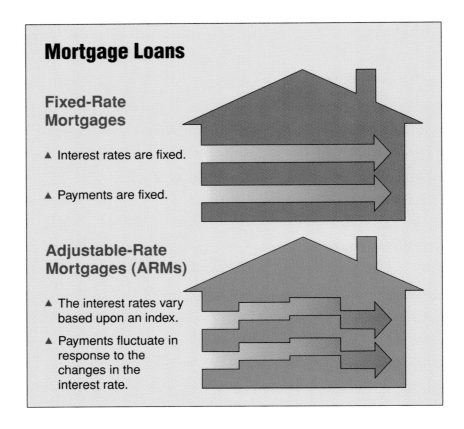

Mortgage Loans

Fixed-Rate Mortgages

▲ Interest rates are fixed.

▲ Payments are fixed.

Adjustable-Rate Mortgages (ARMs)

▲ The interest rates vary based upon an index.

▲ Payments fluctuate in response to the changes in the interest rate.

Adjustable-Rate Mortgage Loans

Adjustable-rate loans have interest rates that are adjusted at specified intervals using a certain index such as the U.S. Treasury bill rate (annual and lifetime interest rate caps generally apply). Lenders like them because it removes a lot of their risk when interest rates reflect current market conditions. Buyers like them because they usually cost less at the beginning of the loan, so adjustable-rate mortgages can be good for home buyers who plan to sell within a relatively short period of time.

Government Loans

The government created the Federal Housing Administration (FHA) in 1934 with the objective of putting more people into better homes. How was it done? By reducing the down payment required. Then, in 1942, Congress created the Veterans Administration (VA) loan benefit

FIGURE 17–6

Elements of Home Finance
Calculating Your Monthly Payment

Before calculating your monthly mortgage payment, you should understand the concept of amortization.

An amortization loan provides for repayment of the debt over a specified time period (term) by means of regular payments at specified intervals (weekly, monthly, bimonthly, annually, etc.). A portion of each payment is applied toward principal reduction and the remainder to interest.

Amortization is the gradual paying off of a debt by periodic installments

Example:
$90,000 loan
@ 8%
for 30 years

90 x 7.34
$660.60 per month

Monthly Payment Necessary to Amortize a $1,000 Loan

Years	5%	6%	7%	8%	9%	10%	11%	12%	13%	14%
1	85.61	86.07	86.53	86.99	87.45	87.92	88.38	88.85	89.32	89.79
2	43.87	44.32	44.77	45.23	45.68	46.14	46.61	47.07	47.54	48.01
3	29.97	30.42	30.88	31.34	31.80	32.27	32.74	33.21	33.69	34.18
4	23.03	23.49	23.95	24.41	24.89	25.36	25.85	26.33	16.83	27.33
5	18.87	19.33	19.80	20.28	20.76	21.25	21.74	22.24	22.75	23.27
6	16.10	16.57	17.05	17.53	18.03	18.53	19.03	19.55	20.07	20.61
7	14.13	14.61	15.09	15.59	16.09	16.60	17.12	17.65	18.19	18.74
8	12.66	13.14	13.63	14.14	14.65	15.17	15.71	16.25	16.81	17.37
9	11.52	12.01	12.51	13.02	13.54	14.08	14.63	15.18	15.75	16.33
10	10.61	11.10	11.61	12.13	12.67	13.22	13.78	14.35	14.93	15.53
11	9.86	10.37	10.88	11.42	11.96	12.52	13.09	13.68	14.28	14.89
12	9.25	9.76	10.28	10.82	11.38	11.95	12.54	13.13	13.75	14.37
13	8.73	9.25	9.78	10.33	10.90	11.48	12.08	12.69	13.31	13.94
14	8.29	8.81	9.35	9.91	10.49	11.08	11.69	12.31	12.95	13.60
15	7.91	8.44	8.99	9.56	10.14	10.75	11.37	12.00	12.65	13.32
16	7.58	8.11	8.67	9.25	9.85	10.46	11.09	11.74	12.40	13.08
17	7.29	7.83	8.40	8.98	9.59	10.21	10.85	11.51	12.19	10.87
18	7.03	7.58	8.16	8.75	9.36	10.00	10.65	11.32	12.00	12.70
19	6.80	7.36	7.94	8.55	9.17	9.81	10.47	11.15	11.85	12.56
20	6.60	7.16	7.75	8.36	9.00	9.65	10.32	11.01	11.72	12.44
21	6.42	6.99	7.58	8.20	8.85	9.51	10.19	10.89	11.60	12.33
22	6.25	6.83	7.43	8.06	8.71	9.38	10.07	10.78	11.50	12.24
23	6.10	6.69	7.30	7.93	8.59	9.27	9.97	10.69	11.42	12.16
24	5.97	6.56	7.18	7.82	8.49	9.17	9.88	10.60	11.34	12.10
25	5.85	6.44	7.07	7.72	8.39	9.09	9.80	10.53	11.28	12.04
26	5.73	6.34	6.97	7.63	8.31	9.01	9.73	10.47	11.22	11.99
27	5.63	6.24	6.88	7.54	8.23	8.94	9.67	10.41	11.17	11.95
28	5.54	6.15	6.80	7.47	8.16	8.88	9.61	10.37	11.13	11.91
29	5.45	6.07	6.72	7.40	8.70	8.82	9.57	10.32	11.09	11.88
30	5.37	6.00	6.65	7.34	8.05	8.78	9.52	10.29	11.06	11.85

program to reward veterans for their service and requires no down payment. Together, these programs account for over half of the home mortgages every year.

Neither of these programs actually make the loans; instead they insure the loans made by banks, savings and loans, and mortgage companies. With the United States government guaranteeing that the loans will be repaid, lenders are more willing to write the mortgages, and Americans find it easier to obtain housing.

FHA Loans. Down payment requirements vary from transaction to transaction and by geographical location for FHA loans, but a good estimate is about 3 or 4 percent of the purchase price. The FHA has liberal qualification standards with no income limitations, but closing costs are high. FHA loans are required to carry mortgage insurance, a one-time premium of 3.8 percent of the loan, payable either in cash or as part of the loan, plus annual mortgage insurance premiums which work out to about .5 percent of the loan paid monthly. The length of time required to carry the insurance goes down with a higher down payment.

The FHA has strict property requirements, purchase price limitations (hovering around $100,000 these days), which are often a small percentage above conventional interest rates, but the reduced down payment makes them especially attractive if you can qualify.

VA Loans. Veterans qualify for VA loans if they have had 90 days of active service during World War II, the Korean War, or the Vietnam War, or 181 days of active service between the wars. Veterans after 1980 have more specific requirements to qualify.

The federal government determines the amount veterans may borrow through the calculation of "entitlement," which is determined by the length of time spent in the service and adjusted periodically as housing prices increase. The current maximum loan amount is $203,000 for VA loans.

The no down payment feature is still the stellar attraction of VA loans, and the qualifying standards are more liberal than conventional loans. The loans carry a fixed rate of interest, so payments remain the same over the life of the loan. The VA charges a funding fee of 1.25 to 3 percent of the loan amount, and it can be financed into the loan if needed. Closing costs cannot be included in the loans, so they must be paid up front and must also be within schedules of permissible fees.

Leasing with the Option to Buy

There is one other way that you can move into real estate without a large down payment, and that is by finding a seller who is willing to consider a lease with an option to buy. This concept is a little complicated, so many real estate agents and sellers shy away from it, but it's not that difficult either. Put simply, leasing with an option to buy is a hybrid between an outright contract to purchase and a lease.

The contract includes the purchase price, the option amount (which is a nonrefundable substitute for a down payment), the option time period, the rent price, and the rent credit. When the option is exercised, the option funds (option amount and rent credits) are applied to the down payment and closing costs. If the buyer chooses not to exercise the option within the term, the seller keeps the money for their trouble.

Using this method, you can make an agreement with an amount considerably less than a typical down payment, then make rent payments for example, 18 months or so. The rent is usually higher than the going rate because a portion of it (the rent credit) goes toward the down payment. After some period of time, you have accumulated a fairly good down payment with the rent credit and can move into the sale.

Terms between the buyer and seller are negotiable, but the buyer's financial parameters usually structure the deal. The buyer has to give the seller an incentive to negotiate in this manner, generally a higher purchase price.

Leasing with the option to buy offers a lot of advantages for special situations. It can help people who can't simultaneously pay rent and save a large amount for a down payment. Buyers who need immediate occupancy can move in and then arrange their financing. Sellers can cover their own monthly expenses on the house and often because they are willing to deal, end up receiving a higher purchase price.

Exposing the Myths about Real Estate Investment

Have you ever been to or heard of one of those programs titled "How I turned $200 into $1 Million in Real Estate"? Sounds fantastic, doesn't it? These programs should be posted with "Caution" signs because the truth is, real estate has attracted billions of dollars over the years for all the wrong reasons: unrealistic tax benefits and unbelievable returns.

Unrealistic Tax Benefits

We believe that the tax benefits of real estate properties have been grossly overestimated by people who have sales programs, books, and tapes to sell. While it's true that the interest on your principal residence is tax-deductible, the tax benefits of other real estate properties are generally restricted and may not be as great as their claims would have you believe.

Unbelievable Returns

Unbelievable returns are just that — unbelievable. If it were that easy, why aren't these salespeople out buying and selling real estate instead of peddling their "How I Made it Big in Real Estate" audio tapes for $9.95? We know the truth is tough, but unbelievable returns dissolve under scrutiny, in our experience. There is money to be made in real estate when you approach it correctly, but don't get taken in. When you consider investing, leave the hawkers at the carnival.

Good Returns

These caveats don't take the attraction out of investing in real estate. Many people have done quite well investing in various types of real estate. Overall, real estate investments have offered good returns, generally outpacing inflation by a few percentage points. And good returns can really blossom with leverage.

Best of all, real estate is tangible. You can walk on it, or plant trees on it. It holds a perennial mystique of feeling comfortable. While we have met a lot of wealthy people who made their money outside of real estate, we have met few wealthy people who didn't own real estate. It's a solid investment.

While we believe that real estate has a part in every investment portfolio in one form or the other, we want to caution you against holding a portfolio of *only* real estate. The risk and liquidity constraints are too confining. Unless your portfolio is exceptionally well-funded, it's difficult to achieve adequate diversification with real estate alone. The numbers are simply too large. And you must be prepared to hold real estate for a long time to realize a good return.

But when you arrange your financial affairs to cope with these drawbacks (and it is quite possible when you build your financial house from the bottom up, as we have shown), then real estate can be an exciting investment opportunity.

Judge real estate on its potential for appreciation and positive cash flow, with tax benefits as a secondary consideration. Remember, the whole idea behind portfolio diversification is to spread the risk, so when one part of your portfolio may be performing poorly, other areas are hopefully picking up the slack. During the 1970s, stocks didn't do well, for instance, but certain areas of real estate were very good investments.

Beyond the Home — Real Estate Investments

Rental real estate holds the alluring promise of letting someone else pay for your investment and, for the most part, it works because you can use leverage. And since lenders continue their love affair with real estate, it is usually fairly simple to find financing for rental property. The tenants are paying the costs of maintenance and debt service. In fact, rental property would be a nearly perfect investment if it weren't for a few little snags that can trip you up. They are landlord responsibility and the possibility of negative cash flow.

Being a landlord involves a little more than making out deposit slips for your bank account. It means collecting rent (sometimes late rent), fixing 3:00 a.m. plumbing problems, handling neighborhood complaints, and making frequent property visits. As a landlord you are also responsible for property damage and illegal activities on your property. Ask anyone who's owned a rental for any length of time; they probably have a few other headaches to add to this list of potential problems.

Suppose you can't find tenants at all or have long periods of vacancy. When that happens, you continue to carry all of the financing costs while the property remains vacant, resulting in *negative cash flow* — you pay out more cash than you take in. Add the cost of maintenance and taxes to these other little things we mentioned, and you begin to see that rental real estate isn't for the faint hearted.

But the faint hearted are never rewarded either, are they? You can negotiate these snags by hiring professional property managers, or by purchasing property close to where you live so you can make frequent visits. One owner of a multi-family housing complex always said the place was a continual headache, but dealing with the tenants was so interesting, it made up for the problems. By the way, he sold it for a bundle after 20 years.

Now that we've given you a general idea of what life as a landlord is, let's consider what some of the ownership options are.

Multi-Family Housing

In contrast to a single-family home, multi-family housing is generally described as a structure with four or more living units that share some common facilities such as hallways, entrances, environmental control devices, laundry facilities, parking lots, and recreational facilities. They are also known as fourplexes, sixplexes, and so on.

Advantages

Less Vacancy Risk.   The main advantage of multi-family housing over a single-family dwelling is quite simple: *more tenants mean less risk*. If you have a vacancy in a single-family home, the vacancy rate is 100 percent. If you have one vacancy in a fourplex, the vacancy rate is 25 percent. If one tenant leaves from a 100-unit apartment, your vacancy rate has increased by only one percent.

Economies of Scale.   In multi-family housing, maintenance costs such as landscaping are spread across a lot of rental payments. Items such as carpeting, appliances, draperies, and similar items can be purchased at volume prices.

Potential Buyers Have Cash.   When it comes time to sell your multi-family dwelling, the most likely buyers have cash. Who are the buyers? Stable buyers such as life insurance companies, pension funds, real estate investment trusts, and real estate limited partnerships.

All of these investors have purchased multi-family dwellings as investments before. Does that tell you anything about the advantages of rental real estate? These companies wouldn't invest in it unless they believed there was a reasonable chance of getting a good return.

Disadvantages

Large Investment Required.   Unfortunately, multi-family dwellings are beyond the reach of most individual investors. They require a greater outlay of cash to begin with and the initial costs of maintenance or repairs may be prohibitive. Then too, financing arrangements for multi-family dwellings can be quite complex (no pun intended).

Full-Time Management Required.   When you consider the time it requires to manage a single-family dwelling and multiply that by the number of units in a multi-family dwelling, it generally means that

The Success Triangle

full-time management is required. Ask yourself whether you're really prepared to spend that much time on your investment.

Tax Benefits Possibly Reduced. Tax deductibility of a multi-family dwelling can be adversely affected if the property isn't actively managed. According to the Tax Reform Act of 1986, deductions for depreciation and operating losses are limited to investments in which the investor is a *material participant.* The Act defines material participation as 500 hours of involvement per year in the operations and management of the property.

Actually, very few investors, who are not the property managers, can meet this requirement. The IRS will also accept as little as one hundred hours of involvement if the property agent or manager can show that he or she did not spend any more time managing the property than the investor. Even then, most investors would still have a tough time meeting the lesser requirement.

Time-Shares

A time-share is a shared proportional ownership in a property, generally in a vacation area, in which the time-share owner is entitled to use the unit for a certain amount of time each year. We do not view time-shares as good investments. They are frequently sold at inflated prices with high commissions by the initial developer and are difficult to sell on the secondary market.

Commercial and Industrial

If living space doesn't appeal to you, you might want to consider a commercial or industrial real estate investment. Some possibilities include office buildings, shopping centers, warehouses, factories, and service centers.

One advantage of commercial real estate investment (if it is in a good location), is the availability of suitable investors. Life insurance companies, foreign investors, pension funds, real estate limited partnerships, and real estate investment trusts are all possible sources of investment capital for commercial property.

Real Estate Limited Partnerships

An alternate solution to the headaches of real estate management that requires less of an investment is to purchase *real estate limited partnerships.* These partnerships purchase a pool of real estate investments.

They also pool financial and managerial resources; that is, investors provide the funds for investment and turn the management over to a qualified real estate management organization. Minimum participation can be as low as $2,000.

Advantages

Professional Management. Real estate limited partnerships help relieve the investor of the management hassles, because a professional real estate organization manages the property and the portfolio.

Investment Selection. Because a limited partnership pools financial and managerial resources, many investments are open to investors who would not otherwise be able to afford them on their own. Partnerships can hold rental property, commercial property, or any other real estate as defined by the prospectus of the partnership.

Limited Liability. The word *limited* in limited partnership refers to the limited liability of the investors. In other words, the investors are only liable up to the amount of the investment.

Disclosure Requirements. Securities regulations on limited partnerships require that a substantial amount of information be made available to the investors. Having this information greatly reduces the risk of a poor investment.

Disadvantages

Investment Risk. As with most investments, real estate limited partnerships involve some investment risk. Should the market decline, the investor may lose part or all of the principal investment.

Illiquid. Plan on holding real estate limited partnership investments for a long time. Once in, it is difficult to get out until the term of the investment is up. On the rare occasion that you are able to sell your interest to someone else, it is usually at a severe loss.

Cash Flow Risk. The three elements of return from real estate investments are cash flow, appreciation, and tax benefits. If a decline in market rental rates occurs (due to over building or economic decline, for example), cash flow from investments may also decline.

Sponsorship Risks. The sponsoring organization may be unable to invest in properties that meet the objectives of the partners within a reasonable time. Then, the capital invested will only earn the rates of return from the money market fund or other temporary investment where the funds have been kept awaiting a suitable investment. In addition, the sponsoring organization may lose the ability to properly manage the investments because of financial pressures or other difficulties.

Real Estate Investment Trusts

A real estate investment trust (REIT) can be compared to a mutual fund that invests in stocks. REIT investors own shares of a real estate portfolio rather than a specific business; however, the management of the portfolio is actually more important than the investments themselves.

REITs have existed on the stock market for 30 years and appeal mainly to those looking for anti-inflationary investments. REIT holdings tend to be more novel or creative real estate investments, because there is fierce competition among bankers, insurance companies, and others who compete aggressively on the price of large projects. Some past REIT holdings include mini-warehouses, health care facilities, and the Rockefeller Center.

Like limited partnerships, REITs involve passive participation. Because there is no official minimum investment, REITs are fairly easy to get into and, therefore, offer better marketability than limited partnerships. Share prices, however, can be volatile.

Summary

Real estate is an important part of any investment portfolio, especially because it is a proven hedge against inflation. It can also be less volatile than the stock market, and the relative stability of real estate investments can help reduce the overall volatility of your portfolio.

Think of your home as housing first, then as an investment. There are lifestyle benefits associated with owning your own home that may supersede normal investment criteria. But when selecting your home, look for characteristics that maximize your investment, such as a good location and proximity to schools, highways, and amenities.

Qualifying for a home mortgage involves your income, your down payment, and usually, a financing package. When the down payment is a concern, alternatives include FHA and VA loans, or leasing with an option to buy.

When investing in real estate, look for potential for appreciation and cash flow, with leveraging possibilities to enhance returns on the investment. Stick with income-producing property to cover debt service and other management expenses. And, if property management doesn't appeal to you, consider a limited partnership or a REIT. Both require less investment expertise, are managed by professionals, and allow you to participate in the sometimes-lucrative real estate market.

SECRETS IN ACTION

Alyssa Ryan earns $3,000 monthly working for an accounting firm. Last summer, she and a friend vacationed in Door County, Wisconsin. Sitting at a sidewalk cafe eating frozen custard, Alyssa wrote, "I would love to own a bed and breakfast here!" on her napkin.

When she was unpacking, she playfully slipped that napkin behind the edge of her mirror. Alyssa continued to file tax returns, but every day, she looked at that napkin. She talked to some realtors and discovered she could purchase a home in Door County for about $200,000.

For months, Alyssa researched the bed and breakfast industry. She drew up a plan. She estimated she would need $50,000 to put down on a piece of property, about $100,000 to furnish and equip the house, and $50,000 in working capital to start her business. With her current earnings and liabilities, Alyssa thought she could save about $400 a month.

After sharing her dreams with a financial planner, she learned that saving $400 a month wasn't enough to reach her goals anytime soon. But she owned her own home, and her planner suggested the creative solution of increasing her mortgage to 80 percent of the value, releasing $80,000 to invest. After deducting the mortgage interest, her net payment was only two hundred dollars more a month.

The planner explained that refinancing increased her risk, but Alyssa had no dependents, and left her cash reserves untouched, so decided she could afford the risk. She invested her $80,000 in a mix of mutual funds worked out with her planner.

Alyssa checked out antique furniture books from the library. After three years, she enrolled in cooking school, and hotel and restaurant management classes at the local technical school. In seven to ten years, Alyssa's home and business would be in Door County.

EIGHTEEN

Retirement Planning
Achieving Financial Independence through Retirement Plans

Retirement Planning Is for Everyone

"The end of labor is to gain leisure."
– Aristotle

The typical American will work more than 90,000 hours during their lifetime. For many people, looking forward to a happy and secure retirement is a key goal as they work all those hours. Sadly, however, most people spend more time planning a vacation or a party than they spend planning their retirement.

In this context, we will define *retirement planning* as saving and investing during your working years to assure that you will have accumulated enough assets to be able to maintain or exceed your preretirement standard of living throughout your retirement years. Obviously, money is only one part of retirement planning, but it is essential to a secure and enjoyable future. After providing for the necessary financial resources for retirement, it becomes more plausible to think about and plan various leisure activities.

A typical American today should plan to spend from 15 to 20 years or more in retirement. Successful retirement planning will help maximize the enjoyment of your retirement years. Whether you are planning for future retirement or are already retired, learn to make the right choices when confronted with inflation, investment alternatives, insurance coverage, decisions about retirement plan options, increasing health care costs, taxes, and estate planning issues (see Chapter 9).

FIGURE 18–1

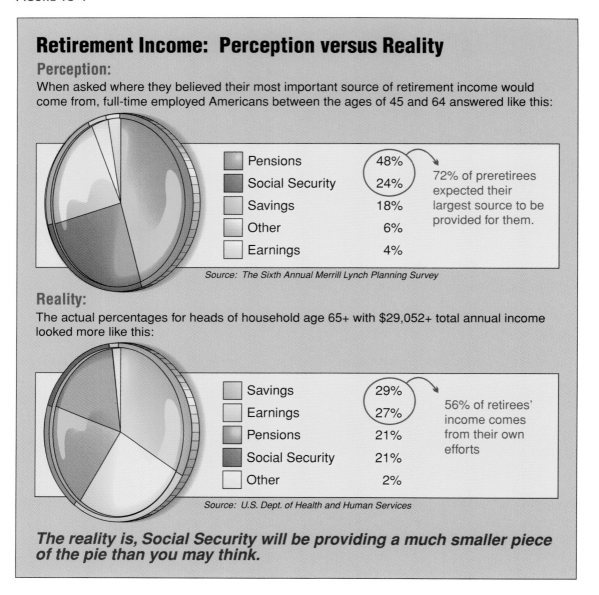

Retirement Income: Perception versus Reality

Perception:

When asked where they believed their most important source of retirement income would come from, full-time employed Americans between the ages of 45 and 64 answered like this:

Pensions	48%
Social Security	24%
Savings	18%
Other	6%
Earnings	4%

72% of preretirees expected their largest source to be provided for them.

Source: The Sixth Annual Merrill Lynch Planning Survey

Reality:

The actual percentages for heads of household age 65+ with $29,052+ total annual income looked more like this:

Savings	29%
Earnings	27%
Pensions	21%
Social Security	21%
Other	2%

56% of retirees' income comes from their own efforts

Source: U.S. Dept. of Health and Human Services

The reality is, Social Security will be providing a much smaller piece of the pie than you may think.

In this chapter we will discuss Social Security, individual retirement plans, and employee sponsored retirement plans. In Chapter 23 we will talk specifics about determining your retirement income needs and developing a savings and investment plan to meet your objectives.

Retirement planning is for everyone. Most people underestimate how much savings they will need for retirement and most people don't even start saving for retirement until they are middle age. It is never too late to start, but with your knowledge of time and compound interest, you know that the sooner you get started, the better. Start now, if you haven't already done so, and make the most of your retirement.

Social Security

Believe it or not, there *is* some good news to tell you about Social Security. The average monthly Social Security check in 1995 was over $700, up quite a bit from $84 in 1966. Poverty among people age 65 and over declined from 24.6 to 12.2 percent in the 20-year period ending 1990, partly because of this increase. One unique benefit of Social Security income, as compared to other retirement income, is that monthly payments increase annually by the percentage increase of the consumer price index. Thus the purchasing power of your Social Security benefits remain fairly constant.

The House of Representatives Select Committee on Aging states that we now have 31½ million people age 65 or over in America. By 2010, that number is predicted to increase to 39 million and by 2030 to 64.5 million.

The problem with this prediction is that there will be fewer and fewer workers to support the ever-increasing senior population. In 1945, there were 42 people working and contributing to Social Security to support each retired person. By 1984, that number had declined to only 3.3 people working for every retired person. By the year 2020, there will only be 2.4 people left working to support each person age 65 or over. This demographic shift is occurring for many reasons, including a declining birth rate, medical advances which enable us to live longer, and the aging baby boomers who are all approaching retirement at once.

How long can this trend continue? Will the Social Security program go bankrupt trying to support all our retired people? We don't think so because in spite of some bad press, the fact is that the Social Security system is financially sound. In recent years Social Security tax receipts have exceeded benefits paid enabling the buildup of a substantial reserve fund from which future benefits can be paid. But, because current Social Security benefits are being paid out of current Social Security tax receipts, it stands to reason that we will need adjustments in the Social Security system's benefit structure.

FIGURE 18-2

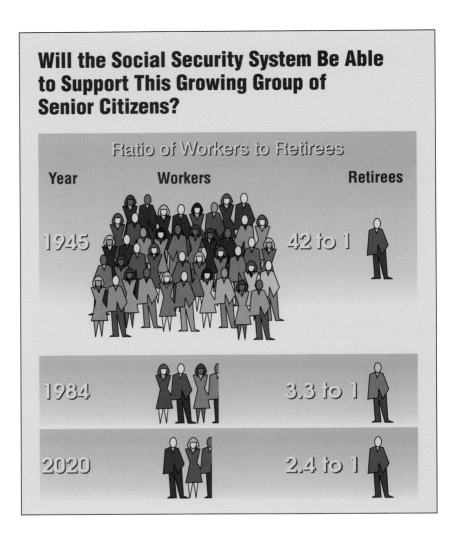

Will the Social Security System Be Able to Support This Growing Group of Senior Citizens?

Ratio of Workers to Retirees

Year	Workers	Retirees
1945		42 to 1
1984		3.3 to 1
2020		2.4 to 1

The biggest problem we see with the Social Security program is that many people mistakenly believe that their benefits will provide an adequate retirement income. Think back to the numbers we quoted earlier. Would you really want to try living on $700 per month? With luck, that might pay your monthly utilities for a cold February in Wisconsin — if, that is, you own your own home, own a new energy efficient furnace, and eat at your daughter's all month! Unless you plan for extra income to supplement your Social Security benefits, the only excitement in your retirement may be in planning how to survive until your next Social Security check arrives.

The Success Triangle

FIGURE 18-3

How Retirement Age Affects Social Security Benefits

Presently, the normal retirement age for receiving full Social Security benefits is age 65. As illustrated here, we can retire at age 62 and receive 80 percent of the normal benefit, or we can delay retirement to age 70 and receive 122.5 percent of the normal benefit. In those cases where an individual or couple hasn't accumulated enough resources to provide the desired income, a delayed retirement can help make up part or all of the shortage in addition to allowing time for further compounding of their investments.

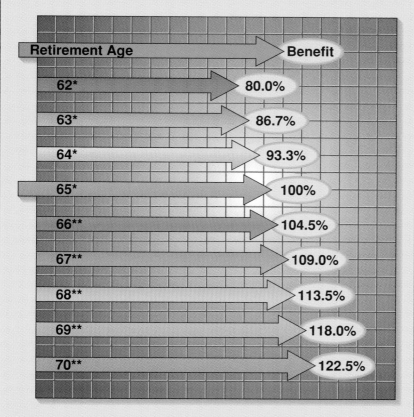

Retirement Age	Benefit
62*	80.0%
63*	86.7%
64*	93.3%
65*	100%
66**	104.5%
67**	109.0%
68**	113.5%
69**	118.0%
70**	122.5%

* Changes are scheduled for those reaching age 62 in the year 2000. Age 67 will be the normal retirement age for those attaining age 62 in the year 2022.

** The delayed Retirement Credit increases from its current level by 1/2% for those attaining age 65 in the year 1996, and every other year thereafter, reaching 8% per year in the year 2008.

You should, of course, avoid this predicament. Think of Social Security as just a nice supplement to your retirement income — the rest is up to you. With a little foresight and planning you can be one of the 3 out of 10 Americans who retire financially secure.

Retirement Investment Plans

When we say "retirement plans" we mean investments that were specifically designed for retirement and as such offer tax shelter benefits. In fact, retirement plans are among the very few remaining investment vehicles which offer substantial tax shelter benefits. Congress has offered tax deferrals to encourage participation in retirement plans, believing that our society will ultimately benefit through more private sector retirement planning.

Employee contributions to retirement plans are generally made on a pretax basis. In other words, you can set aside and invest a portion of your income without it being subject to current income tax. This benefit alone is like receiving an instant *guaranteed* return of 15 to 30 percent or more on your investment. It is safe to say that no other investment offers such monetary rewards with so little risk. You will ultimately pay tax when money is withdrawn, but in the meantime you will have benefited from long-term tax-deferred growth on money that you would have otherwise paid to Uncle Sam.

Because of the tax advantages and possible matching employer contributions, we believe that retirement plans offer some of the best investment opportunities available. Indeed, if people were to wisely invest in these plans starting at an early age, they might even become wealthy.

If we were asked to offer general financial advice that could apply to everyone, we would suggest that after establishing adequate emergency funds, accumulating some liquid investments, and purchasing sufficient insurance coverage, you should then contribute as much as possible to your retirement plans.

However, there are drawbacks to every investment. In the case of retirement plans, the trade-off for the tax advantages is that access to your money is restricted until you reach retirement age. These restrictions really bother some people, but what should bother them even more are the odds of running out of money during retirement. If they could face the cold reality of a not-so-golden retirement for even a short time, they would welcome, not just tolerate, the restricted access to their funds.

Some investors might say that our general advice is a little too simplistic. But the sad truth is that the median annual income (including

The Power of Tax-Deferred Growth through Retirement Plans

The tax advantages available through retirement plans make a much bigger difference in the growth of your investments than you might realize. In comparing a retirement plan, offering tax-deductible contributions and tax-deferred accumulation of earnings, with an investment offering the same rate of return with no tax advantages, the results are dramatic. By investing in a retirement plan such as an IRA or 401(k), you would have 90 percent more money after 20 years, 139 percent more after 30 years, and 200 percent more after 40 years! This chart illustrates the differences.

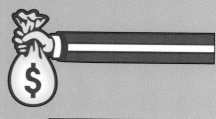

Investment Assumptions
- $2,000 Available for Annual Investment
- 28% Tax Bracket
- 10% Annual Return
- Without Tax-Deductible Contributions, Taxes Reduce Annual Investment to $1,440

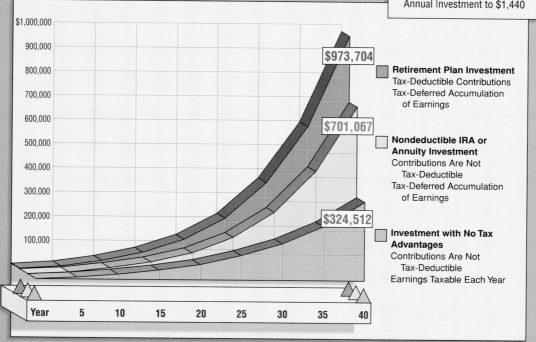

Retirement Plan Investment
Tax-Deductible Contributions
Tax-Deferred Accumulation
of Earnings — $973,704

Nondeductible IRA or Annuity Investment
Contributions Are Not Tax-Deductible
Tax-Deferred Accumulation of Earnings — $701,067

Investment with No Tax Advantages
Contributions Are Not Tax-Deductible
Earnings Taxable Each Year — $324,512

We encourage virtually everyone to take full advantage of tax-deferred growth through available retirement plans such as IRAs and 401(k) plans, and to start saving in these plans as soon as possible.

Chapter 18 / Retirement Planning

Social Security) of males over the age of 65 in America is less than $15,000, giving us a reason for concern. The situation for women over the age of 65 is much worse, even tragic — their median annual income is just over $8,000 a year. These statistics show that Americans not only *need* to save larger portions of their income for retirement, they also *need* to have access to their retirement funds restricted, to discourage using their funds today at the expense of long-term financial security.

Retirement plans usually offer investment choices such as a money market fund, a stock portfolio, or a bond portfolio. Use the same criteria in selecting retirement plan investments that you would to pick other investments. Within the plan, consider risk and diversification. Retirement plans fit into a specific level of the Success Triangle™; they are tax-advantaged investments and generally have a long-term time frame, and therefore should emphasize equities to keep pace with inflation. By definition, retirement plan investments are illiquid, with penalties for early withdrawals.

Let's look at some of the retirement plans that are available to us individually and through our employers, to learn more about their benefits and why you should seriously consider contributing as much, and as early as possible.

Personal Retirement Plans

The most common and popular personal retirement plans are individual retirement accounts (IRAs), annuities, and for self-employed individuals, Keogh accounts which will be discussed in a later section.

Individual Retirement Accounts.   One of the best and easiest ways to accumulate money for your retirement is through an individual retirement account (IRA), a tax-favored savings and investment plan. The first objective of an IRA is to realize a tax savings in the *current year.* IRA contributions are up to 100 percent tax deductible, depending on your income and participation in other retirement plans. Regardless, all earnings on an IRA investment accumulate on a tax-deferred basis. Here are some answers to the most frequently asked questions about IRAs.

Who may contribute to an IRA?   Anyone under the age of 70½ who has earned income (income you receive from rendering services — investment income doesn't count) may contribute to an IRA.

How much can be contributed to an IRA?   An individual may contribute up to $2,000, or 100 percent of his or her earned income, if it is

FIGURE 18–5

Individual Retirement Account (IRA)

A Tax-Favored Savings and Investment Program

An *Individual Retirement Account (IRA)* is a tax-favored savings and investment plan. Congress enacted legislation to encourage individuals to save and invest money for retirement. They have provided tax deductions for most and deferrals for all of those who are willing to set aside a portion of their earnings specifically for retirement (so that 95 percent of our senior citizens won't reach age 65 broke or almost broke).

When you make a deductible IRA contribution, the amount of your contribution is deducted from your gross income, which in turn reduces the amount of your taxable income. This is like having Uncle Sam kick in a percentage of your contribution equal to your marginal tax bracket. If you are in the 28 percent tax bracket, the government reduces your taxes $560 for an IRA contribution of $2,000. This makes your net cost only $1,440 for a $2,000 IRA investment. We look at that as getting an almost immediate 38.9 percent return on your IRA investment!

Family A: *Gross income $42,000*

| No IRA Contribution | $6,700 Deductions $7,650 Exemptions | Taxable Income $27,650 | Federal Tax $4,148 State Tax $? |

Family B: *Gross income $42,000*

Save $600 in Federal Taxes
+ Additional $ in State Taxes

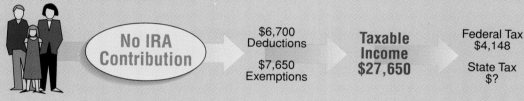

| $4,000 IRA Contribution | $6,700 Deductions $7,650 Exemptions | Taxable Income $23,650 | Federal Tax $3,548 State Tax $? |

Objectives of an IRA

➤ **Tax savings in the current year.** IRA contributions are up to 100 percent tax deductible.

➤ **Earnings accumulate tax-deferred.** There are no current taxes to pay on earnings of the IRA investments. Even though changes in the tax laws restrict the deductibility of the IRA contributions for some people, everyone with earned income can still make a nondeductible IRA contribution and take advantage of tax deferral.

➤ **Retirement income.** Withdrawals can start at any time between the ages of 59½ and 70½.

Who may contribute to an IRA? Anyone under the age of 70½ who has earned income may contribute up to $2,000, or 100 percent of their earned income, if less than $2,000.

1996 tax tables used in making calculations.

less than $2,000. Say that you have a part-time job and you're earning $1,000 or $1,200 or $1,500 — you can put all of that amount into an IRA. A married couple may contribute up to $2,250 if only one spouse has earned income, or up to $4,000 if each spouse has earned income of $2,000 or more.

We've talked to many people who haven't contributed to an IRA because they thought they had to put in the full $2,000. In truth, you can put in any amount — $500, $1,000, $1,500, or whatever your investment will accept. You can also make monthly contributions if you choose, as low as $25 per month with many investments. Or how about $166.66 a month ($2,000 divided by 12 months) — there are a lot of investments that will accept exactly that amount. The important thing is to contribute as much as you can if you can't afford $2,000 per year.

For those who have procrastinated, IRA contributions may be made as late as the April filing date for the prior year. But don't forget the power of time and compound interest — the sooner you start putting your money to work, the better.

How much will be tax-deductible?   The amount of your contribution that is tax-deductible will be determined by your adjusted gross income and whether or not you (or your spouse) participate in a quali-fied retirement plan through your employer. If neither spouse partici-pates in a qualified retirement plan your full contribution, up to the specified limits, will be completely tax-deductible.

In those cases where an individual or either spouse of a married couple participates in a qualified retirement plan, IRA contributions may not be fully tax deductible. An individual with an adjusted gross income of less than $25,000 or a married couple earning $40,000 or less can take the maximum IRA deduction, even if the individual or spouse par-ticipates in a retirement plan at work (a married couple with one work-ing spouse may deduct $2,250, or each spouse may deduct up to the lesser of $2,000, or 100 percent of earned income). For individuals earn-ing over $25,000 or couples earning over $40,000, deduction of IRA contributions may be restricted but they can still benefit by making par-tial deductible or nondeductible contributions (see Chapter 15).

So, what's the big deal about receiving a tax deduction for an IRA contribution? As an example, let's say that you contribute $2,000 and you are in the 28 percent marginal tax bracket. The $2,000 is deducted from your taxable income and, accordingly, your current tax liability is immediately reduced by $560. Thus, in order to put $2,000 to work in your IRA, you actually only need to come up with $1,440 ($2,000 minus your $560 tax savings). Sounds almost too good to be true, doesn't it? Indeed, you will eventually pay taxes when you begin taking money out of your account. In the meantime the money you didn't send to Uncle Sam is working for you, and its earnings and the earnings on its reinvested earnings are not taxable. Once again the magic of compounding and tax deferral is working for your benefit.

Even though you might not be able to deduct your full IRA contribution, don't let that fact overshadow the principal benefit of tax deferral of the earnings of IRA investments. While the law may restrict your ability to deduct your IRA contribution, it does not restrict your ability to make the contribution and benefit from tax deferral.

Do all earnings within IRAs accumulate tax-deferred? All earnings on investments within the IRA will be tax-deferred, whether or not your contribution was deductible. Whatever your IRA earns, whether it is 5, 8, 10, 15, 20 percent, or more, it is tax-deferred until you withdraw the funds. There are no current taxes to pay on an IRA.

The power of combining tax-deductible contributions with tax-deferred growth through an IRA adds up to a lot more money than you may realize. Let's say you'll make 10 percent interest on your investment and you're in the 28 percent tax bracket. Over a 30-year period you invest $2,000 a year, for a total investment of $60,000. If you had to pay current income tax on the contributions and investment earnings, your net investment after taxes would be $1,440 ($2,000 less $560 in taxes) annually. You would accumulate $151,171 in your IRAs by the end of the 30 years.

On the other hand, with tax-deductible contributions and tax-deferral of your earnings, you'd end up with $361,887. That's a difference of more than $210,000 — 139 percent more! There's a lot of power in combining tax-deductibility and tax-deferral, isn't there? And even if you can't deduct your IRA contribution (net annual investment of $1,440), deferring taxes on the earnings would still result in a significant improvement in performance — an increase of almost $110,000 or 73 percent more over the 30 years.

Where should IRA funds be invested? IRA funds can be invested almost anywhere you choose: bank CDs, stocks, bonds, mutual funds, limited partnerships, and certain types of real estate, for example. Life insurance and collectibles are generally not permitted for IRA investments. The investment can vary from year to year and you may split your annual IRA contributions between two or more investment vehicles. You can have as many IRAs as you like, but watch out for account maintenance fees.

When do the deferred taxes become due? As we mentioned earlier, you will have to begin paying taxes on earnings and deductible contributions when you start withdrawals from your IRA. But in the meantime you have kept the money you would have paid in taxes and have also compounded the earnings on it. So the money that you would have mailed to Uncle Sam keeps earning interest, dividends, or capital gains on a tax-deferred basis. Had you sent that money to Uncle Sam instead, it would never have earned one cent!

Withdrawals can start at any time between the ages of 59½ and 70½. Withdrawals that start before or after this age range may be subject to penalties and income tax. You can defer your IRA distributions — and thus your taxes — until age 70½, but you will face a 50 percent tax penalty if you do not begin making minimum required withdrawals by age 70½.

When it's time to withdraw funds from your IRA, don't hesitate to do so. Remember, the IRS is pretty serious about making sure you pull the money out. They don't want tax deferral to go on forever. In fact, failure to liquidate the annual minimum will result in a tax penalty that is 50 percent of the difference between the required and the actual distribution on top of the regular income tax due. If you forget to do it or think, Well, maybe they won't notice if I don't take anything out this year, the penalty for failure to withdraw $4,854 is $2,427. That's a pretty stiff penalty, isn't it? As you approach age 70½, be sure all the paperwork is in order so the withdrawals can be made and penalties can be avoided.

Annuities. Annuities offer individuals another way of deferring taxes on investment returns. However, as we discussed in Chapter 16, before you invest in any annuity, you should first make maximum contributions to available qualified retirement plans, such as 401(k) plans, 403(b) plans, Keoghs, and deductible IRA accounts. Contributions to qualified plans, unlike annuities, are tax deductible. Both qualified retirement plans and annuities offer tax-deferred accumulation of investment earnings. For a complete discussion on annuities refer back to Chapter 16.

Employer-Sponsored Retirement Plans

Approximately 50 million Americans participate in some type of employer-sponsored retirement or pension plan. There are two fundamental reasons that motivate employers to establish qualified retirement plans. The first is to use them as a tax sheltered wealth accumulation vehicle for the owner-employees of the business. The second reason is to provide a genuine employee benefit to reward and help retain good employees and to attract qualified employees into the business. In either case, the contributions are deductible business expenses and both the contributions to the plan and the earnings of the investments accumulate, for the employee free of current income taxes.

In granting the favorable tax benefits the IRS requires that certain criteria or qualifying standards, must be met; hence the term *qualified retirement plans.* These standards require that the plan be a written document and that the existence of the plan be communicated to employees. The plan must be established and maintained by the employer and have limitations on contributions and restrictions on the amount that can be contributed on behalf of the owner-employees relative to employee contributions. The plan must specify vesting requirements, requirements regarding withdrawals and distributions of funds from the plan, and provisions for employee contributions.

Employers are not legally obligated to offer retirement plans to their employees. And if they do offer a plan, little can be done by employees to affect the amount that is contributed on their behalf. In this day of corporate cost cutting, workers can be thankful for whatever amount is invested into their retirement accounts by their employers.

On the other hand, employees should keep abreast of the benefits offered by these plans and encourage their employers to offer them. Small business owners should know how to establish plans that provide for the accumulation of retirement capital and help attract, reward, and retain good employees. Employer-provided retirement plans can be grouped as defined benefit or defined contribution plans.

Defined Benefit Plans. A *defined benefit plan* is a retirement plan from which plan participants are promised a *specified retirement benefit.* The monthly retirement benefit is usually based on the employee's income over a certain time period and may also reflect their years of service. The employer makes contributions to an investment pool from which retirement benefits are paid. The amount that the employer must contribute to the plan is not specified, but because they are obligated to pay the promised benefits, it is only sensible to hire actuaries to calculate the amounts of contributions the employer needs to make to assure that adequate funds are available.

Defined benefit plans are what we traditionally think of as pension plans. Historically, they have been associated with large industries such as manufacturing, mining, and finance and were also often associated with the growth of organized labor. These plans are often expensive for the employer to administer and maintain. The employer assumes all investment risk and must pay the promised benefits even when plan investments perform poorly. Because of these disadvantages, many companies have switched their retirement plans to defined contribution plans.

However, defined benefit plans can be especially beneficial for older employees who lack the long-term preretirement period to benefit from a defined contribution plan. These plans are also useful to older professionals (employee-owners) who need to accumulate substantial retirement savings within a relatively short time frame. Some plans may also allow additional voluntary contributions by employees.

Defined Contribution Plans. *Defined contribution plans* specify the employer contribution amount but do not promise any particular benefit. They are also called individual account plans since each participating employee's funds are either accounted for separately or maintained in an individual account for the participant. The amount of a participant's retirement benefit is determined by the participant's total account value, including investment earnings, at retirement. The employer can make contributions from year to year of from 0 to 25 percent of the participant's pay, depending on limits imposed on the various plans and employer desires.

Profit Sharing Plans.   Profit sharing plans provide a flexible contribution plan for the employer. Contributions are usually made as a percentage of the employee's pay and are usually tied to the profits of the company, although they do not have to be. Maximum annual contributions are the higher of 15 percent of the employee's salary or $30,000. Contributions are not mandatory and may be lowered, raised, or omitted as business conditions dictate. Profit sharing plans may be paired with other plans.

Money Purchase Plans.   Money purchase plans have fixed employer contributions specified in the plan document. These plans are less flexible for the employer because they require that a specified percentage of up to 25 percent of the employee's pay be contributed each year. IRS approval is required to change the determined contribution amount. The certainty of this annual contribution and the higher contribution limits are advantages to plan participants.

Target Benefit Plans.   Target benefit plans are actually a hybrid between defined benefit plans and money purchase plans. They target a particular benefit amount and actuaries calculate the contribution amount needed to hit the target, and contributions are then made at that level. However, depending on investment performance, the actual retirement benefits could be more or less than the targeted amount. Employer contributions are more flexible than in defined benefit plans but contributions must be made each year.

401(k) Plans. These plans were created by Congress in 1978 and carry the name of the IRS code section where they are discussed. Since their creation, 401(k) plans have become very popular. Employee participation in the 401(k) plan is voluntary. The plan provisions allow participants to make pretax contributions to the plan. Some employers offer a 401(k) plan along with or as an alternative to their other retirement plans.

A notable feature about 401(k) plans in general, is that the burden of providing retirement plan benefits has been shifted from the employer to the employee. Under 401(k) plans the employer may make contributions on behalf of employees or an employee may elect to take a salary reduction or forgo a salary increase and have the amount placed in the 401(k) plan. The employee benefits because the contributions are made on a pretax basis and all earnings accumulate tax deferred.

Contributions may be up to 25 percent of the employee's earned income, up to a maximum dollar amount per year. A $7,000 limit was established in 1988 and this amount is periodically adjusted (indexed for inflation) when cumulative adjustments reach $500. The 1996 maximum contribution is $9,500. Here are some of the key advantages of 401(k) plans:

Matching contributions. Employers may match employee salary deferred contributions to a 401(k) plan. For example, they could say, "For every dollar you invest we will contribute 25 cents to your account." Some employers are generous enough to match or even exceed your contributions.

Employer contributions including matching contributions are generally subject to *vesting*. That is, the employee is *not fully entitled* to the employer contributions until they have a specified term of service with the employer. *Forfeitures* are amounts that terminated employees who are not fully vested leave behind in the plan.

Let's say that your employer offers a 401(k) plan and contributes 50 cents for each dollar that employees put into their plans. That's the equivalent of making a 50 percent return on your money the day you contribute to the program. Not too many investments can generate that

FIGURE 18–6

Tax Savings Comparison by Contributing to a 401(k) Plan

	Without 401(k)	With 401(k)
Earned Income	$42,000	$42,000
Other Taxable Income (Interest, Dividends, Rental Income, etc.)	+5,000	+5,000
Total Income	47,000	47,000
Adjustments to Income	–0	–0
Adjusted Gross Income before 401(k) Contribution	47,000	47,000
401(k) Contribution	0	4,000
Adjusted Gross Income	47,000	43,000
* Deductions	–6,700	–6,700
* Exemptions	–5,100	–5,100
Taxable Income	35,200	31,200
* Federal Tax	5,280	4,680
State Tax	?	?
Total Tax	$5,280 + State Tax	$4,680 + State Tax

Save $600 in Federal Taxes
+ Additional $ in State Taxes!!

Investment	**$4,000**
Taxes Saved	**$600 + State Tax**
Your Actual Out-of-Pocket Cost to Make a $4,000 Investment	**$3,400 – State Tax**

*1996 tax tables used in calculations

You will eventually have to pay taxes on your earnings, but only when they are withdrawn from your 401(k) or IRA Rollover. Until then, your dollars will compound on a tax-deferred basis.

kind of return. Finally, when your employer matches your 401(k) contribution, you can add that amount to your tax savings.

No penalty upon death or disability.   Distributions can be made because of death or disability, without penalties.

Early retirement options.   Distributions can also be made from a 401(k) plan if it has an early retirement provision. If the company allows early retirement, for instance, at age 55, you can access funds from your 401(k) at that age without penalty. Any time distributions are taken after the age of 59½ and before age 70½, there are no penalties, regardless of the reason. After the age of 70½ minimum withdrawal requirements must be met and withdrawals must also be kept under the specified maximums to avoid penalties.

Lifetime annuity options.   You may also choose to use the proceeds to purchase a lifetime annuity or have your distributions calculated as such. Instead of taking a lump sum distribution, you would agree to receive a check each month for the rest of your life. In doing so, you will avoid penalties, but you will still have to pay taxes on the amount withdrawn.

Hardship withdrawals.   Depending on the specifics of a particular plan, withdrawals may be available in cases of financial hardship, such as the purchase of a principal residence, to pay tuition and fees for immediate family members, or to pay for medical or funeral expenses. However, they are limited and have some restrictions. You must first demonstrate that you have no other financial resources available. For obvious reasons, we discourage these kinds of withdrawals. Be sure to check with your employer for their availability.

Life insurance.   There is a provision in some 401(k) plans that allows the purchase of life insurance with your 401(k) contributions. If you need more life insurance, that is a good way to purchase it on a before-tax basis, instead of with the usual after-tax dollars.

IRA deductibility.   Contributions to a 401(k) plan will not necessarily prohibit you from making a deductible IRA contribution. As we discussed earlier, a married couple earning under $40,000 a year or an individual earning less than $25,000 will receive a full deduction on both types of accounts. Couples earning between $40,000 and $49,999 and individuals earning between $25,000 and $34,999 will receive a partial deduction for their IRA contributions.

We believe that a 401(k) plan provides one of the best ways to accumulate savings for retirement. If you have a 401(k) plan available to you and are not taking full advantage of it, you should reconsider.

403(b) Plans. Educational institutions or qualifying nonprofit organizations may also establish a tax-sheltered retirement plan for employees. Under Section 403(b) of the tax code, employees' payroll reduction contributions are excludable from taxable income. Payroll reduction is the most favored way to contribute to these retirement programs.

One of the outstanding features of a 403(b) plan is that the contributions can be larger than IRA contributions. The salary reduction amount generally is limited to a maximum of $9,500 per year. Several calculations are necessary to determine the limit; the lesser of the exclusion allowance or 25 percent of compensation would apply, if less than $9,500.

Formerly called *tax-sheltered annuities (TSAs),* 403(b) plans now allow participants to choose between annuities or mutual funds as investment vehicles (hence we prefer to call them 403(b) plans). All earnings accumulate tax-deferred until they are withdrawn. Generous loan provisions and hardship withdrawals are usually available.

In the event you are eligible for a 403(b) plan but haven't taken full advantage of it, a *catch-up* provision may allow you to do so. If you are eligible, this provision permits you to make contributions that exceed the usual maximums. The catch-up provision is unique to 403(b) plans and it can be quite beneficial.

A 403(b) plan also qualifies for rollover into an IRA account, should you terminate employment with your educational or nonprofit employer.

Simplified Employee Pension Plans (SEP-IRA). *Simplified Employee Pension Plans,* or *SEPs,* are really nothing more than individual retirement accounts funded by the employer. Employees set up IRAs and the employer makes annual contributions to these accounts. SEPs have no IRS filing requirements so they are useful for employers who want to avoid the administrative costs of setting up a pension plan. The government developed this plan to encourage small employers to implement retirement programs for their employees. Self-employed people can use a SEP as an alternative to a Keogh.

Deductible contributions to a SEP are higher than under regular IRAs. Up to $30,000 or 15 percent of the employee's income, whichever is less, may be contributed to an individual's account. The total includes employer and elective employee contributions. The employer's contribution to a SEP is fully discretionary from year to year. That is, the employer can contribute from 0 to 15 percent each year, but there is no requirement that contributions be made on a regular basis.

SARSEPs.   Employers with 25 or fewer eligible employees may offer a variation of the SEP called a *salary reduction SEP,* or *SARSEP,* allowing employees to use salary reductions to make SEP contributions. The employee's salary is not actually *reduced* but is *deferred* from taxation by being placed in the plan. Unlike an IRA, in which you make the contribution now and receive the refund once you file your taxes, the SARSEP contribution is deducted from your paycheck *before* it is taxed. Employee salary reduction contributions are limited to a specified maximum ($9,500 in 1996), including the employee's contributions to other plans.

Keogh Plans.   A *Keogh* can be any qualified retirement plan designed for self-employed individuals (business owner-employees) and their employees. Defined contribution plans are most frequently used for Keoghs; contributions are based on compensation and limited each year to a percentage of participating payroll. The annual maximum that can be added to an individual participant's account is $30,000, or 25 percent of compensation, whichever is less.

As a qualified plan, a Keogh is subject to the same nondiscrimination requirements that apply to qualified plans. That is, the plan may not discriminate in favor of officers or other highly compensated employees. The plan usually must include all full-time employees (those who work over 1000 hours per year) over age 21 who have at least one year of service. Contributions made on behalf of the employer (owner-employee) may not exceed the rate of contributions made on behalf of employees.

Which Retirement Plan Is Best?

Some employees will have no choice as to whether or not they participate in their employer's retirement plan. However, many employees may find that they have more than one plan in which they or their spouses may participate. Decisions must be made as to how voluntary contributions should be divided among different options.

Should you contribute all your annual retirement savings to your 401(k) plan or, should you instead, put all or part of it into an IRA? To answer this question, determine whether or not your employer or your spouse's employer offers matching 401(k) contributions and whether or not an IRA contribution would be tax-deductible.

Suppose your company offers a 401(k) plan and your spouse's employer offers a 403(b) plan. Together you are unable to fully fund either plan. How should you and your spouse allocate your retirement savings between the two plans? Again consider such things and whether or not your company offers matching contributions and whether or not the catch-up provision (if offered) through your spouse's 403(b) would be useful to you. For example let's say that you and your spouse expect to be able to make much larger contributions later on. For now, you might consider putting all the money you and your spouse have available for contribution into your 401(k). Then later on, use the 403(b) catch-up provision of your spouse's plan to make contributions in excess of the normally allowable annual limits when the time comes that you can contribute more. Other things to consider are loan provisions available from the various plans, investment alternatives available within the plans, life insurance provisions, the distribution options, and the availability of income averaging on distributions.

It is quickly apparent that the big picture can become quite complex. We think it is imperative that you and your spouse work closely with your financial advisor to completely evaluate your situation. Your future retirement success may depend on making the right choices early in your retirement planning strategy.

Distributions from Retirement Plans

Employees will eventually be faced with taking distributions from their retirement plans, and it could involve situations other than normal retirement. Decisions such as whether or not to take the distribution as a lump sum or from a variety of periodic payment options will need to be made. Making the best choice can often be difficult and once a decision is made, it may be irrevocable. Therefore we always recommend that you consult a professional financial advisor, who has expertise in retirement plans, before making your final decision. Let's look at some of the options.

Lump Sum Distributions

What technically qualifies as a lump sum distribution from an IRS standpoint? A *lump sum distribution* is when the entire balance of the employee's interest in a *qualified retirement plan* is paid to the employee within a single taxable year. If you receive money from a non-qualified deferred compensation plan, it does not qualify as a lump sum distribution.

Some employers may offer retiring employees a choice between a lump sum distribution or a monthly annuity option. Others do not offer a monthly benefit at retirement time. Instead, they pay their employees a one time lump sum distribution. The employer may also offer lump sum distributions if the plan is being terminated by the employer, at termination of the employee's service, if the employee becomes disabled or dies, or if the employer is offering early retirement.

There are substantial benefits to taking retirement plan distributions in the form of a lump sum. For one thing, it allows you to gain control of the entire retirement plan balance. You can decide where it is to be invested and there may be investments you like better than those your employer offers. If instead, the monthly annuity option were chosen, there are no more investment choices to be made.

Taking a lump sum distribution also gives you the ability to access your principal as you desire. You may want money to take a trip around the world, help your kids make a down payment on a house, or fund a once-in-a-lifetime opportunity. You will not have these options if you have opted for a lifetime annuity. In addition, income averaging on your taxes may be used to your advantage in certain situations when you take a lump sum distribution.

To qualify as a lump sum distribution all the money must be received **in one taxable year.** We worked with some clients a few years back who had a problem because their employer paid part of the money in December and the balance in February. Since it was received in two taxable years, it did not qualify as a lump sum distribution.

The distribution **must also represent the entire balance of your account in the plan,** and money **must be received at retirement, separation from service, death, or disability (for self-employed), or termination of the plan itself.**

To qualify for special tax treatment, **you must be at least 59½ years old** when you receive the distribution and you must have participated in the plan for at least five years.

We've been careful in defining what a lump sum distribution is in IRS terms because true lump sum distributions qualify for special tax treatment that can save money at distribution. These include IRA rollovers and special forward averaging provisions; 10-year averaging is allowed for people born before 1936 and 5-year averaging is available for everyone else. Depending on individual circumstances, the tax advantages of forward averaging may result in less taxes than with other distribution methods. Again, consult your financial advisor before making a final determination.

Rollover Options. Almost all taxable distributions from qualified retirement plans are eligible for tax-free rollover to IRAs or other qualified retirement plans. Complex IRS rules apply to rollovers but some general considerations merit discussion here.

When you receive eligible distributions that you intend to roll over instruct your employer to directly deposit the funds to your designated IRA or the qualified plan of your new employer. Otherwise, if you receive the funds yourself, they are subject to a mandatory 20 percent tax withholding, leaving you with only 80 percent of your funds. And even though you only receive 80 percent of your funds, the entire distribution is taxable if the rollover into an IRA or qualified plan is not done within 60 days.

In other words, to roll over 100 percent of your distribution you would have to use other funds to replace the 20 percent which was withheld. If you only roll over the 80 percent of the distribution you receive you will be liable for taxes on the other 20 percent, which was withheld.

Direct rollovers by your employer simplify the whole process and withholding and penalties are avoided. Your rollover can be divided into several different investments and accounts. As always, diversification should be considered.

In addition, if you are under age 59½ any taxable distribution not rolled over will be subject to a 10 percent penalty, except in special circumstances such as disability, early retirement after age 55, using the funds to pay medical expenses exceeding 7.5 percent of your gross income, or distributions to a spouse after your death. If you are over age 70½ the usual minimum distribution rules apply. Finally, be aware that rollover into an IRA is irrevocable. Lump sum distributions exceeding $750,000 will be subject to the 15 percent penalty that applies to excess distributions.

Periodic Distributions — Opting for a Monthly Check

The *monthly annuity option* has advantages that make it a better choice for some employees.

Some people simply do not want to be responsible for a large sum of money. Suppose your employer handed you a check for $80,000. And suddenly, you just don't feel comfortable having that much money at one time to deal with. Some people don't want to worry about where to make investments or they lie awake at night worrying whether their investments are going up or down. They would rather simply receive a check every month.

FIGURE 18–7

The IRS Rollover Snatch

The IRS now requires 20 percent withholding on lump sum distributions from qualified retirement plans. In order to avoid paying taxes on your distribution, you must roll it over into an IRA or another qualified retirement plan within 60 days. The problem is that you receive only 80 percent of your money and you need to roll over 100 percent of the distribution amount to avoid paying taxes. In addition, if you are not yet age 59½ you will pay a 10 percent penalty of the amount not rolled over. The IRS will send you a tax refund if you don't owe what they withheld from you, but in the meantime you will need to come up with the amount the IRS withheld to be able to roll over the full amount of your distribution. To avoid this IRS rollover snatch, you need to make sure that the money never comes directly to you. For most people, the simplest option is to have their distribution transferred directly into an IRA or other qualified retirement plan.

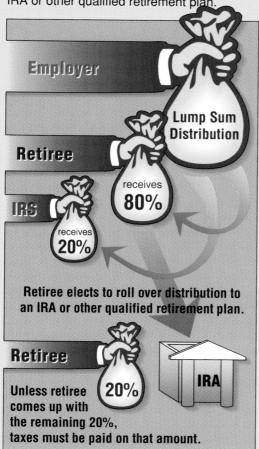

Employer

Lump Sum Distribution

Retiree receives 80%

IRS receives 20%

Retiree elects to roll over distribution to an IRA or other qualified retirement plan.

Retiree 20% IRA

Unless retiree comes up with the remaining 20%, taxes must be paid on that amount.

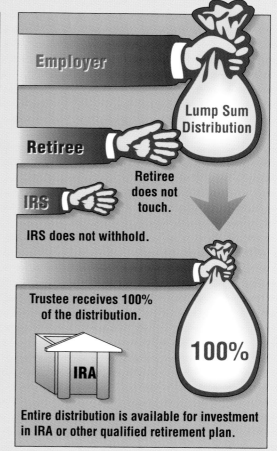

Employer

Lump Sum Distribution

Retiree does not touch.

IRS does not withhold.

Trustee receives 100% of the distribution.

IRA 100%

Entire distribution is available for investment in IRA or other qualified retirement plan.

Many plans provide for automatic cost-of-living adjustments. Your distribution could begin at $500 a month, and increase each year, based on the consumer price index. If there is a lot of inflation in the next 10, 15, or 20 years, the cost-of-living adjustments could be pretty valuable.

A monthly distribution plan could reduce your tax burden in the year of retirement. Instead of getting a lump sum of money all at once to pay tax on, you can have your payments spread out over a period of years. However, you can also eliminate tax in the year of retirement if you take advantage of an IRA rollover, or by not taking any distribution from your plan.

If you come from a family that has a history of longevity, and you worry about using all your money before you die, you can be comfortable knowing that the monthly annuity option provides an income that is guaranteed to last as long as you live.

Given the choice of a monthly benefit or a lump sum distribution, you must wrestle with the pros and cons of each. Let's say that your employer tells you that you're going to receive $1,667 a month for the rest of your life when you retire. Sounds simple enough, but that's not *really* the only choice you have.

Payment Options.   Your plan may offer several payment options upon retirement. Which one you choose will depend on your own financial situation and income needs.

Life Option.   With this choice you elect to receive the maximum monthly benefit with no benefit payable to your spouse or other survivors at your death. You receive a check every month for as long as you live, but when you die, the checks stop. There are no further payments to your spouse, your children, or to anyone.

If you should die one month after you retire, that doesn't appear to be a very good deal. If you live to be 102 years old, it looks like a great deal. This option pays the highest monthly amount available during your lifetime, but a surviving spouse receives nothing after your death.

The Joint and Survivor Option.   With this option, the monthly benefit amount is less than with the life option but it will continue to be paid until the death of both you and your spouse. This income would seem especially important to your surviving spouse if you predecease her or him. In fact, it is a qualified plan requirement that if you want to choose the life option over the joint and survivor option, your spouse is required to sign a form giving you permission to do so.

Joint and Reduced Survivor Option.   This option is a balance between the two previous options. You elect to receive an amount less than you would get from the life option, but greater than you would receive for the joint and survivor option. Then, at your death your spouse will receive a monthly check, but at a reduced percentage of the original amount.

Pension Maximization.   The option you choose is up to you, but before you choose joint and survivorship options, as most people do, consider the financial benefits of choosing the life option and purchasing a separate life insurance policy with the extra money you'll receive in your monthly check. This strategy, called _pension maximization,_ not only gives you more money now, but the higher payments continue if your spouse predeceases you. The joint and survivorship option actually penalizes you if your spouse dies before you do, because you still continue to receive the reduced benefit, even though your reason for choosing it (protecting your spouse) is no longer valid.

Other benefits of the pension maximization strategy include _transferability_ — you can change the beneficiary to a new spouse or other person or charity — and _flexibility_ — you can tap cash values if desired or the surviving spouse can vary income according to current need.

Things to consider before using pension maximization are your general health and inflation adjustments to your company's plan. Maybe the inflation adjustments in your company's plan are attractive enough to select the joint and survivor option.

Another very important consideration is whether your spouse can continue participating in company-sponsored health insurance after your death. If you select the life option, there is no spousal retirement benefit, and this option may disqualify your spouse from receiving company-provided health insurance.

You can see that there are some reasons why you would not want to use this plan and it doesn't always pencil out as the best choice, but definitely explore the feasibility of pension maximization before selecting your pension benefit option.

Before you go with the life option to use pension maximization, be sure a life insurance policy has been issued on your life. We repeat: _do_

FIGURE 18–8

Pension Maximization

Periodic Annuity Payment Options – Without Pension Maximization

Option 1 – Life Option

Retired Worker and Spouse jointly receive $1,667 per month

– at death of retired worker –

Surviving Spouse receives nothing

Option 2 – Joint and Survivor Option

Retired Worker and Spouse jointly receive $1,175 per month

– at death of retired worker –

Surviving Spouse continues to receive $1,175 per month

Option 3 – Joint and Reduced Survivor Option

Retired Worker and Spouse jointly receive $1,500 per month

– at death of retired worker –

Surviving Spouse receives $750 per month

With Pension Maximization Strategy

Choose Option 1
Monthly Benefit: $1,667
Survivor Benefit: $0

$492/month above Option 2 benefit

Purchase $160,000 Life Insurance
Option 1
Monthly Income: $1,667
Less Premium: $385
Net Income: $1,282

$107/month above Option 2 benefit

Life Insurance Policy
$4,614 Annual Premium
$385 Monthly

– at death of retired worker –

Surviving spouse invests insurance proceeds.

$160,000 at 8% return will generate $1,175/month for 30 years.

Same as Option 2 benefit

– if spouse dies first –

Retiree may cancel policy and receive its cash value.

Cash Value

Retiree continues to receive $1,667/month Option 1 income.

not make this decision before you have applied for a life insurance policy and it has been issued.

Early Retirement: Yes or No?

In an effort to reduce salary expenses, many companies are offering their employees early retirement packages. Should you be offered one of these plans, keep in mind that they are designed with the employer's best interests in mind. Early retirement plans are designed to save the company money — and most don't do you any favors, financially speaking. While retiring early may have some psychological appeal, if you are offered an early retirement package consider the following factors carefully before making your decision.

Years to "natural" retirement and expected income. How many years will you work before natural retirement? What is your expected income during that time? You may find that the early retirement package doesn't look nearly as favorable as it originally did, when you total your expected salary over the next 10 or 12 years.

Your life expectancy. Even though your own mortality may be unpleasant to think about, it's important that you realize how long your retirement funds will have to provide your financial needs. If you retire at age 53 and your life expectancy at that age is 83, then you may have 30 years left to support yourself on a fixed income. And if you are still alive at age 83, statistics indicate you could have another 8 years to live: so it turns out you should have planned for a 38-year retirement.

Inflation. What will inflation do to your retirement dollars prior to your death? If you retire now on a fixed income of $1,600 per month and factor in a 4 percent rate of inflation, after 20 years that $1,600 will only be worth $707 in today's dollars. Can you afford to live on that amount?

Potential for layoff. Is there a likelihood that you will be laid off anyway if you don't take early retirement? If your company is going through financial difficulties and layoffs in your area are imminent, an early retirement may be the safest and most financially sound way to "get while the gettin's good."

Other funds at your disposal. What other funds will be available at retirement time? If you have been investing wisely or if you have retirement income due you from a previous place of employment, per-haps your present employer's retirement package isn't too important. In that case, you may not want to retire, even if a layoff is possible. You may choose to take the risk, since you have other retirement assets.

Employment after retirement. Is there another job available, at another company, that will pay the same salary you're currently receiv-ing? Then consider taking an early retirement package from your cur-rent employer. Be aware, however, that it is difficult for most of us to find employment at the same salary range when we're in our high-income fifties. Be sure about that next job (and its security) before you depend on it for income over the next 10 years or so.

Summary

Retirement should be a time to reap the rewards of all the hard work you've done in your earning years. But to live your retirement years to their fullest, take advantage of as many of the retirement plans as are available to you: 401(k)s, IRAs, defined benefit pension plans, and profit sharing plans are just a few of the ways you can prepare for your leisure years. When you understand the benefits of tax-deferred accu-mulation of capital, you will be enthused and inspired to put away all you can in these plans.

When it comes time to take the money out, take a long hard look at your payment options. Will a lump sum distribution work best for you, or would you prefer monthly payments? Consider the payment options too: life, joint and survivorship, or joint and reduced survivorship. Which of these options will best suit your family's financial needs at retirement and for the years to come?

Carefully scrutinize any early retirement packages you're offered. They may seem attractive initially, but factor in inflation, the number of years left in your life expectancy, and other available income into your equation.

SECRETS IN ACTION

After working for the Power Company for 20 years, Cameron Eldridge was offered an early retirement package at age 55. The package was 60 percent of his salary ($45,000 per year) for life plus a $2,000 bonus for each year of service. Cameron was in good health and had planned to work until age 65. But this offer sounded attractive. It would give him time to travel with his wife Margaret, visit their children, and enjoy their hobbies: gardening and golf. After discussing it with Margaret, Cameron decided to accept the offer. After all, he'd be receiving $2,250 per month for life, plus a $40,000 bonus.

After he retired, he discussed his retirement with a financial advisor. The planner had sobering news for him. He told him that at 5 percent inflation, his $2,250 per month would only be worth $624 in today's purchasing power in 25 years, and if he lived to be 85, in 30 years it would only be worth $482.

Cameron began to think he made a terrible mistake in accepting the offer — except that one month later, many of Cameron's coworkers were laid off. If Cameron hadn't accepted the offer, he would have been laid off as well.

Cameron's financial advisor showed him how to harness the power of time with his $40,000 bonus. After 10 years with a 10 percent return, Cameron would have $103,749 and his pension (then worth $1,347 in purchasing power through inflation) could be augmented by a 12 percent annual withdrawal from his $103,749, giving him $12,450 per year extra. This would help support his standard of living for the next 10 years; then he could increase his withdrawal amount to 15 or 20 percent and, provided he maintained a 10 percent return, would not deplete his principal in his lifetime.

NINETEEN

Gold, Glitter, and Glitz
Tangible Assets and Exotic Investments

N ow we come to the upper levels of our Success Triangle™ — Tangible Assets and Exotic Investments. Most of the investments we have talked about in this book, with the exception of real estate investments, involve ownership of *financial* or *intangible assets* — marketable paper documents such as stocks, bonds, and cash — rather than ownership of actual physical items. *Tangible assets* include real estate, precious metals, rare coins, precious gemstones, other collectibles, and other commodities with potential investment value.

For our purposes, we will limit this discussion to those tangible assets that are portable (thus excluding real estate) and that are of widespread interest to the general public. To further simplify our discussion, we will differentiate tangible assets into two loosely defined categories: conventional tangible asset investments and exotic tangible assets. In our *conventional tangible asset investment* category, we include those assets that are readily accessible to the average investor, for which there are well-established markets and that have well-defined standards to which valuation is tied. These assets include precious metals, rare coins, and gemstones.

In our *exotic tangible asset* category, we don't mean time-shares in a tropical resort in Bali. Exotic in our sense means outlandish or intriguingly unusual: investments in collectible tangible asset items such as oriental rugs, fine art, antiques, postage stamps, Chinese ceramics, sports cards, rare books, and — yes — even dinosaur fossils.

"Let us not be too particular. It is better to have old second-hand diamonds than none at all."

– Mark Twain

And, for lack of a better place to put them, we have included a brief discussion of derivatives under exotic investments.

By now you should know that a good investment provides a good return over time. It is easily marketable, meaning its current market value can readily be converted to cash. The items we place in the exotic tangible asset category do not fit neatly into this description. So we're going to say that if you don't complete the highest tier of your Success Triangle™, you're still OK in our book. We say this because these exotic tangible assets may be difficult to valuate and market, and when looked at purely from an investment standpoint, they are riskier than most of the other investments we have discussed. Indeed, in many cases our exotic tangible assets are not owned primarily as investments in the traditional sense — people own them because they are hobbies. When looked at this way, they can be considered *lifestyle assets*, not investments. However, we are not attempting to downplay the fact that many people have accumulated collections that are worth fortunes.

Tangible asset investments are especially appealing to many people because of the richness, beauty, rarity, and mystique associated with them. Ownership of a tangible asset such as a Renoir painting or an 1836 Christian Gobrecht silver dollar offers an emotional feeling of pride of ownership that we just can't imagine someone obtaining through ownership in mutual fund shares. Many collectibles are cultural artifacts from the past with rich historic significance. Aside from their sensual appeal there are some good reasons for you to diversify your investment portfolio by adding tangible assets.

As investments, tangible assets have usually performed well during periods of high inflation, which can be quite damaging to financial assets. When investor confidence goes down, the prices of financial assets follow, but the desire to own tangible assets increases. During the high inflation of the 1970s, tangible assets outperformed financial assets and over the long term, even during periods of normal inflation rates, tangibles have generally kept pace with, or exceeded, inflation. However, short term the investment performance of tangibles can be quite volatile.

Tangible assets offer freedom from government control and have an established history of long-term appreciation. As part of a dwindling supply (like rare coins and collectibles) there is generally an increasing demand for them. Tangible assets are reasonably portable (except for some large pieces of artwork and sculpture); they provide an anonymity of ownership (wealth can be stored secretly without record-keeping or reporting requirements), and they have international value and liquidity.

The Success Triangle

In addition, you can take advantage of tax deferral through ownership of tangible assets. You don't owe any taxes on the appreciation of your investment until you sell the asset and realize a profit, or taxes can be postponed indefinitely if you reinvest your sale proceeds in similar assets under the like-kind exchange rules (see Chapter 15).

Unfortunately, not all of these benefits apply to every kind of tangible investment. For example, the markets for certain tangibles may be created and driven by short-term fads rather than long-term interest. What is hot today may get really hot tomorrow, and then really cold for many years to come. Generally, you must sell a tangible asset before you can realize any return on it. Tangibles don't pay interest or dividends; therefore, your entire potential for profit is dependent upon the asset increasing in market value. When buying tangibles, you will usually be paying the retail price and when selling you will usually receive the wholesale price.

Conventional Tangible Asset Investments

We have included three major types of tangible assets in this category that merit further attention: types that offer investors many of the benefits we've just described. They are precious metals, rare U. S. coins, and gemstones.

Precious Metals

Gold, silver, and platinum are the most popular precious metal investments. These precious metals also have many other uses. Gold is used primarily in jewelry and to a much lesser degree in electronics and dentistry. Silver and platinum, unlike gold, have several important industrial uses. By far the most important use of silver is in photography with relatively small amounts also being used in electronics and jewelry. Platinum is used as a catalyst, for example in automobile catalytic converters.

Gold is the most well known of the precious metals. Early civilizations prized gold for its beauty long before they had developed much use for metals. It was used as early as 9000 B.C. in decorative art. In addition, gold and silver have been used for centuries as direct currency. With the advent of paper currency, gold was still used by most countries as a *currency reserve*, meaning paper money was directly convertible into gold. The original *gold standard*, as it was known, was gradually abandoned and the U.S. dollar eventually emerged as the principal unit of international monetary transactions. In 1934 President

FIGURE 19–1

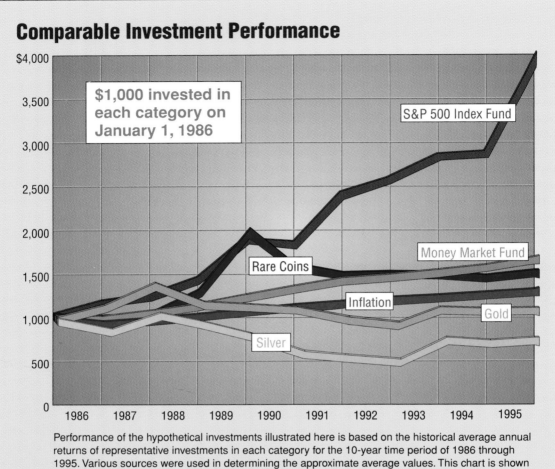

Comparable Investment Performance

$1,000 invested in each category on January 1, 1986

S&P 500 Index Fund

Rare Coins

Money Market Fund

Inflation

Gold

Silver

Performance of the hypothetical investments illustrated here is based on the historical average annual returns of representative investments in each category for the 10-year time period of 1986 through 1995. Various sources were used in determining the approximate average values. This chart is shown to compare performance of the various investment categories, and actual performance of specific investments may have differed from those illustrated here.

Roosevelt fixed the price of gold at $35 per ounce and imposed restrictions on private gold ownership in the United States; a private citizen desiring to own gold could do so only in the form of jewelry or gold bullion coins minted prior to 1933. On January 1, 1975, these restrictions were completely lifted and gold has since traded on the open market, with dramatically fluctuating prices.

Precious metals have historically been used as hedges against inflation. Generally, as the rate of inflation increases so does the price of precious metals; when inflation decreases, precious metal prices fall too. A few comparisons relating the price of gold to the cost of consumer goods are interesting. Throughout the eighteenth, nineteenth, an twentieth centuries an ounce of gold would buy a well-made man's suit, 200 ounces of gold would buy a family home throughout most of the last 200 years, and 25 ounces would buy a Model T Ford in 1927 or would still buy many of today's new car models.

During times of depression, precious metals gain appeal, because people fear losing their money and look to precious metals for increased stability and security. Gold remains the world's most marketable and anonymous currency; in fact many people still believe that gold is the "ultimate" currency. During times of political turmoil or wars, gold is highly desired as a vehicle for maintaining and transporting wealth.

The purity of alloyed gold is expressed by the *karat system*, where the percent of gold by weight is given as a fraction of 24. Pure gold is 24 karat, whereas 18-karat gold is 18/24, or 75 percent gold by weight. This *karat*, spelled with a "k", is not to be confused with the *carat* weight of gemstones, which begins with a "c".

Gold can be purchased as gold bullion, in bars or wafers, or as gold bullion coins such as the Canadian Gold Maple Leaf, South African Krugerands, Australian Kangaroo Nugget, and the American Gold Eagle series. These coins are issued by the various governments that guarantee their gold content and are intended as vehicles in which the metal can be traded in known amounts and purity. The value of these coins is only slightly above that of their precious metal content. For the small investor, gold coins are usually preferable to bullion because gold can be purchased in a smaller amounts in coins and because bullion presents a storage issue. If bullion leaves the possession of the dealer or bank that sold it initially, it may need to be assayed (analyzed to quantify its metal content and purity) before it can be resold. In addition to commissions, storage costs, and assay costs, individuals taking possession of precious metals may also incur sales tax. Some of these costs can be eliminated or reduced if the dealer retains possession of the bullion, in which case the dealer issues a *gold deposit certificate* to the buyer.

The precious metals market is a fickle one, as many investors have discovered. After watching the price of gold soar from under $200 an ounce in 1977 to more than $850 an ounce in early 1980, many investors joined the gold rush, only to see their investment — their supposed hedge against inflation — lose over 50 percent of its value in the next two years. In 1981 gold was worth about $450 and in 1985 it dipped below $300 an ounce. After a rise in 1987 to $450, its value today is again down below $400 an ounce. Silver prices have fluctuated wildly, too, from a high of over $50 an ounce in early 1980, when the Hunt brothers made their failed bid to control the world's silver market, to around $5 an ounce today.

Do we believe the prices of gold and silver will ever rise to their previous peaks? Eventually. But that's small consolation to the investors who plunked down millions of dollars in 1979 and 1980. It will be a long time before they recoup their investments, let alone see any appreciation from them.

Whether or not an investor profits in precious metals (or other tangible investments) is completely dependent on future price increases. Speculators who actively trade in precious metals try to use market timing, because the only way to make money is through capital gains. However, as you may recall from our discussion of mutual fund timing, timing is nothing more than an educated guess. Even the most astute investors have a dismal record in accurately predicting market fluctuations — in stocks, mutual funds, gold, or anything else.

Therefore, as with other equity investments, we like to look at investments in precious metals as long-term propositions — the old buy-and-hold philosophy. We aren't great at making short-term predictions, but we do know that historical facts show, especially if we should again experience high inflation, that a little precious metal in your investment portfolio might prove valuable.

If you are interested in participating in the precious metals market, especially if you require income from your portfolio, you may want to consider stocks in mining companies or a mutual fund that invests in mines or mining shares, instead of buying and holding the actual metals. Keep in mind that mining stocks generally move in the same direction as precious metals prices. And when the price of precious metals moves, the price of mining stocks usually moves more dramatically because of increasing profit margins versus the fixed costs of mining the metals. Because mining stocks often move in the opposite direction of the market as a whole, they can reduce the overall volatility of your portfolio.

Rare U.S. Coins

Coins, of interest to collectors and historians for many decades, have more recently become popular investments. The study or collection of coins is called *numismatics*. A coin collector is a *numismatist*.

The value of a coin is derived from many factors, including its intrinsic beauty, historical interest, condition, metal content, age, and mostly, its rarity. The rarest coins, not necessarily the oldest ones, generally command the highest prices.

Rarity is determined by many factors. One important factor is the original number of a coin that was minted — obviously the more coins that were minted, the more that are apt to survive. Through the passage of time, coins are damaged, melted down for their metal, worn through circulation, or lost. Thus the higher grades become more and more rare.

Countless varieties of coins have been minted by hundreds of issuing authorities throughout the world for about the past 2,500 years. Although many of these coins have collector and investment value, our discussion will be limited to U.S. coins because they hold the greatest interest for our typical investors. Investors in rare U.S. coins are generally most interested in coins minted before 1934, which are in uncirculated or proof condition and of grade MS-64 or Proof-64 or better. The United States government melted down large quantities of coins in 1934 which contributed much to the rarity of pre-1934 mintage.

An estimated 20 million collectors in this country and four to five times that many more worldwide form the basis of the market in U.S. rare coins. The number of collectors continues to grow, and this fact coupled with increasing investor interest has fueled a growing demand for rare U.S. coins. As these millions of collectors and investors compete for a dwindling supply of rare coins, prices move upward. Whenever market conditions cause the price of a rare coin to fall, collectors who are anxious to acquire additional coins often step up to buy at the decreased price, which tends to push the price back up. Market activity provides price support.

Rare U.S. coins have fared much better as investments than their intrinsic precious metals. Following innovative improvements in grading, pricing, and marketing of rare coins over the last few years, new markets have emerged and investor interest has soared.

In 1980 when gold was trading for $700 an ounce, the bid price for a $20 Saint Gaudens Gold MS-65 was more than $2,000. Even though the price dipped to $1,800 in 1982, it soared to $12,000 in 1988 and has a current value today of over $9,000.

Grading Rare U. S. Coins   Rare U.S. coins are a better investment than many foreign coins because of an independent grading system that ensures the condition of the coin. In 1948 Dr. William Sheldon, a well-known numismatist, developed the Sheldon Scale for grading coins. He assigned coins a grade between 1 and 70 with the idea that a 70 would be worth 70 times as much as a 1. A grade 70 is a coin that is in absolutely perfect, uncirculated condition (70s are virtually

FIGURE 19–2

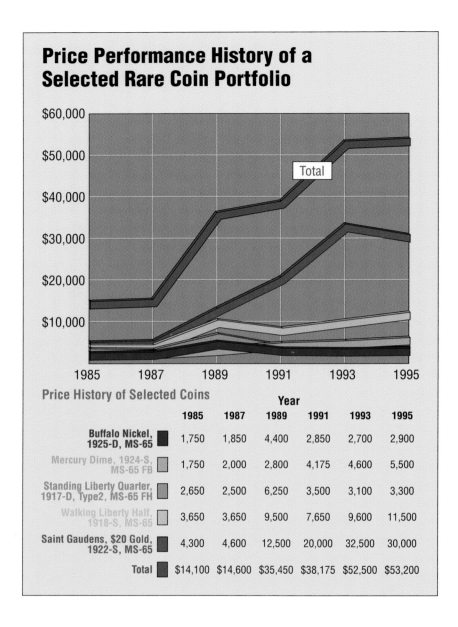

Price Performance History of a Selected Rare Coin Portfolio

Price History of Selected Coins

	Year					
	1985	**1987**	**1989**	**1991**	**1993**	**1995**
Buffalo Nickel, 1925-D, MS-65	1,750	1,850	4,400	2,850	2,700	2,900
Mercury Dime, 1924-S, MS-65 FB	1,750	2,000	2,800	4,175	4,600	5,500
Standing Liberty Quarter, 1917-D, Type2, MS-65 FH	2,650	2,500	6,250	3,500	3,100	3,300
Walking Liberty Half, 1918-S, MS-65	3,650	3,650	9,500	7,650	9,600	11,500
Saint Gaudens, $20 Gold, 1922-S, MS-65	4,300	4,600	12,500	20,000	32,500	30,000
Total	$14,100	$14,600	$35,450	$38,175	$52,500	$53,200

nonexistent) and a 1 is a coin that is so worn it is barely recognizabie. Sheldon's idea that his scale would represent the relative value of coins no longer applies because, for example, a 67 could be worth 30 times a 60 in today's market. However, in spite of this, Dr. Sheldon's scale has been refined and adopted as the industry standard in grading.

FIGURE 19–3

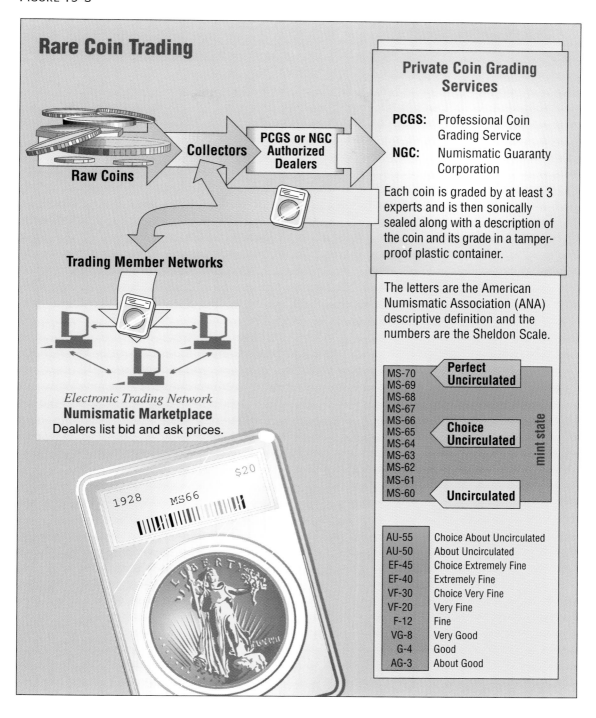

Rare Coin Trading

Collectors

Raw Coins

PCGS or NGC Authorized Dealers

Private Coin Grading Services

PCGS: Professional Coin Grading Service

NGC: Numismatic Guaranty Corporation

Each coin is graded by at least 3 experts and is then sonically sealed along with a description of the coin and its grade in a tamper-proof plastic container.

The letters are the American Numismatic Association (ANA) descriptive definition and the numbers are the Sheldon Scale.

Trading Member Networks

Electronic Trading Network
Numismatic Marketplace
Dealers list bid and ask prices.

1928   MS66 $20

MS-70	**Perfect Uncirculated**	
MS-69		
MS-68		
MS-67		
MS-66		
MS-65	**Choice Uncirculated**	mint state
MS-64		
MS-63		
MS-62		
MS-61		
MS-60	**Uncirculated**	

AU-55	Choice About Uncirculated
AU-50	About Uncirculated
EF-45	Choice Extremely Fine
EF-40	Extremely Fine
VF-30	Choice Very Fine
VF-20	Very Fine
F-12	Fine
VG-8	Very Good
G-4	Good
AG-3	About Good

Two independent grading firms, the Professional Coin Grading Service (PCGS) and the Numismatic Guaranty Corporation of America (NGC) have both adopted the Sheldon Numerical Grading System to describe the condition of a coin. Each firm uses three to five expert graders to evaluate and assign the appropriate grade to each submitted coin, which is then labeled and sonically sealed in an inert tamper-proof plastic case.

A significant risk faced in the past by rare coin investors was that coins purchased might be below the represented grade, and as mentioned above, a small difference in grade can make a profound difference in value. Establishment of an active and credible market requires that the coins investors buy are the grade they are represented to be. These third-party grading services have created an environment in which consumers can participate in rare coin investing with the confidence that they will get what they pay for. In fact, grades assigned by these services are considered to be so reliable that many investors are now willing to purchase the graded and sealed coins sight unseen. The grading and certification process has done much to protect investors who were previously victimized by the intentional or accidental misrepresentation of the grade.

Benefits of Investing in Rare Coins   Rare coins offer the investor some unusual advantages. Your purchases are discreet and confidential, and there are no reporting requirements or cumbersome government regulations. However, we do advise that you keep receipts of your purchases. Unlike some of the other collectibles, rare coins are a highly marketable asset. Your graded and certified coins can be readily sold through dealers at current market prices. Unlike bullion, the supply of rare coins is very limited, and their scarcity is steadily increasing due to coins being damaged or lost.

Rare coin investing provides tax benefits as well. There are no taxes to pay while you own your portfolio, and if your coin investment profits are rolled over into more coins, you receive the full benefits of a tax-deferred "like-kind" exchange. In fact, these transfers are totally confidential and do not require any government reporting. No taxes are due on your profits until you liquidate your holdings and report your net profit as income.

Rare coins are easily stored (we recommend a safe-deposit box), need little space, and require no maintenance. In addition, each coin has its own unique place in history and the coins are truly pieces of art that can be enjoyed for their beauty.

A major reason to purchase rare coins is for diversification in your overall portfolio. According to some Wall Street investment surveys, rare coins have been one of the top-performing investments over the last 20 years. With the increasing investor activity, it seems likely that rare coins will remain a viable investment option.

Investing and profiting in rare coins on your own may require knowledge and experience. But, reputable dealers who sell coins that have been professionally graded and encapsulated by one of the services mentioned above can advise the average investor on assembling a rare coin portfolio that has good investment performance potential. However, try to keep the portfolio diverse. Coins should be purchased from different years, denominations, and metals, because it's difficult to accurately predict which coins investors will be paying top dollar for in the future.

Like nearly all investments, the rare coin market is subject to market cycles. Rare coins should be purchased for a minimum 3-to-5-year holding period. Investors should purchase coins from only reputable dealers. Insist that any coins you purchase have been graded and sealed by one of the professional grading services.

We believe that investment in rare U.S. coins will continue to offer good long-term returns primarily because of the increasing collector and investor base, the dwindling supply, and a well-established market. When you utilize the services of reputable dealers (check them out), numismatic expertise on your part is not required for successful investing. Today, many financial advisors recommend using U.S. rare coins for between 5 to 15 percent of your investment dollars.

Diamonds and Colored Gemstones

Perhaps nothing has fascinated investors as much as the allure and visual appeal of diamonds and colored gemstones. Throughout history, gemstones have been a symbol of wealth and power and have been prized possessions by royalty and common folk alike. Many cultures have ascribed mystical or spiritual powers to gemstones. Gems were useful as a preservation and transport medium for wealth as they were valued throughout the world.

More recently, advertising campaigns have vigorously promoted gems as the ultimate symbol of eternal love and lasting value — this is particularly true of diamonds. Many Americans today will either buy or receive a diamond engagement or wedding ring, and some will own several diamonds or colored gemstones during their lifetimes.

As investments in the traditional Wall Street sense, gemstones are relative newcomers. We will say right up front that, although gemstone investments have a history of providing respectable long-term investment returns, we discourage most people from investing in gemstones.

Diamonds Diamonds are an investment gem whose mystique and rarity date back many centuries. Yet, rarity is only one of the myths associated with diamonds. Although diamond cartels have long promoted them as rare and valuable stones, they are actually very plentiful. In truth, it is the tightly controlled *distribution of diamonds* by these cartels that perpetuates this myth of rarity.

Approximately 65 to 85 percent of the world's diamond distribution is controlled by the famous South African De Beers Consolidated Mines, Ltd., and their selling arm, The Central Selling Organization (CSO). The other major producers have historically cooperated with De Beers, because what is good for De Beers is good for the diamond industry.

Colored Gemstones Colored gemstones are classified into two broad categories: *noble* (which includes rubies, golden and blue sapphires, and emeralds) and *precious* (such as aquamarine, topaz, tanzanite, tsavorite, and tourmaline). Relative to diamonds, colored gemstones are much rarer, but the market is not nearly as well established, monopolized, and controlled as the diamond market.

Grading Gemstones In an effort to accurately describe the quality of gemstones, several international grading systems have been developed. The Gemological Institute of America (GIA) system has gained international acceptance and is the most widely used system in America. The GIA grading laboratory provides a certificate with each stone which gives precise information to fully describe it and verify its authenticity, and a plot that shows the location and type of inclusions and blemishes. Both diamonds and colored gemstones are graded according to four criteria called "The Four Cs."

Carat weight is the first C. Originally, the weight of a carob seed or a grain of wheat was known as a carat, but in 1913 this variable weight was standardized to 0.2 grams (200 milligrams). The largest single diamond ever found, the Cullinan, was discovered in South Africa in 1905 and weighed 3,106 carats (that's about 20 ounces!). The famous deep-blue Hope Diamond, weighing 44.5 carats is in the Smithsonian Institution in Washington D.C. Because the carat is a unit of weight and not size, different types of stones of the same carat

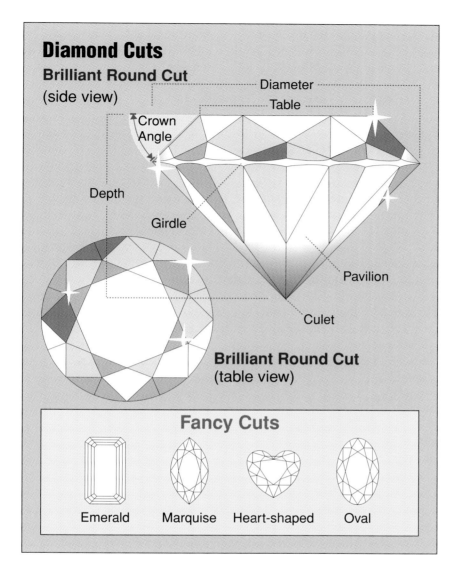

FIGURE 19–4

Diamond Cuts

Brilliant Round Cut
(side view)

Diameter

Table

Crown
Angle

Depth

Girdle

Pavilion

Culet

Brilliant Round Cut
(table view)

Fancy Cuts

Emerald   Marquise   Heart-shaped   Oval

weight may be different sizes: for example, a one-carat emerald is larger than a one-carat diamond and a one-carat ruby is smaller than the diamond. As the carat weight of a stone increases, the price per carat usually increases dramatically for the same quality stone. This is because larger gemstones are much rarer than smaller ones.

The second C is the *cut*. Cut is very important, because it gives the stone its *fire* or brilliance. Properly cut, a round, brilliant diamond has

FIGURE 19–5

GIA Color Scale for Diamonds

D, E, F	G, H, I	J, K, L, M	N, O, P, Q, R	S, T, U, V, W, X, Y, Z	Fancies
Colorless	Near Colorless	Faint Yellow	Very Light Yellow	Light Yellow	Various Colors

⌐···· Investment Grade ····⌐

58 equally proportioned facets (flat polished surfaces cut on a gemstone) to adequately reflect the light. The depth must also be cut correctly in proportion to the width or it will not properly refract light. The round brilliant cut is considered the best cut for investment grade stones as it displays the qualities of the stone to its maximum although fancy cuts (oval, pear-shaped, marquise, heart-shaped, etc.), when well done, don't have much adverse affect on the stone's value. In colored gemstones, the cut will affect both the depth of color and the liveliness of the stone.

Faulty cuts include off-centered or misaligned cutlet, sloping table, poor symmetry, extra facets, girdle too thick, and broken cutlet. Fancy shapes may be too wide or narrow or have an improperly cut pavilion.

The best cut stones have the highest value per carat. Various defects in the cut will adversely affect the stone's value; how much, is dependent on the severity and number of faults in the cut.

The third C is *color*. The finest diamonds are colorless and clear, and the lesser grades have varying tints of dull yellow, brown, or gray. An entire color scale exists between the two extremes. Discolored diamonds are not to be confused with *fancies*, rare diamonds that come in a variety of intense colors and shades. Color is also important in the other gemstones that are evaluated for hue, intensity, tone and distribution of color, but standardized systems for evaluating their colors are not yet as widely used within the industry as those for diamonds.

Clarity, is the fourth and final C. Clarity refers to the presence or absence of internal *flaws* (inclusions) in the stone and external flaws (blemishes). To determine the GIA grade a gemstone is viewed with a jeweler's scope providing 10X magnification and examined for cracks, inclusions, or other little flaws.

FIGURE 19–6

GIA Clarity Scale for Diamonds

FL	IF	VVS-1, VVS-2	VS-1, VS-2	SI-1, SI-2	I-1, I-2
Flawless	Internally Flawless	Very, very slight inclusions	Very slight inclusions	Slight inclusions	Imperfect

Investment Grade .... Quality Jewelry

Stones that are flawless are considered the most valuable investments, more valuable than stones that have more flaws and discoloration in them. Various locations of flaws within a stone will also have a different impact on the stone's value. Flawless colored gemstones are even rarer than flawless diamonds, but in the case of colored gemstones, small and unobtrusively positioned flaws are not nearly as detrimental to the stone's value.

Pros and Cons of Investing in Gemstones   Gemstones, like other tangible assets, generally perform well during periods of high inflation and when investor confidence in the stock market is low. Gems are easily moved and stored, and can be used and enjoyed in jewelry without destroying their value. Like rare coins they provide anonymity of ownership, freedom from government regulation, value worldwide, and tax-deferred increases in value until you sell the gems and keep the profits.

However, successful investing in gemstones requires specialized knowledge, as there are many possible pitfalls for the unwary or uninformed. Determining the quality and authenticity of gems, sometimes challenging for experts, may be impossible for novices. The greatest problem investors encounter is the difficulty in distinguishing real stones from synthetic ones in the flood of lifelike imitations on the market. Unfortunately, outright intentional fraud or innocent misrepresentation of quality and authenticity is not uncommon.

Investors need a relatively large cash outlay and should plan for a holding period of at least 10 years. Investors buy at retail and sell at wholesale with a differential of 15 to 30 percent or more depending on the value of the individual stone. Even larger markups are frequently imposed on less expensive stones. Assessing the current value of a stone can be quite difficult and gems are not liquid — it could take weeks, months, or even years to market gemstones at reasonable prices.

Investors in diamonds or gemstones must demand that the stones *be investment grade.* We're not talking about those used in most of the jewelry we wear — rings, watches, necklaces, an so forth. We're talking about the *highest quality gems.*

You will find that very few diamonds and gemstones are of investment quality. Of all the diamonds mined, 80 percent are used for industrial purposes, over 18 percent are used in jewelry, and less than 2 percent are of investment quality.

Diamond prices are quite volatile, although over the past 20 years investment-grade diamonds have demonstrated average appreciation rates of about four to ten percent. Like precious metals and rare coins, the only opportunity for profit in diamond and gemstone investing is through appreciation. Unlike rare coins, more diamonds and gemstones are discovered in mines every day.

If you feel that you'd like to add diamonds or gemstones to diversify your portfolio, there are a couple of factors that you must consider very carefully before investing your money. Deal only with the most reputable persons and firms. Investors without considerable experience in this area should deal only with those dealers who are affiliated with trade groups or national gemological societies.

No governmental licensing is required to sell gemstones, and an unfortunate consequence of this fact is that many slick scoundrels have entered the marketplace and preyed upon unwary buyers. And by all means, remember this: never buy diamonds or gemstones over the telephone, no matter how convincing the salesperson is!

Determining whether you are getting a good stone is nearly impossible for a layperson. Insist that your stone be graded by an independent gemological laboratory such as the Gemological Institute of America, the acknowledged industry leader. Keep in mind, though, that the grading of stones is not an exact science.

Again, as exciting, interesting, and romantic as gemstones may be, we are not big fans of putting your investment dollars in gemstones. There are too many variables that affect the market, and historically, long-term investment returns on gemstones have lagged behind many less risky and more traditional investments. Considerable knowledge and skill is a real asset, if not a necessity, to anyone considering investing in gemstones. For those who like the appeal of investing in gemstones, consider a holding period of at least 10 years and be aware that it won't be easy to sell your stones at a good price when you are ready to liquidate your investment.

Exotic Tangible Assets

Exotic tangible assets include a wide variety of items. Among the better known are postage stamps, Chinese ceramics, oriental rugs, rare books, sports cards, comic books, antiques of many kinds (furniture, automobiles, dolls), art (old masters, prints, sculpture), cast iron toys, and many others. Nostalgic items are becoming increasingly popular.

Collectibles

Collectibles generally share one or more of the following characteristics: rarity, popularity, craftsmanship, aesthetic beauty, antiquity, and interest in history or culture.

Although some investors can profit in collectibles, one must usually gain considerable expertise in a specific area before any expectation of regular gains can be predicted. Prices of collectibles are very inconsistent and the quality of an individual item may be difficult to determine. As in anything else, there are many reputable dealers and experts who will assist you, and there are many not-so-honest dealers, as well. For the uninformed, the pitfalls are abundant. Therefore, it is prudent to carefully study and evaluate the subject area before you invest.

For most people, collectibles provide interesting and educational hobbies; the investment side is secondary, although we acknowledge that many people have accumulated substantial wealth through ownership and investment in collectibles.

As with other tangible asset investments, the only way to profit in collectibles is through price appreciation and you must sell the item to realize the profit. Many factors contribute to the value of collectibles, the least of which is not the emotional desire that a potential buyer feels for a certain item. There is little accurate information that tells us the investment performance of collectibles, although Salomon Brothers has previously reported on the investment performance of Chinese ceramics and old masters' artworks.

Derivatives — "Exotics" from Wall Street

Derivatives certainly are not tangible assets, but we've placed them in this chapter because many people who don't fully understand them perceive them as being rather exotic.

What are these mysterious creatures anyway? They are mentioned frequently in the press, but it's difficult to actually find a clear definition. We'll give you one here. *Derivatives* are financial instruments whose value is derived from some underlying asset or whose performance is tied to an underlying index that derives its value from underlying assets. They are used primarily as a leveraging tool to hedge against interest rate fluctuations and currency exchange rate fluctuations.

The problem with pinning down derivatives is that they travel by so many names. There are the traditional derivatives — options, futures, and currency forwards that have existed for some time and are actively traded on the exchanges or over-the-counter markets. Other well-known derivatives include collateralized mortgage obligations (CMOs) and Real Estate Mortgage Investment Conduits (REMICs). More recently, the investment banking industry has created some "exotic" or "complex" derivatives from traditional securities such as bonds. These include interest-only strips (IOs) , principal-only strips (POs), inverse floaters, and indexed securities. Sound confusing? They are. But, they can be useful instruments and have firmly established their niche in the investment world.

We firmly believe that investing in derivatives should be left to the pros; however, many of us are already unknowingly investing in derivatives via our mutual funds, many of which use them in their portfolios. Although derivatives have received some recent bad press, this should not alarm you. The use of derivatives in a mutual fund's portfolio may increase the overall yield, if they can be used within the fund's expected risk level. In fact, certain appropriate derivative strategies can actually reduce the portfolio risk. Mutual funds use derivatives for the following reasons:

1. **As a hedging tool.** International stock-and-bond funds regularly use currency options and futures to hedge their currency risk in trading overseas. Fixed-income securities may also use derivatives as a hedge to reduce interest rate risk — they can buy or sell Treasury bond futures without actually selling any of the bonds in their portfolios.

2. **As substitutes for the actual securities.** The derivatives provide the same performance as the underlying securities but it is cheaper to buy the derivatives than the actual securities. For example, rather than buying Treasury bonds, the fund buys Treasury bond futures. Using stock market index futures is a lower cost way to invest in the market for stock funds.

3. **To maintain liquidity.** An index stock fund might use stock futures, requiring just a small deposit to maintain full exposure to the stock market while actually keeping some of their cash on hand to meet redemptions. That avoids the transaction

costs incurred when having to sell individual stocks to meet redemptions. Also, especially during a bull market, a fund manager with considerable cash coming in at a rapid rate could use derivatives to get the cash invested quickly.

4. **To provide yield enhancement.** Derivatives are added to some fund portfolios to increase their yield, although at more risk. For example, since the yields on short-term government bond funds are similar because their investment choices are very limited, a fund manager seeking higher yields might add derivatives from within its category to differentiate their funds from other, similar funds.

5. **To take a position on the direction of certain interest rates.** For example, a fund manager expecting long-term interest rates to rise might buy derivatives tied to less volatile short-term interest rates, to use as leverage in producing the same potential gain (or loss) as if long-term bonds had been purchased.

Of course, some derivatives pose substantial risks. When rising interest rates cause the resale prices of all long-term bonds to drop, the derivatives based in these securities respond in an exaggerated way. A good part of their volatility comes from their leverage aspect; like options and futures contracts, derivatives control a lot of assets with a small amount of money. Leveraging magnifies the impact of derivatives whenever there are price fluctuations in the underlying securities. Overuse and misuse of derivatives can make an investment portfolio especially vulnerable to movements in interest rates, causing disproportionate drops in net asset values.

Summary

Tangible assets and exotic investments may or may not have a place in your portfolio. Three types of tangibles assets — precious metals, rare U.S. coins, and gemstones — might be considered, because they have generally been able to keep pace with or exceed the inflation rate in the past. Many tangible asset investments have a long and well-established history of appreciation. Of these, we believe that precious metals or rare coins are well suited for many people, but investing in gemstones should be left to those who have a strong interest and have acquired specialized knowledge in the area.

Many collectibles should be considered hobbies, rather than serious investments. For example, if you are interested in Southwestern art and have the extra money to spend, definitely invest in it. But don't expect to feather your retirement nest egg that way. Exotic tangible assets are risky for the average investor without specialized knowledge in the area. And there may or may not be a market for them in the future.

Consider each tangible asset investment on its own merits, and before investing, ask yourself three questions. Does this investment provide a good return over time? Is it liquid? Is there a large market of interested investors?

Derivatives are financial instruments that are derived from another underlying investment. Derivatives enable investors to employ leverage and are generally used within a portfolio primarily as a tool to hedge against interest and currency exchange rate fluctuations. Because of the leverage aspect, derivatives can pose risks. In spite of some recent bad press, we believe that proper use of derivatives in a mutual fund or money market portfolio has merit. We advise that investing in derivatives be reserved for the most sophisticated and experienced investors.

SECRETS IN ACTION

Linda Lee, an up-and-coming CPA with a prestigious Northwest accounting firm, is fascinated with diamonds. After ten years with her firm, she owns cash reserves, mutual funds, and contributes to her company pension program. Now she wants an out-of-the-ordinary investment that she can really get excited about.

One summer evening a salesman called to say that she was among a select group of professionals he was contacting to offer a "once-in-lifetime" investment. Then he quickly said, "For a limited time, my firm is offering an unusually low, introductory price on high-quality, investment-grade diamonds for new investors." Her first instinct was to hang up, but she was fascinated anytime the word diamonds came up.

The salesman explained that each diamond was of investment quality and carried a money-back guarantee if she were not completely satisfied. However, the guarantee would be honored only if the diamond was returned to his company still intact in its seal.

Each stone would be accompanied by a signed certificate of authenticity from the Southwest Gemological Institute of California (Linda had never heard of it). As she hesitated, the salesman again stressed the money-back guarantee.

Despite a pressing and convincing sales presentation, Linda decided to speak to her friend Tom, first, who happened to be an investment advisor.

"Never buy an investment such as diamonds over the telephone," Tom told her. He said persuasive salespeople often dupe inexperienced investors by selling them poor-quality diamonds at highly inflated prices. A certification by "gem experts" means nothing, and it is impossible to determine the real value of the stone if you couldn't remove the seal, he added.

Linda realized that diversifying into exotic investments required the expertise of knowledgeable professionals. She was relieved she had waited.

Financial Planning Extras
Putting Your Knowledge into Action

By now, you have probably developed a love affair with compound interest. Your understanding of what money can do has been changed forever. You have learned the seven secrets and understand how they work. You understand what it takes to build a sound financial house and how the different pieces interrelate.

Yet, no matter what you have heard and read about money, it still remains one of life's greatest mysteries. We hope this book has taken most of the mystery out of money for you. But will the seven secrets work for you? Will this knowledge help you become financially successful? You'll never know until you *try*.

Understanding a lot about money doesn't always change your financial life. Although the power to change begins in the mind, real change only occurs when knowledge is put into action.

We didn't write this book to teach you theory alone; we wrote it to provide the tools for successful money management. Will you use them? You have all you will ever need to achieve financial success right here in your hands.

In this final section, we talk about implementation. If you haven't already done so, this is the time to fill out your cash flow form and list your assets and liabilities. We've tried to make this process as easy as possible to accomplish on your own or with your financial advisor.

Success — There are many paths to the top of the mountain, but the view is always the same.
– Chinese Proverb

Chapters 20, 21, and 22 offer some interesting ideas and strategies about some key subjects that are frequently poorly understood or troublesome for many people. We think you will appreciate these chapters because they are packed with solid information about home equity management, college costs, and self-employment issues. In Chapter 23, you will take your list of goals from Chapter 1, the seven secrets, the Success Triangle™, and BEGIN. Getting away from the status quo is never easy. We know it takes courage, especially if you are feeling a bit skeptical of the unknown. Our best advice: just go for it.

If you have dreamed of being financially successful, and dared to believe it is actually possible, then now is the time to actually experience financial success. Will it come easily? No way. Will it require difficult decisions? Of course. Will it be fun? You bet.

Our final chapter puts wings to the dream.

Enjoy.

TWENTY

Cashing In on the Nest
Home Equity as a Source of Money

Your Best Investment?

What has been your best investment? When asked, most people respond, "My home!" Then they point to the equity they've built up in their homes over the years and the appreciation of their property as evidence.

"When I bought my home 15 years ago, I paid $74,000 for it," says one. "It's now worth $190,000." We'd say, "That looks like a pretty good investment — maybe." But if your home were subjected to the same scrutiny other investments usually undergo, we think you might not hold it in such high esteem as an investment.

For some reason, people are much more patient with their homes than they are with other investments. They can't check the price of their home in the daily paper. They tolerate periods of declining prices without raising an eyebrow, and accept minuscule returns on most of their asset dollars without a second thought. After all, the roof does keep the rain off their heads.

It's easy to overestimate a home's actual performance as an investment. For instance, in the example above, the $74,000 home appreciated to $190,000 in 15 years. It sounds like a good investment, at first. Now sharpen your focus and examine it more carefully. An increase in value from $74,000 to $190,000 in 15 years is an average annual appreciation rate of 6.5 percent. Not a terrible investment, if you paid cash.

"Homes aren't built to store cash, they are built to house people."
– Anonymous

In all likelihood, the home was financed, which means closing costs and mortgage payments for 15 years. And after 15 years, do you own the home? Not if the mortgage was a conventional 30-year mortgage. Fifteen years ago, in 1980, mortgage rates were a whopping 15 percent. Any savvy investor would have refinanced the home after mortgage rates dipped again. However, in this example, let's assume that you put 20 percent, or $14,800, down and financed the balance at 15 percent. After 180 monthly payments of $749, the balance on the mortgage is still $53,484.

Now, just what has happened in 15 years? You made a down payment of $14,800, and paid an additional $68,279 in monthly payments, for a total investment of $149,539. Is the house worth $190,000? Yes, upon sale this investment returns the value less the mortgage balance of $53,484. Therefore, the net proceeds from the sale are only $136,516 — $13,023 *less* than the total you paid into the house. Hmmm . . .

But that's not quite right; you and your family lived in it all that time, and if you hadn't, you would have had to pay rent elsewhere. Yes, there is value in a home that surpasses the value of a regular investment. You also had the homeowner's privileges of paying for all the taxes, insurance, making repairs, and the ongoing maintenance on this investment for the full 15 years.

Factor in all these things and the issue of return from your home investment gets pretty cloudy, doesn't it? If you don't already fully understand the differences and the relationships between the *value of your home* and your actual *equity in the home*, you will after reading the next several pages. Your *home equity*, at any point in time, is the current value of the home less any obligations (mortgages or home equity loans) that you have against it. You will see that your amount of equity in the home has nothing to do with the value of the home or how rapidly the home appreciates (or depreciates) in value.

How Does Home Equity Measure Up as an Investment?

When you examine the desirability of a prospective investment, the first three questions to ask are:

1. Is the investment liquid or readily marketable?
2. How safe is the investment? (What is its risk level?)
3. Does the investment provide a rate of return that is attractive when compared to other investment opportunities?

After generations of conditioning, it may be difficult to stop thinking about your home as the best investment of the century. You must separate the emotions surrounding home ownership from the financial aspects. Take a cold calculating look at the current actual dollar value of the equity you have in your home, and then apply the same tough criteria you would to any other investment situation. It's unrealistic to continue thinking of your home and your home equity with the same mind-set as when your ancestors chopped down trees for their log cabins. Because of today's tax considerations and economic complexities, you must carefully scrutinize every investment.

Is Home Equity Liquid?

Remember that we defined *liquidity* in Chapter 4 as your ability to access your money when it is needed. It also refers to how quickly an investment can be converted into cash without suffering a loss. Savings accounts and money market accounts are completely liquid. Stocks and bonds can be converted to cash within a few days, but because you could lose principal in the process if you sell when the market is down, these investments are considered *marketable* rather than *liquid*. In this regard, home equity is usually, though not always, marketable. Unlike stocks and bonds that are readily marketable, it could take many months to sell a home.

In the early 1980s, the city of Farmington, New Mexico, flourished with a booming economy fueled by oil and gas and the petroleum services industry. When the petroleum industry staggered, Farmington, like so many towns in Texas and Oklahoma, became a ghost of its former self. Within three years, unemployment was at a record high — close to 35 percent.

The residents of Farmington weren't bad people, nor did they buy poor real estate. To find new employment, people had to move, and there were so many homes on the market that a great number of them were turned back to the banks in foreclosure. Two of the state's largest savings and loan institutions folded under the pressure. Three years earlier, the possible collapse of the housing market would have been laughable. But, by 1984, it was nearly impossible for the residents of Farmington to convert their home equity into cash because their homes weren't marketable.

Is home equity liquid? Is it even readily marketable? No, it is not.

Is Home Equity Safe?

The residential real estate market is like any other market — it goes up and it comes down. A lot of people in the New England states watched much of their home equity vanish during the late 1980s and early

1990s. And more than 15,000 homes were turned back to the lenders in Houston, Texas, in the 1980s. That didn't happen because 15,000 families became deadbeats overnight. They simply couldn't make their mortgage payments because they had lost their jobs.

We know of one Houston family where the husband was earning more than $100,000 a year. They lived in a house valued at $250,000 with a $100,000 mortgage. Then the husband lost his job. Could he go to the bank and say, "I've lost my job. I'm sure something will turn up eventually. Can I get a second mortgage so that I can make payments until things turn around?" Not on your life. This family had only one option: to sell their house along with thousands of other families who were selling theirs at the same time. This of course, meant selling when the housing supply far exceeded the housing demand.

The best offer our friends received was for less than their mortgage. Eventually, through foreclosure, they ended up turning their house over to the bank — losing their house, their former $150,000 of equity, and their credit rating in the process. Was their $150,000 in home equity safe?

Even when a local economy can sustain property values, home equity is constantly at risk to the erosion of inflation. For years, we counted on inflation to help real estate appreciate, and we also came to rely on real estate as a hedge against inflation. We've used examples in states that were hit hard by a downturn in the oil industry, but it also happened more recently in New England and California. Under certain circumstances, property values stop appreciating, and even decline. At the same time, inflation continues to erode the purchasing power of your equity dollars.

So, is your home equity safe? No, not at all.

Does Home Equity Provide a Reasonable Rate of Return?

What rate of return would you say your equity is earning? Ten percent? Eight? Seven? Try **ZERO.** That's right, ZERO. The value of your home may be appreciating, but there is a distinct difference between the value of your home and the value of your home equity. Only the value of your home appreciates, regardless of how much or how little equity you have built up. The equity in your home is actually earning nothing. Sitting there, unavailable for use in any other way, your equity is whiling away valuable time — earning nothing.

Don't confuse property appreciation with returns on home equity. Admittedly, the calculation of your current equity is closely tied to the appreciation of the property, but the return is coming from the value of the property, not from your equity in the property. Your property will appreciate at the same rate, regardless of the amount of equity in the home. Said another way, appreciation of the property's value has nothing to do with equity. In fact, the less equity there is in your home, the greater the return percentage on your original investment. Refer back to the sections about leverage in Figure 5–1 and in Chapter 17.

We like to compare returns on home equity to burying a dollar in a can in your yard. You have the dollar buried where you can't benefit from it. The rate of appreciation of your house is not affected in any way and when you finally dig up the dollar, it is still just a dollar — it earned nothing.

Does home equity provide a reasonable rate of return? Absolutely not. Home equity provides zero return.

So Why Do We Keep Our Money Tied Up in Home Equity?

If it isn't liquid, isn't safe, and doesn't earn a rate of return, why leave so much money tied up in home equity? Because Americans have a historical bias against mortgages. It's as much a part of our heritage as the tea in Boston Harbor. We have been conditioned by our parents, grandparents, and great-grandparents for years to believe that it is bad to be in debt and that it is good to own a debt-free home. We all admire folks who have their house paid off and hold mortgage-burning parties, and we dream of the day when we no longer have to make house payments.

While we are paying our mortgages down, we gradually lose tax breaks due to the declining deductibility of the interest. A smaller portion of each mortgage payment goes to interest, which is tax deductible. and a larger portion to principal repayment, which is not tax deductible. That raises the after-tax cost of the remaining mortgage payments. But we feel safe. If loss of job or disability occurs, we can't use the equity in our home because no bank in the world would loan money to anyone without the income to repay it. But we feel safe. We can't turn the equity into money for medical bills or retirement income. But we feel safe. When needed the most, we can't use our equity without selling the house we hold so dear. But we feel safe. We defy all sensible rules of investment, especially the law of diversification, by having most or all of our money tied up in a single investment. But we feel safe!

We're not doing ourselves a favor with this line of thinking. We have inherited the attitude, left over from the Great Depression, that unless we own our homes free and clear that we could suddenly become homeless in the face of almost any economic calamity. True indeed, but as our home equity grows and we come ever closer to paying off the mortgage, the very risk we are trying to avoid grows progressively larger. Anytime mortgage payments cannot be met, there is a risk of foreclosure. If a lender found it necessary to foreclose on several mortgage loans, would their interest be served best by foreclosing on homes the defaulting borrowers had a large amount of equity in first, or those with smaller equity build-up?

In the end, feeling safe isn't enough when we end up with no options and no flexibility to manage other changes in our lives. Maybe it's time to step out of the log cabin, out of our depression mentality, leave behind past attitudes, and use that pioneering spirit to push ahead to financial independence and personal wealth. Ready? The key is *equity management.*

Equity Management

Equity management is the process of converting nonworking equity dollars into working equity dollars. Equity management involves looking at home equity completely apart from the home itself, so that we can use the equity, if needed, and also be able to profit from other available opportunities. It involves taking control of your home equity dollars before you really need them. Equity management is truly one of the most powerful financial planning tools available.

Keep in mind that we are not talking about taking all your equity out of your home and escaping to Bali for the next 15 years, as tempting as that may sound. Our methods are designed to simply manage your home equity as you do other investments: to brighten your financial outlook.

When would you be most likely to need the use of your home equity? Some examples would be if you became unemployed or disabled, were having credit problems or were on the verge of bankruptcy, or died and your family needed income. In any of these situations, about the only way you could get the equity out of your home would be to sell it, providing the market is good at the time and the sale could be made quickly. What about going to the bank and borrowing against your equity? Sure, just try getting a loan when you are unemployed, disabled, bankrupt, or dead. Banks are income lenders. They loan money to people who have the income to repay it. They don't loan against assets when there is little or no income.

People who have owned their homes for many years often find that the majority of their total net worth is tied up in their home equity.

We have worked with many people whose home equity comprised 70 to 90 percent of their total assets. So, add lack of diversification to the other disadvantages of keeping your money tied up in home equity. This lack of diversification can really magnify the impact the disadvantages of keeping your money in home equity may have on your financial well-being.

For most people, equity management is a new concept that goes completely against our traditional thinking. It is an area where even many financial advisors haven't yet seen the light. We frequently conduct training classes in equity management for financial services professionals, and it is really fun to feel their excitement as they begin to grasp these powerful concepts.

Equity management strategies can be divided into three general categories: equity development, equity conservation, and equity conversion. Each of these strategies meets specific objectives of homeowners, and we will explain each one in turn. But first, let's talk briefly about home ownership and equity management in general.

Before you get excited about the concepts we're going to outline in this chapter, you must understand that we have no desire whatsoever to contribute to the growing problems of the homeless. We understand that emotional and psychological connections with your home may override investment considerations. Therefore, we caution you to proceed carefully.

None of these strategies should be used until you have a thorough understanding of the principles underlying *The Seven Secrets of Financial Success!* It will be difficult to make the decisions needed for equity management strategies unless you have a working knowledge of the investment world that is outlined in the second section of this book.

In short, you must follow the rules. If you haven't proven that you have the discipline to pay yourself first, wait until you can establish a track record of good judgment and sound personal financial management. You must have an emergency cash reserve fund in place or use an equity management strategy to establish one. And always diversify your investments.

Accessing Your Home Equity

There are only two ways to access your home equity — by selling your home or by taking out a loan against the property. Only you can decide which is best.

FIGURE 20–1

Home Equity Management Strategies

A Strategy for Every Home Owner. Equity Management can be divided into three general categories, each one meeting specific objectives of the individual or family.

Equity Development

- 15-Year Mortgages
- Biweekly Payment Plans
- Additional Principal Payments
- Mortgage Endowment

Equity development involves building equity in the home as quickly as possible through accelerated mortgage payoff. This strategy is most useful for home owners who have yet to build up much home equity and for people who have a strong bias against mortgages.

Advantages	Disadvantages
1. More rapid debt reduction	1. Lack of liquidity
2. Equity increases more rapidly	2. Reduced tax savings
3. Less interest paid	3. No return on equity
	4. Equity at risk

Equity Conservation

- Equity Exchange
- Equity Transfer

Equity conservation involves converting the home equity to cash by taking out a loan against the home and then deploying this money for other uses. Through equity conservation, the property and the equity may appreciate and grow independent of one another. This strategy is useful for people who have a moderate-to-large amount of home equity and the income necessary to make payments.

Advantages	Disadvantages
1. Increase liquidity	1. Bias against mortgages
2. Increase diversification and safety of principal	2. Loan origination fees and closing costs
3. Improve rate of return	3. Temptation to spend redeployed equity
4. Reduce or eliminate consumer debt	4. Must qualify for a mortgage under current conditions
5. Increase monthly cash flow	
6. Potential tax savings	

Equity Conversion

- Reverse Mortgages
- Refinance Mortgages
- Home Equity Loan
- Sale — Lease back
- Trade Down

Equity conversion involves converting the home equity to an income flow. This strategy is appropriate for people who want or need to tap into their home equity to supplement retirement.

Advantages	Disadvantages
1. Can continue living in home while tapping equity	1. Consumes equity
2. Loan proceeds are not taxable	2. May receive equity in lump sum
3. Potential tax savings	3. Potentially disinherits family
	4. Loan origination fees and closing costs

Selling Your Home

When you sell a home, you may suddenly be in an equity management situation without even thinking about it. The choice is to reinvest the home equity into another home or to use it for other purposes. If the whole amount is reinvested, there are usually no tax consequences. However, if any portion of the equity is *not* reinvested into another home, there may be tax consequences depending on whether or not the equity in hand represents a profit from the sale. Many people use their previous home equity to leverage a *trade-up*, that is to purchase a larger or nicer home while others do a *trade-down*, moving to a less costly home. Any equity not reinvested is then put to other uses, preferably invested or used as retirement income.

Obviously, if you wish to continue living in your home, selling is not the preferable option. Assuming that you have the ability to obtain a mortgage or home equity loan, the choice then becomes a question of what kind of loan to obtain.

Taking Out a Loan against Your Property

You may consider refinancing your home with a new mortgage, especially if your mortgage interest rate is above the current rates. When possible, refinancing at a lower rate allows you to access additional equity and lower the cost of payments on the balance of the existing mortgage at the same time. Remember, however, that you may pay origination costs, up-front fees, and/or points when you take out a new mortgage. Don't forget to include these costs in your calculations.

Fixed-rate mortgages are often preferred over variable- or adjustable-rate mortgages because of the fixed monthly payments, but if you plan to live in the home for less than five or six years, an adjustable-rate mortgage may be more economical because of the lower initial interest rate.

If your mortgage is at or below current market interest rates, you probably won't want to refinance that portion of the debt. A second mortgage or home equity loan would then be more appropriate, keeping the lower rate on the first mortgage amount to reduce the overall costs of borrowing. (This section does not apply to Texans, who are not permitted to take out second mortgages or home equity loans.) An advantage is that second mortgages and home equity loans are generally easier and less costly to obtain. They may not require an appraisal, and the process usually takes only 15 to 30 days. The interest on these loans is deductible, just like the first mortgage, up to a $100,000 loan.

If the loan is larger than that, the interest is only deductible if the money is used for home improvements, business expenses, or income-generating investments. If the borrowed money (above $100,000) is used for anything else, the interest deduction is lost.

On the downside, home equity loans have become so easy to obtain that financial experts have become concerned about them being overused in recent years. It's too easy to forget that a larger mortgage puts a home at greater risk. Debt counselors are seeing home equity loans showing up in greater numbers. "It's like being on the edge of a precipice," one *Business Week* article says. "If anything goes wrong or any unexpected expenses come up, you lose the house."

Consumers who use the loans to pay off credit card debts are especially vulnerable to defaults on home equity loans. The numbers are difficult to track, but available evidence shows that 75 percent of those who use home equity loans for debt consolidation find themselves in twice as much debt in two years! After consolidating their loans, they feel so free that they quickly run up more consumer debt and have the same problem again, plus the payment on their home equity loan. And we're actually recommending these things?

We repeat the following advice emphatically. We recommend home equity loans *only* when you have a solid understanding of *The 7 Secrets of Financial Success*, and a proven track record of financial discipline. And you must understand that equity management is for conservation, not consumption.

Employment or Opportunity Cost — Either Way, You Pay

Remember: No matter what you do with your home equity, whether you leave it in your home or take out a mortgage to convert it to cash, you will pay for it. When you take out the mortgage, you will have to pay interest. That is, the cost of putting your money to work in other places, called the *employment cost*. Do you think you could avoid this cost by simply leaving your equity in your home? You can't. If those equity dollars could be earning ten percent in some other investment, then the cost of losing that investment opportunity is ten percent — it is called the *opportunity cost*. Whether it is employment cost or opportunity cost, you pay either way. Another important point is that the cost of a mortgage is simple interest on a declining mortgage balance, but when you leave the equity in the home you are losing the opportunity for compounding interest returns, were it invested apart from the home.

Equity Development

Equity development involves building equity in the home as quickly as possible by accelerating the mortgage payoff. People who haven't built up much equity or who haven't disciplined themselves to save any other way can benefit from this strategy. The primary advantage of accelerated mortgage payoff is that over the term of the loan you will pay less interest.

One strategy to shorten the total term of the loan is to pay one-half of your monthly mortgage payment amount every two weeks (biweekly) resulting in the equivalent of one extra payment every year. By doing so, you reduce the term of a 30-year amortized loan to just under 21 years. Some people choose to make periodic payments of various amounts in addition to their regular monthly payment or to simply make an extra (monthly) payment each year. Any extra money you pay is applied directly to the principal and shortens the time needed to repay the loan. (Whenever you make extra payments, be sure to notify your lender, otherwise it could confuse their bookkeeping process, and your extra payments may be returned to you or not be properly credited.)

Experts often recommend a 15-year mortgage instead of the traditional 30-year mortgage for accelerated equity buildup. If you have a $100,000, 15-year fixed-rate mortgage loan at 7.5 percent interest, you'll pay a total of $166,862 in interest and principal over 15 years, with a monthly payment of $927.01. An equivalent 30-year mortgage would require a slightly higher rate of interest (about 8 percent) and a monthly payment of $733.76, for a total of $264,154 over 30 years. This calculates out to $97,292 in savings with the 15-year loan. Coupled with the lower interest rate on the 15-year mortgage, it looks like a pretty good deal.

But now let's look at the rest of the story. Although accelerated mortgage payment programs offer more rapid debt reduction and more rapid increase of equity, the disadvantages of keeping too much equity in your home are still apparent. There remains a lack of liquidity, reduced tax savings, and lack of flexibility. A shorter-term mortgage may not be your best option in the long run. Let's compare the above 15-year mortgage with the 30-year mortgage to see where you will stand in 15 years.

After 180 payments, with the 15-year mortgage you will have paid $166,862 and own your home free and clear. During the first 15 years of the comparable 30-year mortgage, 180 payments would have totaled $132,077, a difference of $34,785. But, you would still owe $76,783

FIGURE 20–2

EQUITY DEVELOPMENT IN ACTION

Brad and Jennifer Marcus, both age 28, were quite excited about purchasing their first home. They had worked and saved faithfully, accumulating $25,000 for a down payment in just over 3 years. After researching their mortgage options, they decided that a 15-year mortgage seemed to be a better deal than a 30-year mortgage. After all, they could get one at a one-half percent lower interest rate and save over $97,000 in interest over the life of their $100,000 mortgage loan: all for less than $200 more in monthly payment.

However, their financial planner recommended instead that they take out a 30-year mortgage and invest the difference between payments in a side fund. She told Brad and Jennifer about liquidity, safety, returns, tax savings on their mortgage interest deduction, and the other advantages of keeping their equity invested outside of their home mortgage.

$100,000 30-Year Mortgage
Interest Rate = 8.0%
Monthly Payment = $733.76

Year	Annual Total Interest	*Annual Tax Savings	Year-End Mortgage Balance
1	$7,970	$2,232	$99,165
2	7,901	2,212	98,260
3	7,825	2,191	97,280
4	7,744	2,168	96,219
5	7,656	2,144	95,070
6	7,561	2,117	93,826
7	7,457	2,088	92,478
8	7,345	2,057	91,018
9	7,224	2,023	89,437
10	7,093	1,986	87,725
11	6,951	1,946	85,871
12	6,797	1,903	83,863
13	6,630	1,857	81,688
14	6,450	1,806	79,333
15	6,254	1,751	76,783

$100,000 15-Year Mortgage
Interest Rate = 7.5%
Monthly Payment = $927.01

Year	Annual Total Interest	*Annual Tax Savings	Year-End Mortgage Balance
1	$7,373	$2,064	$96,249
2	7,082	1,983	92,206
3	6,768	1,895	87,850
4	6,430	1,800	83,155
5	6,065	1,698	78,096
6	5,672	1,588	72,644
7	5,249	1,470	66,769
8	4,793	1,342	60,438
9	4,302	1,204	53,616
10	3,772	1,056	46,263
11	3,201	896	38,340
12	2,586	724	29,802
13	1,923	538	20,601
14	1,209	338	10,686
15	439	123	0

Monthly Investment =
$193.25
Annual Return = 10.00%

Year	Year-End Account Balance
1	$ 2,449
2	5,153
3	8,142
4	11,443
5	15,089
6	19,118
7	23,568
8	28,485
9	33,916
10	39,916
11	46,544
12	53,867
13	61,956
14	70,892
15	80,764

Results after 15 Years

Total Payments = $132,077
Total Interest Paid = $108,859

Net After-Tax Cost
of Payments = $101,596

Total Payments = $166,862
Total Interest Paid = $66,862

Net After-Tax Cost
of Payments = $148,140

If annual tax savings were also invested, investment would be worth over $100,000.

The Marcuses accepted the planner's advice. At projected return rates, their investment fund would grow to sufficient size to completely pay off their 30-year mortgage within 15 years should they desire or need to do so. After 15 years, they could use a portion of their investment earnings to make their mortgage payments and their investment fund would continue to grow.

*Assumed tax bracket is 28%.

on the home. So, it still appears that the 15-year mortgage is the best deal, right? Not necessarily.

Taxes, as always, muddle the picture a bit. With a 15-year mortgage, the amount of each payment going to principal repayment, rather than interest, increases quickly as the principal is paid down. Consequently, your tax deduction for mortgage interest decreases too. So instead of just looking at the loan payoff in terms of total dollars, let's now look at your after-tax cost of payments, assuming a 28 percent federal tax bracket; that is, how much of your net income (after taxes) will be needed to make your house payments for 15 years? The 15-year mortgage will require $148,140 versus $101,596 for the first 15 years of a 30-year loan, *a difference of $46,544 in after-tax income.* The deductible interest tax savings lost as the principal balance falls quickly makes the actual added cost of paying off the 15-year loan considerably more than the difference we arrived at in the previous paragraph.

Now suppose that you had chosen the 30-year mortgage. Being a disciplined investor who employs the principles of *The 7 Secrets of Financial Success*, you invest the monthly difference of $193.25 in payments, between the 15-year and 30-year mortgages, in an S&P 500 index mutual fund. After 15 years, assuming an after-tax average annual return of 10 percent, the investment would have grown to $80,764. But that's not all. Because a higher portion of the mortgage payment went to interest, the tax savings on the 30-year mortgage were higher than on the shorter-term mortgage. In a 28 percent tax bracket, the investment of the monthly payment savings plus the tax savings (taxes you would have been required to pay if not for the deduction allowed for your mortgage interest) would have grown to over $100,000 in 15 years. State and local tax savings will make the picture look even brighter.

With this nest egg, you could pay off the outstanding $76,782 mortgage balance on your 30-year loan at the end of 15 years. Just like with a 15-year mortgage, you would own your home free and clear in 15 years. But, by choosing the longer-term loan and investing the difference in monthly payments in a side account, you have almost $24,000 you otherwise would not have, had you chosen the 15-year mortgage.

However, since this chapter is about separating your equity from the home, let's not pay off your 30-year mortgage. Instead, keep the investment and pay your mortgage payments from it for the next 15 years. With the 15-year mortgage you were able to stop making payments, so we will let you do the same in this example. At the beginning of the second 15 years, you have over $100,000 accumulated in a mutual fund. If you begin withdrawals of $734 each month to make the mortgage payment, assuming that it performs as projected, not only will it make the monthly payments for 15 years, it will continue to grow to well over $140,000 by the end of your 30-year mortgage.

To summarize, since you chose a 30-year mortgage over the 15-year mortgage and invested the difference in payments and tax savings, you own a house and about $144,000, instead of just a house, for an identical total expenditure. Now, which do you think is a better deal for you — the 15-year or the 30-year mortgage?

To emphasize an important advantage of keeping some of your equity invested separately from your home, let's assume that you experienced a temporary loss of employment at some time after taking out the mortgage. With the 15-year mortgage and no other funds from which to draw, chances are that you might have lost your home and your equity in it to foreclosure. On the other hand, with a 30-year mortgage and an investment fund established with the difference between the monthly payment amounts, you could use the investment to continue making your mortgage payments. This method would, in effect, give you time to get another job and enable you to keep the house, or sell the house and preserve your equity dollars.

Another benefit of a 30-year loan over a 15-year loan is that your monthly payments are less, giving you a lot more flexibility in managing your monthly cash flow. Also, if you want to apply for other loans (hopefully the good-debt kind), your debt-to-income ratios will look better to the lender when determining how much, and at what rate, they would loan you money. A lower monthly mortgage payment tilts the ratio more in your favor.

Of course, in real life we would discourage you from ever paying your house off. You simply do not need to have large amounts of idle equity dollars sitting in your house to realize the full benefits of home ownership. Equity development strategies are intended to help you accumulate equity through the benefits of home ownership, which you can then transfer to other, more productive investments. As your home equity grows, we would advise that you borrow against it and invest your equity dollars apart from the house.

However, if you are having difficulty accepting the idea of not owning a home free and clear because of a well-ingrained bias against mortgages, we understand. Equity development through accelerated mortgage payoff may still be just the ticket for you.

Two things are critical to the success of this kind of long-range planning: You must have the discipline to invest the savings, and you must be able to realize the projected rate of return. Our projection of a ten percent average annual return is not guaranteed, but it is consistent with historical, long-term average returns of common stock portfolios or equity mutual fund investments.

Equity Conservation

Equity conservation involves converting your home equity to cash by obtaining a loan using your home as collateral and then using the cash for investments apart from the home. These strategies work for people who have accumulated moderate-to-large amounts of equity in their homes and have the necessary income to repay the loan. The objectives of equity conservation are to increase liquidity, increase return on equity, and increase cash reserves. Equity conservation also allows you to maximize tax benefits, decrease risk of principal and, often, to consolidate debt. Equity conservation strategies include equity exchange and equity transfer.

Equity Exchange

With *equity exchange,* mortgage or home loan proceeds are used to pay off consumer or other debt, in effect replacing or exchanging bad debt with good debt. People who are house-rich and cash- or cash-flow poor are good candidates for equity exchange. By exchanging short-term, high-interest consumer debt for long-term, low-interest mortgage or home equity financing, monthly cash flow can be improved by lowering monthly payments. It can also be the opportunity to establish an adequate emergency cash reserve fund or to enhance investment portfolios.

After the successful completion of the equity exchange strategy, people find that they still have the same net worth, but their financial flexibility and strength have improved. They have an adequate emergency fund and have been able to increase their diversification substantially. The potential for future earnings is enhanced because the house will continue to appreciate at the same rate it did when all their money was tied up in it, and now a portion of their equity is earning a return on its own.

Freed-up monthly cash flow should be invested. For many people, this is the opportunity to finally begin paying themselves first. Invest in your mutual funds monthly or add to a retirement plan. And as you already know, monthly additions accelerate investment growth because of the magic of time and compound interest. The increased tax deductions from mortgage interest lowers the actual net cost of the mortgage payments, offering additional savings at tax time.

FIGURE 20–3

EQUITY EXCHANGE IN ACTION

Gerry Avila (age 42) and his spouse Adrienne (age 40) have two children, ages 12 and 14, and have a combined income of $80,000 annually. The Avilas have become acutely aware of the need to increase savings for their children's education and their retirement, but their current cash flow already seems barely adequate. They are managing to pay their obligations on time, but otherwise are feeling financially stressed. Together, they examined their current situation and needs and established some financial goals.

Goals

1. Increase emergency cash reserves

2. Reduce or eliminate consumer debt

3. Increase savings dedicated to their children's education and other financial goals

4. Increase savings for retirement

5. Increase their life insurance

Before Equity Exchange

	Asset Value	Liability against Asset Value	Monthly Payment
Home	$240,000	$ 77,000	$ 805
Cash Reserves	3,000		
Consumer Debt			
Auto 1	15,000	13,000	494
Auto 2	12,000	7,000	377
Credit Card 1	0	2,500	100
Credit Card 2	0	3,600	150
Retail Account 1	0	1,700	100
Retail Account 2	0	900	50
Mutual Fund Portfolio	7,500		100
Mutual Fund – IRA	8,700		200
Life Insurance			
Gerry: $50,000 Whole Life	6,000		39
Adrienne: $25,000 Whole Life	4,000		19
Totals	**$296,200**	**$105,700**	**$2,434**

Net Worth = $190,500
(= assets minus liabilities)
Federal Taxes:
Annual $12,108
Monthly $1,009

After this exercise, the Avilas felt that they were in a hopeless situation. But, then they met with a professional financial advisor who told them how they could access and utilize their home equity to meet all these goals.

FIGURE 20–3 (CONCLUDED)

The Avilas acted upon their advisor's recommendations and refinanced their home to access a portion of their home equity. After paying off their original mortgage and costs incurred with the new loan, they used their loan proceeds and subsequent increase in their discretionary income to achieve the following results:

Situation after Equity Exchange

Asset Value	Liability against Asset Value	Monthly Payment	
$240,000	$160,000	$1,175	**Home**
17,300			**Cash Reserves**
			Consumer Debt
15,000	0	0	Auto 1
12,000	0	0	Auto 2
0	0	0	Credit Card 1
0	0	0	Credit Card 2
0	0	0	Retail Account 1
0	0	0	Retail Account 2
47,500		300	**Mutual Fund Portfolio**
8,700		333	**Mutual Fund – IRA**
			Life Insurance
6,000		39	Gerry: $50,000 Whole Life
		300	$300,000 Variable Universal Life
4,000		19	Adrienne: $25,000 Whole Life
		125	$150,000 Variable Universal Life
$350,500	**$160,000**	**$2,291**	**Totals**

Net Worth = $190,500
(= assets minus liabilities)
Federal Taxes:
Annual $10,050
Monthly $838

Results

1. Cash reserves increased to $17,300

2. Eliminated all consumer debt

3. Invested $40,000 in mutual fund portfolio and increased monthly additions to $300

4. Increased IRA contributions to maximum

5. Increased life insurance coverage
   • To meet needs
   • To accumulate retirement funds
   Projected at age 65:
   Spouse A $206,500
   Spouse B $70,000

6. Freed up $143/mo. for discretionary use

7. Reduced federal taxes by over $170/mo. for additional discretionary use

Equity Transfer

Equity transfer is simply using the process of a home equity loan for other investments apart from the home. This strategy is useful for people who have small mortgage balances and little or no consumer debt. Benefits of equity transfer include increasing liquidity for emergencies and opportunities, increasing safety through diversification, improving rate of return, increasing investment portfolio for long-term needs, and potential tax savings.

The best time to borrow against your home equity is when you don't need the money, because as we discussed earlier, lenders are not willing to loan when your needs are most pressing such as during unemployment or disability. Through equity transfer, your money will be readily available when you need it, and in the meantime, you will have more diversification and be earning a rate of return on money that would otherwise be dead equity.

There are a variety of techniques for equity conservation and everyone's situation is unique. Work with your financial planner, look at the options, and decide which are the most appropriate for you. By taking some of the eggs out of your nest, your overall risk level is decreased.

Our basic premise is to keep 20 to 50 percent of your home's value in equity, depending on how aggressive your investment attitude is, and transfer the rest of your equity dollars into other investment positions. The nice thing about this strategy is that you don't have to find investments that are earning a higher rate of return than your mortgage interest rate is for it to work.

You may ask, "Why not pay off the house and invest the amount we have been paying in house payments?" Because by then, you are out of time. Think back to the Third Secret. You need time to fully realize the beauty of compound interest. And time is what your home equity idles away, when you let it. Also, if you have a mortgage payment due, you are likely to pay it. When the house is paid off, you may find seemingly justifiable places to spend all or part of the money you have earmarked for savings and investment. Even for the strong-willed, a mortgage is a good forced monthly savings plan.

Equity Conversion

Equity conversion means to convert home equity into cash that can be used for consumption or other needs. This strategy is used by people with little or no mortgage debt against their home. Equity conversion is especially useful to those who are in their retirement years. Approximately 13 million Americans who are retired today own their own homes free and clear. However, an alarming one-third of them have incomes below the national poverty level. They, too, are house-rich and cash-poor. There are three methods used to tap into home equity without giving up the benefits of home ownership: trade-downs, sale-leasebacks, and reverse mortgages.

Trade Downs

If you are worried about spending down assets to meet living expenses and travel objectives, and are concerned about the rising cost and worry of home maintenance, then trading a big, expensive house for a smaller home or condominium might be the answer. It can reduce housing and maintenance costs, property taxes, and insurance premiums, as well as allow you to convert your equity from the larger home to cash.

Although it requires moving, trading down allows people to maintain home ownership status and increase their monthly income and lifestyle options. The lump-sum proceeds from the sale should be put into income-producing investments. And if neither spouse has used their capital gains exclusion, this is the time to do so.

The capital gains exclusion is one of the few great benefits left in the tax code. As we mentioned in Chapter 17, the IRS allows you to exclude $125,000 of capital gains realized from the sale of your residence from taxation once in your lifetime. You have to be age 55, or older, and the property must have been your primary residence for three of the last five years. There is one hitch: if one spouse has used the exemption before, either as a single person or in a previous marriage, it nixes the exemption for the other spouse.

Use as many dollars as you possibly can for this exemption, because it can only be used once. If you only use $100,000 of the exemption, it's like throwing the other $25,000 away.

It's often a difficult choice to know just when to take this exemption. You can defer capital gains from a primary residence as long as the cost of the new house is greater than or equal to the sale of the previous residence and if you buy or build within two years of sale. If you are planning to stay in the house you trade down to until you die, it's a good idea to take it now.

Trading down increases cash reserves, freeing your money to be used when you want or need to use it. It can increase disposable income through reduced expenses and income from investments. Home ownership and net worth is maintained, and retirement income is increased substantially.

FIGURE 20–4

EQUITY TRANSFER IN ACTION

Harvey and Carolyn Lee, both age 50, have an annual family income of $60,000. Their youngest child has recently completed college and the Lees finally have some excess cash flow that will enable them to begin saving for their retirement, in earnest. They met with a financial planner who evaluated their current situation. Presently, the Lees have humble savings, but no consumer debt. Alarmingly, over 75 percent of their net worth is in their home equity. The planner helped the Lees establish some financial goals.

Goals

1. Provide for an adequate retirement income

2. Diversify assets

3. Increase returns on current assets

4. Reduce taxes

5. Purchase additional life insurance to meet their needs

Before Equity Transfer

	Asset Value	Liability against Asset Value	Monthly Payment
Home	$200,000	$45,000	$ 580
Cash Reserves			
Certificate of Deposit	20,000		
Money Market Fund	9,000		800
Investments (Retirement-Specific)			
Mutual Funds – IRA	14,000		167
Variable Annuity Portfolio			
Other Investments			
Mutual Fund Portfolio			
Tax Exempt Bond Portfolio			
Life Insurance			
Harvey: $50,000 Whole Life	16,500		107
Carolyn: $25,000 Whole Life	5,400		90
Federal Taxes			651
State Taxes (at 8%)			255
TOTALS	**$264,900**	**$45,000**	**$2,650**

Net Worth = $219,900
(= assets minus liabilities)

These goals seemed like a lot to accomplish with their current income. However, their financial planner showed the Lees how they could refinance their home and utilize their equity from it to accomplish all these goals and provide a financially secure future.

The Lees acted on their planner's recommendations and refinanced their home for $150,000. After paying off their original mortgage and cashing in their CD, they had $125,000 to work with. From this, they increased their liquid cash reserves, opened a variable annuity account to take advantage of

FIGURE 20–4 (CONCLUDED)

tax-deferral on their reinvested earnings, purchased reducing-term life insurance on each spouse, purchased a portfolio of tax-exempt bonds, and opened a mutual fund account. The following results were achieved:

After Equity Transfer

Asset Value	Liability against Asset Value	Monthly Payment		Results
$200,000	$150,000	$1,110	**Home**	**1. Retirement planning objectives fulfilled**
			Cash Reserves	Projected values at age 65: Variable annuity portfolio = $306,000
			Certificate of Deposit	IRA (fully funded for both spouses) = $263,000
15,000			Money Market Fund	Life insurance cash values = $67,000
			Investments (Retirement-Specific)	**2. Assets well diversified**
28,000		333	Mutual Funds – IRA	Home equity, money market fund, IRAs,
60,000		200	Variable Annuity Portfolio	annuities, life insurance cash values, bonds, and
			Other Investments	mutual fund portfolio.
30,000			Mutual Fund Portfolio	**3. Majority of assets placed in equity investments for higher potential returns**
15,000			Tax-Exempt Bond Portfolio	
			Life Insurance	**4. Liquid cash reserves increased**
16,500		107	Harvey: $50,000 Whole Life	
5,400		90	Carolyn: $25,000 Whole Life	**5. Life insurance needs met**
		150	$200,000 Term on Each Spouse	**6. Mutual fund portfolio established**
		454	**Federal Taxes**	
		206	**State Taxes** (at 8%)	**7. Taxes reduced**
$369,900	$150,000	**$2,640**	**TOTALS**	Larger mortgage interest deduction and increased contribution to IRA accounts save $246 per month in taxes, which is added to investments.

Net Worth = $219,900
(= assets minus liabilities)

Where will this leave the Lees 15 years down the road at retirement? Their investments will have grown to almost $700,000, enough to produce a substantial monthly retirement income. If desired, they could pay off their mortgage balance of approximately $115,000, and still have a nice chunk of change left over. During all of that time, they will enjoy the advantages of being able to invest their home equity and can readily access their money if they need it. Their home will continue to appreciate at the same rate, whether they owe $45,000 or $150,000 against it. At age 65, their projected total net worth will exceed $1,100,000, largely because they learned the difference between property and home equity appreciation.

FIGURE 20–5

EQUITY CONVERSION – TRADE-DOWN IN ACTION

Patrick and Amelia Wade, both age 65, were awakening to some of the harsh financial realities of maintaining their preretirement lifestyle. Soon after Pat's retirement from his $70,000 a year position with a large manufacturing company, their retirement savings were being quickly depleted. They were taking out about $1,000 each month from their investment principal, a rate that would completely exhaust their savings within just a few years. To solve their dilemma, they attended a retirees' financial seminar at their local community college. They discovered other problems they hadn't considered, such as inflation's adverse impact on their future buying power and how long-term health care could devastate them financially. The Wades saw their retirement dreams fading fast, but became hopeful during the discussion of home equity management. Following the seminar, the Wades had a private consultation with the instructor, a professional financial advisor who analyzed their situation and helped them establish these financial goals.

GOALS

1. Realize an adequate retirement income from current assets
2. Reposition current assets to increase return
3. Provide for possible long-term health care needs
4. Maintain their independence
5. Purchase a motor home
6. Preserve some of their estate for their children

The goals seemed impossible, given their current income. Like many retirees, the Wades were in a house-rich, cash flow-poor position. Their financial advisor showed them how a trade-down of their home could help them utilize their home equity to accomplish all these goals.

Within several weeks, the Wades were able to sell their large home and purchase a new, smaller one in a planned retirement community. These transactions freed up $184,000. Using their new wealth and other savings, the financial advisor helped them establish a conservative investment and insurance portfolio compatible with their needs and goals. They added $68,000 to their mutual fund portfolio, purchased $56,000 in bonds with varying maturity dates, and invested $50,000 among several blue chip income-producing stocks. They purchased long-term health care insurance policies and still had enough cash remaining to buy the motor home they had dreamed of for years.

1. Increased monthly retirement income from assets
2. Decreased fixed monthly expenditures
3. Diversified assets among income-producing investments
4. Purchased long-term health care insurance
5. Maintained the benefits and independence of home ownership
6. Purchased motor home
7. Investment principal will be preserved

RESULTS

FIGURE 20–5 (CONCLUDED)

	Situation before Trade-Down			Situation after Trade-Down		
	Asset Value	Monthly Expense	Avg. Monthly Income/ Withdrawals	Asset Value	Monthly Expense	Avg. Monthly Income/ Withdrawals
Home	$300,000	$ 805		$120,000	$ 660	
Taxes, Insurance, & Maintenance	(w/$86,000 Mortgage)	475		(w/$90,000 Mortgage)	210	
Cash Reserves						
Certificate of Deposit	50,000		$ 208	10,000		$ 42
Money Market Account	12,000		40	12,000		40
Investments						
Mutual Fund Portfolio	12,000		600	80,000		667
Bond Portfolio	24,000		650	80,000		467
Blue Chip Stock Portfolio				60,000		325
Motor Home				40,000		
Long-Term Health Care Insurance						
Spouse A					108	
Spouse B					125	
Retirement Income						
Social Security, Spouse A			1,213			1,213
Social Security, Spouse B			606			606
Pension Income, Spouse A			950			950
Totals	**$398,000**	**$1,280**	**$4,267**	**$402,000**	**$1,103**	**$4,310**

Net Worth = $312,000 (= assets minus mortgage)

Net Worth = $312,000 (= assets minus mortgage)

The Wades had not planned well for retirement, but fortunately purchased a home and accumulated considerable equity in it. By accessing and investing their home equity, they realized sufficient income to enjoy a comfortable retirement and preserve their investment principal. They also took advantage of their one-time $125,000 capital gains exclusion from the sale of their home. Anyone considering an equity conversion strategy needs to fully evaluate the possible tax consequences first.

Sale-Leasebacks

A sale-leaseback involves selling your home to an investor, then leasing it back from them. Now, who would be willing to do that? Your own adult children are the most likely candidates. The sale-leaseback allows you to remain in the home while realizing income from its sale. You can take advantage of the $125,000 capital gains exclusion and at the same time reduce the size of your taxable estate. Future appreciation in your home's value goes directly to your children instead of enlarging your estate.

A sale-leaseback can provide your offspring with the tax benefits of home ownership, and provide them with a great tenant: you! (Get some legal and tax advice here. The IRS has rules on how much of a price break you can give your children.) This technique offers dramatic benefits, so be sure it's done correctly.

Reverse Mortgages

A reverse mortgage works the opposite of conventional mortgages. Instead of making a monthly payment to a mortgage company, the mortgage company makes payments to you, which are applied against the equity in your home. This strategy allows people to remain in their homes while receiving nontaxable income, for the most part.

The nicest thing about reverse mortgages is that you don't have to meet income qualifications to get one, and there are no restrictions on the use of the money. Reverse mortgages come with a lot of flexibility as to how you receive the money. It can be in a lump sum, as a line of credit to access your equity as you need it, or in regular monthly payments.

Reverse mortgages do consume equity, an important consideration if you plan to pass your home to your heirs at your death. If all your equity is used up, you could potentially disinherit family members.

From our point of view, that would be fine because your own independence is a gift to your children. Reverse mortgages charge higher rates than conventional mortgages because they are fairly uncommon and because the paperwork must be done in reverse, creating an additional burden. The lender doesn't know in advance the extent of the liability they are assuming or the length of time until pay-back. This uncertainty is reflected in higher interest rates.

Recently the Federal Housing Administration and the U.S. Department of Housing and Urban Development have taken steps to make reverse mortgages easier to obtain. They are now available in 48 states, but only a few banks actually offer them. Candidates must be 62

Financial Planning Extras

years old and own their home free and clear or have only a small mortgage balance. FHA insurance protects reverse mortgage holders against the borrower's owing more than the value of the home. In other words, you can never owe more than an agreed-upon loan value, or the value of the home, whichever is lower.

If you are relatively young, there is a risk of using up all your equity, leaving nothing to draw upon when you are older. These mortgages are really best for people in their 70s. The up-front fees can be disproportionately high, especially if the mortgage is held for only two or three years. The loan must be repaid if you sell or move. If you die, your estate must pay the note.

Before getting a reverse mortgage, you must go through a counseling session to make sure it is right for you. Limits on the amount that can be borrowed are low, so it's difficult to pocket more than 40 or 50 percent of your equity. And since bankers are rightfully conservative, up-front costs and mortgage rates are both higher than normal.

Despite their shortcomings, reverse mortgages free up money that retired people couldn't use otherwise. The American Association of Retired Persons has published a brochure about reverse mortgages and can offer help in finding a lender.

Summary

Even though most of us have been programmed to keep as much equity as possible in our homes, it could be a distinct disadvantage and detriment to achieving personal wealth. Evaluate your home equity using the same criteria applied to other investment opportunities. It could mean there should be a change in the way your largest investment is managed.

Equity management strategies can be used in almost every situation to achieve investment objectives. These strategies are based on the sound financial principles outlined in this book. Most strategies require converting equity to cash, either by selling or taking out a mortgage against your home.

Equity development strategies employ shorter-term mortgages or additional payments to conventional mortgages. Equity development builds equity at a faster pace, but reduces tax savings, investment options, and liquidity.

Equity conservation strategies remove a portion of your home equity and exchange or transfer it to other positions to improve liquidity, reduce taxes, establish cash reserves, consolidate debt, or contribute to investments.

Equity conversion converts home equity into disposable income, to increase financial flexibility and monthly income. Reverse mortgages and sale-leasebacks allow retired people to remain in their original homes and, in some cases, save a portion of their assets from future estate taxes.

TWENTY-ONE

Investing in Posterity
Planning for College Costs

ducation has its critics, but few will argue that a college degree ever *hurt* anyone's chances for success. Glance through your local newspaper's Help Wanted section and you'll see that many jobs, which 20 years ago were filled by high school graduates, are now open only to college graduates. Bookkeeping, secretarial, and service industries often require job applicants with college degrees. In today's world, a degree isn't a luxury — it's almost a necessity.

In 1960, about 21 percent of high school graduates went on to college. By 1981 (the first year that more women than men graduated from college) that number had grown to 31 percent, then moved up to 45 percent in 1992. This trend will continue as the changing job market demands better educated employees.

Along with more job opportunities, a college degree usually means higher income. On the average, college graduates earn between $250,000 and $500,000 more in their lifetimes than do nongraduates. Median income comparisons by the U.S. Bureau of the Census show that females with college degrees earn almost $10,000 more per year than female high school graduates. Males with college degrees earn nearly $14,000 more per year than male high school graduates. Average lifetime incomes of college graduates with bachelor's degrees are two to three times higher than those with high school diplomas alone. When the result of a college education rings in at a half-million dollars plus, there is no question that the price of that education is a worthy investment.

> *"We must open the doors to opportunity. But we must also equip our people to walk through those doors."*
>
> *– Lyndon B. Johnson*

Attending college has advantages other than increased job opportunities and a greater lifetime income. It also provides exposure to new ideas and experiences, fosters self-discipline and a feeling of community, encourages camaraderie, and develops personal as well as professional contacts they can draw on for a lifetime. The whole college experience is background, background, background.

The Cost of a College Education

"Okay, you've convinced me," you say. "But can I *afford* to send my children to college?" It's true that the cost of college tuition has soared. Today, attending top private schools such as Cornell, Duke, and Stanford costs about $100,000 for a four-year degree. State residents will pay from $24,000 to $40,000 or more over four years to attend public universities such as the University of Texas in Austin or the University of Michigan in Ann Arbor. In recent years, the costs of attending college have been increasing at twice the inflation rate. Using a 6 percent average annual college cost increase, future projections push the costs to earn a bachelor's degree at a state school to around $80,000. By the year 2012 the same degree at a prestigious private college or university will cost well over $200,000.

However, the situation isn't really as bad as it may seem at first glance. Let's look a little closer at the projections for future college costs. In truth, the cost to attend college as a percentage of median family income isn't much different today than it was 35 years ago. In 1960, the average tuition and other costs to attend a public institution were about 15 percent of the median family income, and today they're still under 16 percent. Annual costs to attend a private college now consume up to 40 percent of median family income, up from 27 percent in 1960, although private colleges are now offering more financial aid. In many cases cost increases have flattened out, and in some cases have dropped, as college administrators realize that increases in tuition don't necessarily improve their bottom line.

For example, let's say that your child was born in 1992. At the current rate that college expenses are increasing, the cost of a four-year degree (tuition, books, room and board) could be somewhere between $80,000 and $250,000 or more (depending on whether it is a state or private college) by the time your child enters college.

However, prudent parents who understand *The 7 Secrets of Financial Success* don't panic. They start planning early, and save and invest what they can for as long as they can. The good news for those with young children is that time is on your side. With all the years ahead to save and invest, you can likely accumulate most of the needed dollars for little Bradley's B.A. in art history. For the rest of us, the situation is still far from hopeless as there are many options available to help pay for college costs. Sure, it's nice to have all the necessary cash waiting when your child heads off to college, but the fact is that most people don't. If your children are currently in high school and you've done little or nothing to prepare for their college education, you're not alone. Whether college costs are way down the road or upon you within the next few years, few parents will be able to pay for their children's education solely from savings.

Sources of College Funding

Funding for college will most likely come from several different sources: parents' savings, parents' current income, student's savings or summer jobs, student's work while attending college, financial aid including grants and/or scholarships, short- or long-term loans, and other more creative sources we will cover later. In short, most people believe that every type of funding is worth pursuing for a college education. Although it may take some hard work and ingenuity, parents and students working together can make financing a college education possible in most situations.

Our current system is based on the assumption that each family has the primary responsibility for meeting college costs. Financial aid is intended to fill in the gaps only after the family has done as much as it reasonably can. Then, you may be eligible to receive some kind of financial aid: loans, grants, scholarships, or cooperative education programs through the college or university. With the current provisions in federal and other student loan programs, everyone is eligible for some sort of financial aid, regardless of family income. Loans must be repaid of course, but when combined with other sources of college funding they help ensure that everyone with the desire can manage to obtain a college education.

With the current cost-cutting mode of Congress, there may be less financial aid available in the future. In addition, with college enrollment rising there will be more students competing for the available aid. This situation means that you may need to accept a greater share of your child's college costs. The theme throughout this book has been one of self-reliance and personal responsibility. We believe that you are always in a better position and will have many more options when you have planned ahead and have your own savings and investments from which to draw. However, we do not discourage you from utilizing available financial aid when needed to ensure that your children can attend college.

Parents' and Student's Savings

It is natural to want to save money to provide for your children's education. We hope that you will, but there are some important factors to consider. Many parents, with the best of intentions for their children, make unwise decisions that ultimately jeopardize their own financial security. For those who begin planning and saving early, accumulating adequate money for their children's education is not that difficult. However, as selfish as this may sound, we believe that you must consider your own financial future before saving for your children's education.

We have known people who spent most of their savings to put their children through college. Then suddenly they are in their late forties or fifties and find themselves with insufficient time to accumulate enough money for their expected comfortable retirement lifestyle.

As we have discussed in earlier chapters, the best place for saving and investing is in qualified retirement plans. These plans greatly enhance the growth of your investments through the benefits of tax-deductible contributions and tax-deferred accumulation of earnings. When applying for financial aid, money in retirement plans is not considered among the parents' assets and therefore doesn't reduce the amount of aid your student is eligible for. Preparing for retirement should always be your number one financial goal. You should fully fund your retirement plans before saving for other purposes.

If necessary, you might be able to access the money in your retirement plans to help pay college costs. Some 401(k) plans will allow you to borrow from your retirement funds at favorable rates. And in the near future, Congress is expected to allow people to withdraw funds from their IRA accounts, without penalties, to finance college education for their children. The benefits of investing your savings in retirement plans will likely offset the costs you might incur later if you need to borrow for college funding. By taking care of yourself first, you will probably find that in the long run you are in a much better position to help your children with their college funding needs.

Another common practice that is not always wise, is to save money destined for college funding in the children's names. When applying for financial aid, colleges expect that 35 percent of the child's money be used for college costs each year, but only about 5.6 percent of the parents' assets. In other words, money saved in the child's name reduces their eligibility for financial aid. So unless you are certain that no financial aid will be needed, it is usually best to keep college savings in the parents' names.

For many people, especially those with two or more children, it may be difficult or unrealistic to expect to save 100 percent of education costs. It may even be unnecessary, because there are so many options and funding sources available. A realistic goal might be to save enough for 50 percent of anticipated costs and plan to make up the difference through other sources. However, the more money you have accumulated for education, the more choices your child will have and the less you will need to borrow later on.

The best way to fund a future college education is to invest early, invest often, think growth, and don't lay awake nights worrying about those outlandish college cost predictions. If you start saving $100 a month for your infant and manage to average about 10 percent interest, you will have more than $60,000 at college enrollment time. That will go a long way in reducing the enormous cost of college funding to a reasonable level. Also, remember that you don't have to pay the entire cost of college on the first day of your student's freshman year. You still have a few years left to accumulate additional savings and investment returns before the whole amount is needed.

In our experience, there are a couple of things to watch for in saving for college. First, many investments that are tagged for *college costs* are invested too conservatively or inappropriately to produce the kind of growth needed in the length of time you have. Think growth!

Some financial advisors advocate accumulating money for college funding in life insurance policies. Money accumulates tax-deferred within the policy, although you still have to pay taxes on earnings when it is cashed in. We are not big fans of life insurance on children and recommend that, if you do choose the life insurance route, the insurance is placed on the parents. Also, we prefer variable universal life when accumulation of principal is the primary goal, because of the more favorable returns that are possible. Think growth!

Of course, exactly how you should invest will depend on how many years you have available for the magic of compound interest to work. Let's look at some of the possible strategies.

Newborn to 10 Years of Age   If your child is newborn to 10 years of age, there are 8 to 18 years to accumulate the needed capital. This time frame allows you to invest aggressively for growth. Consider common stock and stock mutual funds. They may be more volatile than other

FIGURE 21–1

Calculate Approximate Savings Needed for College Funding

1. Your child's age.

2. Years to college (18 minus child's age).

3. Current annual cost of tuition, fees, room, board, books, supplies, transportation, and personal expenses.* Enter your own estimate.
   a. $8,562 average at public school for 1994/1995
   b. $17,846 average at private school for 1994/1995

4. College cost inflation. Select the anticipated inflation rate and find the appropriate inflation factor for your time horizon from the table below.

5. Future total cost of college. (Multiply Step 3 by Step 4)

6. Select the appropriate after-tax anticipated rate of return and locate the applicable return factor for your time horizon from the table below.

7. For the annual amount you will need to invest, divide Step 5 by Step 6.

8. For the monthly amount to invest, divide the annual amount by 12.

1. Age 4
2. 14 years to college
3. Public $8,562
4. (7%) x11.4485
5. $98,022
6. (8%) ÷34.1842
7. Annual $2,867
8. Monthly $2,867÷12
   $239

Years to College	Anticipated Inflation Rate			Anticipated Rate of Return			
	5%	7%	9%	6%	8%	10%	12%
0	4.3101	4.4399	4.5731	5.4875	5.5707	5.6561	5.7440
1	4.5256	4.7507	4.9847	5.2937	5.3760	5.4609	5.5485
2	4.7519	5.0833	5.4333	6.5426	6.7140	6.8927	7.0788
3	4.9895	5.4391	5.9223	7.8662	8.1594	8.4689	8.7950
4	5.2690	5.8199	6.4553	9.2689	9.7210	10.2041	10.7200
5	5.5009	6.2272	7.0363	10.7554	11.4078	12.1142	12.8790
6	5.7760	6.6632	7.6696	12.3306	13.2297	14.2170	15.3006
7	6.0648	7.1296	8.3599	14.0003	15.1982	16.4317	18.0170
8	6.3680	7.6286	9.1122	15.7699	17.3244	19.0803	21.0644
9	6.6864	8.1627	9.9323	17.6451	19.6214	21.8858	24.4827
10	7.0207	8.7340	10.8263	19.6323	22.1024	24.9745	28.3180
11	7.3718	9.3454	11.8006	21.7389	24.7828	28.3743	32.6210
12	7.7404	9.9996	12.8627	23.9713	27.6779	32.1183	37.4493
13	8.1274	10.6996	14.0203	26.3371	30.8057	36.2399	42.8674
14	8.5338	11.4485	15.2821	28.8446	34.1842	40.7778	48.9476
15	8.9604	12.2499	16.6575	31.5021	37.8337	45.7737	55.7713
16	9.4085	13.1074	18.1567	34.3188	41.7760	51.2740	63.4306
17	9.8789	14.0250	19.7908	37.3037	46.0348	57.3305	72.0286
18	10.3728	15.0067	21.5720	40.4676	50.6350	63.9989	81.6804

*Source: The College Board

investments, but have proven to be winners over the long term (growth mutual funds have averaged 13.6 percent over the last 10 years). Time is on your side.

Ages 10 to 14   If your child is within this age bracket, you have four to eight years to invest. Consider a balanced investment portfolio consisting of both high growth stock and stock mutual funds, and limited maturity bonds and bond funds (government bond funds averaged 10.6 percent over the last 10 years). A portfolio such as this will give you the advantage of equity growth with the security and decreased volatility of bond funds.

Over Age 14   With less than four years to accumulate capital, invest for both income and liquidity. This strategy means income-oriented funds, Treasury bills, limited maturity bonds and bond funds, and tax-free limited maturity bonds and bond funds. These investments will provide growth without sacrificing stability and liquidity.

Use the concepts of diversification you have learned to spread your risk. As the time to begin using the money nears, just lighten up on stocks and move into either fixed-income securities maturing when the tuition is due or short-term bonds. This strategy will protect you in the event of a major market reversal shortly before you need the money. But don't go overboard, because there are still three years until it is time to pay the senior year's tuition. Don't abandon your growth positions entirely.

Parents' Current Income

How much you can contribute depends, of course, on your income level and other expenses. We believe that if you have implemented the seven secrets that you will have adequate discretionary income to supplement your child's college costs, if needed. Also with one less teenager to house and feed, your costs at home will go down somewhat! Many people, those with their financial house in order, are able to pay 100 percent of their child's education from current cash flow.

Student's Income

A student who contributes toward his or her own education has an even greater stake in it, which we believe enhances the student's commitment to success in college. There is a lot to be said for Junior pitching in with a part-time job or a work-study program to pick up his incidental costs such as movies, dates, pizza, and beverages. We believe a higher value is placed on things that are earned. Besides, learning to handle money, even being frugal, is an important life skill. It may even be more valuable than Chemistry 101 in the long run.

We prefer that students focus their attention on their studies and other worthwhile college activities, but working for four to eight hours a week is not a great distraction and the money earned is a significant contribution. Most college towns seem to have plenty of part-time jobs to go around. The Root kids held a variety of part-time jobs throughout their college years, including working in restaurants and dorm cafeterias, cleaning horse and livestock barns on campus, selling advertising for the school newspaper, and driving a school bus. Special work-study job programs are available through the school, depending on financial need requirements.

Summer jobs have long been a mainstay for college students. While acknowledging that the best jobs usually go to those who start their search first, we believe that any ambitious student can find worthwhile summer employment. Many students pay a significant portion of their college expenses with income from their summer wages.

Financial Aid

For families that are not able to meet college costs, there is financial aid available from a variety of sources, including the federal government, state governments, colleges, and private organizations. Financial aid helps pay college costs, including direct educational costs (tuition, books, fees) and personal living expenses incurred while attending college. Financial aid includes gift aid (grants and scholarships) and self-help aid (loans and work). There is about $45 billion worth of aid available annually in the United States, 75 percent of which comes from the federal and state governments.

The total financial aid package that is offered by a college to a student will generally combine aid from two or more sources. The amount of aid a student receives depends on the student's calculated need, which is based on the costs of the college the student is attending and the *expected family contribution*. This contribution is the amount that the family and student are expected to pay and is determined from the *Federal Methodology* formula that considers the family's and student's income and assets. The resulting financial aid package is made up of different layers.

Federal Pell Grants   Federal Pell Grants (formerly called *Basic Educational Opportunity Grants*) make up the first layer of the financial aid package for undergraduate students. This is Uncle Sam's largest gift program to college students and is designed to help qualifying families take the bite out of college tuition. To qualify for the program, the family income must not exceed $28,000 per year and the expected family contribution must be $2,100 or less per year. Don't get excited if you're just under the income cutoff: the higher your expected family contribution, the less you will qualify for. Pell Grants are awarded in amounts ranging from about $400 to $2,340 per year to qualifying students. Although these grants fall far short of meeting college expenses, they are a good start.

Private Scholarships   Private scholarships are the next layer of the financial aid package. These scholarships do not affect eligibility for Pell Grants, but they do affect the amount of other need-based aid a student may receive. (We'll talk more about scholarships a little later.)

State Grants   State grants make up the next layer of the aid package. These grants are usually available only to state residents attending in-state colleges and are usually based on need.

Other Federal Aid   Other federal aid is administered at the campus level. This aid includes the Federal Supplemental Educational Opportunity Grant (FSEOG) for undergraduate students who have exceptional financial need. Students can receive as much as $4,000 a year, depending on the school they choose and available funding. Also included are the Federal Work-Study Program and 5 percent interest Federal Perkins Loans, which don't begin charging interest until 9 months after graduation.

Many people who could really use the money don't apply for financial aid, thinking that they won't qualify. However, keep in mind that *need* is a relative term determined by the costs of the college your student is attending. Your family may have little or no need if your child is attending a state college costing $9,000 per year, but you might have substantial need if she or he is considering a private college that costs $24,000 per year.

There is money available for students at almost all income levels. Even though federal aid is almost exclusively reserved for students who have financial need, we advise that you apply for it no matter what. We make this recommendation because many other possible sources of financial aid are simply not available until you have been turned down for federal aid. Application for federal aid is made through the Free Application for Federal Student Aid.

FIGURE 21–2

COLLEGE PLANNING IN ACTION

Brooklynne Levasa was one of the top students in her high school class. She hoped to attend a highly regarded private college and major in architecture. Her parents, Roger and Kimberly, believing that they were over the income limits for financial aid, were quick to point out that there was just no way that they could afford to send Brooklynne to that college; they suggested that she attend the less expensive state university instead. However, because of Brooklynne's persistence, the Levasas agreed to visit the private college and investigate their college funding options. They met with a representative of the financial aid office who was able to assemble a viable financial aid package for Brooklynne. It included a college scholarship, a private architectural scholarship for minority students, work-study, and a subsidized Stafford loan — that, with the expected family contribution, would cover most of Brooklynne's anticipated college costs. The family, excited about Brooklynne's newly discovered prospects said that, if necessary, they would take out a PLUS loan to make up the difference. The Levasas, previously thinking that they were not eligible for financial aid, learned that need is relative to the costs of the chosen college. They now advise their friends to carefully investigate all financing options before putting the student's college dreams aside.

Financial Need = Cost to Attend College − Expected Family Contribution

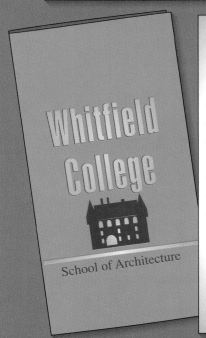

	Standard State University	Prestigious Private College
Total Annual Cost of Attendance	$9,000	$24,000
Expected Family Contribution	−8,000	−8,000
Financial Need (Aid Eligibility)	$1,000	$16,000
Financial Aid Package Offered		
Pell Grant	$ 0	$ 0
Private Scholarship	0	2,000
Institutional Scholarship	0	6,000
State Grant	0	0
FSEOG	0	0
Work Study	0	3,375
Perkins Loan	0	0
Subsidized Stafford Loan	1,000	2,625
Total Aid Package	**$1,000**	**$14,000**
Amount Not Covered by Aid	**0**	***$2,000**

* The amount not covered by aid at the private college can be borrowed using a PLUS loan or other private loan source, paid from current cash flow, or taken from investments or savings.

Financial Planning Extras

For more specifics on applying for financial aid, contact your high school guidance counselor or the financial aid office of the college your student will attend. However, we do want to emphasize that this process must be started early. The application should be submitted immediately after January 1 of the year your student will enter college. Because there is a limited amount of aid available, this is a situation where the early bird does get the worm.

Loans

Loan money is available for people of all income levels and, depending on the specific loan program, may or may not be based on need. Student loans available through the Federal Family Education Loan Program include Stafford Loans, Unsubsidized Stafford Loans, and the Parent Loans to Undergraduate Students (PLUS) Loans. The Direct William D. Ford Student Loan Program (currently available at about 500 colleges) includes the Direct Stafford, Direct Unsubsidized Stafford, and Direct PLUS Loans. The difference between these programs is that the federal government itself is the lender for the direct loans. Banks, S&Ls, credit unions, insurance companies, and other private lenders provide the funds for the other loans.

The federal government's student loan programs offer favorable interest rates and repayment terms that make them hard to beat.

Stafford Loans Subsidized Stafford Student Loans are only available to students who demonstrate financial need and are offered at below-market interest rates with the federal government making up the difference. In addition, the federal government will pay the interest while the student is in school and for six months afterward. Unsubsidized loans are less restrictive and aren't need-based, so anyone can qualify, but the interest is at higher rates and accrues while the student is attending school. Subject to eligibility, college freshmen can borrow up to $2,625 for the first year and borrowing can total up to $23,000 for undergraduate work. In the second year, the limit is $3,500. Third and fourth-year students can borrow up to $5,500. If you're a quick study in math, you'll notice right away that the total for these four years adds up to less than $23,000. The difference is that money is included for summer school sessions.

To apply for a Stafford Loan, you must first fill out a Free Application for Federal Student Aid (FAFSA), which is available at any college financial aid office or high school guidance office. Some schools also require a Financial Aid Form (FAF). In four to six weeks after the form(s) have been completed, you will receive the Student Aid Report (SAR) to verify the information. Again, we emphasize that when applying for financial aid, the rule-of-thumb is to apply as early as possible after January 1st. January is better than March. Late applications don't mean that you won't receive aid, but early applications receive priority funding and can end up with higher loan amounts.

After all the paperwork requirements are completed and accepted, you will receive an award letter that details the aid package. When you receive the letter, you must then apply at your local bank or other financial institution for the actual loan. Here again, the financial aid office will probably have all the necessary paperwork and can make helpful recommendations.

Payments on either the principal or interest, or both, are deferred until six months after graduation or the student leaves college. Repayment may be stretched out from 12 to 30 years. Under certain circumstances such as loss of a job (limited to three years), economic hardship (limited to three years), or going back to school, payments can be deferred or temporarily suspended. Under certain less severe hardship conditions that do not qualify for deferment, there is a provision to temporarily postpone or reduce the principal payments. The loans are authorized to be canceled upon death or permanent disability of the borrower. There is also a Federal Loan Consolidation Program for loans over $7,500. Be sure you understand all the conditions of the loan, and whenever there is a problem in repaying it, communicate with your lender.

The Federal Student Loan programs seem to be under constant reconsideration and revision. Interest rates, eligibility requirements, loan limits, and repayment provisions may be changed. The amount of loan money available during each year depends on the generosity of Congress and on how well former students repay their loans, thus replenishing the loan pools. Currently, about $65 billion is outstanding in student loans.

In the past, many people did not take their obligation to repay their student loans seriously and the programs suffered substantial losses. Uncle Sam has since instituted serious measures to crack down on defaulters. Defaulted loans are reported to national credit agencies and eventually assigned to the federal government for collections. Internal Revenue Service tax refunds can be withheld and applied to the loan balance, your wages could be garnisheed, and certain professional licenses could be lost. The continued existence of these programs, which have been of tremendous benefit to millions of people, is dependent upon people fulfilling their obligations to repay their student loans.

PLUS Loans for Parents PLUS (Parent Loans for Undergraduate Students) loans are the responsibility of the parents alone and are not based on need, whereas Stafford loans are taken out and repaid by the student. PLUS loans have reasonably competitive rates, but should be considered only after other sources such as grants, scholarships, available income, and guaranteed student loan (GSL) options have been exhausted. PLUS loan rates are tied to the Treasury bill rates. There is no set dollar limit on a PLUS loan; you can borrow the entire cost of college minus any other financial aid received. Although eligibility is open to all income levels, a solid credit record is necessary to obtain a PLUS loan.

Other Loans There are also many private or nonfederal education loans available such as the EXCEL[sm] loan from Nellie Mae, the largest nonprofit provider of education loans in the country. Also many colleges have their own loans available for students who cannot cover their educational costs by other means.

Scholarships

Scholarships are a source of free money that doesn't have to be repaid, and they come in a wide variety of sizes, shapes, and colors. They are made available by many nonprofit groups, corporations, and foundations, as well as by the colleges themselves. Most scholarships are not the full-ride kind, but instead offer a smaller sum. However, every little bit helps. Many scholarships have narrowly defined selection criteria, so searching out the right ones can be quite a trying but worthwhile task. Check with your employer, your church, any organizations you or your student belongs to, and your college for the availability of scholarships. There are also many reference sources and books listing hundreds of available scholarships. Many scholarships are not awarded because no one applies for them.

Colleges have their own pools of funds which they use to attract and help students that they want to attend their colleges. These include academic, athletic, music, and talent awards.

Merit-based scholarships are awarded based on specified criteria and many are also need-based. They generally have well-defined requirements, and criteria for awarding the scholarships can depend on such things as field of study, age, race, or service in the armed forces. For example, in the state of Wisconsin, there are scholarships available to women studying journalism and to children of Korean War Veterans. In addition, many corporations award scholarships to the children of their employees.

However, many merit scholarships are awarded based on academic achievement and/or SAT or ACT scores instead of need. It may be very financially worthwhile to have your student spend some extra time or even take a review course to prepare for the SAT or ACT exams. Students who do, usually get higher scores. The cost of a special preparatory course may be a good investment. Also keep in mind that these exams may be repeated. Good grades are more than academic indicators; they can really pay off when seeking funding for a college education.

Some states have special programs to help finance college education. In Georgia, for instance, the state lottery-funded program HOPE (Helping Outstanding Pupils Educationally) offers students who have a 3.0 grade point average and are from families earning less than $100,000 a year, free tuition at any Georgia public institution.

When you are searching out scholarships, the password is persistence. Seek them out. Use many reference sources. You have to find scholarships before you can apply for them.

Reserve Officers Training Corps (ROTC)

The armed forces offers some great scholarship opportunities for those who are interested in military service through the Reserve Officers Training Corps (ROTC) programs on many college campuses. Students accepted into these programs may receive full-ride scholarships plus a monthly spending allowance. Following graduation, the student will owe the military a certain number of years of service, which is a good opportunity to get some on-the-job experience and additional training plus other military benefits.

Home Equity as a Source of Money for College

Many parents of college-age children may find themselves in the position of being house-rich and cash-poor that we discussed at length in Chapter 20. After student loans, the next least-expensive source of loans to finance college is probably tapping into your home equity. Home equity is not considered in the calculations for federal financial aid and if you borrow against it, the loan proceeds are not counted as income. You can spend many years paying off a mortgage or home equity loan, lessening the burden of trying to pay for college in a tight time frame.

The interest on home mortgages is tax deductible, so take the tax savings into consideration when you are borrowing against home equity. In a 31 percent tax bracket, a home equity loan at 11 percent is a better deal than a PLUS loan at 8.38 percent.

Saving on College Costs

So far we have talked about coming up with the money to pay for college, but now we want to shift our focus to some ideas that can reduce the amount of money you need for college costs, while still providing your student with the education he or she desires.

Community College — Benefits Close to Home

Community college is a great way to cut college costs by about 40 percent. You can save a bundle in tuition and room and board if your child attends a local community college the first two years.

Accredited community college courses are transferable to state and private colleges and universities. The first two years in most college degree programs are generally spent satisfying general education requirements — courses that are essentially taught the same everywhere. When saving money is important, attending community college for the first two years really makes sense. Your child will receive the same four-year college degree, whether he or she spends all four years at the same college or transfers from a community college.

Community colleges are also good places to explore career interests. Whether or not your child has chosen a field of study, chances are he or she will change majors at least once during the next four years. After two years, when it is time to transfer to a four-year college, your student will probably be more certain about a major. Changing majors in a four-year college can be expensive, sometimes adding a year or more to the total studies.

Viewing college financing with the tough investment criteria you have learned points to another benefit of community colleges: less investment risk. About one third of the students who enter college do not graduate. They drop out after one or two semesters and take jobs, get married, or perhaps enter military service. Community college is a good place to try out and become accustomed to the college experience without too much expense. After students make it through two years of college, they will have a better idea of whether college is the right track for them, wisdom better gained at community college prices.

Stay on Track

Degrees are awarded when the requirements for the degree are completed. Whenever signing up for courses for each term, students need to plan carefully to be certain that they are keeping on schedule for their degree requirements. Most degree programs are designed to be completed in four years. However, it is easy to fall behind in taking required courses and additional terms may be necessary. This additional time costs money.

Accelerate Studies

Students who can handle heavier course loads can shorten the time needed to complete their degrees. Graduating a semester or a quarter early can result in significant savings as well as give the graduate a head start over his or her classmates in the job market. Some colleges even offer formal three-year bachelor's degree programs. One of the Root children completed his bachelor's degree in just 3 years and one summer term — saving one full year of college costs.

Some students are able to accelerate their studies by taking advantage of Advanced Placement (AP) courses in high school and then passing exams to qualify for college credits in certain subjects. About 150 high schools in the United States even take this process to the next level: an intensive college preparatory program leading to an International Baccalaureate (IB) diploma. This diploma is worth as much as one year of college credits at many colleges and universities.

UTMA and UGMA

No, these are not characters from *Clan of the Cave Bear*. The Uniform Transfer to Minors Account and the Uniform Gifts to Minors Act are ways to transfer small to medium-sized *tax-advantaged* investments to minor children. A portion of all the earnings within these accounts are taxed at the rate of the minor, not the parent. Refer back to Chapter 15 for more details.

Anyone can gift $10,000 per person per year without paying gift tax. ($20,000, if given jointly with your spouse.)

Because of the tax advantages, it would seem as though these minor's accounts would be the answer to college savings. But they are best made to older children — and we'll show you why.

Prior to age 14, the first $600 of investment income is tax-free, and the next $600 is taxed at the child's rate of 15 percent. For example, there would be $90 in federal tax due on an investment held in the name of a minor if it earned $1,200 a year. If the same account were held by parents who are in the 31 percent tax bracket, their tax would be $372. The catch here is that any amount over $1,200 is taxed at the parent's rate. Some parents compromise by transferring only an amount that returns $1,200 into the child's name. Assuming earnings of 10 percent, they achieve the maximum tax benefit.

At age 14 and beyond, though, all investment income under $21,450 is taxed at the child's rate. Therefore, at that age there would be tax advantages to having much more money held in the child's name. But wait, that may not always be the wisest course. Be aware that one of the drawbacks of these accounts is that they are irrevocable upon the age of majority of the child (age 18 in most states), and are truly the property of the child, who may or may not use the money as you intended. There is no guarantee that it will be used for college.

Alternative Investments for College Savings

You already know that we think the best places to invest savings for college are in growth mutual funds. They will accept small monthly investments, and because there is such a tremendous variety to choose from, you can invest in just about anything you are interested in. There are also other options to investigate.

EE savings bonds are safe and exempt from state and local taxes. If they are used to pay tuition, and if your earnings are less than $61,850 as a couple or less than $41,200 as a single parent, they are also exempt from federal taxes. A 4.25 percent exempt bond is equivalent to a 6.85 percent taxable yield.

Nearly two dozen states offer college savings bonds, sometimes called baccalaureate bonds, that are state-backed zero-coupon bonds. These bonds currently have a yield to maturity of about 5 percent, and the earnings are exempt from state and federal taxes. They can be used for any purpose , not just to pay tuition. But be aware that they are subject to market risk. When interest rates go up, the value of bonds goes down. If that were the case, when it is time to use the money you may have to sell at a loss.

Ten states — Alabama, Alaska, Florida, Louisiana, Missouri, Ohio, Oklahoma, Pennsylvania, West Virginia, and Wyoming — offer prepaid tuition plans that allow you to lock in tuition costs by paying in advance. In Florida, which has the largest program with 240,000 contracts, you can pay a lump sum of $5,667 (1995) or $121 a month for 55 months to guarantee four years of tuition at any of the states' nine state university campuses. Benefits are transferable to a sibling, and if the child doesn't choose a state institution, the public tuition cost can be transferred to a private school. Even though these plans sound like a good idea, chances are that you could do better investing the same amount of money elsewhere.

Ready, Set, Go

First, keep in mind that student loans aren't distributed until a beginning student is in school for 30 days. The people at the college are aware of this provision and will arrange deferred payment when financial aid is coming.

Second, if you are contributing to the cost of tuition, use the money from the investments that are held in your child's name first. Standard financial aid contribution formulas require students to use 35 percent of the money from their accounts as part of the estimated family contribution. Yet, parents are only required to use 5.6 percent after various allowances. Using the child's money first delays invading other assets, and the student is eligible for more aid after his or her money is gone.

Finally, keep in mind that selling stocks or mutual funds to finance tuition might be double trouble. You will be taxed on any gain and the income will count against you in the financial aid formula. Depending on the return on the investment and the cost of borrowing, it may be better to borrow money using the investment as collateral. When school is over, draw from the investment to repay the loan.

Summary

Most people want to provide a college education for their children because it offers so many advantages: increased job opportunities, the ability to earn a much higher income than those without college degrees, self-discipline, and many personal and professional contacts they can maintain for the rest of their lives. But college costs continue to mount each year, making it necessary to plan well in advance of college years. In fact, you cannot begin planning too soon.

Besides the savings you accumulate toward your children's education, there are many types of financial aid available to soften the financial impact: scholarships, grants, and loans. It is well worth the time to carefully investigate all sources of outside financial aid.

Don't overlook some of the ideas that can cut the overall costs of obtaining a degree. These include sending your children to a local community college for the first one or two years of college, advanced placement courses, and accelerating studies.

Information Sources

The Federal Student Aid Information Center: 1-800-4-FED-AID
Higher Education Information Center: 1-800-442-1171
Nellie Mae, Braintree, Massachusetts: 1-800-634-9308

TWENTY-TWO

Financial Planning for the Self-Employed
An Entrepreneurial Primer

"You'll never get rich working for someone else."

– (Just About)
Everyone's Father

Have you always dreamed of being your own boss? There is a special allure to being self-employed that is exploding in our country. Of the more than two million new businesses that Dun & Bradstreet researched last year, over 20 percent were one- or two-person companies. More people are becoming self-employed than are getting married!

We are not sure whether this trend can be attributed to corporate downsizing or global economic forces, but we think most of these people are simply seeking a better quality of life than they can have working for big companies. They are looking for a sense of job security that doesn't exist elsewhere in the business world, and they want to be part of the action.

Today's self-employed business owners are better educated than in prior times and their businesses are more sophisticated. A large percentage are service or consultant-style businesses, run by people who understand how technology and electronic networks are changing industry. They understand how computers and communications equipment make it easy for the little person on Main Street to deliver goods and skilled services to the big companies on Park Avenues around the world.

These people are not looking for leisure workdays or instantly inflated incomes, because both are scarce among the self-employed. In fact, if you prefer a chain of command, a clearly defined job description, and carrying out orders, being self-employed is probably not for you.

Being self-employed means that you do it all: empty the garbage, type your own letters, and make your own cold calls. Above all, self-employed people take risks. By now you know what that means: high rewards can only come with high risk. We have been self-employed for many years, and we know that whatever the headaches and risks, the freedom and rewards are unmatched in the nine-to-five corporate world.

The bad news is that only one out of every five new businesses will make it. Will yours be the one? Or will it be one of the four that failed? Being self-employed requires discipline and dedication. Zeal and a sense of mission will only take you so far. You have to prepare, prepare, and prepare before you decide to be self-employed. If you are already self-employed, upgrade your skills and business knowledge at every opportunity. Raise your head and be aware of the direction your business is taking.

The good news, on the other hand, is that you are already more prepared than most people because you are reading *The 7 Secrets of Financial Success*. Remember the quote we used about managing your money like a business? You guessed it: most of the tools you need to succeed at being self-employed are in this book. In this chapter, we'll look at the *basic* issues and strategies that come with self-employment.

We're going to assume that you've already test-marketed your product or service and have done the necessary research on pricing, related expenses, and break-even points. What? You haven't? Just because you can build widgets doesn't mean that anyone is going to buy them. If you are going to rely on the business for your livelihood, we think you should approach it as a business, not a hobby.

So, what is the first step in getting off to a good start? Seek professional advice. It is vital to your success in business. Secret number seven, if you remember, is to seek professional advice, but concerning self-employment, it should be number one.

Seek Professional Advice

Yes, entrepreneurship is for mavericks, but there are some things that it doesn't pay to try to do alone. You probably decided to go into business because of your knowledge in a particular area. But you can't be an expert in every field, right? Getting professional advice in specific areas of expertise will help you avoid costly mistakes. Your own field of expertise and your experience will dictate which advisors you should seek out when starting your business. Consider these professionals your business management team.

Attorney.   An attorney is a must to help choose and set up the most appropriate structure for your business (sole proprietorship, partnership, corporation, or limited liability company, in some states). He or she will advise you about federal and state regulations that affect your industry and help file the necessary licenses and permits. Your attorney should draw up or review contracts and other legal documents and suggest steps to help avoid lawsuits.

> ***"One who is not wise himself cannot be well advised."***
> **Machiavelli, The Prince, XXIII**

As many as 60 to 80 percent of businesses fail upon the death of the key business owner. At the outset, meet with your attorney and insurance agent to be sure your business can be passed to your heirs in the manner you wish, and that there is cash available to cover the costs of finding and training a replacement.

Bookkeeper/Accountant/Tax Advisor.   If you are the creative type, but are not good at record keeping, you may want to hire a full-time bookkeeper, accountant, or both, or use their services on an as-needed basis. They will help you choose and set up an accounting system, computerized or not, that will simplify tax work and allow you to make timely business decisions. Small business owners run their businesses by watching cash flow and their bottom line. Do yourself and your business a favor — keep accurate records and stay current!

Your accountant or tax advisor will tell you how and when to file tax reports and help set up a payroll program, if you have employees. Handling multistate revenue is especially tricky, so if you do business in more than one state, you will need extra help.

> **"He that refuseth to buy counsel cheap, shall buy repentance dear."**
> *Anonymous*

Insurance Agent.   Businesses are subject to certain liabilities of which you may not be aware. In addition, the personal insurance coverage your employer carried will stop when you become self-employed. In this complex and expensive area, you need the services of a business insurance expert.

Small Business Administration.   Representatives from the SBA have a wealth of knowledge at their fingertips. Take advantage of their knowledge and experience, and meet with them as often as necessary. Consider them your mentors. You'll find their free help invaluable in the start-up phase of your business.

Start Small

If you want to include a potentially high income-producing investment that holds a high degree of risk in your portfolio, how can you best minimize the risk? By making it a small part of your overall portfolio. The same is true with your business. If you're not 100 percent positive that you can earn an income that will equal your current income — or better yet, outperform it — ease into your new business gradually.

Work Part-Time.   When you run a business part-time and work part-time (or full-time) for someone else, you may put in 60-hour weeks, but you have the best of both worlds: the stability of a full-time position along with the freedom and tax incentives of operating your own business.

Don't Hire Unnecessary Help.   If you can run your business by yourself (or with the help of a family member), don't hire unnecessary employees who will add tax, insurance, and liability headaches. For help during your busy season, try temporary workers hired through a qualified temporary agency, and let them deal with payroll deductions and other details.

Work from Home.   Keeping an office in your home has many advantages, not the least of which is convenience. You will save money on space rental, commuting, and utilities, and also realize the tax advantages associated with a home office. Be sure you are aware of any zoning restrictions and get the necessary permits to operate a business from your home.

Lease or Rent Equipment.   Don't spend a lot of cash for equipment you might need to replace or repair later at great cost. Lease and rental fees are 100 percent deductible if the equipment is used strictly for business purposes. Your cash can then be used for operating costs.

Business Structure

Professional advice is critical when choosing the structure of your business. It is a difficult decision — a vital first step — and must be done before you establish a track record of what works best. Different structures have different treatment of gains and losses, and of course, tax treatment is the most important consideration in choosing which structure is best for your business.

Generally speaking, you have three or four options, depending upon the availability in your state: incorporation, sole proprietorship, partnership, and limited liability company (not yet available in all states). Each structure has advantages and disadvantages in the areas of management, transferability of ownership, personal liability, set-up cost, and benefits for owners. Again, we must stress this point: don't try to do the job alone. Seek professional help!

Incorporation

The choices for incorporating your business are as an ordinary C corporation and as a Subchapter S corporation.

A corporation is an entity that is authorized by law to stand alone, with various rights and duties. One of the rights is the right of succession. In other words, it can be sold, traded, or passed to heirs. Incorporation has traditionally been used by small businesses to shield personal assets from business liabilities. (However, this protection is not absolute, and much of the time, you will still be personally liable to some degree.)

Incorporation also vastly increases the deductions that can be taken for pension plans, and income can be spread out over several years using good years to make up for lean years, thereby reducing taxes. One advantage of a C corporation in the base or start-up year is that you can choose your fiscal year. It does not have to be the calendar year. Corporations are not privileged by Fifth Amendment rights and have fewer rights than individuals in a tax audit.

An ordinary C corporation can be owned by one person or many people. Common and preferred stock can be issued and the net or taxable income is taxed at the corporate level. This tax may be less than at the personal level because salaries are an expense that reduces corporate taxable income. Of course, you pay personal taxes on your salary. Keep in mind that corporate profits are taxed twice: once at the corporate level, and again when dividends are paid out to the shareholders.

Ownership of a Subchapter S corporation is limited to 35 individuals or certain trusts, and only one class of common stock can be issued. Sub S corporate earnings pass through to the individual owners and are taxed as personal income. Employee benefits for shareholder-employees may also pass through and not be fully deductible. The Sub S name comes from the 1958 IRS code that authorizes qualified corporations to be taxed like partnerships. As you can see, Sub S corporations have the benefits of being incorporated without the major disadvantage: double taxation.

Whichever corporate structure you choose, you must be aware of and follow all the rules to avoid pitfalls.

FIGURE 22-1

Business Organizational Structure

Sole Proprietorship

A *sole proprietorship* is an unincorporated business owned by one person, the proprietor. This is the simplest form of business ownership. Sole proprietorships are generally relatively small businesses, although some have hundreds of employees.

- One owner
- Income reported on the owner's tax return
- Income is taxed at the owner's tax rate
- The owner accepts all the business risks

Advantages
1. The owner is the boss
2. Lowest organizational costs
3. Easy to start or end
4. Owner maintains control
5. All profits go directly to the owner
6. Avoids "double taxation"
7. Keogh retirement plan available

Disadvantages
1. Unlimited and unshared liability
2. The owner assumes ultimate responsibility
3. Limited ability to raise capital
4. Profits are taxed at a rate higher than the corporate rate
5. Business terminates upon death of proprietor

Partnership

A *partnership* is a voluntary association of two or more persons who combine their resources and talents to conduct business. The proportion of ownership is determined by agreement between the partners. There should be a written partnership agreement.

- More than one owner
- Income is reported on each owner's individual income tax return
- Income is taxed at each individual owner's tax rate

Advantages
1. Combines the skills and resources of the partners
2. Low organizational costs
3. Easy to start
4. Profits flow directly to partners
5. Avoids "double taxation"
6. Keogh retirement plan available

Disadvantages
1. Disagreements among partners
2. Unlimited personal liability
3. Phantom income
4. Profits taxed at a higher rate than for corporations
5. Limited ability raise capital
6. Business continuation problems
7. Benefits may not be deductible

Incorporation

A *corporation* is a legal entity which is looked upon as a separate "person" by the law. The corporate entity has its own rights, privileges, and liabilities distinct from those of its owners. Ownership is defined in terms of shares of stock owned by one, a few, or large group of individuals. The life of the corporation continues beyond the life of the shareholders income.

- Three Forms of Corporations
  Close or Private
  Open or Public
  Nonprofit
- The corporation files its own tax returns
- Shares of stock issued to owners

Advantages
1. Limited liability of shareholders
2. Easy to transfer ownership interest
3. Greatest ability to raise capital
4. Indefinite life
5. Corporate tax rate is lower than personal tax rate

Disadvantages
1. Possible double taxation
2. Higher organizational costs
3. Requires complex records and many filings
4. Higher legal and accounting fees
5. Increased government regulations

Sole Proprietorship

Operating as a sole proprietor allows self-employed individuals to claim business income and expenses on a Schedule C, and it is the simplest method of operating a small business. As with Sub S corporations, employee benefit deductions for owners are restricted. Since a schedule C is filed with the owner's personal tax return, the operating year must generally be a calendar year.

Partnership

A customer of ours once said, "A partnership is a ship you shouldn't sail." From our personal experience, that statement is true. Being a partner can be *very* difficult and, on the other hand, has benefits such as being able to take advantage of the expertise and experience of more than one person.

Generally, partnership taxable income and expense items pass through to the partners who are taxed at their respective individual tax rates. The operating year is most often a calendar year and partnerships have tax benefits and restrictions similar to Sub S corporations.

Limited Liability Company

A fairly new business structure that is not yet available in all states is the limited liability company (LLC). This structure is taxed like partnerships, but has the protection of corporations.

The Business Plan

The first financial success secret in this book is to set your personal financial goals. The same holds true for your business. A study done by AT&T showed that businesses are more likely to fail when they begin without a business plan. The business plan forces you to make explicit assumptions about the operation of your business, and then allows you to challenge those assumptions.

Whether your business plan is a simple mission statement or a complicated document with staged growth and earnings projections, review it often and make revisions as conditions dictate. As you know, focusing on your goals creates success.

FIGURE 22–2

Steps to Successful Business Planning

Financial planning for business owners and professionals is a comprehensive process through which business owner(s) and advisor(s):

- Evaluate the business's needs in areas such as structure and organization, risk management, employee benefits, retirement planning, and tax planning.

- Set goals and develop a plan that will maximize the financial benefits to the business and its owner(s).

- Implement the plan through appropriate legal and company documents, investment vehicles, and insurance programs which will take maximum advantage of pre-tax and after-tax dollars.

- Provide continuous monitoring of investment performance, tax laws, and changes within the business so that appropriate adjustments to the business plan are made, when necessary, to keep it on track.

- Coordinate the business owner's personal and business financial matters for optimum advantage of each.

- Evaluate estate plans and documents, especially when the owner wants to keep the business in the family.

Coping with Erratic Income

One of the most frightening things about being self-employed is learning to cope with an erratic income. Payday doesn't arrive on the first of the month anymore, but rather when your customers decide to pay their bills. Unfortunately, there's no guarantee that it will be the same time that your house payment is due.

Sometimes seeing a large balance in your checking account for the first time causes temporary insanity. Remember your suppliers and payroll when success comes and take advantage of the opportunity to save for the lean times.

When we started our business, we were often crippled before we completely understood the need for a cash reserve. The foundation of The Success Triangle™, that rainy day stash, is even more critical to the smooth operation of business. Why? You not only have to prepare for unexpected emergencies on the expense side; when you're self-employed, you also have to prepare for nasty surprises on the income side.

One of the worst mistakes a newly self-employed business owner can make is to inflate fixed expenses in the high income years. Don't burden yourself with excessive debt right away and don't rush to upgrade your lifestyle before you have proved your mettle. Many small businesses have failed because of expensive offices, new cars, fancy equipment, and such.

Concentrate on Your Core Business

After all we have said about diversification, you might find it odd that we don't think diversifying is the answer when you start a business. If the business depends on the expertise of a key person, spreading yourself too thinly spells disaster.

Instead, concentrate on your core business. To succeed, stay focused and keep a clear idea of what business you are really in, what product you are really selling, and what energies really create revenues. You may have heard the old adage that 20 percent of your output determines 80 percent of your income. We have never come across anything that disproves that point. Determine which activities create revenue, then concentrate on them. Make the most of your most precious asset: your time.

Financing and Debt

Lenders usually want you to leave them the keys to your house and your first-born child before they will consider extending credit to self-employed people. They don't like customers with huge income swings (the hallmark of the self-employed) and they aren't used to dealing with people who don't fit the mold. And can you blame them? Statistics show that small businesses do not have a good record for staying in business. If it is any consolation, professional athletes often find themselves in a similar position when they are trying to obtain credit, in spite of their giant salaries.

When you are trying to obtain credit, your cash reserve will be an important asset. You must be able to prove to a lender that you can successfully manage a variable income, and if you have followed our advice and used your emergency funds wisely, that's not too difficult to prove. Expect to put up some type of collateral and personal guarantees for any loan.

When things are going well and you have had a couple of successful years in a row, set up a business line of credit before you need it. If the world were perfect, you might never have to use it. It's nice to have it anyway, though, because it is nearly impossible to obtain a loan when you really need it.

Insurance Concerns

Besides the necessary insurance specific to your business, you will probably want to consider a business liability policy, or umbrella policy, to cover other areas of vulnerability. Even when you are working from home, you will need specific insurance to cover your business assets. Be aware that homeowner's insurance will not cover business losses, and your automobile insurance will not cover business equipment such as a camera or a portable computer when you travel.

Currently, sole proprietors, partnerships, and S corporations can only write off 25 percent of the costs of owner/partner health insurance at the individual level. The full amount is a deductible expense to C corporations.

If you were participating in a company health care plan as an employee, you can keep it at your own expense for 18 months after leaving. Be sure to compare coverages and rates; you may be able to find a better deal on your own, especially if you are young and healthy. If you don't run to the doctor for every ailment and keep your emergency fund in place, you can save money by using high deductibles.

It can be a disastrous mistake to neglect disability insurance when you are self-employed. Your most important asset is your income-producing ability. The chances of your being disabled for more than three months are much greater than the risk of a significant loss on your house or auto. You wouldn't think of not having homeowner's or auto insurance. Why gamble with your future income?

You may find it easier to purchase an individual, noncancelable disability policy while you are an employee, because some insurance companies want to see a year's self-employed earnings before they will provide coverage. Try to replace 60 to 70 percent of your total income. If partial disability allows earning some income, most disability policies make up the difference between your reduced earnings and your previous earnings. Here again, if you have that precious six-month emergency reserve, you can save on premiums by opting for a six-month waiting period.

Taking Advantage of Tax Deductions

Tax advantages are one of the most exciting aspects of owning your own business. When you purchase equipment such as a portable computer or a fax machine, or even a painting to decorate your office, the entire cost is a deductible business expense. If you are in the 31 percent tax bracket, this deduction is like getting the IRS to kick in 31 percent on every business expense.

This idea is so intriguing to some people that they create sideline businesses that lose money just so they can enjoy the tax deductions. Does this strategy sound wise? Not to us. Remember, we don't choose an investment simply for the tax benefits. The IRS looks at businesses closely and will want to see a profit in three out of five years — otherwise they'll classify your business as a hobby and won't allow deductions. However, if a consistent reduction in losses can be demonstrated, you may still qualify. Fortunately, the IRS accepts a broad interpretation of a business. Consider the tax benefits of having a business that you enjoy a blessing. And be sure to see your tax advisor for details.

Keep Accurate Records

Successful, self-employed business people stockpile records as diligently as they pursue their customers, not only to efficiently operate their businesses, but also to prove deductions. The IRS can veto any deductions you can't prove are helping to build your business, so look upon your business records as your best friends.

Computerized bookkeeping systems are inexpensive and easy to use, taking much of the pain out of record keeping. Whatever system you use, create a thorough paper trail. Always pay by check, save every receipt and invoice, and keep a log of business travel mileage. A few minutes a day can make a big difference at tax time. A good tax advisor won't let you get away with buying so much as a box of paper clips without getting a receipt.

Home Office Deductions

Choosing to work from home is not just a convenience, it can also help you realize significant tax savings. For instance, if you set aside a portion of your home (or apartment) strictly for business purposes, 100 percent of the costs associated with that portion of your dwelling are deductible.

The same holds true for utilities, repairs, cleaning fees, taxes, home-owner's insurance, and mortgage interest. A pro rata portion of any expenses relating to the whole dwelling can be deducted as business expenses.

The IRS will not allow deductions for home office expenses if most of the income-producing work is done on the clients' premises. For instance, if you repair computers and work primarily at your customers' offices, you would not be eligible for home office deductions.

If you own your home, the portion used for an office can be depreciated over a 31½-year period, but remember that it reduces the cost basis on your home and increases capital gains at the time of sale. And capital gains from that portion of the house cannot be rolled over. If you are planning to move in the near future, think again about the depreciation expense.

Accelerate Deductions; Defer Income

Being self-employed gives you the unique advantage of being able to plan expenditures and, to some extent, to plan to realize income in a way that will be the most advantageous, tax-wise. Plan purchases of equipment to take maximum advantage of the annual equipment tax break. The allowed portion of the costs can be expensed instead of depreciated over a longer period. Time major purchases over a two-year period.

Is it better to realize a significant business expense in December of the current year or the following January? Usually in December, because *time is money*. Every dollar you save in taxes this year is worth a dollar plus the rate of inflation next year. Then, too, the IRS isn't known for giving back extra tax dollars paid if you make a lot of money this year and lose money next year. Take the deductions as soon as you can, unless you *know* your tax liability will be significantly greater next year. In that case, push the expenditure forward into the next year.

Let's say that you have the opportunity to realize income either in December of the current year or the following January. Which would be better from a tax standpoint? The following January is almost always the better choice. You may think this recommendation violates the logic we've just described, because if a dollar is worth more now, why not realize the income in December?

Financial Planning Extras

A dollar earned in December will be added to the taxable income for the entire year. Why pay taxes on it in December when you can wait an entire year? Remember the time value of money — put off paying taxes!

Hire the Kids

If you have minor children who would like to earn some money, why not pay them to stuff envelopes and lick stamps, deliver flyers, or answer the phone? Their wages are a legitimate expense and you don't have to pay unemployment taxes or Social Security for minor children. Be sure to keep adequate time records and pay appropriate wages for the tasks they perform, or the IRS may take a dim view of your business practices. Another benefit is that children pay no income taxes on a portion of their earned income.

Claiming Auto Expenses

To claim expenses for automobile usage, you must keep a detailed log of all business travel in order to separate it from personal use. A per-mile rate is not available to owners, so the true cost method must be used. The cost of oil, gas, repairs, license fees, car washes, and auto club dues are deductible.

The business use portion of your auto can be depreciated, usually over five years or a longer period. Here again, though, the depreciation reduces the cost basis, and thereby increases gains at the time of sale. Mileage logs are available at any office supply store, and a quick note in the log can become as much a habit as buckling your seat belt. Don't miss out on this deduction because you don't want to take ten seconds to make a note.

Meals and Entertainment

In spite of the stories you may have heard about writing off tropical cruises as a business expense, you can only legally deduct 50 percent of business meals and entertainment. This deduction applies to country club fees, fine dining, or theater events, but you must prove that the expenses are directly related to promoting new business, critical to maintaining a business relationship, or that they directly result in sales. Keep your receipts and note on them whom you entertained, the purpose of the expenditure, and the result.

Self-Employment: A Taxing Situation

You are probably wondering why we are so concerned about scouting out all the business deductions possible. It is because the tax laws hold a few nasty surprises for the self-employed. When you are an employee, FICA (Social Security) and Medicare taxes are deducted from your wages, and your employer pays a matching amount as their tax burden. But who pays your tax burden portion when you're self-employed? You guessed it; you pay twice the amount that an employee pays.

Half the amount paid for these taxes is deductible on page one of your 1040 form, but you still pay more than 70 percent more than when you were employed by someone else. After adding the self-employment taxes to state and federal income taxes, you are paying approximately 50 percent of your income out in taxes. You might want to reread the earlier section about deductions.

When self-employed, you are required to project your annual income and pay 90 percent of the estimated taxes on a quarterly basis. The four deadlines for paying these taxes are April 15, June 15, September 15, and January 15 of the following year. If you do not make quarterly payments, a penalty and interest will be charged from the date it is due. In effect, these excess changes can really add up.

The penalty can be avoided by paying 100 percent of last year's tax bill, but be careful when estimating this amount. If your adjusted gross income is over $75,000 and is more than $40,000 above last year's income, you are not protected by the 100 percent-of-income rule. In that case, you must pay 90 percent of the current year's liability by January of the following year and the shortfall must be paid in full by the April tax filing deadline.

Paying estimated taxes really isn't as difficult as it may sound at first. You will soon become accustomed to dealing with the deadlines. Use your accountant! Concentrate on your business and use his or her expertise to file quarterly reports and tax returns, and to keep up with any changes that affect you and your business.

Surviving a Tax Audit

Even though the audit rate for small businesses is about 1.8 percent of filed returns, the IRS is taking a hard look at Schedule C returns. In truth, the IRS doesn't trust the self-employed to pay everything they owe. Salaried workers generally pay 92 percent of the taxes they should. But the compliance rate for the general population is only 82 percent. This points directly to independent business owners and sole proprietors as the culprits. Actually, small corporation owners have the highest level of noncompliance with the tax laws.

Therefore, the IRS has set up the Market Segment Specialization Program to deal with the common compliance problems of the self-employed. Special agents have been trained to audit business returns and are armed with statistics of average earnings and expenses and an awareness of common tax dodges.

Bed-and-breakfast owners can no longer furnish the house with antiques and use the cost as a deduction, and vacations can't be disguised as buying trips. Crafty practitioners can't claim a $10,000 salary and use $200,000 of living expenses as business deductions. The result is that the IRS has published audit guides for businesses that are available to the public. We recommend that you read the guides that are relevant to your business.

If you are subjected to a tax audit and have followed our advice, you have little to worry about. Current and accurate record keeping will again prove a wise business practice. The IRS will match 1099s with reported income and home office deductions, entertainment expenses, and significant charitable deductions will receive the closest scrutiny. Business expenses that are disproportionately large in relation to income and Schedule C gross receipts over $100,000 will be examined carefully.

Not all audits end up with taxpayers owing more money. Sometimes there is no change at all. A correspondence audit means that the IRS wants to examine one or two items in your return, and the audit can be dealt with by mail. Office audits have a broader scope.

When you receive a request for information, don't become defensive. Provide the information asked for, but offer no more. The IRS has the right to force you to produce records, but the Taxpayer Bill of Rights of 1988 does assure you some rights of privacy, confidentiality, courtesy, and consideration. You should be able to explain each item in question, and detailed mileage logs, notations, and receipts will likely be adequate.

Finally, meet all the required deadlines. If you don't, taxes may be assessed on nonaction. Again, use your accountant! He or she is familiar with audit procedures and usually doesn't suffer the emotional apprehension that you could feel.

Retirement Accounts

It is nice to move on from the bitter medicine of taxes to the sweet rewards that are out there for the self-employed. Those who want to provide for their retirement can take advantage of specific plans that are not available to the general public. These plans include Keoghs and SEP-IRAs, both of which allow greater annual contributions than traditional IRAs, as well as more sophisticated plans. The benefits of these plans are covered in detail in Chapter 18, so here we will focus on the particular concerns of the self-employed.

Self-employed people who have erratic incomes tend to be better at saving for retirement than employees; they don't have false illusions about having a miraculous safety net. The same characteristics that make them independent business people make them willing to take on the responsibility of their own retirement. But saving for retirement isn't easy. When earnings are down and health insurance premiums are high, it may be difficult to fund a retirement plan. The tax benefits of doing so make it a wise choice.

Contributions to retirement plans are deducted from self-employed earnings before they are taxed. That's right, it is an adjustment to income on page one of the 1040 form.

SEP-IRAs (Simplified Employee Pension Plans) allow contributions up to 15 percent of an employee's income or $30,000, whichever is less. They require less administrative paperwork than Keoghs, but employees, even part-time workers, must be included in the plan.

SEP-IRAs have an advantage over traditional IRAs in that employees may be able to use salary reduction to make contributions. In other words, the contributions are deducted from the employee's income *before* they are taxed. A major advantage of choosing a SEP-IRA over a Keogh is that contributions can be skipped in a year when income is down.

Keogh plans involve a defined contribution and the maximum contribution is $30,000 or 25 percent of compensation, whichever is less. You must contribute for full-time employees, but part-timers can be excluded.

Both Keoghs and SEPs are available to moonlighters for the portion of income earned from self-employment, even when you are participating in a pension plan or a maxed-out 401(k) at a nine-to-five job. SEP-IRAs are simple to set up and have annual fees of as little as $15. We think it is a good place to start. If you want to contribute more, or your employee situation indicates it, choose a Keogh.

If you have a 401(k) plan and leave the company to become self-employed, leave the plan in place, especially if it is well managed and earning expected rates of return. It is better protected from creditors where it is. Otherwise, it can be transferred into a rollover IRA, which should be done through a trustee-to-trustee transfer so there is no doubt that you did not touch the money.

There are other pension plans available to the self-employed that tend to be more costly to administer, but they do have the advantage of greatly expanding the scope of retirement planning. Suppose that you are retiring and have the opportunity to earn consulting fees from your previous employer. If the fees are substantial, by using a defined benefit pension plan, which requires a pension specialist and about $5,000 to set up, you will be able to defer taxes much of the income.

You are also eligible for a regular IRA if you have a SEP-IRA or a Keogh plan, but it is not always deductible. The advantage of having a nondeductible IRA is that the earnings accumulate tax-deferred within the plan, compounding without current taxes. IRAs are fully deductible for joint self-employed filers if income is less than $40,000, or less than $25,000 for single taxpayers. It is partially deductible between $40,000 and $50,000 for joint filers and between $25,000 and $35,000 for single filers.

Damage Control

Small businesses are not inviolable (secure from violation). As the thousands of small businesses victimized by the 1993 Midwestern floods can testify, small businesses are vulnerable to floods, hurricanes, riots, and explosions, to say nothing of smaller disasters such as fires. Catastrophes beyond your control can strike any business. That's why we think damage control should be part of every business plan.

This strategy is to prevent disaster, to control disaster in the face of catastrophe, and to foresee opportunities that can arise out of disaster. Contemplating events that have only the tiniest chance of ever occurring may sound like overkill, but it is only prudent to protect against the unexpected.

Keep your insurance up to date. Be aware of what is and is not covered under your business insurance. Install fire extinguishers and alarm systems, and consider storing your inventory in more than one location to mitigate damage. The primary asset of businesses such as law practices, accounting firms, and many others is their records. Protect computerized data by making periodic backups and store them off site.

When the loss of one or more persons would cripple the business, obtain key-person life and disability insurance to cover the costs of replacing them.

Self-Employed in the Next Century

We believe you have only three important assets when you are self-employed: your customers, your employees, and your good name. When you and your employees are mutually committed to the basic values of doing business, you enhance your products and services. These values are what makes small businesses survive and can carry you into the next century.

It is no longer enough to work hard. You have to work smart and stay smart. Your business isn't insulated from the consequences of a global economy. Think and act globally to recognize and access international resources.

Take a tip from the Japanese. Instead of working to increase revenues, use technology to whittle expenses in order to maximize your available resources.

When your short-term goal is customer satisfaction, your long-term result will be customer loyalty. Someone can always beat your price or build a better widget, but it is more difficult to break emotional bonds.

Future employment scenarios project a shortage of skilled workers in a work force that is dominated by minorities, women, and older workers. Be fair and flexible with your employees. Your response to their needs and the needs of your customers, your suppliers, and your community will determine your future success.

Set yourself apart by striving for a unique niche in your market. There are really only two ways to distinguish yourself: by price or by value. So if you can't make the cheapest pizza in town, create the most mouth-watering pizza anyone could imagine. In an age when Main Street circles the globe, you have to be more than another mom-and-pop store.

Most important, become accustomed to dealing with constant and rapid changes in unexpected directions. You can't plan on things being the same tomorrow as they were yesterday. Structures will vary, people will shift, but your business will continue to thrive if you learn to deal with change.

The Payoff

The path of the self-employed person defies conventional wisdom. In our business, we left the well-traveled road to pursue something we enjoy and love, when the payoff wasn't insured. We found unbelievable gratification and an incredible potential for financial rewards. We have put in long, hard hours — many more than we would have if we had stayed in our former positions. We have struggled financially, and along the way we have learned much.

Some of the payoff of being self-employed is in the freedom and independence that it provides, a certain sense of job security, and an unending potential for improvement and self-fulfillment. The uphill battle is long and arduous, but the view from the top is incredibly worthwhile.

> **"There is only one success — to be able to spend your life in your own way."**
>
> Christopher Morley, *Where the Blue Begins*

Summary

Owning and operating your own business has many rewards — and risks. To minimize your risks, start slowly by working part-time or by using your business as a secondary source of income until you become established. You can lease or rent equipment instead of purchasing it, establish your office in your home to save on rental space, and take advantage of home office deductions for tax purposes. You'll also want to seek competent advice in such areas as taxes, the law, record keeping, and insurance.

To maximize your rewards, know what tax deductions you're entitled to. Two tax strategies include deferring income and accelerating deductions. During day-to-day operations, keep precise records of business expenses and business mileage. Take advantage of retirement plans available specifically for the self-employed by investing in a Keogh or a SEP-IRA retirement account.

TWENTY-THREE

Implement the 7 Secrets
Pull It All Together for Financial Success

hether the seven secrets are all new to you, add to what you already know, or are simply confirmation of your knowledge, we hope your sense of your overall financial success is sharpened. If you feel as though you are holding both hands full of puzzle pieces but haven't been allowed to look at the puzzle box cover, this chapter will help pull it all together.

The power of *The 7 Secrets of Financial Success* does not lie in knowing the secrets, but in implementing them. Applying this knowledge to your own situation probably seems a bit overwhelming right now, but it's really not all that difficult. Just stand back and look at yourself, your job, your income, your family, your financial attitudes, and your aptitude for achieving success. Carefully examine every aspect of your entire financial life. This self-examination will point out the areas that need improvement. This process requires honesty, maybe even a little painful self-criticism, persistence, and determination.

We're certainly not suggesting that you do your financial planning alone. Involve your spouse and children too, if appropriate, or anyone who impacts your financial situation or is impacted by it. When your family is involved in the planning process, their support will make success all the more likely.

We have provided several simple worksheets in this chapter. When you have completed them, review them with an experienced professional financial advisor. Filling out the worksheets will help you collect

"You can be as romantic as you please about love, Hector; but you mustn't be romantic about money."

– George Bernard Shaw

your thoughts, organize your financial data, identify your strengths and weaknesses, and gain a better idea of what a financial advisor will be looking for.

Everything in this book is copyrighted material, but you have our permission to make photocopies of the worksheets in this chapter for your own personal use. It will take time, but you will realize the value of this exercise when it is complete. Plan to repeat the process periodically to monitor your progress.

Evaluate Your Present Situation

A surprising number of people have an unrealistic idea of exactly how much money they handle and control. Do you know what your gross income is? What is the difference between gross and net income? What tax bracket are you in, and how much interest and investment income can you earn? Until you know how much money is coming in, you cannot accurately plan your expenditures, savings, and investments.

Evaluate Your Income and Income Potential (Inflows)

Your primary income source is probably the money you earn at your job or business. People choose jobs and careers for reasons more important than money, then generally become comfortable with their earnings and adjust their lifestyles accordingly. A critical look at your earnings may reveal that you aren't taking full advantage of your earnings potential.

While you are compiling the information for the form in Figure 23–1A using payroll stubs and tax reports, think about your future income possibilities. Have you maximized your earnings potential? Do you anticipate a salary increase or promotion? Are you in line for an inheritance of any sort? And if you usually receive an annual bonus, include that in your planning too.

Would additional education or training result in increased income in your current position or a promotion within your company? After all, one of the best investments you can make is in your own income-producing capability.

Consider, too, the possibility of a career change or a move to another company. It is easy to become comfortable in your present situation, but taking a little personal risk can yield big dividends in terms of your future income. Beyond additional income, a major job or career change can offer new opportunities for personal growth.

In the 1990s (and beyond), lifelong jobs are rapidly becoming a thing of the past. In this radically changing world, you must adapt to the rapid alterations in business resulting from advances in technology and changes in our society. If you constantly strive to upgrade your skills, you will be more valuable to your employer or your own business, which of course, results in higher income.

If you love your current position but are presently having difficulty meeting your financial goals, work overtime or take a part-time job, at least temporarily. By increasing your income just $10 each working day, you can earn and save $2,500 a year. You already have a good idea what that amount could be worth when invested at even a modest rate of return until your retirement. If you are employed as a shift worker for $12 an hour, five hours a week of overtime at time-and-a-half is $90 a week. In your 20s, just that much invested over the long term can grow to a million dollars, as you know. Or the income from overtime or a part-time job one or two nights a week for several months or so may be all you need to completely remove the albatross of *bad debt* from your life.

The changes that are needed to increase your income will probably be immediately apparent after you have completed the worksheets.

Financial Statement

Your *balance sheet*, a listing of your assets and liabilities (see Figures 23–2A and 23–2B), together with a listing of your income and expenditures (see Figures 23–1A and 23–1B) for a given period of time makes up your *financial statement*. Almost everyone prepares a financial statement from time to time. If you haven't, you should do so every year. Your net worth, total assets minus total liabilities, is your scorecard as you begin to achieve financial success. Make it a goal to increase your net worth every year.

You may be distressed to find that you have a negative net worth; that is, your total liabilities add up to more than your total assets. Therefore, a share of your future income is already committed to your debts.

It is not uncommon for young people just starting careers, businesses, or families to have a negative net worth. If you are in this position, implement the seven secrets early and you will see that your net worth soon becomes positive and grows quickly from there on.

For other people, a negative net worth could be a sign of real trouble. If that is the case, fully investigate and understand the reasons for the negative net worth. Manage your income carefully and gain control of your expenditures to assure that you are living within your means. While you are paying off debts, it is important to build up your cash reserves at the same time.

FIGURE 23–1

Your Monthly Cash Flow

Income and Earnings

	Yours	Spouse or Partner
1. Salary, Wages, and Bonuses		
2. Net Income from Self-Employment		
3. Interest Income:		
Taxable		
Nontaxable		
4. Investment Income:		
Dividends		
Capital Gains		
5. Rental Income		
6. Royalty Income		
7. Partnership Income		
8. Income from Trusts		
9. Social Security		
10. IRA/Keogh Distribution/Withdrawals		
11. Pension or Annuity Income		
12. Other		
Subtotal: Individual Income		
Combined Total Income		

Monthly Additions to Savings and Investments

	Yours	Spouse or Partner
1. Savings Accounts		
2. Money Market Accounts or Funds		
3. Stocks, Bonds		
4. Mutual Funds		
5. IRA, Keogh, 403(b)		
6. 401(k), Other Profit Sharing		
7. Annuities		
8. Other		
Subtotal: Individual Savings and Investments		
Total Savings and Investments		

FIGURE 23–1 (CONCLUDED)

Your Monthly Cash Flow (concluded)

Expenditures

Fixed Expenditures	1. Housing:	Mortgage or Rent
		Property Taxes
	2. Insurance:	Life
		Auto
		Homeowners
		Medical/Dental
		Disability
		Other
	3. Car Payments:	All Cars
	4. Other	
	Subtotal: Fixed Expenditures	

Variable Expenditures	1. Food:	Groceries/Dining Out
	2. Installment Debt:	Credit Cards/Other
	3. Auto Expenses:	Fuel/Maintenance
	4. Utilities:	Electric/Telephone/Fuel/Other
	5. Home Maintenance	
	6. Education	
	7. Other	
	Subtotal: Variable Expenditures	

Discretionary Expenditures	1. Clothing
	2. Entertainment/Recreation/Vacation
	3. Charity/Gifts
	4. Other
	Subtotal: Discretionary Expenditures

Taxes	1. Federal Income
	2. State Income
	3. FICA - Social Security
	4. Other
	Subtotal: Taxes

Total Expenditures

FIGURE 23-2

Balance Sheet - Part 1 - Assets

Cash reserves (see figure 10-1) **/Liquid Assets**
 1. Cash
 2. Checking Accounts
 3. Savings Accounts
 4. Certificates of Deposit
 5. Money Market Accounts/Funds
 6. Life Insurance Cash Values
Subtotal: Cash Reserves/Liquid Assets

Home and Real Estate
 1. Home (Current Market Value)
 2. Other
Subtotal: Home and Real Estate

Investments
 1. Retirement Plans [IRA and 401(k) accounts]
 2. Stocks and Mutual Funds
 3. Bonds
 4. Annuities
 5. Tangible Assets
 6. Other
Subtotal: Investments

Personal Property
 1. Household (furniture, electronics, appliances)
 2. Automobiles
 3. Jewelry, Artworks, etc.
 4. Other
Subtotal: Personal Property

Miscellaneous
 1. Money Owed You
 2. Other
Subtotal: Miscellaneous

Total: Assets

FIGURE 23–2 (CONCLUDED)

Balance Sheet - Part 2 - Liabilities

Current Consumer Credit

1. Auto A
2. Auto B
3. Credit Cards   A:
           B:
           C:
4. Retail Accounts   A:
           B:
           C:
5. Bank Credit Line
6. Other Bank Loans
7. Personal Loans
8. Medical Bills
9. Taxes Owed
10. Other

Subtotal: Current Consumer Credit

Long-Term Liabilities

1. Real Estate:
        Mortgage Balance
        Second Mortgage or Home Equity Loan Balance
        Home Improvement Loan
2. Student Loans
3. Other

Subtotal: Long-Term Liabilities

Miscellaneous

1. Loans against Life Insurance Cash Values
2. Other

Subtotal: Miscellaneous

Total: Liabilities

Net Worth (= Total Assets − Total Liabilities)

Are your assets appreciating assets (real estate and investments) and increasing the asset side of your balance sheet, or are they depreciating assets (autos and other consumer goods) that could push your net worth in the wrong direction? Your net worth increases when you increase your assets or when you decrease your liabilities. When you implement the second secret, of paying yourself first, remember that you can work on both sides of your balance sheet at the same time — decrease your liabilities while you increase your investment assets.

Your financial advisor will analyze your personal financial statement the same way a business is analyzed. Is your income adequate to cover normal living expenses and pay off debts? Was the debt incurred to purchase assets or education that will lead to future growth? The goal of analyzing your family financial statement is to make you look like a successful business that would attract investors and, ultimately, financial success.

Is your debt level consistent with your income and your ability to make payments? Do you have debts that could be refinanced at a lower interest rate? If so, your financial advisor can make helpful recommendations.

Your financial advisor can help calculate the current yields and estimate future yields of your investment portfolio. You may be perfectly happy with your current position, but with the things you have learned in this book, you will most likely want to reposition at least some of your investments to coincide with your risk tolerance level and to earn a higher rate of return.

Determine Your Risk Tolerance Level

The secret of diversification creates many repositioning opportunities, so many that it can seem like a maze. Clearly defining your risk tolerance level gives you a little road map, narrowing the opportunities to the ones that fit with your personality and investment goals.

As you know, we don't define aggressive investing as a trip to the race track. We define it as a willingness to accept greater short-term volatility to receive higher investment returns over a long-term holding period. When you have only a short-term holding period, stay conservative in your investment choices.

You should be comfortable with your investment strategy, whether it is aggressive, conservative, or somewhere in between. It goes back to the sleep factor we discussed many chapters ago. Be guided by your risk tolerance level when diversifying your assets.

Financial Planning Extras

FIGURE 23-3

Determine Your Risk Acceptance Level

Circle the number in each row that best describes your attitude toward investing. After you have circled a number in each of the seven rows, total them.

How Important Is the Objective to You?

Investment Objective	Extremely	Highly	Somewhat	Very Little	Not at All
High Total Return	10	8	6	4	2
Long-Term Deferred Gains	10	8	6	4	2
Tax Benefits	10	8	6	4	2
Current Investment Income	2	4	6	8	10
Stability of Principal	2	4	6	8	10
Absence of Short-Term Losses	2	4	6	8	10
Liquidity	2	4	6	8	10

Total Score =

If your risk tolerance score totals less than 30, concentrate on investments that are low risk. By accepting comparably lower earnings from your investments, you will be more at ease.

If your score is between 30 and 50, choose medium-risk investments: perhaps the best of both worlds. You may give up some of the returns of the high flyers, but you won't settle for the lowest either.

If your score is above 50, you have the risk tolerance to sustain occasional or periodic losses in exchange for higher returns over time. This score indicates that you have a *go-for-it* attitude.

Review Your Tax Situation

Taxes have a large impact on your earnings. If you don't already know how to figure your tax bracket, learn to do it. You must know it to figure after-tax yields or to estimate future net income. We've developed a short calculation method to help you, and have included the 1996 Federal Income Tax schedules.

Every year at tax time, we inevitably hear people bragging about receiving large tax refunds. If it happens once, you can feel good about it, but after that, it's an indication of little or no planning and ignorance of what money must do to make money.

If you are getting a tax refund every year, it is time to have your withholdings reduced. We believe in paying the taxes we owe (America, apple pie, and so forth), but overpaying your taxes year after year is simply poor planning. Uncle Sam appreciates the interest-free loan, but wouldn't you rather be benefiting from the use of the money yourself?

Implement the First Secret — Set Goals

Did you follow our advice in Chapter 1 and write down your goals? Get them out now, and see if reading the rest of this book has changed your thinking about anything. Now that you have had a little time to become accustomed to these goals, you might want to prioritize them differently, or completely change some of them.

If you didn't actually take the time to put your goals on paper, go back to Chapter 1 and work through the process. Break down your long-term goals into short-term subgoals. Set a time frame for each, and make each of them explicit. That is the starting point for pulling it all together.

Writing down your goals is simply answering a series of questions. What do you want to accomplish during your life? How can your income and your assets contribute to your goals? At what age do you want to retire? What kind of lifestyle is important during your retirement? How much money will you need to support that lifestyle? Do you have children to put through college? Do you have adequate cash reserves or any cash reserves at all? Think back to the Success Triangle™, and remember that the foundation for everything above risk management rests on cash reserves.

The result of answering these questions as you write out your goals is probably a cross between a mission statement and a business plan, because life goals and financial goals are so closely related. Goal setting will always be the cornerstone of implementing *The 7 Secrets of Financial Success*. Never underestimate the power of setting goals and clearly ranking your priorities in order of importance.

Financial Planning Extras

Implement the Second Secret — Pay Yourself First

Writing down your goals makes it easy to implement the second secret. How can you achieve your financial goals? By paying yourself first. If necessary, change your financial habits to accommodate your goals.

Study the monthly cash flow data that you created in Figures 23–1. It may be necessary to track outflows for several months or look back at last year's records to get a realistic picture of expenses, especially occasional or inconsistent ones.

Does this picture show that you are paying yourself first? Do you have a monthly investment plan? One of your first goals should be to contribute the allowed maximum into tax-qualified plans such as IRAs or 401(k)s, then look for additional investment money.

Is there more money going out than coming in? If so, why? Will that still be the case when you align your spending habits with your goals? If you aren't living within your means, the answer is obvious: decrease your spending or increase your income.

Is there a big difference between what you earn and what you keep? This situation could be what your grandmother was talking about when she spoke of frittering away your money. Think about the difference between your necessary expenditures and your discretionary expenditures. The difference could be the source of money for savings and investments.

What can be done when you know how much you have to invest to achieve your goals, but it doesn't seem possible when you look at your income? Should you give up? Not on your financial life.

Of course it's possible. You have five options for action, besides increasing your income:

1. Defer gratification; free up money to save and invest by reducing your current standard of living.
2. Reduce insurance costs and invest the savings.
3. Reposition your investments to earn higher rates of return.
4. Reduce taxes and invest the savings.
5. Change your goals.

Reallocating Your Income

On the average, we spend 58 percent of our income on our standard of living: food, shelter, clothing, education, entertainment, medical, and all those tennis shoes we buy. About 26 percent of our income is paid out in taxes and about 12 percent goes to insurance. That leaves only 4 percent, just four cents out of every dollar, for savings and investment.

FIGURE 23-4

1996 Federal Income Tax Schedules

Married, Filing Jointly

If taxable income is:

More than $_____, but not more than $_____, federal tax is $_____ +_____% of the amount over $_____.

More than $	but not more than $	federal tax is $	+ %	of the amount over $
0	40,100	0	15	0
40,100	96,900	6,015	28	40,100
96,900	147,700	21,919	31	96,900
147,700	263,750	37,667	36	147,700
263,750	---	79,445	39.6	263,750

First $40,100	$40,100 to $96,900	$96,900 to $147,700	$147,700 to $263,750	over $263,750
Tax Bracket 15%	28%	31%	36%	39.6%

Unmarried Taxpayer

If taxable income is:

More than $_____, but not more than $_____, federal tax is $_____ +_____% of the amount over $_____.

More than $	but not more than $	federal tax is $	+ %	of the amount over $
0	24,000	0	15	0
24,000	58,150	3,600	28	24,000
58,150	121,300	13,162	31	58,150
121,300	263,750	32,739	36	121,300
263,750	---	84,021	39.6	263,750

First $24,000	$24,000 to $58,150	$58,150 to $121,300	$121,300 to $263,750	over $263,750
Tax Bracket 15%	28%	31%	36%	39.6%

Head of Household

If taxable income is:

More than $_____, but not more than $_____, federal tax is $_____ +_____% of the amount over $_____.

More than $	but not more than $	federal tax is $	+ %	of the amount over $
0	32,150	0	15	0
32,150	83,050	4,823	28	32,150
83,050	134,500	19,075	31	83,050
134,500	263,750	35,024	36	134,500
263,750	---	81,554	39.6	263,750

First $32,150	$32,150 to $83,050	$83,050 to $134,500	$134,500 to $263,750	over $263,750
Tax Bracket 15%	28%	31%	36%	39.6%

FIGURE 23–5

Figure Your Own Tax Bracket

Married, Filing Jointly

Gross Income	$ _____
Less Deductions	– _____
Adjusted Income	_____
Less Exemptions	– _____
Taxable Income	_____

⬇

Find your income in appropriate table from Figure 23–4.

⬇

Tax on first

$ _____ is $ _____

Amount over

first $ _____

is $ _____

× _____ % = $ _____

Total Federal Tax $ _____

Federal Tax Bracket _____ %

Unmarried Taxpayer

Gross Income	$ _____
Less Deductions	– _____
Adjusted Income	_____
Less Exemptions	– _____
Taxable Income	_____

⬇

Find your income in appropriate table from Figure 23–4.

⬇

Tax on first

$ _____ is $ _____

Amount over

first $ _____

is $ _____

× _____ % = $ _____

Total Federal Tax $ _____

Federal Tax Bracket _____ %

Example: Married, Filling jointly (Family of Four)

Gross Income	$	68,000
Less Itemized Deductions	–	7,400
Adjusted Income	$	60,000
Less Exemptions (1996 = $2,550 each)	–	10,200
Taxable Income	$	50,400

Tax on first $41,100 is $ 6,015

Amount over first $40,100 is $10,300 × 28% = $ 2,884

Total Federal Tax $ 8,899

Federal Tax Bracket (28%)

Example: Single Taxpayer

Gross Income	$	36,000
Less 1996 Standard Deductions	–	4,000
Adjusted Income	$	32,000
Less Exemptions (1996 = $2,550 each)	–	2,550
Taxable Income	$	29,450

Tax on first $24,000 is $ 3,600

Amount over first $24,000 is $5,450 × 28% = $ 1,526

Total Federal Tax $ 5,126

Federal Tax Bracket (28%)

This amount is probably grossly inadequate to meet your worthwhile financial goals.

Making minor adjustments in your expenditures can greatly improve your financial outlook. (See Figure 23–6.) If your taxes could be reduced to 20 to 24 percent of your income, and your insurance expenditures to 6 to 10 percent, instead of the usual 12 percent, your savings and investments could be increased to 10 to 14 percent without altering your current standard of living.

Reread the chapters on taxes and insurance if you have to, and take advantage of some of our recommendations. For example, investing in a retirement plan not only increases your assets, but also reduces your taxes. A mere 2 percent change here and there can make a huge difference. Remember, excellent results are obtained when you save and invest just the first 10 percent of everything you earn.

Implement the Third Secret — Harness the Power of Time

What must be done to make the changes we're recommending? Meet with your financial advisor? Call your insurance agent? Fill out a few forms with your employer? You can't afford to wait. Do it *now.*

Procrastination is the bitter enemy of financial success. Knowing this fact, and understanding the power of compound interest, why would you wait even one day longer to make changes?

We're not scientists, but we understand the simple laws of physics that apply here too. The greatest amount of energy is needed to overcome inertia, but once moving, it doesn't take much to keep things going. Payroll deduction plans are amazingly painless. When your employer matches your contribution in a retirement plan at work, you get a 100 percent return the first day. It's a rare investment that can match that. Take advantage of it today!

Increase the hours you work or make other changes to increase your income. Let time work for you by doing everything you can now, today; then make periodic adjustments as time goes on.

Procrastination kills financial dreams. Let time and compound interest work their magic for you. Don't wait. Do it *now.*

Implement the Fourth Secret — Diversify Your Investments

Think back to Chapter 4 about diversification. The concept of *don't put all your eggs in one basket* is simple enough, but perhaps you are still wondering just what baskets you should be putting your eggs into. Random diversification can reduce risk, but use care in selecting your baskets to increase your overall investment returns.

FIGURE 23–6

Reallocating Your Income

Moves You from Here...
(where your money is allocated now)

4¢   12¢   26¢   58¢

To Here...
(where your money should be allocated)

10¢-14¢ 6¢-10¢ 20¢-24¢   58¢

Savings and Investments

Insurance
Auto, Home, Health, Disability, Life

Taxes

Standard of Living
Shelter, Clothing, Transportation, Education, Entertainment, Medical, Church, Etc.

The goal of reallocating your income is to maintain your standard of living while increasing the amount of money you save and invest to at least 10 percent of your income. Through careful analysis and planning, many people are able to find the dollars needed to reasch their savings and investment goals by simply reducing their taxes and insurance costs.

The Success Triangle as Your Guide

The Success Triangle™ is a simple guide to follow when choosing diversification vehicles. As each step in the triangle is completed, you will see that your assets are pretty well diversified. You will have money for three to six months of living expenses in cash reserves in guaranteed accounts that feature stability of principal. You will have money in liquid investments including both fixed-income accounts, which emphasize income and current yield, and equity investments, which feature long-term appreciation. Money destined for retirement will be invested to take advantage of tax-deferred growth. And you may have some money in tangible assets that tend to perform well during periods of high inflation or other economic instability.

Diversification isn't just for reducing risk. All investments, even the so-called *safe* ones, are exposed to risk. But don't look at all risk as bad. Some riskier investments also offer the highest potential for returns. Diversification allows you to invest more aggressively. All your investments won't be stellar performers, but some will be, and over the long term your investment returns will be increased.

Don't plan your investment strategies to protect yourself from market downturns. Historically, there is very little precedence to base this strategy upon. Even in the stock market crash of 1929 and the following depression years, investors didn't lose their shares. The shares just lost their value. When the economy rebounded, share values also rebounded.

We see no good reason to build investment portfolios based on *safe* investments that provide low returns. Some people stay away from equity investments because they confuse safety with stability of principal and risk with market volatility. Diversification smoothes out the bumps between market cycles. It reduces your overall risk and has been proven to increase long-term returns.

Asset Allocation

Asset allocation is today's popular buzzword for the old-fashioned concept of diversification. In practice, it generally means taking diversification to the next level. It involves diversifying your assets among categories of investments that generally behave differently in market cycles. It's a way of trying to take advantage of the schizophrenic relationships that exist among the classes of securities that make up the marketplace.

For example, gold prices usually go up when the stock market is sliding, and when stocks go up, gold usually goes down. The asset allocation theory dictates that it would be wise to own some of both. In

Financial Planning Extras

FIGURE 23–7

Investments and Their Positions in the Success Triangle™

Exotic	Commodities, Collectibles (Art, Antiques, Oriental Rugs, and Ceramics, Stamps, etc.)
Tax Shelters	Oil & Gas Drilling, Federal Housing Tax Credits, Historic Rehabilitation Tax Credits
Tangible Assets	Metals, Rare Coins, Gems
Tax-Advantaged Investments	Municipal Bonds, Tax-Deferred Annuities, Limited Partnerships (Real Estate, Cable TV, Equipment Leasing, Energy Income)
Liquid Investments	Treasury, Corporate, and Municipal Bonds, Preferred & Common Stock, Mutual Funds
Cash Reserves	Passbook Savings, Certificates of Deposit, Treasury Bills, Money Market Funds
Foundation Estate Conservation/Risk Management	Life Insurance, Disability Income Insurance, Long-Term Health Care Insurance, Estate Planning (Wills, Trusts, Gifts)

other words, your assets should be apportioned among various investment categories in percentages that are in line with your own risk tolerance level (See Figure 23–3). And of course, the goal of asset allocation is for your overall portfolio to produce the highest possible return at a given level of risk. We are always looking for ways to get a higher rate of return with less risk. But the truth is higher potential returns are usually tied to higher levels of risk.

Many financial planning books cover asset allocation and feature fancy pie charts to illustrate what percentage of your investment portfolio should be allocated to various investment categories, according to your age. It is simple, but we believe that when put into practice it falls short of meeting your actual objectives.

Investors in their 20s are generally advised to put a large percentage of their investment dollars in long-term growth equity investments. If retirement is the goal, that is fine, but if they are saving for a down payment on a home in three years, we would recommend less volatile investments. Investors in their early 60s are advised to keep most of

FIGURE 23–8

Investment Categories

Guaranteed Accounts

Investments Featuring Stability of Principal

Passbook Savings
Money Market Accounts (Daily Interest)
Certificates of Deposit
U.S. Savings Bonds
Treasury Bills
Money Market Funds
Fixed Annuity (or Fixed Account in Variable Annuity)
Cash Values (Whole Life Insurance)
Guaranteed Investment Contracts (GIC)

Loanership Investments

Fixed-Income Accounts

Investments Featuring Income and Current Yield

Bonds
Ginnie Maes
Collateralized Mortgage Obligations (CMO)
Mortgages
Bond Mutual Funds
Variable Annuities (Bond Portfolios)
Variable Life (Fixed-Income Accounts)
High Yielding Stocks
Real Estate Investments Trusts (REIT)
Unit Investment Trusts
Mortgage Limited Partnerships
Equipment Leasing Limited Partnerships

Ownership Investments

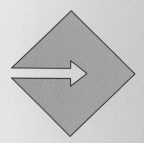

Equity Accounts

Investments Featuring Appreciation and Inflation Hedge

Common Stocks
Preferred Stocks
Growth Mutual Funds
Variable Annuities (Equity Accounts)
Variable Life (Equity Accounts)
Real Estate
Real Estate Investment Trusts (REIT)
Real Estate Limited Partnerships
Tangible Assets

FIGURE 23–9

Asset Allocation

Many factors must be considered before deciding what type of investments should be made, and how much to invest in each. Your age, financial resources, liabilities, and tax bracket should be considered. Most important, however, are your own goals and risk tolerance levels.

This chart is designed to illustrate possible portfolio allocations across the three broad investment categories. It should not be considered specific investment advice.

Your Total Risk Acceptance Score from Figure 23–3	Percentage of Portfolio Invested in Each Category		
	Guaranteed Accounts	Fixed-Income Accounts	Equity Accounts
68-70	5%	5%	90%
56-66	10%	10%	80%
42-54	20%	20%	60%
32-40	30%	30%	40%
22-30	40%	40%	20%
14-22	50%	40%	10%

their money in more conservative investments for stability of principal and current income. The problem we see with this advice is that people in this age group today can plan to live another 20 to 30 years. They are not going to need all their retirement money on the first day they retire, and unless they plan for some long-term growth, they could out-live their money.

Your age alone should not determine how your investment dollars are allocated. We prefer to look at your investment time frame — the time to achieve your goals, your risk tolerance level, and your outlook on where you think the economy is headed (severe inflation, deflation or depression, or normalcy). Because of the many variables involved, you can see that it is really difficult for us to spell out hard-and-fast rules for asset allocation. We encourage you to work closely with your financial advisor on this subject.

Diversifying with Mutual Funds

You are already quite familiar with our preference for mutual funds. Part of this preference is due to the built-in diversification you get with them. As you remember from Chapter 12, there are mutual funds designed to meet an almost endless variety of specific objectives. Depending on their objectives, the investments in a given fund may be limited to small company stocks, blue chip stocks, gold mining stocks, technology stocks, pharmaceutical company stocks, high-grade corporate bonds, junk bonds, tax-exempt bonds, money markets, foreign stocks or bonds, or a mixture of these investments. And of course, many mutual fund companies offer a family of funds, each having specific objectives that offer excellent features such as no-fee or low-fee transfers between the funds within the family.

Because of the options mutual funds offer, you can do a lot of asset allocations within a single family of funds. For example, cash reserves can be kept in a money market fund, bond funds and high-yielding stock funds produce income, and growth or aggressive growth funds produce long-term equity growth. When your situation or objectives change, transfer your assets to other funds within the family that meet your current objectives.

Remember that any strategy which reduces volatility also reduces potential gains. The weak performers dilute the strong gainers. Don't diversify to the point of confusion for the sake of diversification. As stated before, 90 percent of the theoretical benefits of diversification can be achieved with 13 to 15 different investments.

Implement the Fifth Secret — Manage Your Credit Wisely

This piece of your financial puzzle analyzes the liabilities side of your balance sheet (Figure 23–2, Part 2) and the management of your credit. We have spent a lot of time exposing the destructive consequences of living beyond your means, which inevitably burdens the liabilities column of your financial statement. Many people spend years of their lives trying to get out of debt. Some finally work their way out while others are eventually forced into a fresh, though tarnished, start through bankruptcy.

Implementing the fifth secret first demands that you live within your means. This proves to be the most difficult change for many people to make, but once accomplished, you are liberated to pursue financial success in earnest. A good place to start is by removing the temptation of spending what you do not have by getting rid of your credit cards. Keep just one for making telephone or electronic purchases, car rentals, hotel reservations, and so forth; then pay the balance in full every month.

Separate your liabilities into categories of good debt and bad debt, with the objective of completely eliminating the bad debt (refer back to Chapter 5). Seek out methods of lowering interest rates even while you are paying off your debts. There are credit card companies whose interest rates are close to prime that will take over your other higher-interest card debts. Moving debt from a credit card account charging 18 percent interest to one that charges only 8 percent represents quite a savings.

Now look at your good debt. Are you carrying loans that are above current market rates? Could they be refinanced at a lower interest rate? Would refinancing your mortgage be appropriate?

If the credit and debt piece of your financial puzzle is an impossible challenge and gives you ulcers, reread Chapter 5, and seek out a credit counselor, if appropriate. They can help you work out arrangements with your creditors and they can also help clean up a poor credit record.

Implement the Sixth Secret — Safeguard Your Future

Insurance is vital to securing your financial future. It is also a subject that you may not be comfortable with. As a result, you may be under-insured or over-insured and in either case you could be paying too much for your coverage. A subject that is approached with even less enthusiasm than insurance is estate planning. An estate planning attorney is an absolute necessity because of the complexity of planning your estate and the tax consequences that are involved in this planning process.

Evaluate Your Insurance Coverage

You will probably have to get out some of those old insurance policies and actually read them (what a novel idea!) to answer some of the questions in Figure 23–10. If insurance is still a murky subject, go over Chapters 6 and 8 again.

Your mission is to determine whether your coverage is commensurate with your goals. One of your goals is to decrease your insurance premiums. Eliminate duplicate coverage, and investigate paying premiums through a payroll deduction plan. Increasing deductibles also reduces the premiums, but remember that you can only afford higher deductibles when your emergency funds (cash reserves) are in place.

FIGURE 23–10

Evaluate Your Insurance Coverage

Present Life Insurance
Type: UL = Universal Life; W = Whole Life; T = Term; M = Mortgage

Company Name	Name of Insured	Type	Beneficiary	Face Amount	Cash Value	Loans	$ Annual Premium

Group Term
    Spouse A
    Spouse B

Disability Income Insurance

Existing Coverage Personal/Group	Company Name	Monthly Benefits	Waiting Period	Maximum Benefit Period	$ Annual Premium

Spouse A

Spouse B

Medical/Dental Insurance

Existing Coverage Personal/Group	Daily Hospitalization	Amount Copay	Prescriptions	$ Annual Premium

Spouse A

Spouse B

Automobile Insurance

Liability Limits/ Accident	Medical Limits/ Accident	Uninsured Motorest Coverage	Collision	Deductible Amount	$ Premium

Auto 1

Auto 2

Homeowners Insurance

Dwelling	Other Structures	Personal Property	Personal Liability	$ Premium

Long-Term Health Care
Current need?
Policy currently in force?

If you are underinsured, there would not be enough money to cover losses from accidents or disasters or to meet the needs of your family in the event of your death. If you are over-insured, you are paying too much in premiums for unnecessary insurance coverage. It could be invested instead to meet your future needs, and in effect, you will be self-insured.

Safeguarding your future also includes providing for the future of those you love. In the event of your death, you would most likely want to provide an income for your spouse and minor children, provide an education for your children, and be sure your heirs receive your assets according to your wishes. Again, meet with your financial advisor/estate planning attorney.

Implement the Seventh Secret — Seek Professional Guidance

We have presented this entire chapter as an exercise in data gathering and a method of gaining insights into your own financial situation. But we have never expected you to do it alone. Perhaps the seventh secret is the most valuable advice we can give: seek professional advice.

These professionals devote their entire lives to keeping up to date on the latest changes in the tax laws and on a multitude of investments and investment options. In Chapter 7, we outlined our criteria for choosing an advisor that you feel comfortable with and who understands your needs and objectives.

At this point we want to emphasize the need for a financial advisor. Choose one and use his or her services on a regular basis. One of the reasons 80 percent of the people fail to plan their financial future is that it is not an easy task.

In addition to periodic meetings with your advisor, read books and periodicals and attend money management seminars. Keeping abreast of developments in the financial marketplace is one way of fine-tuning your financial plan.

Designing a Strategy

Your advisor is an expert in designing strategies for financial success. Take a list of your goals, these data collection forms, and the notes you have taken while working through these forms when you meet with your financial advisor. With his or her help, you can further identify your problem areas and what changes need to be made. A new baby, a promotion, failing health, or an inheritance can quickly change your objectives; that's why frequent review is necessary.

You know where you want to go, and your advisors can help you get there. So now, complete the implementation of *The 7 Secrets of Financial Success* by implementing your strategy. Sometimes, just getting it all down on paper is enough to jump-start a winning attitude.

Summary

We have presented *The 7 Secrets of Financial Planning* sequentially, but in truth, the secrets work together as a whole. Even as we examine how one secret works, the other secrets will color our decisions.

Implementing *The 7 Secrets of Financial Success* means putting the principles and ideas in this book into action. You know what needs to be done to achieve financial success. So — just do it, now!

TWENTY-FOUR

Become a Millionaire
Yes, You Can!

— STOP —

If you turned to this chapter first, go back and read the entire book! It's quite possible to ensure your financial success and become a millionaire, but there are no short-cuts, and you need a solid financial foundation to get there.

his is an exciting and energizing book about money — getting it, keeping it, saving it, protecting it from taxes and infla- tion, and passing it on to the appropriate people. So you may be sur- prised at our next statement. *There are more important things in life than money.*

What's more important than money? You know. It's the answer to these questions: What would you be worth if you lost every cent of your money? What would you have left? Your health? Your family? Your talents and skills? Only you know the answers. We are confident that you will not be confused about the difference between riches and wealth and that you will give top priority to the things that make you truly *wealthy.*

Joan Didion, journalist and astute observer of American culture, said, "The secret point of money and power in America is neither the things money can buy nor power for power's sake, but absolute per- sonal freedom, mobility, privacy."

"I have a surefire plan for becoming a millionaire: First, get a million dollars. Then…"

– Comedian Steve Martin

We believe every law-abiding, tax-paying citizen in America is entitled to these freedoms. And while Thomas Jefferson didn't list it as an unalienable right in the Declaration of Independence, we believe financial security is an essential part of this pursuit of happiness that we are all guaranteed. But financial security doesn't mean setting out to become rich.

In fact, studies have shown that people who set out to simply make a lot of money are usually failures. Someone who enters a business or career with the primary goal of getting rich is seldom able to keep focused on what it takes to succeed. When storms come along, they simply head off in another direction, never demonstrating the patience, creativity, and perseverance required for success.

On the other hand, for the many people — those who love their chosen professions, who believe that they are making a positive contribution to society, and who enjoy helping other people achieve their needs and desires — success is almost inevitable.

Why? Because diligence is a magnet for money, and because the conditions for success in any chosen field are the same as those required for financial success. Abraham Lincoln spent years studying the law before he achieved fame as a brilliant debater. Musicians practice long hours of boring exercises before becoming masters at their craft. Athletes run lonely miles in the early dawn before becoming Olympians.

What is important to these people? Fame? Riches? A glamorous lifestyle? Perhaps, to some degree. But all the successful people we know of had a deep inner conviction that they *could* succeed and were willing to do what was necessary to achieve success.

Wealth Is an Attitude

Did you know that 80 percent of the millionaires in America today are first-generation millionaires? They didn't inherit their wealth. They *earned* it. With hard work and discipline. And, quite surprisingly, many of these millionaires are also first-generation Americans.

Motivational speaker Zig Ziglar often quotes the fact that, "Legal immigrants are four times as likely to become millionaires as native-born Americans." Why? Because these immigrants don't take the freedoms of our country for granted. They come to this country seeking opportunity and, in doing so, find it.

Successful immigrants aren't afraid to work at more than one minimum-wage job. They aren't shackled by a false sense of pride. They simply do what is necessary to achieve their goals — even if it means packing sardines, driving taxis, or flipping hamburgers. By the time they become adjusted to American culture and the blasé attitude many have, it's too late. They already know what can be achieved if they keep striving toward their goals and practicing what many others are unwilling to practice.

We once had the opportunity of helping a Vietnamese family who escaped from a war-torn Saigon. They came out of their country with the clothes on their backs and their lives — nothing else. It was a large family, and they were very grateful for our cast-off clothing and the towels we didn't like.

During high school, the children worked at part-time jobs for anyone willing to hire recent immigrants. They all worked several jobs, and when they could, they went to night school. One of the children became an engineer, and after about five years, the family had accumulated enough money to build a large house in an upscale neighborhood.

We wondered how it had happened. How had they managed to achieve so quickly what the rest of us were working toward? Their jobs were not the ones we wanted. The obstacles they faced and overcame were obstacles none of us had ever grappled with. Consequently, their success was even met by some of us with suspicion and jealousy.

A close relationship with our Vietnamese family, however, made us realize that they had personal characteristics we have come to recognize in all successful people. Successful people are motivated by results. Call them dreams, if you will. They are not content with the results that come from only doing what they *want* to do. Instead, they aggressively seek out the results that come from doing what others *don't* want to do. They take simple, basic principles and practice them until they become second nature.

You don't have to do the extraordinary to become successful — you *only* need to do the ordinary extraordinarily well.

Successful people don't succumb to the temptation of hoping — hoping problems will solve themselves, hoping to win the lottery, or hoping Prince Charming will swoop down on a white horse and deliver them. By making the best of what comes their way, developing their talents and refusing to compare themselves to others, they take full responsibility for their future.

Successful people know that success is a series of little accomplishments, a goal that can be broken down into subgoals. This approach makes success possible. In short, it is nearly impossible to separate a person like this from financial success.

Financial Success Is an Attitude

Financial success is a decision you make. We have focused on it from the beginning, and now it's time to say it outright. Decide to be financially successful, then do it. How? You hold all the tools in your hands with this book. You know the most important financial secrets of all time. Using these secrets as your guide, decide to become a millionaire.

A *Millionaire?* Why not? You'll make a million dollars (and probably a lot more) in your lifetime. If you work at a job earning $25,000 a year for 40 years, that's a million bucks. How much of that you decide to keep is entirely up to you. Through modest but diligent saving and keeping a close eye on the money your money earns, you will grow a substantial investment portfolio. Our message is this: *Yes, you can!*

Once you truly decide to achieve a goal, be it an academic degree or financial security, you have leaped the largest hurdle. Apply your intelligence, persistence, and enthusiasm to your commitment, and nothing can stop you from succeeding.

Because you are persistently working and earning money, you have the flexibility of breaking your large goals down into smaller ones that can be achieved over time (covered in Chapter 1, on setting your goals). We have heard millionaires say that the first $100,000 was the most difficult sum of money to accumulate. We believe that the first $10,000 is really the hardest, or for some people, it may even be the first $1,000.

What does financial success mean to you? In our experience, you are financially successful if you have enough money to maintain your standard of living, pursue your interests, keep cash reserves within your comfort level, and buy adequate insurance to protect your assets.

For some, it may mean earning a consistent, modest income that is guaranteed for life. For others, financial security is a lump-sum dollar figure of $100,000, $500,000, or $1,000,000 at retirement. You really don't have to have a million dollars to be rich. But admit it, there is something wonderfully satisfying about the very idea of becoming a millionaire.

What about My Million Bucks?

When you are young, everything is so easy. Time is on your side, and all you have to do is let the time value of money work for you. If you are older, the magic of time value is still there, but when there is less time, it takes more investment dollars to become a millionaire.

Financial Planning Extras

FIGURE 24–1

Monthly Investment Required to Accumulate a Million Dollars

% Rate of Return	Years									
	5	10	15	20	25	30	35	40	45	50
3	15,430	7,138	4,395	3,038	2,237	1,712	1,345	1,077	875	718
4	15,033	6,769	4,050	2,717	1,939	1,436	1,091	843	660	522
5	14,644	6,413	3,726	2,423	1,672	1,197	877	653	491	373
6	14,261	6,072	3,421	2,154	1,436	991	698	500	361	263
7	13,887	5,744	3,137	1,909	1,227	815	552	379	262	182
8	13,520	5,430	2,871	1,686	1,045	667	433	285	188	125
9	13,160	5,129	2,623	1,486	885	542	337	212	134	85
10	12,807	4,841	2,393	1,306	747	439	261	157	95	57
11	12,462	4,566	2,179	1,145	629	353	201	115	66	38
12	12,123	4,304	1,982	1,001	527	283	154	84	46	25
13	11,792	4,054	1,800	873	440	226	117	61	32	17
14	11,468	3,815	1,632	760	367	180	89	44	22	11
15	11,151	3,589	1,477	660	304	143	67	32	15	7

Become a Millionaire through Monthly Investing

Since our income is often received in monthly increments and most of our bills are paid monthly, saving in monthly increments is the most logical method of achieving savings goals. A target of accumulating a million dollars becomes quite reasonable when you learn how little you actually need to set aside every month. Look carefully at Figure 24–1. It only takes a relatively meager monthly investment to become a millionaire when time is on your side.

Choose a reasonable interest rate within your risk-level comfort zone. We like to use a 10 percent rate in projections because it is reasonable, based on past market performance, and easy to work with. But we are aggressive investors. You might feel more comfortable with a 7 or 8 percent projection.

To Become a Millionaire:

In 10 years — Invest $62,745 per year for 10 years ($4,841 per month) at 10 percent.

In 20 years — Invest $17,460 per year for 20 years ($1,306 per month) at 10 percent.

In 30 years — Invest $6,079 per year for 30 years ($439 per month) at 10 percent.

In 40 years — Invest $2,259 per year for 40 years ($157 per month) at 10 percent. Isn't that amazingly close to simply funding your IRA every year? That's all it would take to become a millionaire. You see, it's just that easy.

Become a Millionaire with a Lump Sum Investment

Let's assume that you have saved a lot of money, received a lump sum distribution from a retirement plan, received an inheritance, or sold a business. Now you have a lump sum to invest. Study Figure 24–2. You may be surprised to find that you already have the seeds of a million dollars.

Empower Yourself

When quoting Joan Didion, we took the idea of money and power for power's sake and expanded it to mean personal freedom, mobility, and privacy. We have talked a lot about power and empowerment in this book. The real empowerment behind *The 7 Secrets of Financial Success* is that each of them expands to encompass all areas of your life.

The ideas behind paying yourself first, for example, expand to discipline, diligence, and even patience. Behind compound interest is the power of investigating new/old ideas with an open mind and growing by increasing your knowledge. The idea of diversification expands to an ability to adapt and change with agility and confidence.

You empower yourself when you refuse the negative pull of society and allow ideas to root, spread, and flourish. We sincerely hope that the principles described in our book expand to financial success for everyone.

FIGURE 24–2

Lump Sum Investment Required to Accumulate a Million Dollars

% Rate of Return	Years									
	5	10	15	20	25	30	35	40	45	50
3	862,609	744,094	641,862	553,676	477,606	411,987	355,383	306,557	264,439	228,107
4	821,927	675,564	555,265	456,387	375,117	308,319	253,415	208,289	171,198	140,713
5	783,526	613,913	481,017	376,889	295,303	231,377	181,290	142,046	111,297	87,204
6	747,258	558,395	417,265	311,805	232,999	174,110	130,105	97,222	72,650	54,288
7	712,986	508,349	362,446	258,419	184,249	131,367	93,663	66,780	47,613	33,948
8	680,583	463,193	315,242	214,548	146,018	99,377	67,635	46,031	31,328	21,321
9	649,931	422,411	274,538	178,431	115,968	75,371	48,986	31,838	20,692	13,449
10	620,921	385,543	239,392	148,644	92,296	57,309	35,584	22,095	13,719	8,519
11	593,451	352,184	209,004	124,034	73,608	43,683	25,924	15,384	9,130	5,418
12	567,427	321,973	182,696	103,667	58,823	33,378	18,940	10,747	6,098	3,460
13	542,760	294,588	159,891	86,782	47,102	25,565	13,876	7,531	4,088	2,219
14	519,369	269,744	140,096	72,762	37,790	19,627	10,194	5,294	2,750	1,428
15	497,177	247,185	122,894	61,100	30,378	15,103	7,509	3,733	1,856	923

Make a Commitment

When you think about it, you probably know a lot of millionaires. In truth, becoming a millionaire is pretty commonplace today. We know a millionaire who once worked as a bellhop for $3 a week. He saved enough money to buy a small business that turned into five golf courses in two states. We know another millionaire who started as a farm hand at age 12 for 25 cents a day and eventually turned a job as a carpenter's assistant into a land development company.

When asked, any of them will say that at one point in their lives, they made a commitment. Maybe it wasn't a commitment to becoming a millionaire. Maybe it was a commitment to not live in poverty. Maybe it was a commitment to getting out of debt and staying out of debt. But one day, every millionaire we know decided to get on top and stay on top of their financial situation. That's right. *They made a decision.*

What are you going to do after you finish this book? Are you going to think, Now wasn't that a pleasant little mental exercise? Or are you going to commit to financial success? Are you going to sit down and actually plan your goals or are you going to *talk* about setting goals? Are you going to work through Chapter 23, which shows you how to pull it all together?

We wrote this book to share *The 7 Secrets of Financial Success* with you. And all the time we were writing and sharing the magic of setting goals, paying yourself first, taking advantage of compound interest, and safeguarding your future, we knew that the magic wasn't really found in these things. The secrets are tools. The magic is in *you*.

Only *you* can achieve financial success for yourself, one step at a time. Make decisions that go beyond the status quo and leap over the barriers that we all put up to keep from changing.

Now, what are these barriers? We call them the *barriers to performance*. In our world, the first barrier people invent is the *consumption barrier*: "I can't invest because the rent is due, the kids need tennis shoes, or the house needs painting." The consumption barrier will never disappear. It is what drives income. But we've shown you how to leap over the consumption barrier by paying yourself first.

Some people invent the safety barrier: "I can't go forward because I don't want to do anything that is not safe." We have shown that you can harness the power of time and diversify your investment portfolio that is compatible with your comfort level. We have painstakingly shown you how to safeguard your future and also suggested that you may have been deceived about safety. The safety barrier should disappear with this knowledge.

Other people are simply afraid of large numbers. You might think, A *number barrier*? You have probably thought about what you would do if you won the lottery. One man in the Midwest who won a $5 million lottery announced to the world that he was going to buy a pickup truck. Did he understand that he could buy hundreds of pickup trucks? Probably not.

Your path can only lead where your mind has gone before, so stretch your mind to envision large numbers. Take courage and *believe* that you can be a millionaire. Six zeros behind the one. *Yes, you can.*

FIGURE 24–3

Seven Main Reasons People Fail Financially

1 Procrastination.

2 Failure to establish goals.

3 Ignorance about what money must do to accomplish these goals.

4 Failure to understand and manage credit.

5 Failure to understand and apply our tax laws.

6 Failure to properly prepare for the unexpected.

7 Failure to develop a winning financial attitude.

Conclusion

Your future is too important for you to procrastinate anymore.

Believe in and apply *The 7 Secrets*. You know what you must do. You know the secrets work! Just begin to use them now and benefit from their almost magical power to transform your economic life and ensure your financial success!

Go forward with our best wishes. Decide to be financially successful. Decide to become a millionaire. Do it *now!*

Index

B

Babson, Roger W., 123
Baccalaureate bonds, 369
Bachelard, Gaston, 249
Balance sheet, 393, 396, 397
Bank loans, 56, 57
Bankruptcy, 64
Barriers to performance, 422
Basic educational opportunity grants, 360
Bear market, 143
Bears, 143
Bed and breakfast, 272
Beneficiary, 114
Bequests, 220
Bid price, 160
Black Monday, 77, 142, 143
Boesky, Ivan, 137
Bond funds, 201-210
  advantages, 204-206
  commissions and expenses, 208
  differences in, 207, 208
  disadvantages, 206
  performance charts, 205
  portfolio of funds, 209
  reasons brokers like them, 203
  reasons to invest, 202, 203
  secrets in action, 210
  suggestion, 202
  summary, 209
  unit investment trusts, 203, 204
  what are they, 201, 202
  which is best, 208, 209
Bonds, 179-200
  benefits of, 180-183
  collateralized mortgage obligations, 196
  corporate, 181, 190-192
  credit risk, 186-188
  defined, 180
  deflation, and, 182
  diversification, and, 181, 182
  interest rate risk, 184-186
  investment income, 180

Bonds—*Cont.*
  junk, 187, 189, 207
  market risk, 183
  mortgage-backed, 193-196
  municipal; *see* Municipal bonds
  premiums/discounts, 185
  ratings, 187, 188
  risk, and, 183-188
  smart investing, 188, 189
  staggering maturity dates, 189
  tax-exempt vs. taxable yields, 107, 208, 209
  tax-free capital building, 182, 183, 196
  taxable, 190, 191
  terminology, 180
  treasury, 181, 192, 193
  types, 190, 191
  yield to maturity, 186
Brothers, Joyce, 51
Bull market, 143
Bulls, 143
Bypass trusts, 115-118

C

C Corporation, 375
Capital appreciation, 141
Carat weight, 314
Cash reserve vehicles, 124
Cash reserves; *see* Rainy day money
Cash value, 95
Cash value insurance, 94, 95
Catch-up provision, 290
Certificate of deposit (CD), 132, 133, 237, 238
Certified financial planner (CFP), 77
Certified public accountants (CPAs), 77
Charitable giving, 219-221
Charitable lead trusts, 220
Charitable remainder trusts, 220
Chartered financial consultant (ChFC), 78

Index